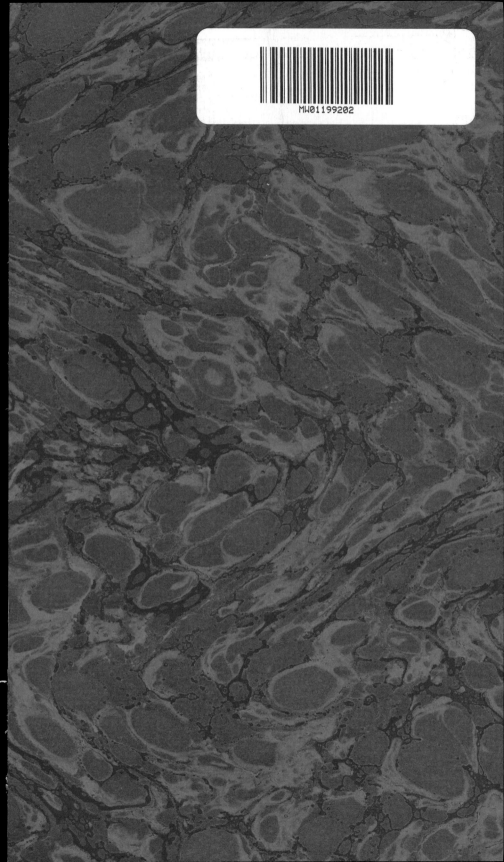

27 Dec 1985

MAY YOU FIND PLEASURE AND ENJOYMENT IN THIS BOOK.

THANKS FOR THE EYE EXAMS. MOST OF ALL, THANKS FOR BEING MY FRIEND. I APPRECIATE YOUR FRIENDSHIP AND HOPE WE WILL BE ASSOCIATED A LONG TIME.

BEST TO YOU ALWAYS.

Clayton Petty, MD

THIS SPECIAL EDITION OF

PRACTICAL OBSERVATIONS

ON THE

Diseases of the Eyes

BY ANTONIO SCARPA

HAS BEEN PRIVATELY PRINTED

FOR THE MEMBERS OF

THE CLASSICS OF MEDICINE LIBRARY

PRACTICAL OBSERVATIONS

ON THE

PRINCIPAL DISEASES

OF THE

E Y E S:

ILLUSTRATED WITH CASES.

TRANSLATED FROM THE ITALIAN

OF

ANTONIO SCARPA,

PROFESSOR OF ANATOMY AND PRACTICAL SURGERY IN THE UNIVERSITY
OF PAVIA, FELLOW OF THE ROYAL ACADEMY OF BERLIN, OF THE
ROYAL SOCIETY OF LONDON, OF THE JOSEPHINE MEDICO-
CHIRURGICAL SOCIETY OF VIENNA, AND OF THE
MEDICAL SOCIETY OF EDINBURGH, &c. &c.

WITH NOTES,

By JAMES BRIGGS,

MEMBER OF THE ROYAL COLLEGE OF SURGEONS IN LONDON,
AND ASSISTANT-SURGEON OF THE PUBLIC DISPENSARY.

LONDON:

PRINTED FOR T. CADELL AND W. DAVIES, STRAND.

1806.

Je fçais que la plûpart des chirurgiens négligent de s'appliquer aux maladies des yeux; parceque elles font fi nombreufes qu'on s'en fait un monftre, et que l'on croit qu'elles demandent toute l'application d'un homme, et une addreffe toute finguliere pour exercer les opérations qui leurs conviennent. Il n'eft rien de tout cela; elles font nombreufes à la verité, mais elles font trés-faciles à apprendre à un chirurgien déja éclairé dans fa profeffion : elles n'ont point d'autres regles pour leur traitement que celles que l'on fuit pour guérir les autres maladies; pourvû feulement que l'on ait égard à la nature de l'œil; et il n'eft befoin que d'une addreffe médiocre, et d'un peu de jugement pour en faire les plus difficiles opérations. *Maître-Jan Traité des maladies de l'œil.*

T. Bensley Printer,
Bolt Court, Fleet Street, London.

TO

JOHN PEARSON, Esq. F. R. S.

As a fmall Tribute of Gratitude for the ufeful Inftructions,

and friendly Affiftance which he has derived

from him in the Purfuit of his Studies,

And as a Teftimony of Refpect for his Talents and Erudition,

and of Efteem for his Integrity,

THIS WORK

IS INSCRIBED BY

THE TRANSLATOR.

TRANSLATOR'S PREFACE.

THE comparatively flow advancement of fur-gery, in common with the other branch of medicine, is principally to be attributed to the great diverfity and extent of the facts upon which it is founded, and to their irregular and uncertain occurrence. But, independently of thefe obftacles to its improvement, which are naturally infeparable from the ftudy of it, it would feem as if the flow progrefs of this department of the healing art had been in no inconfiderable degree owing to an imperfection in the manner of cultivating it; by furgeons either limiting their obfervations to the difeafes of fome particular part of the body, or by directing their fole attention to fome particular difeafe.

Thofe who have applied themfelves to the ftudy of difeafes of the eye, have too frequently confined

themfelves

themfelves to the mere confideration of fuch
affections, without any regard to furgical difeafes
generally; as if the diforders of the eye had fomething in their nature totally diftinct from thofe
of other parts; or as if there were no analogy
between fimilar difeafes affecting different parts
of the body. It has been frequently imagined
likewife, that the operations which are performed upon the eye require greater fkill or
dexterity, than thofe which are executed upon
other parts of the body. And it has been rather
upon fome fancied improvement in the methods of operating, than upon any acknowledged
peculiarity in the nature of the difeafes which
affect this organ, that thofe who have termed
themfelves oculifts, have generally refted their
pretenfions. Whether there be, however, any
greater difficulty in thefe operations, than in
thofe which are executed upon the body generally, thofe who have had the moft extenfive opportunities of performing both, are beft able to
determine. It ought alfo to be recollected, that
the term dexterity can fcarcely be applied with
propriety to furgical operations, in the fame

fenfe in which it is employed in the mechanic arts; the fuccefs of an operation depending more upon a diftinct knowledge of what ought to be done, than upon any adroitnefs in the performance of it.

The cuftom of confidering the difeafes of the eye as a diftinct province of the healing art, and of confining the ftudy of them to a few individuals, appears to be no lefs unfounded in nature, than prejudicial to the general advancement of furgery. Nor can any thing analogous to this be difcovered in the other departments of fcience, the principles upon which they are formed, being drawn from the moft comprehenfive view of the objects which they embrace. If, indeed, we take a view of the improvements which have been introduced into this branch of furgery, we fhall find that, they have been almoft exclufively confined to thofe, who, with extenfive opportunities of inveftigating the morbid affections of the eye, have united an enlarged knowledge of other difeafes. And it is to this application of the general principles of furgery, and to a more correct anatomy, both of the

natural

natural and difordered ftate of this organ, than has been hitherto attained, that the greater part of the difcoveries contained in this work are to be attributed.

In attempting, therefore, to render the writings of an author more generally known, who has fo greatly contributed to enlarge our knowledge of the difeafes of the eye, and to eftablifh the treatment of them upon the moft rational principles, the tranflator is unwilling to believe that any particular apology is neceffary, or that his labour has been ufelefs or mifapplied. His principal folicitude in the execution of it, has been to render it as clofe an imitation of the original as the genius of the two languages would admit.

It has not been thought neceffary to diftinguifh the notes which the tranflator has added to it by any particular defignation, fince they are neither numerous nor important; and are in no danger of being confounded with thofe of the very able author.

It was originally the tranflator's intention to have fubjoined to the work, the "additional obfervations"

obfervations" of the French editor, Monf. Le-
veillè. Further confideration, however, convinced him, that the greater part of the remarks
contained in them, are to be found in writings
which are acceffible to moft Englifh readers; and
that in this refpect he would have departed from
the author's original plan, who does not propofe to offer a complete treatife of the difeafes
of the eye, but only fuch facts and obfervations
as his extenfive practice has afforded him an
opportunity of making in the moft important
of thofe diforders which affect the organ of
vifion. The tranflator, however, has availed
himfelf of that gentleman's notes, which he
has diftinguifhed by affixing his name to
them.

As moft of the names of the pharmaceutical
preparations which the author has ufed in the
courfe of the work are falling gradually into
difufe, it has been thought proper, for the
fake of uniformity, to employ thofe which are
at prefent adopted by the London College.

It may be proper to mention, that the two
principal errata which occur in the original
work

work, and which fhould have been incorporated in the tranflation, unfortunately were not difcovered, until that part of it was printed off in which they ought to have been inferted.

THE

THE

AUTHOR's PREFACE.

IN the practice of furgery, I have been uniformly in the habit of comparing my own obfervations with thofe of the moft eminent writers of every age; and I have been frequently gratified to find, in their writings, facts and obfervations which my own experience confirmed. It was only on the difeafes of the eyes, that in a very confiderable number of cafes and variety of circumftances, the refults of my practice did not accord with their fair promifes and fpecious inftructions, by following which I was very frequently difappointed of the fuccefs which I had expected. It has appeared to me alfo, that the greater part of modern furgeons who have written complete fyftems of furgery, or treatifes on the difeafes of the eyes, have rather employed themfelves in collecting a number of formulæ of medicines, or in minutely detailing all the methods of operating which have been at any time propofed for the cure of thofe difeafes, than in determining, from obfervation and experience, which of the numerous remedies and

variety

variety of operative methods ought to have the preference. Profeſſed oculiſts, who have entirely devoted themſelves to this department of ſurgery, from whom great and important improvements might juſtly have been expected, have only contributed new theories, which for the moſt part have been diſproved by a minute anatomical inveſtigation of the eye, or they have merely furniſhed us with hiſtories of cures little leſs than miraculous. And it is to be regretted, that, even in the preſent day, ſome who have been regularly educated in ſurgery, no ſooner aſpire to the celebrity of oculiſts, than they immediately attach themſelves to the marvellous, and cannot be withheld from inſerting in their writings ſome trait leſs characteriſtic of the ſurgeon than the empiric; than which nothing can be more injurious to the welfare of mankind, to the advancement of ſurgery, and to the honour of him who practiſes it. Theſe inconſiderate promiſes being readily embraced by the young and inexperienced, who ignorant of the many, and ſometimes inſuperable difficulties which they have to encounter, proceed with ardour and intrepidity, and in the end embarraſs themſelves, to the prejudice of their own reputation and the ſafety of others.

The following obſervations, therefore, which are the reſult of my own practice and experience, have been publiſhed with a view to ſeparate

rate from this important branch of furgery whatever is untrue or exaggerated, and to affift the
young furgeon in the treatment of the more
important difeafes of the eyes, not only by a felection of the moft efficacious remedies hitherto
known, but, as far as the prefent ftate of our
knowledge admits, of the moft fimple and ufeful methods of operating, in the feveral cafes in
which they are requifite. Divefted of every
prejudice, and having frequent opportunities of
employing the moft approved remedies, and the
various modes of operating which have been
hitherto propofed for the cure of thofe difeafes,
which moft frequently affect the organ of vifion,
I have been made fully acquainted with the utility of fome of thefe methods of treatment, and
the inefficacy or imperfection of others, though
equally commended and extolled; and on thefe
points, therefore, I am enabled to pronounce de-
finitively. In making thefe refearches I ought
to confefs, that on feveral occafions I could not
but acknowledge the juftnefs of fome of the
practical doctrines tranfmitted to us by the ancients, which have been entirely neglected by
the moderns; as well as obferve how unjuftly
fome of their methods of operating have been
difcredited and laid afide, to give place to
others which experience proves to be greatly
inferior.

Relin-

Relinquifhing every hypothefis which is incon-
fiftent with the anatomical ftructure of the eye;
and practical obfervations on the difeafes of this
organ, I have endeavoured to explain with con-
cifenefs and perfpicuity thofe appearances which
I have obferved to be moft certain and conftant,
with refpect to the nature of the difeafes that
affect this important part of the human body,
as well as the fafeft method of treating them.
And, in order to render the methods of operating more intelligible to the young furgeon, I
have thought it proper to add to the greater part
of the chapters contained in the work, the detail of a fmall number of cafes; exprefsly felect-
ing from the great number, which I might have
adduced under feveral of the heads, the hiftories
of fuch as have been regiftered in my practical
fchool of furgery, in the prefence of a great
number of pupils. Examples without precepts
are generally uninterefting, and precepts without examples are for the moft part obfcure, and
of little utility. I entertain, however, the fulleft
confidence, that whoever will exactly follow the
plan of cure which I have laid down in the
treatment of this clafs of difeafes, both with refpect to the remedies and operations, will not
only eafily underftand what I have advanced,
but will alfo find that the event will generally,
if not always, accord with what I have afferted;
which,

which, in the healing art, is the moſt that can be promiſed.

Nor am I diſpoſed to believe that the moſt able practitioners of the preſent day will regard this work as uſeleſs, merely becauſe it may probably not contain any thing which to them may be ſufficiently important or novel. Their correct judgment in the knowledge of diſeaſes, as well as the operations which are beſt ſuited to each of them, and the frequent opportunities which they have had of comparing, at the bedſide of the patient, the numerous remedies and methods of operating which have been propoſed for the cure of diſeaſes of the eyes, have doubtleſs led them, as well as myſelf, to eſtabliſh their practice on a ſolid baſis, and to make a ſelection of whatever is moſt certain and uſeful in the exerciſe of this branch of ſurgical ſcience. But this is not the caſe with the ſtudent who enters on this career, and ſtands in need of a faithful guide, to prevent him from being ſeduced by the oſtentatious promiſes of ſome, and the magiſterial precepts of others, who, attached to ſome particular opinion, founded only upon theory, or upon ſome particular and extraordinary caſe, have eſtabliſhed upon it a general rule.

It ought to be obſerved, however, that in writing this work I have not propoſed to give a complete treatiſe of the diſeaſes of the eyes, but only

only to speak of the principal affections of this organ, which I have sedulously and repeatedly attended to, since there are some which I have never met with; such are, for instance, the prolapsus of the eye-ball, from external violence, the hypopion, without being preceded by an evident inflammation of the internal membranes of the eye, and, as it is called by metastasis, the union of the internal membrane of the eye-lids with the eye-ball. I have not mentioned, besides, the congenital or accidental coalescence of the eye-lids, the carbuncle of the eye-lids, wounds dividing the cartilage of the tarsus, extraneous substances introduced between the eye-lids or fixed in the eye, and other similar accidents; because, from the simple nature of these subjects, they do not admit of discussion, and because they have been already explained with the greatest precision and clearness by almost all the writers who have treated of them.

It will be seen, in many instances, that I have included diseases in the same chapter, which, although treated of by the greater number of writers under separate heads, are not in reality essentially different, and, notwithstanding the distinct denominations which have been given to them, are nevertheless cured by the same remedies and the same operations. In speaking of the artificial pupil alone, I have confined myself to the consideration of

that

that particular cafe of contracted or obliterated
pupil, which occafionally takes place, after the
extraction or depreffion of the cataract ; principally in confequence of the violent *internal* ophthalmia, excited by thofe operations, becaufe
my experience has not yet fufficiently inftructed
me in the beft method to be purfued in the
other cafes of that difeafe.

For the fame reafon I have not entered into
a defcription of the cancer of the eye, fince I
have never met with more than two inftances
of this difeafe, which only ferve to eftablifh a
fact already fufficiently known, the inefficacy
of extirpating the eye-ball, whenever the cancerous diathefis has, in the fmalleft degree, extended beyond the ball itfelf, or its appendages.
The firft of thefe cafes occurred in a boy 13
years of age, in other refpects ftrong and healthy,
in whom, befides the eye-ball being fchirrous
and projecting out of the orbit, there was a tubercle of the fame nature fituated between the
internal angle of the eye-brow, and the root of
the nofe. I extirpated the eye and removed
every part within the orbit which was indurated,
or difeafed, in the moft careful manner, together
with the tubercle fituated between the fupercilium and root of the nofe : every thing went
on well, and the wound was completely healed.
Two months after the child had returned home,
which was in the province of Cremona, two

b   new

new indurated tubercles appeared in the cellular membrane of the fupercilium of that fide, to- wards the temples, and fungus afterwards ger- minated from the bottom of the orbit. This unfortunate child was then feized with conti- nual pain in the head, afterwards with flow fever and general convulfions, which fhortly terminated in death. The fecond cafe was that of a man 50 years old, ftrong, and in every other refpect perfectly healthy, in whom the cancerous fungus had attacked, not only the eye-ball, but alfo a portion of the upper eye- lid. I removed the eye-lid with the greateft poffible exactnefs, clofe to the arch of the orbit, where it appeared perfectly found, and along with it the globe of the eye, and all the other parts contained in the orbital fofla. The cure went on very well until the 40th day, and the cicatrix gradually advanced from the external margin of the orbit towards the bottom of that cavity. In the midft, however, of the moft promifing hopes the wound became ftationary; a fungus began to appear in various points of the bottom of the orbit, which I endeavoured, but in vain, to deftroy, firft with the favin- powder, afterwards with the cauftic; the pa- tient was ultimately attacked with acute pains in the head, and by a kind of nervous fever, he became infenfible and died.

For

For the greater advantage of students I have thought it neceffary to add three plates. The firft reprefents the via lachrymalia, and particularly the exact fituation and extent of the lachrymal fac. For as the perfect fuccefs of the operation for the fiftula lachrymalis depends greatly on the lachrymal fac being laid open freely through its whole extent, from below the tendon or ligament of the *orbicularis palpebrarum* to the loweft part of it, and on the incifion being made exactly in the direction of its axis; it is neceffary that the young furgeon fhould know precifely the true fituation and direction of thefe parts; which perhaps would not be eafily learnt from the plates which we have at prefent, fince they confift at moft of fmall fections of the face, in which the relative fituation of the via lachrymalia with the furrounding parts and the reft of the head is loft. The fecond plate gives a reprefentation of fome difcafes of the eyes, which appear to me never to have been accurately delineated. The third plate fhows the inftruments, which with the fyringe of Anel, and thofe of the pocket cafe, with which every furgeon is provided, form, in my opinion, the whole apparatus that the furgeon-oculift requires.

With the hope that this work may not prove ufelefs or uninterefting, efpecially to young furgeons, for whofe ufe it is principally intended,

b 2   I propofe,

I propofe, upon the fame plan, to communicate
fucceffively to the public, fuch important obfervations or ufeful refearches, as I may hereafter
make in the other departments of furgery.

C O N T E N T S.

PRACTICAL OBSERVATIONS, &c.

CHAP I.

OF THE PURIFORM DISCHARGE OF THE PAL-PEBRÆ, AND OF THE FISTULA LACHRY-MALIS.

Surgeons are generally agreed that a *fiftula lachrymalis* exifts, whenever a difcharge of a vifcid, curdly, yellowifh matter, refembling pus and mixed with tears, iffues from the *puncta lachrymalia*, on compreffing the fpace fituated between the internal canthus of the eye and the nofe.

If the term *fiftula lachrymalis*, when applied to the difeafe of which I am about to treat, were a mere verbal inaccuracy, and had no influence on the diagnofis and treatment of the complaint, it would be a matter of little importance : but, fince it involves a real error, and one which may eafily miflead the young furgeon in the diagnofis and treatment of this and other difeafes of the *via lachrymalia*, I think it neceffary that fome diftinction fhould be made between thefe two morbid affections. Whenever, therefore, on preffing the lachrymal fac, though in other refpects in a found ftate, a vifcid, curdly, yellowifh matter, refembling pus, flows from the *puncta lachrymalia*, I give to

B   that

that morbid ftate of the *via lachrymalia* the ap-
pellation of the puriform difcharge of the palpebræ; and I would reftrict the term *fiftula lachrymalis* to that form of difeafe, in which the
lachrymal fac is not only greatly diftended, but
ulcerated, and in a fungous ftate on its internal
furface, where there is likewife an external
opening, which is fometimes accompanied with
a caries of the *os unguis*.

The vifcid, curdly, yellowifh humour mixed
with the tears, which in the firft inftance flows
back again through the *puncta lachrymalia*, is
not wholly produced by the fac, as is commonly
believed; but is for the moft part tranfmitted
to it from the eye-lids by the *puncta lachrymalia*,
from which it regurgitates, and confequently appears again upon the eye and eye-lids whenever
the fac, which is gradually filled with this humour, happens to be preffed upon. This puriform humour is principally furnifhed by the
internal membrane of the palpebræ; and comes
more particularly from the lower eye-lid along the
tarfus, and from the glands of Meibomius: the
febaceous matter peculiar to thefe glands being
not only fecreted in larger quantity, but alfo
acquiring an acrid and irritating quality. This
morbid ftate of the febaceous glands is very frequently derived from a catarrhal flux, from a
fcrofulous taint, from the fmall pox, and from cutaneous eruptions improperly repelled. In addition

tion to the febaceous matter which is copiouſly
fecreted by thefe glands, a quantity of thin mucus
is poured out from the internal membrane of
the palpebræ, which greatly contributes to increafe the quantity of vifcid humour which, in
thefe cafes, is diffufed over the eye and eye-lids.*

That the puriform humour which iſſues from
the lachrymal fac on the application of preffure
originates from thefe fources, is rendered evident by everting the affected eye-lids, particularly the inferior one, and comparing them with
thofe of the found fide. For the internal membrane of the former is invariably found redder
than natural, and prefents a villous appearance,
efpecially along the tarfus; the edge of the eye-
lid is tumefied and difcoloured with innumerable fmall varicofe veffels; the glands of Meibomius are more turgid and projecting than in a
natural ſtate, and not unfrequently, when examined with a powerful glafs, appear to be
flightly ulcerated.

This villous ſtructure, then, which the furface
of the internal membrane of the palpebræ
affumes in thefe cafes, becomes an organ, fecreting a larger quantity of fluid than ufual,
refembling vifcid lymph, which being mixed
with the febaceous matter, copiouſly effufed
from the glands of Meibomius, conſtitutes the

* Rudolphus Vehrens has called this difeafe *Epiphora Se-
bacea.* See Haller's addenda to Boerhaave's *Methodus Studii
Medici.*

　　　　　　　　whole

whole of that tenacious fluid with which the eye-lids are imbued, and which is continually carried by the *puncta lachrymalia* into the fac, fo as to fill, and fometimes even diftend, that cavity enormoufly.

If indeed the lachrymal fac is emptied of this matter, by means of compreffion, and the eye and internal furface of the palpebræ are carefully wafhed, fo that none of the glutinous humour preffed from the fac fhall remain upon them, and the eye-lids are everted half an hour afterwards, the internal furface, efpecially of the lower one, will be found covered with a frefh effufion of mucus mixed with febaceous matter, which has evidently not flowed back from the lachrymal fac towards the eye, but has been generated between the eye and the palpebræ, having been there poured out by the villous furface of their internal membrane, and the glands of Meibomius. That the internal membrane of the palpebræ affuming a fungous or villous appearance, changes its natural functions, and becomes an organ fecreting an immoderate quantity of mucus, we have an inftance in that fpecies of puriform difcharge of the palpebræ, produced by the incautious application of the matter of gonorrhea to the edges of the eye-lids. For in this cafe the eye and palpebræ are firft of all inflamed, the internal membrane of the latter then becomes tumefied, and affumes a villous

lous appearance, and a prodigious quantity of
viſcid, yellowiſh humour, is afterwards poured
out, ſimilar to that which is diſcharged from the
urethra in a venereal gonorrhœa.

In the puriform diſcharge of the palpebræ,
however, of which I am treating, and which is
commonly met with in practice, the ſecretion
of mucus from the internal membrane of the
eye-lids, and the glands of Meibomius, is not
ſo conſiderable as in that ariſing from the application of the matter of gonorrhœa; nor is it
always preceded like that with ſymptoms of the
moſt violent inflammation. In general it takes
place ſlowly, and in proportion as the puriform
fluid is ſecreted, it partly lodges upon the eye
and palpebræ, and partly deſcends through the
puncta lachrymalia into the ſac, where being accumulated, it inſtantly flows back upon the eye
when any preſſure is made upon that cavity.

As a further proof that the lachrymal ſac has
no other ſhare in this diſeaſe than that of receiving, together with the tears, the puriform
humour which is tranſmitted to it from the
affected palpebræ, it is ſufficient to obſerve, that
if the morbid ſecretion of the eye-lids is retarded or ſuppreſſed, either accidentally or by means
of external applications, little or none of this
viſcid curdly humour is collected in the lachrymal ſac, or can be forced from the *puncta la-*
chrymalia by the application of preſſure. In-

B 3 deed,

deed, if in the highest degree of this disease the eye-lids are accidentally attacked with inflammation, as in the case of erysipelas of the face, the effect of which, as of all other inflammations, is to supprefs every kind of secretion in the parts affected with it, the accumulation of puriform matter in the fac ceafes altogether, which returns as soon as the inflammation of the palpebræ has abated, and the morbid secretion of their internal membrane, and of the glands of Meibomius, is reproduced. I have frequently afcertained that the fame effect is produced when an inflammation of ·thefe parts is artificially excited, by the introduction of any ftrongly-irritating fubftance between the palpebræ and the ball of the eye: as I have alfo conftantly obferved that the puriform difcharge may be radically cured by merely correcting, at an early period, the morbid fecretion of the internal membrane of the palpebræ, and of the febaceous glands fituated along the tarfus.

If, however, notwithftanding what has been advanced, fome may yet be inclined to believe that the puriform humour in this difeafe is rather formed by the internal membrane of the fac than the palpebræ, it may not be improper for them to confider, that the internal membrane of the lachrymal fac is exactly fimilar to that which lines the frontal and ethmoidal finufes, being a very delicate membrane entirely defti-

4   tute

tute of febaceous glands, and fitted to fecrete a
thin mucus, but not a febaceous, unctuous matter,
fuch as that which in this difeafe forms fo confiderable a part of the fluid which iffues from the
lachrymal fac. It is not, indeed, improbable
that a fmall part of the thin mucus which lu-
bricates the internal membrane of the fac may
be mixed with the puriform humour tranfmitted
to it by the *puncta lachrymalia*; but we are not
warranted to affert from thence that the principal part of the puriform humour is formed
in the fac.

If the origin therefore of this difeafe be not
principally in the lachrymal fac, but in the internal membrane of the palpebræ, and in the
febaceous glands of Meibomius, it is very evident how much they are miftaken who con-
found this difeafe of the *via lachrymalia* with
the *fiftula lachrymalis*; and confequently, how improperly they propofe in the treatment of the
puriform difcharge of the palpebræ to heal an
ulcer of the internal membrane of the fac,
which does not exift, or to open a paffage for
the tears into the nofe by the dilatation of the
nafal canal, which they imagine to be entirely,
or in a great meafure, obftructed. For in thefe
cafes, the nafal canal cannot properly be faid to
be obftructed, unlefs' either relatively with refpect to the denfity and tenacity of the puriform matter, which attempts to pafs from the

palpebræ

palpebræ towards the cavity of the noftrils, or becaufe the irritation which this matter produces, in the courfe of the *via lachrymalia*, occafions a flight degree of thickening, or tumefaction of the membrane of the noftrils which lines the nafal canal.

And in order to proceed with this fubject in as clear a manner as poffible, upon which, it feems unfortunately, the more that has been written, the greater has been the obfcurity and doubt which has been introduced into it, I have thought it proper to divide the puriform difcharge of the palpebræ into four ftages. The firft, is that in which the puriform oily mucous matter, fecreted by the internal membrane of the palpebræ and the glands of Meibomius, is carried into the lachrymal fac, and accumulates there; but defcending eafily through the nafal canal is for the moft part difcharged into the nofe, and occafions no manifeft diftenfion of the fac, which, when compreffed, only gives iffue to a moderate quantity of vifcid matter. The fecond ftage of the puriform difcharge of the palpebræ, is that in which the matter flowing from the eye-lids not being entirely difcharged, or without great difficulty into the nofe, from its exceffive quantity and denfity, as well as from the tumefaction of the internal membrane of the nafal canal, produces gradually, and in the courfe of fome years,

a con-

a confiderable diftenfion of the lachrymal fac, fo
as to deftroy its natural elafticity, and caufe
it to project in the form of a tumour. The
third ftage, is that in which the vifcid matter, in confequence of its abundance, denfity, and acrimony, and perhaps ftill more
from its exceffively diftending the parietes of
the lachrymal fac, caufes an inflammation,
erofion, and fuppuration of that cavity, and
of the integuments covering it; and thereby
occafions an ulcer of the *via lachrymalia*, extenfive internally, but narrow externally, from
which is difcharged a mixture of puriform
matter and true pus. This third ftage of the
puriform difcharge of the palpebræ; is that to
which the term *fiftula lachrymalis* properly
belongs, efpecially if the ulceration has been
for a long time neglected, or improperly treated.
Laftly, the fourth ftage of this difeafe, is the
fame as the *fiftula lachrymalis*, but accompanied with a caries of the *os unguis*.

From the confideration of this feries of pro-
greffive ftages of the puriform difcharge of the
palpebræ, the difference between this difeafe
and the *fiftula lachrymalis* muft be very obvious,
and confequently what is the true and principal
origin of the latter. And fince, from what has
been ftated, the primary and principal caufe of
the *fiftula lachrymalis* does not exift either in
the fac or the nafal canal, as it has been hitherto
believed,

believed, but in the morbid ftate of the palpebræ, it muft neceffarily follow that every method of treatment of the *fiftula lachrymalis*, which is merely directed to heal the ulceration of the fac, or to overcome the obftruction of the nafal canal, can never effect a permanent cure of this difeafe, unlefs fuch practice be conjoined with other meafures which are calculated to correct effectually the morbid fecretion of the palpebræ, from which the *fiftula lachrymalis* is derived.

With refpect to the treatment of the firft ftage of the puriform difcharge of the palpebræ, when it is recent, and when the vifcid humour tranfmitted from the palpebræ through the *puncta lachrymalia* into the fac, though it is fomewhat detained in the latter, does not however diftend it fenfibly, nor elevate it externally, the cure may be effected without having recourfe to the divifion of the fac, or any other painful operation. The plan of treatment under fuch circumftances confifts in reftraining the immoderate fecretion of the glands of Meibomius, and internal membrane of the palpebræ, and at the fame time in affiduoufly wafhing the *via lachrymalia* through their whole extent, in order to prevent any of the acrid, febaceous, and grumous matter from lodging in them.

This may be obtained by means of ftimulating and aftringent medicaments applied to
the

the margin and internal membrane of the palpebræ, and by deterfive injections thrown into the *puncta lachrymalia.* The beft local, ftimulating, and aftringent remedy in this cafe, is the opthalmic ointment of Janin,* employed at firft with a larger quantity of lard than is directed in the formula, until the patient's eye is accuftomed to this kind of ftimulant; a portion of this ointment, equal to the fize of a barley-corn, fhould be introduced upon the point of a blunt probe morning and evening, between the palpebræ and ball of the eye, near the external angle, and the whole margin of the eye-lid fmeared with it; the patient fhould then be directed to clofe the eye, and rub the palpebræ gently, fo that the ointment may be equally diftributed upon the whole of their internal furface; a comprefs and bandage fhould be applied over it, and the patient defired to keep his eye-lids clofed in this manner during two hours. At the expiration of this time, the eye fhould be wafhed with cold water, and a few drops of a collyrium, confifting of four ounces of plantain water, five grains of vitriolated zinc, and half an ounce of the mucilage

---

* Take of hog's lard half an ounce, prepared tutty and armenian bole, of each two drams, white precipitate, (calx hydrarg. alba) a dram. The hog's lard, having been wafhed three times in rofe water, fhould be intimately mixed in a glafs mortar, with the other ingredients previoufly reduced to a fine powder.   *Memoires fur l'Oeil.*

of quince-feed, fhould be inftilled into the eye three or four times in the courfe of the day.

When, in addition to the affection of the glands of Meibomius, and the villous appearance of the internal membrane of the palpebræ, there are fmall fuperficial excoriations upon the edges of the eye-lids, it will be advantageous to employ at the fame time the *unguentum nitratis hydrargyri* of the Edinburgh Pharmacopœia. This remedy fhould be ufed by warming it a little in a fmall veffel till it liquifies, and then with the point of the finger fmearing it upon the edges of the eye-lids at the time when the patient goes to bed. If this fhould be infufficient, recourfe muft be had to the *argentum nitratum,* as employed by S. Yves, which fhould be drawn gently along the edges of the 'palpebræ, wafhing the eye immediately afterwards with new milk.

In order to preferve the canal in a permeable ftate, the furgeon, previoufly to the ufe of the ftimulant and aftringent applications, fhould inject diftilled plantain water, rendered more active by the addition of a little fpirit of wine, through the *puncta lachrymalia,* morning and evening, by means of Anel's fmall fyringe; and this injection fhould be repeated at each time of dreffing the eye, until it is evident that the fluid thrown into the *puncta lachrymalia* has paffed into the noftril.

The phænomena which ufually prefent them-

felves

felves during the treatment of the firft ftage of
the puriform difcharge of the palpebræ, are the
following: The fecretion of puriform matter is
at firft more copious than before, provided the
irritation produced by the ointment does not
exceed certain limits, and occafion an inflammation of the palpebræ.* The edges of the
eye-lids, efpecially of the inferior, which before
were tumefied and rigid, now become gradually
thin, foft, and flexible; the glands of Meibomius infenfibly diminifh, and the internal furface of the palpebræ, which had previoufly a
villous appearance, and was almoft in a fungous
ftate towards the margin of the eye-lid, gradually recovers its natural fmoothnefs, and becomes pale. As thefe favourable changes fucceed each other on the internal furface of the
palpebræ, the puriform difcharge diminifhes in
quantity, and from being vifcid, tenacious, and
grumous, becomes thinner and more fluid, and
no longer imbues the palpebræ and cilia. If
the fac be compreffed afterwards at different
intervals, there only iffues from the *puncta lachrymalia,* a difcharge of turbid tears; and finally,
when the natural fecretion of the palpebræ is

---

* In order that this remedy may produce its proper effect,
however, it is neceffary that it fhould induce a certain degree
of irritation exciting a little warmth and rednefs in the palpebræ and *conjunctina*, during the whole time it remains upon
the eye.

entirely

entirely reftored, the regurgitation of puriform matter ceafes altogether, or there is only a dif-charge of a few pure and limpid tears. Thefe advantages are obtained for the moft part in fix weeks, if there be no obftinate caufes depend-ing on the patient's general conftitution, which, towards the end of the treatment, occafion a re-turn of the difeafe, as too frequently happens in thofe who are in the laft ftage of fcrofula, efpe-cially on the approach of fpring and autumn, or in thofe who are otherwife unhealthy, or who have been affected with a fevere *variolous metaftafis* to the eyes. Thefe cafes require a longer continuance of the treatment than the others, although a cure may be ultimately obtained, if, in conjunction with the external means already mentioned, a feton is made in the neck, and fuch internal remedies employed as are fuited to correct the morbid predifpofition. Of thefe I fhall have occafion to fpeak in the chapter on Ophthalmia.

From thefe principles relative to the firft ftage of the puriform difcharge of the palpebræ and the method of treating it, we are enabled to form a correct judgment of the cafe related by Fabricius Hildanus, in his Cent. IV. Obf. XX. of a lady about thirty years of age, who had been afflicted with a *fiftula lachrymalis* for two years, which he cured in four months, merely by making a feton in the neck, and by the frequent

ufe

ufe of an appropriate collyrium. This cafe of *fiftula lachrymalis* of which Fabricius fpeaks, appears to have been only a puriform difcharge of the palpebræ, which, although of two years ftanding, had not proceeded beyond the firft ftage; and in confequence of the determination made to the neck and the action of the collyrium, which was probably aftringent, applied to the eye-lids, the puriform difcharge was fuppreffed, and confequently ceafed to taint the eye, and obftruct the *via lachrymalia.* A great number of fimilar examples may be met' with both among ancient and modern writers on the difeafes of the eyes, which have been improperly confidered as cafes of *fiftula lachrymalis.**

As the difeafe in this firft ftage does not produce any remarkable pain or tumefaction in that part of the integuments fituated between the internal angle of the eye and the nofe, and only occafions a flight weeping of the eye in the daytime, and during the night, fome degree of cohefion of the eye-lids; and as this difcharge of tears becomes even more tolerable to the patient, if he have the precaution to prefs occafionally upon the internal canthus of the eye,

* I have very frequently feen, fays Pott, cafes of incipient *fiftula lachrymalis* cured merely by means of a good diet, and the application of the vitriolic collyrium.

Obferv. on the Fift. Lachrym.

and

and to force the puriform matter confined in the fac back again through the *puncta*; fo it very frequently happens, that not only the lower claffes of people, but alfo the more opulent, neglect this form of the difeafe 'for a confiderable length of time, and feldom have recourfe to furgical affiftance, until the difeafe has arrived at the fecond ftage, or when it is accompanied with diftention and manifeft tumefaction of the lachrymal fac; for the cure of which, befides the local remedies already enumerated, it is requifite to perform a furgical operation.

For, in the fecond ftage of the puriform difcharge of the palpebræ, when the vifcid matter, fecreted by the eye-lids, has gradually, and, in the courfe of fome years, diftended the fac, and elevated it externally in the form of a tumour, although the primary indication which the furgeon ought to fulfil, be, in every period of this difeafe, to correct the morbid fecretion of the palpebræ, yet the fulfilment of it, under thefe circumftances, is not alone fufficient to effect a complete cure of the difeafe; on account of the atony or flaccidity fuperinduced upon the membranes of the lachrymal fac, which requires the employment of appropriate means. This circumftance demands the greater care and attention, as in the firft place the diminifhed vitality of the membranes of the lachrymal fac, in confequence of the diftenfion tenſion which they have ſuffered diſpoſes them, as well as the integuments, to ulcerate from the ſlighteſt attack of inflammation in the ſurrounding parts; becauſe, in the ſecond place, although the morbid ſecretion of the palpebræ be perfectly corrected, yet, whenever the lachrymal ſac remains conſiderably dilated, ſo that the tears are retarded in it, the further diſtention and dilatation of it, and conſequently the perpetual weeping of the eye, are inconveniences abſolutely inevitable. It is evident, that to avoid this diſcharge of tears, it is not only neceſſary that the naſal canal ſhould be ſufficiently open into the cavity of the noſtrils, but alſo that there ſhould be a certain proportion between the caliber of this canal and the capacity of the lachrymal ſac; otherwiſe, if the latter exceed its uſual dimenſions, the tears poured into it from the *puncta lachrymalia,* as all fluids propelled through narrow tubes into large ones loſe much of the motion originally communicated to them, are retarded, accumulate in the preternaturally dilated ſac, and conſequently flow back upon the eye; nor is the weight of the tears alone ſufficient to make them deſcend through the naſal canal and diſcharge themſelves into the noſe, in the ſame quantity in which they are abſorbed and poured by the *puncta lachrymalia* into the ſac.

To fulfil this indication, that is, to prevent

c   the

the accumulation of the puriform matter and tears in the diftended fac, which all furgical writers have confidered as important, it has been propofed to make ufe of aftringent lotions, confifting of a ftrong folution of alum in the infufion of oak-bark; others have fuggefted a firm and long-continued preffure upon the dilated fac, by means of a fmall inftrument refembling a tourniquet. Both thefe methods are, however, altogether inadequate to the purpofe, for feveral reafons, which it is of little importance at prefent to examine. The only method of treatment which has been found really efficacious, is that of making an incifion into the fac, and introducing into it fuch remedies as are calculated to conftringe its cavity, either by reftoring the actions of its membranes, or diminifhing their extent, principally by the ufe of cauftic applications.*

For

* A cafe of this fecond form of the difeafe lately occurred at the Public Difpenfary, in which the lachrymal fac was immoderately diftended, and the integuments covering it difcoloured and tender to the touch, yet by merely employing the *unguentum hydrarg. nitrat. mitius,* which was introduced between the eye-lids twice a-day, and directing the patient to empty the fac as often as there was any accumulation of matter in it, by preffing upon it with the finger, the fymptoms gradually difappeared, and the difeafe in the courfe of fome weeks was removed; a flight difcharge of tears, however, occafionally took place whenever the eye was expofed to cold air.

For the cure then of the ſecond ſtage of the
puriform diſcharge of the palpebræ, or when
it is attended with a conſiderable dilatation of
the lachrymal ſac, the patient being ſeated, and
his head properly held by an aſſiſtant, the ſurgeon ſhould direct him to cloſe his eye-lids,
and gently preſſing upon thoſe of the affected
ſide with the index and middle finger of one
hand, with the other he ſhould carry the point
of a ſtraight biſtoury immediately below that
ſmall whitiſh ſpot of the integuments, which is
naturally ſeen on the ſide of the noſe, a little
below the internal commiſſure of the palpebræ, covering the tendon or ligament * of the
orbicular muſcle; and preſſing the knife freely
forwards, muſt penetrate the cavity of the lachrymal ſac; he ſhould then continue the inciſion from above downwards, in the direction of
the fold which the lower eye-lid makes at
that part, and which nearly correſponds to that
of the *oſſeous ſulcus* in which the lachrymal ſac
is ſituated.†

And, to make the operation fully ſucceed, if
the ſurgeon is ambidextrous, he ſhould open the
lachrymal ſac of the left ſide with his right

air. This inſtance would ſeem to prove that, however judicious the operation here propoſed by Profeſſor Scarpa may be,
in the generality of caſes, it is not abſolutely neceſſary in all.
And the propriety of proceeding to any operation before ſuch
meaſures have been employed, may be reaſonably doubted.

* Plate I. c. † Plate I. c. b.

hand,

hand, and *vice verſa* that of the right ſide with
his left hand, when the diſeaſe is on that ſide :
always taking particular care that the point of
the biſtoury fall perpendicularly upon the *os
unguis,* and never paſs obliquely from without
inwards, between the margin of the orbit and
the globe of the eye. In performing this operation the young ſurgeon ſhould, in no inſtance,
depart from the rule here laid down, of commencing the inciſion of the ſac, by plunging
the point of the biſtoury immediately below the
whitiſh ſpot of the integuments, which is ſeen
between the internal angle of the eye and the
noſe. For in morbid dilatations of the ſac,
which are always attended with tumefaction of
the neighbouring parts, the uncertainty of penetrating with preciſion into that cavity, and of
extending the inciſion accurately in the courſe
of it is ſo great, that even the beſt anatomiſts
may, by not paying attention to this circum-
ſtance, eaſily get out of the direction of the ſac,
or not open it in the moſt convenient manner
requiſite. Under this ſmall whitiſh ſpot of the
integuments, the ſac never deviates from its
natural poſition, however diſtended and altered
by diſeaſe, ſince it is firmly confined in its
ſituation at this part by the ligament of the
orbicularis muſcle. When the point of the
biſtoury has fairly penetrated the upper part of
the cavity of the ſac, the reſt of the inciſion
may

may be executed without difficulty, by following the direction of the inferior arch of the orbit
where the natural fold of the eye-lid has been
effaced by the tumefaction of the ſac. The
practice of laying the ſac open through its whole
extent * is of the greater importance for obtaining a complete cure of the diſeaſe, as by this
method only are we enabled to make ſuch applications to it as are neceſſary; and experience
has proved, that a ſmall inciſion of the ſac, only
ſufficient to admit a ſeton or tent through it
into the noſe, does not fulfil the original intention for which it ought to be made.

The ſac being divided longitudinally, ſo as to
expoſe the whole of its internal ſurface, the
ſurgeon ſhould introduce into the loweſt part of
it a moderate ſized probe, which he ſhould
puſh through the naſal canal into the correſponding noſtril, giving the inſtrument a ſlight
inclination from without, inwards. After having
withdrawn the probe, he ſhould introduce into
the naſal canal a bougie of a proper thickneſs,
an inch and a half long in the caſe of an adult,
preſſing it gently forwards, until the extremity
which has entered the noſtril, is incurvated towards the fauces, and the other end being
ſecured by a waxed thread, has deſcended ſo
deeply as to be concealed at the loweſt part of
the lachrymal ſac, and preciſely at the entrance

* Plate I. c. b.

of

of the nafal canal; in fhort, that the bougie
may preferve the dilatation of the nafal canal
without occupying any part of the cavity of the
lachrymal fac. A piece of elaftic gum tent, of an
equal length and thicknefs, anfwers extremely
well, inftead of the bougie, both on account of
its great fmoothnefs and flexibility. A bougie,
or elaftic gum tent, an inch and a half long, for
an adult, is preferable to one fhorter, and only
proportioned to the length of the nafal canal;
as the one being incurvated in the noftril towards the fauces, remains conftantly in its fituation at the loweft part of the fac, and is entirely
concealed in the nafal canal, while the other by
its fhortnefs is eafily forced upwards and outwards through the incifion, and prevents the
dreffings from remaining long at the bottom of
the fac. Nor is it a matter of indifference
whether the paffage of the nafal duct be preferved open or not, during the whole time required for the cure of the diftended and flaccid
fac; as we know from experience the great
tendency which there is in the canals and ex-
cretory ducts of the animal body, to contract
and become obliterated, when the fluid which
they are accuftomed to convey ceafes, even
for a fhort time, to pafs through them. Of
this we have an inftance in the fiftula of the parotid duct, the anterior portion of which, no
longer

longer receiving any faliva from its appropriate gland, very foon contracts and clofes itfelf.

Having thus filled the nafal canal, the fur-geon fhould examine the whole preternatural extent of the lachrymal fac, with a bent probe, efpecially that part of it which is fituated above the tendon of the orbicular mufcle,* and which has not been included in the incifion; this will ferve him as a guide for calculating afterwards the progrefs of the contraction of the whole fac, which is the principal object in the treat-ment of the fecond ftage of the puriform dif-charge of the palpebræ. Laftly, the whole ca-vity of the lachrymal fac fhould be filled with foft lint, which fhould be retained in its fitua-tion by means of a comprefs and the monoculus bandage.†

On the third day, if the lips of the wound have begun to fuppurate, the dreffing fhould be renewed; and this fhould confift in wafhing the wound, and filling again in the moft exact manner the bottom of the cavity of the dilated lachrymal fac, with foft lint dipped in a lini-ment, confifting of the hydrargyrus nitratus ruber and mucilage of gum-arabic. This efcharotic is very gentle in its action, and correfponds to what are commonly called mild or *indolent cauftics:*

* Plate I. a.

† For the defcription and method of applying this bandage, fee Heifter's Surgery, Part III. fect. i. p. 357.

it

it gives the patient little uneafinefs, and produces daily a greater contraction of the lachrymal fac; whether it effects this by fimply ftimulating it, or by promoting an abundant difcharge of humour, with which, in this fecond
ftage of the difeafe, the membrane forming the
fac is loaded, the fact is, that at every application the doffil of lint, introduced into the cavity
of the fac, is covered with a whitifh flough refembling cotton; and that by perfifting in this
treatment the capacity of the fac is gradually
diminifhed.

If it fhould appear to refift thefe applications
the whole cavity of the fac fhould be filled with
the hydrarg. nitrat. ruber, either alone or mixed
with a little alum, and fhould be alfo repeatedly
touched with the argentum nitratum, if neceffary.
By means of thefe powerful efcharotics the internal furface of the fac will be reduced to the ftate
of a fimple ulcer, the healing of which muft be
neceffarily attended with a correfponding contraction of its cavity.

The moft fcrupulous attention ought to be
paid at each dreffing, that the external edges of
the wound are kept open, and only fuffered
to contract in proportion to the reft of the
fac, either by the introduction of lint or
fponge. While thefe means are employed for
the purpofe of reducing the fac to its natural
fize, it will be proper to introduce between
the

the eye-lids, morning and evening, the ophthalmic ointment of Janin, and to direct the
patient to inſtil into the eye a few drops of the
vitriolic collyrium three or four times a-day, in
order to correct the morbid ſtate of the palpebræ; without which a complete cure of the
diſeaſe cannot be obtained in any of its ſtages.

As ſoon as the ſac is nearly reduced to its
natural capacity, which may be aſcertained by
examination with the point of a probe, the uſe
of eſcharotics ſhould be ſuſpended, and lint
dipped in a mixture of aqua calcis and mel roſæ
ſubſtituted in the place of them. Afterwards
when the proceſs of cicatrization has evidently
proceeded from the edges of the inciſion to the
bottom of the ſac, and the diſcharge of matter
from it has ceaſed; in ſhort, when the internal
ſurface of the ſac is healed, it will be proper to
withdraw the bougie or elaſtic gum tent from
the naſal canal, in which it had been placed from
the beginning of the treatment, and to ſubſtitute
in its place a tent formed of lead, the upper
extremity of which ſhould have affixed to it a
ſmall plate of the ſame metal,* about four lines
in breadth and rather more than one in thickneſs.
The body of this tent being perfectly ſolid will
continue to keep the naſal canal open for ſome
time, and by its weight cauſe the ſmall plate
reſting on the whole external ſurface of the ſac

* Plate III. fig. 9.

to

to make a continual preſſure upon it from without inwards.

This important part of the treatment was not
neglected by the ancient ſurgeons, I mean the
application of a moderate degree of preſſure upon
the ſac, after its contraction and complete cicatrization internally. Among the moderns Guerin * appears to be the only one who has properly appreciated this practice of the ancients.
For although the paſſage for the tears into the
noſe may have been ſufficiently kept open, and
cauſtic applications have alſo been employed to
reſtore the ſac to its natural ſize, and to obtain on
its internal ſurface a perfect and ſolid cicatrix;
neverthelefs it may eaſily happen that the ſac,
from having been greatly dilated, (notwithſtanding the means which have been employed)
may not have acquired ſufficient power, towards
the end of the cure, to reſiſt a new impulſe
of the tears from any little difficulty which they
may meet with in paſſing into the noſe. In
order therefore to prevent ſuch an accident,
nothing is more advantageous, towards the end
of the treatment of this form of the diſeaſe, than
the application of a gentle degree of preſſure
upon the external ſurface of the ſac, in order to
reſtore its natural tone, and enable it to reſiſt
any accidental impulſe of the tears, after every

* Eſſai ſur les maladies des yeux, p. 160.

kind

kind of application has been removed. I have obferved, however, that preffure made upon the fac, by means of graduated compreffes and the monoculus bandage, or by the fmall machine of *Aquapendente*, however altered and improved, does not fpeedily anfwer the purpofe; fince both thefe methods are very inconvenient to the patient, are eafily removed from the point of compreffion, and, however carefully applied, never exercife an uniform degree of preffure upon the external parietes of the fac. By means of the fmall plate, affixed to the extremity of the leaden tent, this intention is anfwered in the moft complete and fimple manner; fince, as I have before ftated, it refts precifely in the direction of the fac, and being conftantly preffed downwards by the weight of the tent, makes a gentle and equable preffure upon its external part, without occafioning the fmalleft inconvenience to the patient.

So great is the advantage derived from a conftant and regular preffure made upon the external part of the fac, whether fimply dilated, or accompanied with ulceration, by means of this inftrument, that in a lady in whom the lachrymal fac was very much dilated, and had recently fuppurated and burft externally, but who had not courage to fubmit to an operation, after having enlarged the aperture of the fi-

nus,

nus, by means of a piece of catgut, and
paffed into the nofe a tent of a large fize
furnifhed with an external plate, I fucceeded
in the courfe of eight months in leffening the
lachrymal fac, fo as to reduce it to its natural
fize; and, by deftroying at the fame time the
fungus which formed around the fiftulous
opening, and within its cavity, fometimes by
the hydrargyrus nitratus ruber, at other times
by the argentum nitratum, the difeafe was
perfectly cured : which I am certain would not
have been effected by the mere dilatation of
the nafal canal, or it would have relapfed fhortly
afterwards, from the permanent dilatation and
flaccidity of the lachrymal fac.

When after fome time the furgeon fhall perceive that by means of this plate the lachrymal
fac, inftead of projecting outwards, on the contrary finks within the fulcus of the *os unguis*, the
leaden tent fhould be completely withdrawn,
and the external aperture of the lachrymal
fac, now reduced to a fize only large enough to
admit it, be fuffered to clofe, without employing any means to remove the callus which fur-
rounds the margin of the opening; and that for
the following reafons : if the tears, no longer
mixed with the puriform humour of the palpebræ, pafs directly through the nafal canal, and
defcending without any confiderable obftruction
are difcharged into the nofe, the cure is completed ;

pleted; and no vestige of this opening remains externally, as its edges, although callous,
approximate and contract so as scarcely to be
perceptible. If, on the contrary, notwithstanding the nasal canal having been kept dilated,
the tears meet some obstruction, in consequence of any unusual foldings of the *via lachrymalia*, they neither accumulate in the
sac, so as to distend it, nor flow back upon
the eye, but pass partly through the nasal
canal and partly through this small external
aperture, which has been left conveniently open,
from which they issue at intervals in the form
of small drops, without even the patient, or
those around him, perceiving it; this small discharge, added to that by the nasal canal, being
sufficient to preserve the eye constantly clear
and free from tears. In process of time, however, the whole of the tears resume their course
through the nasal canal, and the external aperture disappears. Some years ago a medical stu-
dent informed me that he had had, from his ear-
liest infancy, a small aperture upon each lachrymal sac, sufficient to admit the point of a needle,
and so small as to be scarcely perceptible to
the naked eye. He told me that whenever
the secretion of tears was greatly augmented by
exposure to very cold air, smoke, or other similar causes, a small quantity of tears issued from
this aperture in the form of dew or drops of
sweat;

fweat; but that it was not attended with any inconvenience, and that when it took place no defect could be perceived in the part. I am poffeffed of an extenfive feries of facts, which point out the advantages of this practice. For, as I have faid, either the tears pafs freely through the nafal canal into the cavity of the noftrils, and the external aperture, although callous, contracts fo clofely as to be no longer diftinguifhable; or the tears for fome time are flightly obftructed in their paffage through the nafal canal; and, although, they accumulate in the fac, do not diftend it immoderately or occafion a relapfe of the difeafe; or, laftly, the difeafe of the *via lachrymalia* is fuch, that even after the moft methodical treatment, their paffage from the bottom of the fac into the nofe is altogether, or in a great meafure, permanently intercepted; and, in this cafe, it is better for the patient that a few drops of tears fhould occafionally efcape from the external aperture of the fac, as in the cafe of the ftudent before mentioned, than that he fhould be fubject to a new diftention and ulceration of the fac, and a perpetual reflux and inundation of the tears upon the eye. I can, however, affert that in the greater number of cafes which have come under my obfervation, in which, after the treatment of the *fiftula lachrymalis,* a paffage has remained open for a few fmall drops of tears through

4   the

the callous aperture of the fac, it has produced no remarkable inconvenience to the patient, and has ceafed fpontaneoufly after a few months. From what has been ftated it will be eafy for the ftudent to comprehend what I have to fay refpecting the treatment of the third and fourth ftages of the *puriform difcharge of the palpebræ,* or rather of the *fiftula lachrymalis.*

When the *puriform difcharge of the palpebræ* is accompanied with an abfcefs of the parietes of the lachrymal fac, or an ulceration of its membranes opening externally, this conftitutes the true *fiftula lachrymalis.* If we recollect that this difeafe derives its origin from the puriform humour which is abundantly fecreted by the glands of Meibomius, and the internal membrane of the palpebræ, and that this thick and tenacious humour being retained and accumulated in the fac, partly by diftending and partly by irritating it, has produced an inflammation and confequent fuppuration and ulceration of its membranes, and the integuments covering it; the method of treating the *fiftula lachrymalis* will not be different from that laid down in the fecond ftage of the puriform difcharge of the palpebræ. The primary indication, therefore, in the treatment of the *fiftula lachrymalis* will be invariably to correct the morbid fecretion of the palpebræ; to lay open the lachrymal fac through its whole extent, and to place

a boua bougie or elaftic gum tent in the nafal canal, fo that it fhall occupy no part of the cavity of the fac ; and, laftly, to remedy the flacci‐ dity, fuppuration, and ulceration, by efcharotic and detergent applications, and by compreffion. As the fpontaneous rupture of the abfcefs or the ulceration moft frequently takes place in a part not favourably fituated for dividing the lachrymal fac, with precifion, through its whole extent, in fuch cafes, therefore, the furgeon fhould not attend to the orifice formed by the abfcefs or ulcer, but fhould lay it open longitudinally, precifely according to the rules already delivered.   In fuch cafes, efpe‐ cially in ulcerations of the internal membrane of the lachrymal fac of long ftanding, this membrane is conftantly found converted into a fungous fubftance, and in fome parts of it hard and callous.   The furgeon having therefore placed the bougie or elaftic gum tent, fecured by a waxed thread, in fuch a manner as to occupy the nafal canal only, fhould imme‐ diately have recourfe to efcharotics, fuch as the hydrargyrus nitratus ruber, either alone, or conjoined with a fmall quantity of alum, or to the argentum nitratum, with which the cavity of the fac fhould be fprinkled and filled at each dreffing, until the fungus and callus are entirely deftroyed, and the ulcer which

which remains is ſuſceptible of a ſolid cicatrization.

To this very important part of the treatment
of the *fiſtula lachrymalis* the ancient writers in
ſurgery paid the moſt ſcrupulous attention:
Ægnieta, Ætius, Avicenna, and the moſt celebrated practitioners of the ſucceeding age, have
ſpoken of it diffuſely, and have, with much
reaſon, regarded it as one of the moſt eſſential
points in the cure of the diſeaſe. The cauſtics
which they employed for this purpoſe were the
unguentum *isis,* an ointment compoſed of ce-
ruſe and the hydrarg. nitrat. rub. the unguentum
ægyptiacum (oxymel æruginis), the trochiſci de
minio and the cuprum vitriolatum. This practice, however prudent or advantageous, fell into
diſuſe when the new theory came into vogue,
which taught that the *fiſtula lachrymalis* was
derived from no other cauſe than the obſtruc-
tion of the naſal canal; and that therefore, in
order to effect a radical cure of it, it was only neceſſary to clear and dilate this canal, or to make
a new paſſage for the tears into the noſe. The
frequent relapſes which have taken place ſince
the introduction of this mode of treatment, and
the doubts which even at the preſent time are
occaſionally raiſed by ſurgical writers of the

* The two principal ingredients in this ointment, according to Galen, are the ærugo æris (cuprum vitriolatum) and
alumen uſtum.

higheſt

higheft repute, of the poffibility of the radical
cure of the *fiftula lackrymalis*, fufficiently demon-
ftrate the contrary, and prove how improperly the ancient method of employing cauftics
in a prudent manner has been abandoned in
the treatment of this difeafe. This very ufeful practice of the ancients has been revived
among us' by the elder Nannoni,* with this
difference, however, that this able furgeon has,
in my opinion, propofed too free an ufe of the
cauftic, in the treatment of the *fiftula lachrymalis*,
that is fo as to deftroy the fac entirely, *and con-
vert it into a completely folid and callous body*; and
this he attempted to do the more confidently,
from a perfuafion, that, " *when the lachrymal
fac is converted into a folid body, the tears occafion
little or no inconvenience*:" an opinion, which
indeed ftands in perfect oppofition to obfervation and the anatomical ftructure of the parts.
But as he adduces inftances of perfons, in whom,
after fuch treatment, there remained no weeping of the eye, it is reafonable to conclude
that the cauftic in thefe cafes had deftroyed the
fungus of the fac, and facilitated the healing
of its internal furface, not that it had obliterated the cavity, which, notwithftanding fuch
deftruction, had preferved its continuity with
the nafal canal.

This is precifely what the furgeon ought

* Trattato Chirurg. fulla femplicità del med. Offerv. xxxi.

to have in view in the treatment of the
fiftula lachrymalis, otherwife, by the total deftruction and obliteration of the lachrymal fac,
he would only be converting it into another
difeafe equally troublefome, the perpetual reflux
and accumulation of tears and matter upon the
correfponding eye. The action of the cauftic
fhould be therefore regulated in fuch a manner
as only to deftroy the fungus, and difpofe the
internal furface of the fac to heal. After this
has been accomplifhed, the bougie or elaftic
gum tent fhould be withdrawn from the nafal
canal, and the reft of the treatment conducted
in the manner before directed, by compreffing
the external part of the fac, by means of the
plate affixed to the tent of lead, and after it is
withdrawn, allowing the tears the greateft
poffible opportunity of difcharging themfelves
into the nofe.

The fourth ftage of the puriform difcharge
of the palpebræ, commonly called by furgeons
fiftula lachrymalis cum carie, is a difeafe lefs
common than was formerly imagined, but
which, however, I have had frequent opportunities of feeing, in the courfe of my practice;
and from my own obfervations on this fubject,
it appears to me that this ftage of the *fiftula lachrymalis* prefents itfelf under two diftinct forms.
The firft is that in which the fac, having been
for a confiderable time enormoufly diftended,

and filled with a mixture of matter, tears, and
the puriform humour of the palpebræ, is entire
externally, but opens internally into the cor-
responding noftril through the *os unguis*, which
is carious and eroded, and in which the deftruction of the *via lachrymalia* is fo great that the
nafal canal is obliterated and deftroyed, and may
be confidered as having no connection with the
lachrymal fac. The other form of the difeafe is
that in which the ulcerated fac opens externally,
and the *os unguis* in its pofterior part is denuded
and carious, but not perforated, and where the
nafal canal is indurated and filled with fungus,
fo as to be nearly clofed and feparated from the
reft of the *via lachrymalia*.

The firft form of this difeafe may be known, by
obferving, that when the fac, which is very large,
is even gently compreffed, a fmall portion only
of the purulent humour contained in it iffues
through the *puncta lachrymalia* upon the eye,
while the greater part of that fluid is difcharged
into the nofe, and the capacious fac at the fame
time fubfides and difappears, and the matter
which iffues abundantly from the correfponding
noftril emits a fœtid odour which is peculiar to
carious bone. The fecond form of this difeafe is
rendered evident by the introduction of a probe
into the fac, by which the *os unguis* is found
denuded, and which being preffed downwards
in all directions, inftead of entering the nafal
canal,

canal, comes in contact only with fungous, indurated, and contracted parts.

The firft of thefe forms of the *fiftula lachrymalis*, is not beyond the reach of art, and allows
us to hope for a perfect cure, provided the difeafe
only includes the *os unguis*, with a fmall part of
the ethmoidal cells. For if the fac be laid open
through its whole extent, without any regard to
the reftoration of the nafal canal, and its cavity
cleared by means of efcharotic and detergent
applications, as the aqua calcis with mel rofæ, the
feparation of the carious and perforated bone, and
the contraction of the cavity of the fac, are neceffary confequences. The puriform difcharge of
the palpebræ ceafes by applying upon the internal
furface of the eye-lids, from the commencement of
the treatment, the unguentum ophthalmicum, the
action of which remedy may be affifted, according to circumftances, by the internal ufe of fuch
medicines as are adapted to correct the particular
diathefis, by which the morbid fecretion of the
palpebræ has been produced or kept up. Thefe
advantages being obtained, and the internal furface of the fac healed, and nearly reduced to its
natural fize, if the edges of the external wound
are permitted to approximate and contract, fo
that there is no longer any veftige of it, the
opening which remains in the pofterior part
of the lachrymal fac, communicating with the
correfponding noftril, is fo large, from the defi-

D 3   ciency

ciency of the *os unguis* and the pituitary membrane which covers it on the fide of the nofe,
that the tears carried by the *punɕta lachrymalia*
and lachrymal canals into the fac are immediately difcharged into the nofe, fo that the
cure may be confidered as complete, fince the
patient is no longer incommoded by the over-
flowing of the tears.

The fame method of treatment is attended
with equal fuccefs in the fecond form of the
fiftula lachrymalis, accompanied with denudation
of the *os unguis*; with this difference, that as
the *os unguis* is only denuded and not perforated,
and the pituitary membrane covering it on the
fide of the noftril is entire, and as there is no hope
of being able to reftore the office of the nafal canal,
in this cafe it becomes abfolutely neceffary to
make a new and permanent paffage for the tears
into the nofe, by perforating and deftroying the
denuded *os unguis* and the correfponding portion of the pituitary membrane. Experience
has fhown, that the mere perforation of the *os
unguis* and pituitary membrane, without a de-
ftruɕtion of a portion of the latter to fome extent around the place of perforation or feparation of the bone, does not fufficiently anfwer
the purpofe, fince this opening in procefs of
time becomes too fmall for the difcharge of the
tears, and continues gradually contraɕting until
it is entirely clofed.   A very common exempli-
fication

fication of this preſents itſelf in the caries of the palate from a venereal cauſe. When the carious portion of bone is ſeparated, a communication ſometimes remains between the noſe and mouth, ſufficient to admit the point of the finger; this aperture, however, gradually contracts itſelf, ſo as ſcarcely to admit a writing quill, and it ſometimes even cloſes up entirely, in conſequence of the approximation of the membrane of the palate, which has been divided, but not much injured by the preceding ulceration attending the caries of the ſubjacent bone. If this takes place under ſuch circumſtances the cloſing of the pituitary membrane is much more to be expected after the ſimple perforation of it by the trocar, which is employed for the purpoſe of piercing the *os unguis.* The tubes, which have been propoſed for keeping this perforation of the pituitary membrane conſtantly open are not to be confided in, ſince even thoſe which are beſt conſtructed for producing ſuch an effect are very frequently, after a ſhort time, forced upwards againſt the anterior part of the lachrymal ſac, or they fall into the noſtrils too ſoon, or in the ſpace of a few months they are filled with an earthy ſubſtance which renders them completely impervious and uſeleſs. The perforation and ſeparation of the denuded *os unguis,* therefore, as well as the deſtruction of a portion of the pituitary membrane around the

part

part where *os unguis* has been detached, are the
only certain and efficacious means hitherto difcovered, which can fecure a permanent paffage
for the tears into the nofe : to anfwer which
purpofe no mode of treatment appears better
adapted than the application of the actual cautery, which, though certainly too freely employed by the older furgeons, has been too
haftily rejected by the moderns.* Men's opi-
nions generally run into extremes. The ancients cauterized the *os unguis* and pituitary
membrane, in every cafe of *fiftula lachrymalis*,
and very frequently without neceffity ; the moderns, notwithftanding its evident utility and
neceffity, neglect it altogether.

For the purpofe of applying the cautery, the
fac fhould be divided through its whole extent,
and its cavity filled with foft lint, which fhould
be retained in its place by means of a comprefs
and bandage. At the end of two days the
dreffing fhould be removed, and the cavity of
the fac and denuded bone made perfectly dry.
A canula † being introduced within the fac,
and placed upon the *os unguis* in a direction a
little oblique from above downwards, and the
patient's head firmly fupported, the furgeon
with one hand fhould hold the canula, and with
the other pafs the cautery ‡ as far as the *os*

* Of this opinion alfo is Richter. Obf. Med. Chirurg. ch. x.
† Plate III. fig. 5.   ‡ Plate III. fig. 6.

unguis,

unguis, upon which he fhould make a moderate degree of preffure, in order that the point of the cautery may not only pafs beyond it, but alfo deftroy the pituitary membrane which covers it internally. And as it is a matter of the great-eft importance for the complete fuccefs of the operation, that this part of the membrane fhould form an efchar, and be completely detached around the opening in the bone, if the furgeon therefore perceive that the point of the cautery cools too quickly, he fhould carefully apply a fecond, which he fhould have in readinefs for that purpofe. The cavity of the fac fhould be afterwards filled with foft lint fpread with an emollient ointment, fuch as that confifting of wax and oil, and the patient be directed to draw up his noftrils frequently in the courfe of the day the aqua malvæ in a tepid ftate. If, on the following day, the patient feel much pain and there be confiderable tumefaction of the nofe and palpebræ, they fhould be covered with a poultice of bread and new milk. As foon as a fuppuration is eftablifhed between the found and cauterized parts, the efchar of the pituitary membrane will be difcharged through the nofe, and the fragments of the *os unguis* will pafs partly along with the matter by the external opening of the fac, and partly by the noftril. Through this new open-ing into the nofe the furgeon fhould now in-

troduce

troduce either a bougie or a fmall findon of fine
linen tied with a waxed thread, to prevent its
falling into the noftrils, the fize of which fhould
be increafed in proportion as the new opening
becomes larger by the loofening of other portions
of the efchar of the pituitary membrane or particles of bone. Befides the application of the
ophthalmie ointment of Janin, in order to fup-
prefs the puriform difcharge of the palpebræ,
efcharotics fhould be employed at the fame
time, with a view to deftroy the fungous and
indurated parts of the fac, and to obtain a contraction of its cavity nearly to its natural fize.
When the whole internal furface of the fac is
nearly healed, if there be any appearance of
fungus around the artificial opening in the nofe,
it fhould be repreffed by touching it frequently
with the argentum nitratum ; nor fhould this be
omitted until the margin of this internal opening be as perfectly healed as the reft of the cavity of the fac. After which the lips of the
external wound fhould be fuffered to clofe without fcarifying their edges,

It may not be unneceffary to obferve here,
that the treatment of this, as well as of the fecond ftage of the puriform difcharge of the palpebræ is of long duration, and that the cure is
feldom completed in lefs than four months,
even where the moft diligent attention is paid,
and the patient, in other refpects, is perfectly
healthy.

healthy. But this delay is fufficiently compenfated by a perfect and lafting cure.

From what has been delivered in this chapter
we are enabled to draw the following conclu-
fions.

1. That the difeafe generally termed *fiftula*
lachrymalis, which is divided by fome very accurate writers into the *fimple,* the *compound,* with
atony or flaccidity of the fac, and the *complicated*
with caries of the *os unguis,* is principally derived from the morbid fecretion of the glands of
Meibomius and the internal membrane of the
palpebræ.

2. That it is impoffible to obtain a perfect
cure of this difeafe in any degree, ftage, or com-
plication, unlefs the morbid fecretion of the
palpebræ be at the fame time permanently
corrected by the application of topical remedies
upon the margin and internal furface of the
affected eye-lids, and by the ufe of fuch internal
medicines as are calculated to correct the particular predifpofition from which the morbid fecretion of the palpebræ is derived.

3. That in the fecond ftage of the difeafe attended with atony and evident diftention of the
fac, although the morbid fecretion of the palpebræ be corrected, and the action of the
nafal canal perfectly reftored, the weeping of
the eye will neverthelefs continue, unlefs the
fac be reduced to its natural fize, by laying it
open

open through its whole extent, and by applying upon its internal furface efcharotics, and afterwards detergent and aftringent remedies, fo as to reeftablifh a certain proportion between the capacity of the fac and the caliber of the nafal canal.

4. That the *fiftula lachrymalis*, accompanied with caries and perforation of the *os unguis*, and of that portion of the pituitary membrane which covers it, together with an obliteration of the nafal canal, provided the caries has not penetrated too deeply within the ethmoidal cells, particularly in unhealthy conftitutions, admits of a perfect cure, without any inconvenience remaining from the weeping of the eye, by merely deftroying the fungus within the cavity of the fac, by promoting the feparation of the edges of the carious and eroded bone, and by reftoring the cavity of the fac to its natural fize, and healing it internally.

5. That in the *fiftula lachrymalis*, with denudation of the *os unguis*, and an infuperable obftruction of the nafal canal, in which it becomes neceffary, in order to effect a perfect cure of the difeafe, to make a new paffage for the tears from the fac into the nofe, the application of the cautery is preferable to the fimple perforation of the bone and pituitary membrane by means of the trocar; fince the paffage in the *os unguis* does not remain fufficiently and conftantly

ftantly open, unlefs the portion of pituitary
membrane which covers it be alfo deftroyed.

6. That at the end of the treatment of the
fecond, as well as of the third and fourth ftages
of the difeafe, it is an ufeful precaution not to
fcarify the edges of the external orifice of the
fac, which is now healed internally, but to fuffer them to contract fpontaneoufly, until at leaft
there are the moft certain indications that the
tears meet with no obftruction in the fac, and
either pafs completely through the nafal canal',
or through the artificial opening made in the
os unguis and pituitary membrane.

CASE I.

A young lady of Pavia, 17 years of age, of a
delicate and fenfible fibre, began to experience
an unufual difficulty in opening the right eye,
in confequence of a preternatural tumefaction
of the palpebræ of that fide, accompanied with
a weeping of the eye, and an accumulation of
gum, efpecially in the morning. She was directed to wafh the eye frequently with elder-
flower water. After four months the difeafe
had greatly increafed, and on being confulted,
I found, that on preffing the lachrymal fac a
very confiderable quantity of puriform matter
iffued from the *puncta*. On everting the palpebræ of the right fide, the internal furface,
efpecially of the inferior eye-lid, near its margin,

was

was evidently more tumefied than natural, and
had a villous appearance, the glands of Meibomius were more turgid and elevated than ufual,
and interwoven with fmall varicofe veffels:
which appearances were not perceptible, or in
a very fmall degree, upon the internal furface of
the left fide.   The right ala of the nofe in this
young lady alfo had been for feveral months
very red and fwollen, and the internal furface of
the correfponding noftril incrufted and dry.

Having preffed out all the puriform matter
contained in the fac, I attempted to inject fome
water through one of the *puncta lachrymalia*,
and at the fourth attempt the water paffed into
the nofe and fauces.   And as the lachrymal fac
was not perceptibly more diftended than natural, I directed all my attention to divert the
difcharge, to diminifh and correct the morbid
fecretion, and at the fame time to ftrengthen
the varicofe veffels of the internal membrane of
the affected eye-lids.

I therefore ordered the patient to take, in the
courfe of the day, a pint of milk whey, with a
dram of the cryftals of tartar, and half a grain of
tartarized antimony, which did not difagree with
the ftomach, and procured one, and fometimes
two copious evacuations every day.

As a local application, a fmall quantity of the
ophthalmic ointment of Janin was introduced
between the eye-lids, prepared exactly according

to

to the author's formula. The irritation which
this remedy produced in the prefent cafe was fo
violent, that in little more than an hour, notwithftanding the parts were repeatedly wafhed
with milk, the eye-lids became enormoufly
fwollen and inflamed. During the inflammation, which continued four or five days, the
puriform difcharge was entirely fuppreffed, nor
could any thing be forced from the fac, though
preffed upon at different intervals, except pure
tears. On the fubfidence of the inflammation
the puriform difcharge of the palpebræ returned
nearly as before. The ophthalmic ointment was
again applied, which was rendered lefs active by
adding a double quantity of lard, of which a
portion equal to a grain and a half of wheat was
applied morning and evening, the *via lachrymalia* being previoufly cleared by an injection of
plantain water with a fmall quantity of fpirit of
wine added to it, and a few drops of the vitriolic collyrium were inftilled into the eye three
or four times a day.

By this treatment, at the end of three weeks
the puriform difcharged was greatly diminifhed,
and confifted of little more than tears rendered
turbid by mucus, and the right ala of the nofe
was no longer incrufted, but refumed its natural
appearance. The internal membrane of the
eye-lids became gradually pale and fmooth, the
glands of Meibomius recovered their natural

4   fize,

fize, and the varicofe veffels difappeared; the ufe of the whey with the antimon. tart. was now fufpended.

About the fortieth day, on preffing upon the fac, there only iffued from it pure tears, and the injection paffed with the greateft facility from the *puncta lachrymalia* into the nofe. The tears, however, continued to meet with fome obftruction, and the patient, on expofing herfelf to cold air, or reading by the light of the candle, was obliged to wipe the eye frequently. As this inconvenience did not appear to arife from an atony of the fac, and as the patient conftantly complained of a fullnefs of the pituitary membrane of the right noftril, by which the extremity of the nafal canal fuffered fome degree of conftriction, I ordered her to draw up her noftril frequently in the courfe of the day the vapour of vinegar and water, and to take a little fnuff. This expedient fucceeded very well, for in ten days the difcharge from the nofe was reeftablifhed, and the weeping of the eye entirely ceafed.

Case II.

Maria Bordoni, of Sᵃ Chriftina, a girl 12 years old, who had been fubject in her infancy to frequent attacks of ophthalmia, in one and fometimes both eyes, was affected for eight weeks with a weeping of the right eye, and a confiderable

rable discharge of apparently purulent matter. She was brought by her parents to the
hofpital, not fo much on this account, as in confequence of a fmall hard, red, and painful tumour which had made its appearance, within
fix days, between the internal angle of the eye
and the nofe.

The edges of the eye-lids, of the right fide
were confiderably tuméfied, their internal furface red, and prefenting a fungous appearance, and
the glands of Meïbomius greatly increafed in fize.

A poultice of bread and milk was applied upon
the tumour, as the membrane of the fac appeared to be in a ftate approaching to fuppuration; in a few days, however, the inflammation
was diffipated, the tumour fubfided, and the
puncta lachrymalia, which before appeared to be
retracted towards the caruncle and were concealed, now feparated from the commiffure of
the palpebræ, and refumed their natural pofition. On preffing now upon the lachrymal fac
the puriform matter iffued in great abundance
from the *puncta lachrymalia* upon the eye.

I began immediately to employ the ophthalmic ointment of Janin night and morning in a
quantity not exceeding the fize of a barley-corn.
By this application the puriform difcharge of
the palpebræ was at firft increafed, but in the
courfe of a month diminifhed fo confiderably,
that there only iffued from the fac a diluted

E   mucus.

mucus. As foon as the edges and internal furface of the eye-lids had recovered their natural ftate, I began to inject through the *puncta
lachrymalia*, plantain water, with a little of the
vitriolic collyrium, added to it, which had
been filtered, and the injection paffed into the
nofe. The child was treated in this manner for
twenty days more, and then difcharged from
the hofpital perfectly cured.

CASE III.

A country boy, 10 years of age, after a variolous metaftafis to the eyes, with which he had
been attacked two years before, was affected
with a weeping of both eyes and a gumming
of the eye-lids. The palpebræ were thickened
and deprived of their lafhes, and their internal
furface was of a dark red colour, and had a
villous appearance; the glands of Meibomius
were more elevated than ufual, and on preffing
the fac on each fide, which, however, did not
appear to be more diftended or elevated than
natural, a confiderable quantity of curdly, yellowifh, puriform matter iffued from the *puncta*.
This child had, what is commonly called, a
grofs habit of body.

I began the treatment, by ordering ten ounces
of the decoction of the triticum repens, a dram
of the cryftalli tartari, and half a grain of the
antimonium tartarizatum, to be taken every day
at

at intervals; and if the medicine ſhould purge him too much, he was directed to take only half the quantity for a few days following. I directed alſo that the ophthalmic ointment of Janin ſhould be applied morning and evening between the palpebræ of both eyes, which, as uſual, conſiderably increaſed the ſecretion of puriform matter. Finding that at the end of two weeks the diſcharge did not diminiſh, I made a ſeton in the neck which preſently ſuppurated and greatly relieved the eyes. From this period, by continuing the application of the ophthalmic ointment, and frequently purging the patient with ſmall doſes of the antimonium tartarizatum, the puriform diſcharge gradually diminiſhed, the edges of the eye-lids ſubſided and recovered their natural flexibility, and the internal ſurface began to aſſume a pale colour, and to loſe its villous appearance. The daily and frequent uſe of the vitriolic collyrium, and the injection of plantain water with a little ſpirit of wine through the *puncta lachrymalia* was never omitted. The injection at the firſt paſſed with ſome difficulty, but it afterwards deſcended freely into the noſe on both ſides; and towards the end of the third month the child left the hoſpital completely cured.

CASE

Case IV.

A girl, four years of age, of **Parpanefe**, was
affected after the fmall-pox with an habitual
ophthalmia of the right eye, accompanied with
a turgefcence. of the edges of the eye-lids, a
copious difcharge of puriform matter, and great,
fenfibility of the eye to a very moderate degree
of light. After an ineffectual treatment of feveral months, the child was brought to Pavia, in
the beginning of December 1798. The internal furface of the palpebræ was red and villous,
and on compreffing the fac a thick, yellowifh
matter mixed with tears, iffued from the *puncta
lachrymalia,* fimilar to that with which the eye-
lids were continually imbued. The lachrymal
fac, however, did not appear larger or more elevated than natural. It is proper to remark that
the lymphatic glands of the neck were enlarged
and indurated, the abdomen turgid, and that
the child had an extraordinary voracity for every
kind of food. Added to this, there was a conftant difcharge of a whitifh matter from the
parts of generation, fimilar to the fluor albus.

I ordered, at firft, a good diet, and directed that
the child fhould take every day, in fmall dofes,
a pint of the decoction of the triticum repens,
with a dram of the cryftalli tartari, and half a
grain of the antimonium tartarizatum. This
remedy occafioned at firft a copious vomiting
of

of vifcid, yellowifh matter, but afterwards it excited only a flight naufea, and two or three
evacuations in the courfe of the day, without
inducing debility. A few days afterwards I
directed three drops of the Tinctura Thebaïca
of the London Pharmacopœia to, be inftilled
into the eye for feveral fucceffive nights,
which excited great pain at the firft, but after a
few minutes it ceafed entirely, and left the
eye in a better ftate than before, having
rendered it lefs impatient of the light. After
purfuing this treatment for two weeks, I made a
feton in the neck, which prefently produced a
copious fuppuration, and was attended with a
confiderable diminution of the chronic ophthalmia. The ufe of the antimonium tartarizatum
was continued in fmall dofes, and the ophthalmic ointment of Janin fubftituted for the Thebaïc tincture, at firft only in the evening, but
afterwards morning and evening, and the vitriolic collyrium was dropped into the eye every
three hours in the day.

By the ufe of thefe remedies the chronic ophthalmia was entirely diffipated, the edges of
the eye-lids recovered their form and natural
ftate, and the quantity of puriform matter which
iffued from the *puncta lachrymalia* upon the eye,
by preffing upon the fac, was gradually leffened.
Towards the end of February of the fame year,
the regurgitation of matter ceafed altogether, as

well

well as the cohesion of the eye-lids during the night. The tumefaction of the abdomen and lymphatic glands of the neck was very much diminished; the child improved in its appearance, and was satisfied with a moderate quantity of food; there was yet, however, a little discharge from the genitals. In the beginning of March I ordered the child to take two ounces of the tincture of the cinchona three times a day.* Towards the middle of April she was dismissed perfectly cured, without any fear of the puriform discharge of the eye-lids degenerating into the *fistula lachrymalis.* The seton was kept open for several months afterwards.

Case V.

Signora Angiola P..., a lady, 40 years of age, living in the vicinity of this city, neglected a puriform discharge of the palpebræ for more than 11 years, which by degrees produced an enormous dilatation of the lachrymal sac. When I examined her the first time, the lachrymal sac was full, the tumour which it formed externally was rather larger than a filbert, and on being pressed gave issue to a large quantity of viscid, curdly, greenish matter. The edges of the eye-lids of the same side were tumid, and

---

* I suspect the author here means a watery tincture or infusion of the bark, as such a quantity of the spirituous tincture could not fail to have been attended with unpleasant effects.

internally

internally red and fungous, and the febaceous glands greatly enlarged.

I laid open the lachrymal fac through its whole extent, from the ligament of the orbicularis mufcle to the loweft part of it, and having paffed a fine probe through the nafal canal, and afterwards one of a larger fize, I introduced into it a bougie an inch and a half long, tied with a waxed thread, in fuch a manner that its upper extremity fhould remain entirely concealed in the nafal canal; and I filled the whole cavity of the fac very exactly with foft lint, which I confined in its fituation by means of a comprefs and the *monoculus* bandage.

At the end of two days I took off the dreffings, without removing the bougie from the nafal canal. I found the whole internal furface of the fac in a fungous ftate. I filled its cavity with a doffil of lint fpread with a liniment, confifting of the hydrargyrus nitratus ruber, and mucilage of gum arabic. On the following day the doffil of lint came away covered with a thick whitifh or cottony cruft, and this fubftance continued to come away in an increafed quantity by the ufe of the hydrargyrus nitratus ruber, with which the cavity of the fac was filled feveral times in the courfe of three weeks. From this time, by the repeated application of the cauftic powder, the fungus of the internal furface of the fac

began

began to difappear, and its cavity to contract. I withdrew the bougie for the firft time from the nafal canal in order to clean it and immediately replaced it.

This treatment was continued during twenty days longer, occafionally increafing the activity of the hydrargyrus nitrat. rub. by the addition of a fmall quantity of alum, and keeping the external opening of the fac dilated by the introduction of lint, and fometimes fponge, and that with the fame advantage as before, with refpect to the deftruction of the fungus and the contraction of the atonic and flaccid fac. The dreffing afterwards confifted in filling the cavity of the fac very exactly with lint moiftened in the aqua calcis and mel rofæ. I then withdrew the bougie from the nafal canal for the fecond time, for the purpofe of cleaning it, and immediately replaced it as before.

The cicatrix began to extend from the edges of the external opening of the fac towards its internal furface, which in a month after this period was nearly reduced to its natural capacity. There remained, however, here and there fome points not healed, which appeared rather difpofed to throw out a fungus ; and that part of the fac fituated above the tendon of the orbicularis mufcle,* which had not been included in the incifion, was not yet diminifhed, in pro-

* Plate I. a.

portion

portion to the reſt of the ſac. The cure was completed three weeks afterwards, by the oc- caſional application of the argentum nitrat. and dry lint.

At the expiration of this time the bougie was entirely withdrawn from the naſal canal, and the leaden tent with its plate* intended to compreſs the anterior part of the ſac ſub- ſtituted in its place. I directed her to wear this for a full month, and to clean it every day, and waſh the eye with plantain water mixed with a little ſpirit of wine.

The palpebræ having recovered their natural ſtate by the application of the ophthalmic oint- ment of Janin, which had been employed from the beginning of the treatment, and there being only a diſcharge of limpid tears from the orifice of the ſac, I removed the leaden tent entirely, the plate of which had ſo completely compreſſ- ed the ſac, that inſtead of threatening a new elevation, it was even more depreſſed within the ſulcus of the bone than natural. The edges of the orifice of the ſac, which before were callous and elevated around the cylinder of the tent, immediately contracted, although they had nei- ther been ſtimulated nor ſcarified, without leav- ing ſcarcely any veſtige of the inciſion made in the ſac; and the tears immediately paſſed into the naſal canal. It is proper to remark that,

* Plate III. fig. 9.

except

except during the firſt fifteen days from the operation, the patient conſtantly attended her family affairs as uſual, and that ſhe has now en-
joyed five years of the moſt perfect health, ſuf-
fering no inconvenience either from the weeping of the eye or the diſcharge of matter.

Case VI.

Signor Francefco Bochioli, of S. Angelo Lo-
digiano, a robuſt man 50 years of age, was
affected for about 10 years with a puriform difcharge of the palpebræ of the right eye, attended with atony and great dilatation of the lachrymal fac, which occaſioned a continual diſcharge
of tears, and frequent attacks of acute ophthalmia on that ſide. When I ſaw him, the tumour formed by the lachrymal fac was the ſize
of a nut, ſlightly inflamed and painful; the
edges of the eye-lids were tumefied as uſual,
their internal ſurface was florid and villous, and
the glands of Meibomius enlarged.

A poultice of bread and milk was applied for
two days upon the affected palpebræ and lachrymal fac, to diminiſh the rigidity of theſe parts,
and at the ſame time to leſſen the ſlight degree
of inflammation and tenſion of the integuments.
The operation was then performed as in the
preceding cafe, by laying the fac open through
its whole extent, from the tendon of the orbicularis mufcle to the loweſt part of it, and introducing

troducing a bougie an inch and a half in length into the naſal canal, without its upper extremity projecting into the cavity of the ſac.

The fungus of the internal ſurface of the lachrymal ſac was very conſiderable, in order to deſtroy which I was under the neceſſity of employing, for thirty ſucceſſive days, ſometimes the eſcharotic liniment abovementioned, occaſionally the hydrarg. nitrat. rub. alone or mixed with alum, by means of which there came away at each dreſſing a ſtratum of a white thick ſubſtance reſembling cotton.

Having deſtroyed the fungus, the ulcer which occupied the internal ſurface of the ſac produced healthy granulations, and the ſac was diſpoſed to contract in every direction. As the opening was too narrow, and prevented the commodious introduction of the doſſil of lint into the cavity of the ſac, it conſequently became neceſſary to have recourſe for a few days to the prepared ſponge.

On attempting to withdraw the bougie for the firſt time from the naſal canal, the thread with which it was tied broke, probably from being too much macerated, and the bougie was left in the canal and entirely forgotten, until the cavity of the ſac was perfectly healed and contracted. This was obtained in the courſe of 40 days, by only introducing dry lint into the ſac, and occaſionally touching the bottom of

the

the wound with the argent. nitrat. The cicatrix, as ufual, commenced from the edges of the
wound, and by degrees extended over the internal furface of the fac, which was now reduced
nearly to its natural capacity. The edges of
the palpebræ of the right fide had alfo recovered
their natural ftate and flexibility from the uninterrupted ufe of the ophthalmic ointment of
Janin.

The internal furface of the fac being now
completely healed, I introduced a thick probe
through the fac into the nafal canal, in order to
pufh the bougie downwards, and make it pafs
out by the nofe or fauces; but, contrary to my
expectation, the probe paffed freely into the nofe,
and the injection even more fo, which led me
to fufpect that the bougie had recently defcended into the fauces and ftomach during the patients fleep, without his having perceived it.
I fubftituted in its place a leaden tent furnifhed
with the fmall plate for compreffing the anterior
part of the fac, which the patient wore for 50
days; during this time he attended his bufinefs,
and took it out and replaced it himfelf occafionally. The plate by means of the weight of the
leaden cylinder, having depreffed the anterior
part of the fac confiderably towards the fulcus
of the bone, I withdrew the tent entirely,
and the external orifice of the fac clofed with-

out

out its edges being fcarified, and the tears paffed through the nafal canal.

CASE VII.

Dominica Roffi, a female peafant 30 years of age, a native of the Genoefe Mountains who lived in this city in the capacity of a fervant, of a ftrong and fanguineous temperament, but who had been formerly fubject to herpetic eruptions and eryfipelas of the face, had during feveral years a weeping of the left eye and a gumming of the eye-lids, with tumefaction of their edges and enlargement of the correfpond-ing febaceous glands. The lachrymal fac of that fide had gradually increafed to the fize of a filbert, and on being preffed gave iffue to a confiderable quantity of puriform matter. In this ftate fhe was admitted into the practical fchool of furgery, the 9th of December 1796.

Although, from the great diftenfion and tume-faction of the lachrymal fac, no doubt could be entertained of the neceffity of commencing the treatment by laying it open, yet in order fully to convince the ftudents that the puriform mat-ter which iffued copioufly from the fac upon the eye, was not generated in the fac itfelf, but was principally tranfmitted to it from the in-creafed morbid fecretion of the palpebræ, I merely endeavoured to correct or reftrain this morbid fecretion of the eye-lids, by the applica-

tion

tion of the opthalmic ointment of Janin, and the frequent ufe of the vitriolic collyrium. At the end of three weeks, the difcharge having been almoft entirely fuppreffed by thefe local remedies, there only iffued from the diftended fac limpid tears, or which were rendered flightly turbid by a fmall quantity of thin mucus.

I then proceeded to the radical cure, by laying the fac open through its whole extent, and introducing a bougie into the nafal canal in the manner before mentioned, and laftly by filling the cavity of the fac with dry lint, which was maintained in its fituation by a comprefs and bandage.

Two days after, the dreffings were removed and the cavity of the fac filled with a doffil of lint fpread with the liniment, confifting of the hydrarg. nitrat. rub. and mucilage of gum arabic. This remedy gave the patient a good deal of pain, which is not the cafe in general, and occafioned a confiderable tumefaction of the cheek; in confequence of which I was under the neceffity of defifting from it for fome days. It was, however, afterwards renewed with a larger proportion of mucilage. By the corroding action of this application I obtained in the courfe of a month a floughing of the internal membrane of the fac, and a confiderable contraction of its cavity, the internal furface of which fhowed a very favourable difpofition to heal.

heal. The lips of the orifice were carefully
prevented from cloſing too quickly by the frequent introduction of ſponge inſtead of lint. As
ſoon as the cavity of the ſac was reduced to its
natural ſize, and completely healed internally,
the bougie was withdrawn from the naſal canal,
and the leaden tent with its compreſſing plate
introduced in the place of it. The ſac and
the reſt of the *via lachrymalia* were daily waſhed,
ſometimes with plantain water and ſpirit of
wine, at other times with the aqua calcis and
mel roſæ.

'Towards the middle of May, the external
part of the ſac being ſo much depreſſed by the
plate as to leave no fear of its yielding to the
impulſe of the tears, every application was removed from it, and its external orifice ſuffered
to cloſe. The tears were diſcharged into the
noſe; with this difference, however, that if by
any accident the lachrymal fluid was ſecreted
in larger quantity than uſual, a few drops iſſued
from this ſmall and almoſt imperceptible aperture in the ſac, and thus preſerved the eye conſtantly dry. This occaſional diſcharge continued during ſome months after the patient had
left the hoſpital; it afterwards diſappeared entirely, and ſhe has remained perfectly well ever
ſince. It is proper to obſerve, that, before the
operation, and for ſeveral weeks afterwards the
ophthalmic ointment of *Janin* was made uſe of

at

at night until the morbid fecretion of the palpebræ was completely fuppreffed; and that
during the treatment the patient was frequently
purged either with fmall dofes of the tartarized
antimony and cryftals of tartar, or with the refolvent pills of Schmucker.*

Case VIII.

Maddalena Marinoni of Scaldafole, a girl 19
years of age, was admitted into this hofpital in
January 1792, on account of a puriform difcharge of the eye-lids, attended with a fmall
degree of elevation of the lachrymal fac. By
the conftant ufe of the ophthalmic ointment of
Janin morning and evening, and occafionally of
the collyrium vitriolicum, the morbid fecretion
of the eye-lids entirely ceafed, but the eye remained conftantly watery, and the fac as much
elevated as at firft, which, on being preffed,
difcharged by the *puncta* an abundant quantity
of limpid tears. The puriform difcharge of the
palpebræ was changed into that difeafe, which
is generally called by furgeons *the dropfy of the
lachrymal fac.* Being perfectly fatisfied, that, in
order to reftore to the fac its natural elafticity
and fize, little advantage would be derived either
from aftringent injections, or compreffion, I determined to lay it open longitudinally, which
I found internally fmooth, and without the leaft

* See the Chapter on Amaurofis.

appearance

appearance of fungus. After having examined
the nafal canal I introduced into it a filver
tube, which was to remain there permanently,
exactly fimilar to that recommended by Bell;*
and having injected fome warm water, in order to cleanfe the infide of the fac and canula,
I brought the lips of the wound together, and
retained them in contact by means of fome
ftrips of adhefive plafter, a comprefs, and the
monoculus bandage.

The fubfequent inflammation of the fac and
palpebræ was very confiderable, and it was neceffary to take away blood copioufly, to cover
the parts with an emollient and anodyne plafter, and to confine the patient to a low diet.
In a week the inflammation abated, and the
lips of the wound were united and confolidated;
in fhort every thing went on furprifingly well;
there was no longer any weeping of the eye,
and three weeks after the operation the patient
was difcharged from the hofpital perfectly
cured. After continuing well for a year, fhe
began to complain of a fenfe of weight and
pricking between the internal angle of the left
eye and the nofe, and the weeping of the eye
again returned. A fmall tumour appeared in
the fituation of the lachrymal fac, which on
being preffed gave pain, and gradually inflamed.

* A Syftem of Surgery, vol. iv. plate 42, fig. 5, 6.

F   It

It ultimately fuppurated and burft externally, difcharging matter mixed with tears. In this ftate the girl returned to the hofpital about 19 months after the divifion of the fac and introduction of the tube into the nafal canal.

On preffing this tumour, even flightly, it was eafy to difcover that it contained an extraneous body, and I had no doubt that this was the metallic tube which had been formerly placed in the nafal canal. Without therefore regarding the opening formed by the abfcefs, I laid the fac again completely open, from the tendon of the *orbicularis palpebrarum* to the loweft part, and found the tube lying acrofs it; I extracted it and found that it was completely filled with a compact calcareous fubftance; after which I only filled the fac with foft lint and covered it with a comprefs and bandage.

On removing the firft dreffing, which was two days after, the whole internal furface of the fac exhibited a florid, irregular, and fungous appearance. The probe however paffed with perfect facility through the nafal canal into the correfponding noftril, and I therefore introduced into it without delay a bougie one inch and a half in length, tied with a waxed thread, and pufhed fo far downwards that its upper end might not project into the cavity of the fac. For the purpofe of deftroying the fungus formed by the internal furface of the fac, I employed at

firft,

firft, for feveral days, a doffil of lint dipped in the liniment, confifting of the hydrarg. nitrat. rub. and mucilage of gum arabic; I afterwards filled the whole cavity of the fac repeatedly with the hydrarg. nitrat. rub. in powder.

At the end of feven weeks the cicatrix began to extend from the margin of the wound towards the bottom of the fac, which was now almoft reduced to its natural fize. The dreffing only confifted of dry lint, or fometimes of lint dipped in the aqua calcis and mel rofæ, with a few drops of fpirit of wine added to them. In 20 days more the cavity of the fac was completely healed, nor was it neceffary to ufe the argentum nitratum more than twice or three times. I now withdrew the bougie from the nafal canal and introduced a leaden tent mounted with a plate, which the patient wore for a month, when it was removed, and the external orifice of the fac fuffered to clofe without fcarifying the edges.

The tears paffed into the noftril and no longer regurgitated from the *puncta*, and collected upon the eye. Injections alfo thrown into the *puncta* paffed freely into the nofe. If, however, from any caufe the fecretion of tears was increafed, a fmall portion of that fluid iffued from the contracted aperture remaining in the fac, which occafioned no fenfible inconvenience, as the eye remained conftantly clear. This fmall

and

and occafional difcharge from the almoft imperceptible aperture in the fac gradually diminifhed, and after four months completely difappeared. To this laft inftance I might add a
great number of fimilar hiftories, which I omit,
not only for the fake of brevity, but becaufe
they would not afford a clearer illuftration of
what has been advanced on this fubject.

CASE IX.

An elderly woman, 55 years of age, was admitted into the practical fchool of furgery from
the country, on account of a fmall and fomewhat indolent tumour, the fize of a fmall nut,
which fhe had had for a confiderable time,
fituated between the internal angle of the right
eye and the nofe. In prefling upon this tumour, which readily yielded, a confiderable quantity of greenifh offenfive matter iffued from the
correfponding noftril; and a fmall quantity of
the fame vifcid fluid from the *puncta lachrymalia*
upon the eye.

The woman ftated, that fhe had been affected
with this difeafe during 15 years, and that it began with an immoderate gumming of the eye,
which fhe had never attended to; that the tumour had frequently burft externally, attended
with relief, and clofed again fpontaneoufly;
that within the laft year, after much fwelling
of the whole face and violent pains within the

root

root of the nofe, fhe was relieved by the difcharge of a confiderable quantity of fetid matter from the right noftril, but that notwithftanding the tumour continued to increafe every
day more and more. The edges of the eye-lids
of the right fide were rigid, indurated, red, and
in a fungous ftate internally, and the febaceous
glands enlarged.

I pufhed the point of a biftoury immediately
below the tendon of the *orbicularis palpebrarum,*
and directed the inftrument againft the *os unguis*; then, following the fold of the inferior eye-
lid, I laid the fac completely open. In the act
of dividing it a confiderable quantity of matter
gufhed out; oppofite the incifion I found the
os unguis wanting, and round this part there
were portions of the ethmoid bone denuded.
The opening which was formed by the deficiency of the *os unguis*, was large enough to admit
a thick writing quill, and communicated directly with the right noftril. The pituitary membrane around this opening was equally deftroyed;
I took great pains to difcover the nafal canal, but
without fuccefs. The cavity of the tumour
was filled with lint, and a poultice of bread and
milk applied upon the eye-lids, in order to foften
their hard and rigid edges.

On removing the dreffings the following day,
I found the whole internal furface of the fac
converted into a fungous ulcer. I filled the

cavity

cavity very exactly with lint dipped in the cauftic liniment mentioned in the preceding cafe; and, in order to prevent it from paffing into the noftril, I previoufly introduced into the opening formed by the deficiency of the bone, a fmall findon with a waxed thread paffed through the centre of it, fimilar to that which is ufed after the operation of trepanning the cranium. Befides a copious difcharge of matter from the enlarged fac, pieces of flough and fometimes particles of carious bone came away at each dreffing. The parts where the fungus was more prominent than the reft, were fprinkled with the hydrargyrus nitratus ruber alone, or mixed with alum, and occafionally touched with the argentum nitratum.

By continuing this treatment for 30 days the ulcer affumed a healthy and granulating appearance, and had a tendency to contract in every direction. The treatment afterwards confifted in dreffing the wound with dry lint, and occafionally touching the edges of the large orifice, leading from the fac into the noftril, with the argentum nitratum.

Towards the 60th day the ulcer was completely healed, and the fac nearly reduced to its natural fize, and by the uninterrupted ufe of the ophthalmic ointment of Janin, morning and evening, and the vitriolic collyrium three or four times a day, the palpebræ had recovered
their

their natural healthy condition. The edges of
the external orifice of the fac were now permitted to clofe, the tears being directly difcharged into the noftril through the large opening formed in the posterior part of the fac by
the deficiency of the *os unguis,* and the woman
left the hofpital perfectly cured.

CHAP.

CHAP. II.

OF THE HORDEOLUM.*

THE hordeolum, ſtrictly ſpeaking, is only a ſmall bile which forms upon the margin of the palpebræ, moſt frequently towards the great angle of the eye.

Like the furuncle, this ſmall tumour is of a dark red colour, highly inflamed and much more painful than might be expected from the ſmallneſs of its ſize; which ariſes partly from the violence of the inflammation, by which it is produced, and partly from the exquiſite ſenſibility and tenſion of the ſkin which covers the edges of the eye-lids. Hence it is that the hordeolum, in perſons of delicate and ſenſible habits, frequently occaſions fever and reſtleſſneſs ; its ſuppuration is ſlow and imperfect, and when matter is formed in it, it does not appear diſpoſed to burſt.

This particular form of inflammation, which might be called *furuncular,* differs in ſeveral reſpects from common *phlegmonous* inflammation. The former commences in the ſkin, extends itſelf downwards into the ſubjacent cellular membrane, and produces a more or leſs extenſive deſtruction of it; the *phlegmonous* in-

* Κριθη, χαλαζα, grando, ſtye, ſtithe, or ſtian.

flammation

flammation, on the contrary, originates in the
cellular membrane, the vitality of which it does
not deftroy, and is afterwards propagated externally to the fkin. The *furuncular* inflammation is quickly arrefted, and forms a fmall, cir-
cumfcribed, hard, and very painful tumour,
which, though elevated upon the fkin, does not
contain extravafated coagulable lymph, but is
completely filled with mortified or diforganized
cellular membrane; while on the other hand
the *phlegmonous* inflammation is difpofed to pro-
pagate itfelf extenfively through the cellular
membrane, into the cells of which a confiderable quantity of coagulable lymph is inceffantly
poured, which occafions the tumefaction. In
confequence of the furunculus being completely
filled with mortified or diforganized cellular
membrane, fuppuration either does not take
place in it, or very imperfectly, and never in
the centre of the tumour, but at its circumference where it is in contact with the found parts;
while in the phlegmon a true and complete
fuppuration is formed precifely in the centre of
the inflamed cellular membrane, which, when
the matter is difcharged, fpontaneoufly contracts and recovers its natural ftate and functions.
In the fecond ftage of the furunculus, the fkin
which covers it ulcerates and burfts in one or
more points, and difcharges a very fmall quantity
of ferous fluid, afterwards the fmall portion of
mortified

mortified cellular membrane, which formed the body and bafe of the tumour, comes away in the form of an extraneous fubftance, and the cavity which remains clofes and heals in a fhort time. All thefe phœnomena, peculiar to the *furuncular* inflammation, are common to the Hordeolum, the nature of which does not confequently differ from that of the furunculus.

The treatment of the Hordeolum therefore, as well as that of the furunculus, when the tumour occupies the fubjacent cellular membrane, forms an exception to the general rule, that the beft termination of inflammatory tumours is that of refolution. For whenever the *furuncular* inflammation has extended fo deeply as to deftroy a portion of the cellular membrane, the refolution of the tumour cannot in any manner be effected, or at moft imperfectly; hence this mode of termination would be rather injurious, fince a greater or fmaller portion of the cellular fubftance deprived of vitality would be left ; which fooner or later muft occafion a reproduction of the hordeolum, or degenerate into a hard and indolent fubftance, which would deform the margin of the eye-lid.

The refolution of the incipient hordeolum may be accomplifhed in that ftage of it, in which the inflammation affects only the fkin, and not the fubjacent cellular membrane, as happens on the firft appearance of the difeafe ;

in

in which cafe repellent applications are advantageous, efpecially the repeated application of cold to that part of the margin of the eye-lid, which is beginning to appear red, by means of a convenient piece of metal, as the extremity of a key, a piece of money, or what is ftill preferable, ice. But if the difeafe has already affected and deftroyed a fmall portion of the fubjacent cellular membrane, every repellent application is not only ufelefs but injurious, and recourfe fhould be had to the affiduous ufe of local emollient and anodyne remedies.

In the fecond ftage of the difeafe therefore the hordeolum and palpebræ fhould be covered with a warm poultice made of bread-crumb boiled in new milk, with a little faffron or melon-pulp added to it, and renewed every two hours, and even oftener in the winter feafon.

The appearance of a white fpot upon the moft elevated part of the hordeolum fhould not induce the furgeon to be hafty in opening it, in order to give iffue to the very fmall quantity of ferous matter which is formed between the fkin and the difeafed and mortified cellular membrane. It will be better that he fhould wait until the fkin furrounding this whitifh fpeck become confiderably thinner, that it may burft and open itfelf fufficiently to allow of the fmall quantity of ferum, and of the whole of the fmall portion of corrupted cellular membrane, which formed

the

the principal part of the tumour, being eafily difcharged. If the portion of membrane be flow
in coming away through this aperture, the furgeon, by preffing lightly upon the eye-lid, at
the bafe of the fmall tumour, fhould force it
out; by this means all the fymptoms of the
difeafe will difappear, and the cavity left by
the mortified cellular membrane, which formed
the centre of the tumour, will be entirely clofed
and healed in 24 hours.

It fometimes, though rarely, happens, that
this procefs of nature, defigned to feparate the
mortified portion of the cellular membrane
from that which is found, is but imperfectly
performed, and that a fmall portion of yellowifh diforganized cellular fubftance ftill remains
at the bottom of this fmall cavity, which by
adhering prevents the fmall tubercle from being
completely healed. In thefe cafes, in which
little or no advantage can be derived from
continuing the application of the emollient
poultice, the furgeon fhould touch the bottom
of the cavity with the point of a camel's hair
pencil dipped in the fulphuric acid, one or
more times, until this remaining portion of cellular membrane deprived of life be alfo completely detached from the found parts and ex-
pelled; after which the fmall cavity that remains will very fpeedily clofe.

If,

If, after the cure of the hordeolum the eye-lid upon which it was fituated, remain a little tumefied and edematofe, it may be eafily removed by the application of the aqua lytharg. acet. comp. with a little fpirit of wine added to it.

There are fome perfons who are particularly fubject to this difeafe. This arifes moft frequently from fordes in the primæ viæ, in confequence of their living on acrid and irritating food, and indulging in fpirituous liquors. Such perfons fhould obferve a better regimen than that which they have been accuftomed to, and fhould take occafionally a pint of the decoction of the triticum repens, or of milk whey with a grain of the antimon. tartariz. in divided dofes, particularly when fymptoms of indigeftion of the ftomach are prefent. As a local and prefervative remedy, the vitriolic collyrium may be dropped into the eyes, and the eye-lids wafhed with it once a day.

CHAP.

CHAP III.

OF ENCYSTED TUMOURS OF THE EYE-LIDS.

ENCYSTED tumours are very frequently formed
in the eye-lids. Some writers indeed pretend
that they are more frequently met with in the
eye-lids than in other parts of the body, in conſequence of the former being more abundantly
furniſhed with ſebaceous glands, as thoſe of
Meibomius, from the preternal increaſe of ſome
of which they have preſumed theſe follicular
tumours to originate.

As ſuch a diſcuſſion is of no practical advantage, I willingly omit it, and ſhall merely obſerve
that the glands of Meibomius occupy the edges
of the palpebræ, while ſmall encyſted tumours
do not appear more frequently in this than in
other parts of the eye-lids, where theſe glands
do not exiſt; and that it is alſo proved that
follicular tumours originate as well from the
cells of the reticular membrane, as from theſe
glandular bodies.

An encyſted tumour of the eye-lids in its
commencement is not larger than a millet-ſeed

or

or a fmall pea, and it is only after a confiderable
time that it arrives at the magnitude of a bean,
and fometimes of a filbert. Thefe tumours do
not in general excite pain, but only occafion
fome uneafinefs, when having acquired a confiderable bulk they prevent the free motion of the
eye-lid, produce a partial depreffion of it, or
prefs upon the globe of the eye.

With refpect to the feat of thefe tumours it
appears to me, from numerous obfervations, that
they are, from their commencement, moft frequently lefs covered by the internal membrane.
of the eye-lids, than by the integuments and
mufcular fibres ; fo that their bafes are in general fo fuperficially placed upon the internal furface of the eye-lids, that when the latter are
everted, thefe tumours are feen as it were uncovered, and the yellowifh follicule appears tranfparent through the fine internal membrane of
the palpebræ which covers them.

The frequent unavailing attempts which I
have made to obtain a refolution of thefe encyfted tumours on their firft appearance, fometimes by employing the remedy fo much extolled by Morgagni,* confifting of the aqua re-
ginæ, or elder-flower water, and a moderate
quantity of the aqua ammoniæ, fo as not to excite any heat or uneafinefs in the fkin of the

* Epift. anat. xiii. 2.

eye-lids; at other times by applications of re-
ſolvent gums and local mercurial frictions; have
convinced me that the only effectual method of
curing this diſeaſe, eſpecially when it has exiſted
for ſome months, is the extirpation of the tumour.

And as theſe follicular tubercles are generally
much more ſuperficially ſituated towards the internal than the external ſurface of the palpebræ,
ſo I am authorized, from obſervation and experience, to believe that the beſt method of removing theſe tumours is to extract them from the internal ſurface of the eye-lid, although it has been
even lately aſſerted to the contrary by ſurgeons of
high and deſerved reputation. For, by extracting the ſmall follicular body from the internal
ſurface of the eye-lid, the inciſion which is required is entirely ſuperficial; the ſeparation of
the cyſt from the ſurrounding parts is eaſily effected; the after-treatment is of no importance;
and there does not remain the ſmalleſt veſtige
upon the integuments of the palpebræ, either of
the preceding diſeaſe, or of the operation which
has been performed.

The only exception of any importance which
can be offered to this method of treatment, is
in the caſe where the encyſted tumour is ſo ſituated upon either of the palpebræ, that the
eye-lid cannot be everted ſufficiently to expoſe
the baſe of the tumour, and to admit of its

6   being

being completely removed : as in the cafe where the tumour is fituated immediately under the external or internal commiffure of the eye-lids, fo as to extend under the arch of the orbit, a circumftance which has occurred to me oftener than once.

It may not be improper on this occafion to relate the hiftory of a cafe of encyfted tumour fituated deeply in the orbit which was treated by Meffrs. Bromfield and Ingram. This tumour, after having caufed pain at the bottom of the orbit of the eye during feveral years, diminution of fight, and afterwards total blindnefs, ultimately forced the eye-ball out of its focket, and produced an everfion of the lower eye-lid. On examining the protruded eye-ball with the finger, thefe furgeons perceived, on the external and lower fide, a fluctuation, which they imagined to arife from an encyfted tumour; and it was agreed that it ought to be opened. For this purpofe Mr. Bromfield, having directed that the lower eye-lid fhould be preffed upwards as much as poffible, and held very firmly in that pofition, divided the integuments with a fcalpel, in the direction of the inferior edge of the orbit, beyond the conjunctiva, and of a fufficient extent to enable him to introduce his finger behind the ball of the eye, precifely upon the feat of the cyft. The operator guided by his finger pene-trated the cyft, and there iffued from it a pellu-

G   cid

cid fluid, fufficient in quantity to fill a fmall wine glafs. Having paufed a little he drew the empty cyft towards him by means of two fmall hooks, removed it and filled the wound with foft lint. In 24 hours the head and neck became enormoufly fwollen; this fymptom however was relieved, by the ufe of internal antiphlogiftic remedies and mild applications, and the wound healed in lefs than a month. The lower eye-lid gradually returned to its natural pofition, and the eye-ball retired within the orbit. The narrator adds, that having an opportunity of feeing this patient again, five months afterwards, he found that he could diftinguifh, with the eye which had been fo dangeroufly affected, a ftrong light from darknefs. *Medical Obferv. and Enquiries, vol.* iv. *page* 371. A cafe fimilar to this is related in the treatife on the difeafes of the eyes, by Saint-Yves, chap. 21, under the title, *Opération d'une tumeur fingulière dans l'orbit.*

But thefe are rather to be regarded as encyfted tumours of the parts in the vicinity of the eyelids, than of the eye-lids themfelves; and even if it were defirable to clafs thefe particular cafes with the latter, they would not in the leaft detract from the propriety and utility of the method of treatment here recommended.

Suppofing then the encyfted tumour to occupy the upper eye-lid, the patient being
                                        feated

feated and his head firmly fupported, an able affiftant, placed behind or on one fide of him, fhould turn out the upper eye-lid, in fuch a manner that by placing the point of the fore-finger of one hand upon the tumour, and the fore-finger of the other covered with a piece of fine rag, upon the everted margin of the palpebra, the follicule may be made to project as much as poffible from its internal furface. The furgeon ftanding before the patient, with a lancet or fmall convex-edged fcalpel * fhould, with the hand unfupported, divide the fine internal membrane of the palpebra covering the follicule, in the direction of the edge of the eye-lid, and for a fufficient extent to allow of the tumour paffing eafily out and projecting beyond its internal membrane: the follicule being then taken hold of with the forceps,† or a fmall hook, fhould be drawn out and completely feparated from all its attachments to the furrounding parts, either by the fcalpel or by a ftroke of the curved fciffars.‡ The eye-lid then being returned to its fituation fhould be covered with a comprefs dipped in the aqua lythargyri acetati comp. fupported by the *monoculus* bandage.

If the encyfted tumour be fituated in the lower eye-lid, the affiftant fhould place himfelf before the patient, and the furgeon behind, or

---

* Tab. III. fig. 12. † Tab. III. fig. 8.
‡ Tab. III. fig. 4.

on one ſide, as he may find moſt convenient, and proceed to the operation in the manner already deſcribed. In operating on children, whether on the upper or lower eye-lid, the moſt convenient poſition is to lay them on a table of a convenient height, with the head raiſed by a pillow, and the hands and feet firmly held by aſſiſtants.

When the ſurgeon is deprived of an intelligent aſſiſtant, the operation may be performed in the following manner. The operator ſhould turn out the eye-lid with the point of the fore-finger of his left-hand, and place the extremity of the thumb of the ſame hand upon its everted margin, in order to hold it more ſecurely, and to make the root or baſe of the follicule projeƈt as much as poſſible from the internal ſurface of the eye-lid. Then, with a lancet or ſmall convex-edged ſcalpel in the right hand, he ſhould make a ſlight inciſion through the internal membrane upon the tumour, in the direƈtion from one canthus of the eye towards the other, and with the point of the ſame inſtrument, inſinuated obliquely between the cyſt and internal membrane of the palpebra, ſhould ſeparate it from all its ſurrounding adheſions. Having done this, with the point of the index finger of the left hand, which had been placed from the beginning behind the tumour, he ſhould preſs upon it ſo as

4

to

to make the cyft pafs completely through the incifion made in the internal membrane of the eye-lid, which had before covered it. Then laying afide the fcalpel, and taking hold of the curved fciffars, he fhould include the bafe of the follicule in them, and at one ftroke fepa-rate it entirely from its remaining attachments, and immediately return the eye-lid to its natu-ral pofition.

In employing this method of extirpating encyfted tumours of the eye-lids, it is not neceffary to be fcrupulous about the feparation of the very minute particles of the cyft, when it is opened or burfts during the operation. For when the principal part of the follicule is removed, and the eye-lid reftored to its fituation, the tears, efpecially if the lower eye-lid be operated on, enter and fill the cavity left by the tumour, and confequently prevent the lips of the wound from uniting by the firft intention. When the procefs of fuppuration therefore is eftablifhed, there is no neceffity to employ any other means, as the fmall particles of the follicule which have accidentally remain-ed behind, adhering to the bottom of the ulcer, are gradually loofened and thrown off with the matter which is difcharged from it. If, how-ever, this procefs of nature fhould not fpeedily take place, and the integuments be not readily depreffed and contracted, in confequence of hav-

ing

ing been too much diftended during the continuance of the difeafe, the cure may be accelle-
rated by everting the eye-lid, and touching the
bottom of the cavity of the wound with the
argentum nitratum, taking care to wafh the eye
immediately afterwards with new milk. In
general, however, this expedient is unneceffary, as
every external veftige of the difeafe commonly
difappears in the courfe of four days from the
operation, and on everting the eye-lid, the part
where the incifion was made is found covered
with a mucous matter, the bottom of the fmall
cavity nearly on a level with the internal furface
of the eye-lid, and in the courfe of eight days
it becomes perfectly healed.

It is very fingular that fome of the moft diftinguifhed writers in furgery of the prefent day
fhould feem fo adverfe to this method of removing encyfted tumours of the eye-lids, while
they recommend the extirpation of fimilar follicular tumours of the cheek from the infide of
the mouth, not only to avoid an external wound
of the parotid duct, but, becaufe, according to
their own obfervations, thefe tumours are much
more fpeedily cured when they are removed
from the infide of the mouth, than when the
operation is performed externally. The fame
advantage of a fpeedy cure is equally obtained in
the extirpation of encyfted tumours from the
internal furface of the palpebræ, which is not
lefs

lefs authorized by practice, and is more eafily executed.

I fhall conclude this chapter with fubjoining fome obfervations relative to a particular fpecies of encyfted tumour of the eye-lid, which in fome refpects differs materially from that which I have already fpoken of, and which is not unfrequently met with in practice. This is a fmall, hard, and indolent tubercle, generally rather larger than a millet-feed, which arifes precifely upon fome part of the edge of the eye-lid among the cilia, and is of a white colour, refembling the white of a boiled egg. When this tubercle is of long ftanding it contains a fubftance exactly fimilar to that of the albumen ovi when boiled, and is merely covered with a very thin and tranfparent fkin, which is clofely united with the denfe matter contained within it.

M. Aurelius Severinus,* who has given a more accurate defcription of this difeafe than any other writer, fays: *Tuberculi cujufdam exigui in clivo palpebræ ciliari nafcentis, et fe cum pilis oblique proferentis ; quo magnitudine, duritieque mihi fementulam refert, fi tantummodo flavum hujus colorem in exquifitum alborem intelligas mutatum.— Corticulam duriorem, ac ferme corneolam huic tuberculo adverti ; ufque adeo ut medicamentis acer-*

* De novis obferv. abfces. § De miliolo exterioris palpebræ tuberculo.

rimis,

*rimis, id eft liquidis caufticis, tentatum, nullam vel
tactûs vel coloris mutationem fenferit.*—*Continet
molleculam chartæ bombicinæ madidæ fimilem por-
tiunculam.*

The fituation of this tumour on the very edge
of the eye-lid, the extreme finenefs of the pellicle which covers it, as well as the fmallnefs
of its fize, and the hardnefs of the matter which
it contains, render it moft convenient to remove
it from the external furface of the eye-lid. This
may be eafily executed by including it exactly
at its bafe, with the curved fciffars, or by paffing
the point of a lancet through the root of it, .fo
as to remove the whole tubercle clofe to the
edge of the eye-lid. When the bleeding has
ceafed the divided parts may be covered with
a fmall piece of court plaifter. On the following day the wound may be touched with the
argentum nitratum and the reft of the cure left
to nature. On the exfoliation of the efchar the
part will be found completely healed.

CASE X.

A child, the daughter of a nobleman of Pavia,
had had for a year and a half an encyfted tumour of the upper eye-lid of the right fide, the
fize of a fmall pea.

For the purpofe of extirpating it, I placed the
child upon a table of a convenient height, with
the head fupported upon a pillow, and the arms
and

and legs firmly held, by two affiftants. I defired
the affiftant fituated behind the head of the
child to evert the eye-lid by placing the point
of the fore-finger of his left hand upon the integuments and the tumour, and one finger of
the right hand covered with a piece of fine
cloth upon its everted margin.

Having placed myfelf on the fide of the patient, with the hand unfupported I divided the
internal membrane of the palpebra longitudi-.
nally, at the part covering the bafe of the tumour, which was diftinguifhable by its yellowifh colour. Through this incifion, which
was little more than three lines in length, almoft
the whole of the folliciule immediately paffed
out; I took hold of it with the forceps, and having raifed it, completely detached it. The eye-
lid was then replaced, and covered with a comprefs dipped in the aqua lytharg. acetat. comp.
and a bandage.

The child, which had been unruly, became
quiet, and almoft immediately fell afleep. On
the third day the eye-lid was a little tumefied
and inflamed ; I directed a fmall bag of emollient herbs boiled in milk, to be applied upon
it, and the child remained out of bed as ufual,
and was perfectly cheerful. On the feventh
day the tumefaction of the eye-lid had entirely
fubfided, and on carefully everting it I found
the wound perfectly healed. There was not
the

the fmalleft veftige of the difeafe on the external part of the eye-lid.

CASE XI.

Signor Luigi Gozzani, of Novara, a medical
ftudent in this univerfity, defirous of being freed
from the inconvenience and deformity occafioned by an encyfted tumour, nearly the fize of
a bean, fituated upon the left fuperior eye-lid,
fubmitted to the operation in the prefence of a
great number of his fellow-ftudents in medicine
and furgery.

Having placed himfelf in a chair, I turned out
the upper eye-lid with the point of the fore-
finger of my left hand, and retained it in this
pofition by applying the point of my thumb
upon its internal margin. I made an incifion
with a lancet in that part of the internal membrane of the palpebra, which covered the bafe
or root of the yellow follicular humour, and carrying the point of it circularly between the tumour and the internal membrane of the eye-
lid, feparated it entirely ; then, by making a
greater degree of preffure on the tumour with
the point of the fore-finger of my left hand, I
forced it almoft entirely out through the incifion, and by including its bafe in the curved
fciffars, removed it at a fingle ftroke, and returned the eye-lid to its fituation.

This

This gentleman said, that the pain attending the operation was very trifling, and not greater than that occasioned by bleeding: during the two following days the eye-lid was slightly inflamed and swollen, and bags of emollient herbs were applied upon it. On the fifth day the patient found himself completely well, without its being possible to distinguish in which of the upper eye-lids the tumour had been situated; and on the seventh he returned to his studies as usual.

Case XII.

A poor woman, 40 years of age, came to the practical school to consult me on account of an encysted tumour, the size of the end of the finger, which she had had for several years upon the left superior eye-lid towards the external angle, and which for some weeks had occasioned an unusual sense of weight, and prevented the eye from being sufficiently opened. I proposed the operation, to which she assented, but for some particular reasons refused to remain in the hospital after the operation, proposing to follow in other respects whatever I might direct.

The patient being seated, I everted the upper eye-lid with the fore-finger and thumb of my left hand, holding the point of the fore-finger firmly against the tumour, in order to make it project as much as possible towards the internal membrane

brane of the eye-lid, and having flightly divided the internal membrane upon the bafe of the tumour with a convex-edged fcalpel, the follicule immediately paffed out of the incifion. I carefully feparated it from the furrounding parts, by infinuating the point of the fcalpel obliquely, and carrying it round between the follicule and internal membrane of the palpebra, and then embracing the tumour as clofely as poffible to the fubftance of the eye-lid with the curved fciffars, I removed it at one ftroke. The eyelid was then returned to its fituation, and covered with a dry comprefs and bandage, and the patient returned home.

I waited in vain for a week, flattering myfelf that the patient would give fome account of herfelf, and at length fhe was found, and appeared perfectly well. On being afked what inconvenience fhe had fuffered after the operation, fhe replied none, except a little fwelling and inflammation of the eye-lid during the firft three days; which, however, had not prevented her from attending her family affairs.

Case XIII.

In the act of dividing the internal membrane of the palpebra for extracting an encyfted tumour, of a fize rather larger than a pea, fituated on the lower eye-lid of a child 10 years of age, I accidentally opened the cyft at the fame time,

from which the whole of its contents, confifting of a little milky concrete fubftance was
immediately difcharged. I laid hold of the cyft
in feveral places with the forceps, firft freeing it
as much as poffible from its attachments to the
furrounding parts ; but it eluded me, nor could
I by any means detach it with fuch exactnefs, or
remove it with the curved fciffars clofe to the
fubftance of the eye-lid, as not to leave fome
fmall particles of it adhering to the bottom and
fides of the cavity. After having removed,
however, a fmall portion of the edges of the incifion made in the internal membrane, the eye-
lid was returned to its fituation.

During the two firft days the eye-lid was a
little tumefied and inflamed as ufual, and on
everting it, towards the end of the fourth day, I
found the bottom of the wound covered with
a glutinous matter. On the feventh day the
cavity was quite fuperficial, contracted, and
nearly healed ; and on the ninth the patient was
perfectly cured, without any elevation or deformity of the eye lid remaining externally. I
might here have related a very confiderable number of cafes fimilar to this.

CASE XIV.

A fhoe-maker's boy had for feveral years an
encyfted tumour, nearly in the centre of the
right inferior eye-lid, which gradually increafed

to

to the fize of a nutmeg. It began alfo to produce an everfion of the eye-lid and a weeping
of the eye.

I removed it from the internal furface of the
eye-lid in the manner above-mentioned; but as
the tumour was full of a milky fubftance, half
concrete and half fluid, in making the incifion
the cyft was punctured, and the whole of the
matter contained in it was immediately difcharged. I was unable to feparate the cyft
from the neighbouring parts with the exactnefs
that I could have wifhed ; I removed, however,
as much of it as I could, and returned the eye-
lid to its fituation, in expectation that nature by
means of fuppuration would complete the reft
of the cure. During the two following days
the eye-lid was fwollen and inflamed, upon
which I applied a poultice of bread and milk.
On the fifth day the mucous fuppuration appeared, the bottom of the cavity then began to
affume a florid appearance, to contract and approach the internal furface of the eye-lid. After
fome days the ulcer became ftationary, and
there yet remained a little elevation of the eye-lid
at the part where the tumour had been fituated.
I turned out the eye-lid and touched the cavity
with the argentum nitratum which only occafioned a temporary heat in the patient's eye, as I took
care to drop a little milk immediately afterwards
between the palpebræ and eye-ball, and continued

nued the ufe of it for half an hour. On the following day the eye-lid became again tumefied and inflamed, and the mucous fuppuration appeared again in greater quantity than at firft. In the courfe of eight days more the cavity left by the encyfted tumour clofed and entirely difappeared, both externally and internally; and the patient was difcharged from the hofpital perfectly cured, without the leaft trace of the difeafe by which he had before been disfigured.

CHAP.

CHAP. IV.

OF THE CILIA WHICH IRRITATE THE EYE.

THIS difeafe, which is termed Trichiafis, prefents itfelf under two diftinct forms : the firft is where the cilia are turned inwards, without the tarfus having changed its natural pofition and direction; the fecond confifts in a morbid inclination of the tarfus, and confequently of the eye-lafh towards the ball of the eye.

The firft form of this difeafe is very rare, nor has it come under my own obfervation more than once, and in this inftance only fome of the hairs had changed their direction. The fecond fpecies or form of *Trichiafis*, or that which confifts in a folding inwards of the tarfus and cilia at the fame time, is that which is commonly met with in practice. This may be either complete, affecting the whole of the tarfus; or incomplete, occupying only a certain portion of the edge of the eye-lid, and moft frequently near the external angle of the eye; fometimes the difeafe is confined to one eye-lid only, at other times it affects both, and occafionally the patient is afflicted with it in both eyes.

To thefe two fpecies of *Trichiafis* fome writers have added a third, which they call *diftichiafis,*

chiafis, and which they fuppofe to be produced by a double and unufual row of hairs. But this third fpecies is only imaginary, and the reafon of fuch fubdivifion feems to have arifen from a want of recollecting what was long ago remarked by Winflow * and Albinus † on the natural arrangement of the cilia; that although their roots appear to be difpofed in one line only, they neverthelefs form two, three, and in the upper eye-lid even four ranges of hairs, unequally fituated, and as it were confufed. Whenever, therefore, in confequence of difeafe a certain number of hairs are feparated from each other in a contrary direction and diforderly manner, the eye-lafh will appear to be compofed of a new and unufual row of them, while in fact there has been no change either with refpect to their number or natural implantation.‡

It is not an eafy matter to determine precifely what are the caufes which fometimes occafion a fmall number of the hairs to deviate from their natural direction, while the tarfus remains in its pofition. They are generally attributed to cicatrices which take place upon the tarfus in confequence of previous ulceration, by which the cilia fall off, and thofe which are naturally

* Expofition Anatom. Trait. de la téte, § 278.

† Acad. Annotat. lib. iii. cap. 7.

‡ Maître-Jan made the fame obfervation, a long time ago, as may be feen in his Traité des maladies de l'œil, p. 494.

Léveillé.

growing

growing are prevented from taking their proper
direction. But it is proper to remark, that this
cause is not the only one, since in the case which
occurred to me, two or three hairs were turned
inwards against the eye-ball, although there had
been neither ulceration, nor cicatrization of any
part of the tarsus.

For my own part I am inclined to think, that
the small ulcers and cicatrices, which are occasionally formed on the internal margin of the
tarsus, rather give rise to the second form of the
disease, or the inversion of the edge of the eye-
lid, and consequently of the cilia towards the
ball of the eye. As these ulcers are of a corroding nature, and when neglected destroy the
substance of the internal membrane of the palpebræ near the tarsus, it necessarily follows, that
in proportion as they heal and contract themselves, they draw along with them and turn inwards the tarsus, and consequently the hairs
which are implanted in it. And as these small
ulcers do not always occupy the whole extent
of the internal margin of the eye-lid, but are
sometimes confined to a few lines in the middle
or extremity, near the external angle of the
eye-lid, so after the cicatrices are formed, the
whole of the hairs are not always turned inwards, but only a certain number of them which
correspond to the extent of the ulcers previously
situated along the internal margin of the tarsus.
                                                    Indeed

Indeed in every cafe of imperfect trichiafis, in confequence of a cicatrix of the internal furface of the edge of the eye-lid, a very flight examination will fhow, that the tarfus and cilia are every where in their natural fituation, except oppofite the part where the ulcers had formerly exifted; and if the eye-lid be everted, it will be evident that the internal membrane near that part of the margin correfponding to the feat of the trichiafis is pale, rigid, and callous, and that from this contraction the inverfion of its cartilaginous border is evidently derived, as well as the morbid inclination of the hairs towards the globe of the eye.

Befides thefe caufes, there are others capable of producing the fame injurious effect. In the firft place the chronic ophthalmia of long ftanding, as that which arifes from fcrofula or the fmallpox, which becoming gradually worfe and worfe, keeps the integuments of the eye-lid for a confiderable time in a ftate of diftenfion and œdema, and induces a relaxation of them, by which the cartilaginous border of the eye-lid ultimately lofing a proper and firm fupport in the integuments, inclines towards the eye-ball, and afterwards turns inwards, and draws the cilia along with it in the fame improper direction. The fame unpleafant effect, independently of the relaxation of the integuments, is frequently produced by a foftening of the cartilage of the tarfus, in confequence of a

copious

copious and long continued puriform difcharge from the ciliary glands, by which the cartilage of the tarfus becomes either wholly or partially incapable of fupporting itfelf erect, or of preferving the curve neceffary to its perfect coaptation with the tarfus of the other eye-lid; hence the cartilage, either in the whole, or a part of its extent becomes relaxed and folded inwards, and draws along with it the correfponding hairs againft the ball of the eye.

Thefe caufes are not unfrequently found combined together, and they are alfo often accompanied with cicatrices of the membrane which invefts the internal margin of the tarfus. * Some pretend that the trichiafis is occafionally produced by a fpafmodic contraction of the orbicularis palpebrarum. But I muft confefs that this has never come under my own obfervation, and it is difficult to believe that the fpafm of this mufcle, however violent, can produce a folding inwards of the tarfus and cilia, much lefs that it fhould continue to act as a permanent caufe of the difeafe.

The degree of uneafinefs which muft neceffarily refult from the hairs perpetually preffing upon the cornea and white of the eye, may be eafily calculated even by thofe who are little acquainted with furgery. To aggravate this evil ftill more, it very frequently happens, that

* Bell's Syftem of Surgery, vol. iii. p. 276.

the

the hairs bent inwards acquire a much greater
length and thicknefs than thofe which retain
their natural pofition. And although the difeafe
be confined to one eye, yet from confent, both
are ufually affected, and the found eye cannot
be moved without occafioning pain in that
which is fubjected to the irritation and friction
of the inflected hairs. In general it may be faid
that both the eyes in perfons affected with this
difeafe are very irritable and impatient of the
light. As the patient, in cafes of incomplete
trichiafis, retains fome little power of opening
the eye-lids for the purpofe of feeing, and that
moft frequently towards the internal angle of
the eye, the head and neck are frequently inclined in an awkward manner, producing in
children, at length, a diftortion of the neck and
fhoulders, which is with difficulty corrected,
even after the trichiafis is cured. Children
befides, impatient of the irritation which the
inflected cilia produce, are inceffantly rubbing
the eye-lids, which contributes in no fmall degree to increafe the evils confequent on the
trichiafis; fuch are the *varicofe chronic ophthalmia,* the *nebula,* and the *ulceration of the cornea.*

The cure of the fecond fpecies of this difeafe,
or that which is commonly met with in practice, and which confifts in a morbid inclination
of the tarfus, and confequently of the cilia towards the ball of the eye, whether in confequence of a cicatrix and contraction of the in-

H 3   ternal

ternal membrane of the palpebra in the proximity of the tarfus, from ulceration of the internal
margin of the edge of the eye-lid, or in confequence
of a relaxation of the integuments, a foftening of
the tarfal cartilage, or from all thefe caufes combined; is effected by artificially everting the tarfus, and re-eftablifhing it firmly in its natural pofition, together with the cilia, which were irritating the ball of the eye.   This indication is completely anfwered by the excifion of a portion of
the fkin clofe to the edge of the eye-lid, of fuch
a breadth and extent that when the cicatrix is
formed, the tarfus and margin of the eye-lid
may be turned outwards, and fufficiently feparated from the eye-ball, and may find a point of
fupport in the cicatrix of the integuments fufficiently firm to retain them in their natural pofition and direction.   After fo many ufelefs attempts, I do not believe that there are any among
modern furgeons, who, with a view to the radical cure of this difeafe, place any confidence of
fuccefs, either in the mere evulfion of the morbidly inflected hairs, in bending them outwards,
and retaining them by means of adhefive plaf-
ters, or in plucking them out and deftroying
their roots with cauftic or the actual cautery;
much lefs in extirpating the edge of the eye-
lid along with the hairs, or dividing the orbicularis mufcle on the internal furface of the
eye-lid, under the fuppofition that the difeafe
is fometimes produced by a fpafmodic contraction

tion of it. All thefe hypothetical methods
have been rejected from practice, either as infufficient, or dangerous, and rather calculated
to aggravate than cure the difeafe, or to occafion affections of the eye-lids, no lefs ferious than
the trichiafis itfelf.*

The moft efficacious method for the complete cure of this difeafe, which has been hitherto employed, not excluding that recommended by Kokler,† and known as far back as
the time of Rhafes, confifts, as I have already
ftated, in the excifion of a certain portion of the
fkin of the affected eye-lid, clofe to the tarfus; an
operation which, when reduced to the fimplicity
which I fhall propofe, by excluding from it not
only the apparatus of inftruments formerly in ufe,
but the employment of the bloody future, is eafily
executed by the furgeon, attended with little inconvenience to the patient, and is invariably followed with immediate and certain fuccefs.

The patient being feated in a chair, if an
adult, or, if a child, laid on a table of a conve-

---

* I am certain that thofe who have propofed to confine the
application of the actual cautery to cafes in which two or
three hairs only were turned inwards towards the eye-ball,
have never performed it. For befides the great difficulty, after
the hair has been extracted, of introducing the heated needle
precifely into the foraminula from which the hair has been
plucked, it is ftill more difficult to find the root of the extirpated hair, which may be at fome diftance from the point
which the furgeon propofes to cauterize.

† Verfuch einer neven Heilart der trichiafis. Leipzig,
1796.

nient

nient height, with the head raifed, and firmly
held by an affiftant placed behind, the furgeon
fhould turn out the hairs which irritate the eye
with the point of a probe, then with the forceps,
fuch as are ufed for anatomical purpofes, or with
the point of the fore-finger and thumb, which
anfwers equally well, and in many cafes even
better, he fhould raife a fold of the integuments
of the affected eye-lid, being particularly careful
that the part taken hold of correfpond exactly
to the middle of the fpace occupied by the
trichiafis; fince, as I have already obferved, the
whole of the tarfus is fometimes turned inwards,
at other times one half of it, and occafionally
only a third part of it. The furgeon fhould
raife the fold of the integuments with his left
hand, more or lefs, according to the greater or
lefs degree of relaxation of the integuments of
the eye-lid, and inverfion of the tarfus, and
for this evident reafon, that the extent of the
incifion is always proportionate to the quantity
of fkin raifed. If the patient be an adult, when
the fold of the fkin has been raifed to a certain
extent, he fhould be defired to open the eye, and
if in this ftate the tarfus and cilia refume their
natural fituation, the fold of the integuments
will be fufficiently elevated for the purpofe.
As children very feldom fubmit to fuch an experiment, we are under the neceffity of doing it
by guefs. The forceps of Bartifch of Verduin, and

thofe

thofe improved by Rau, which were formerly
in ufe, have the inconvenience of raifing the integuments of the eye-lid equally from one end to
the other, and therefore of occafioning too much
fkin to be removed towards the angles of the
eye, and not a fufficient quantity in the middle of it. On the contrary by ufing the diffecting forceps and raifing the fkin precifely in the
centre of the whole extent of the trichiafis, it
neceffarily follows that the incifion made in the
integuments forms an oval, the broadeft part of
which is exactly in the middle, or nearly fo, of
the eye-lid, the narroweft towards the angles or
commiffures of it. This contributes very materially to make the cicatrix correfpond to the
natural fold of the eye-lid, and prevents a difeafe contrary to that which it is intended to
remedy from taking place in the angles of the
eye-lid, namely, an everfion of the commiffures
of the palpebræ.

Befides this caution relative to the fituation
and figure of the fold of the integuments to be
removed, particular attention fhould be paid,
that the divifion of the fkin be made fufficiently
near the inverted tarfus. Without attention to
this circumftance, the furgeon may be difappointed after the healing of the wound to find
the eye-lid fhortened upon the whole from the
eye-brow to the place of excifion, but not in an
equal proportion in the fpace between the edge
of

of the eye-lid and the cicatrix of the integuments; consequently, the tarsus will remain
folded inwards as before, or not sufficiently
everted to prevent the hairs from coming in
contact with the eye; which inconvenience
would subject the patient to a second excision
of the integuments of the eye-lid lower than
the first.

Matters being thus arranged, the surgeon
holding the fold of the integuments with his
left hand, by means of the forceps, should carefully include it in the crooked (probe) sciffars *
well sharpened, and being certain that one of
the blades of the sciffars is applied close upon
the external margin of the tarsus, should remove it at one stroke. If both the eye-lids, or
both eyes be affected, the operation should be
repeated upon each severally, without delay,
with such precautions and in such proportion
as the extent of the disease, and the degree of
inversion of the tarsus of each eye-lid may require. Afterwards, laying aside the method employed by the greater part of surgeons, of uniting the wound by sutures, it will be sufficient
to keep the supercilium depressed, if the operation have been performed upon the upper eye-
lid, or if upon the lower, to support it upon the
inferior arch of the orbit by pressing it from be-

* Plate III. fig. 2.

low

low upwards, to prevent the lips of the wound from feparating; which fhould then be placed in perfect contact by means of ftrips of adhefive plafter, which ought to extend from the fuperior arch of the orbit to the zygoma; and for the greater fecurity they fhould be maintained in that pofition by means of two fmall compreffes, one applied upon the eye-brow the other upon the zygoma, and covered with the *uniting* * bandage, which fhould be applied in the direction of the *monoculus*.

It appears to me that furgeons have been induced to employ the future, from obferving that after the excifion of the fold of fkin, of the upper eye-lid for inftance, the integuments were drawn fo much upwards towards the fupercilium, and downwards towards the tarfus, that the eye-lid might be faid at the moment to be denuded, and entirely deprived of fkin. But this is merely fo in appearance, for when the fupercilium is depreffed by means of fmall compreffes and the *uniting* bandage, the eye-lid is immediately covered with fkin as before, and the lips of the wound are eafily brought into perfect contact without the neceffity of employing futures. Gendron † is one of the few, who in thefe cafes prefer the ftrips of adhefive plafter to the ufe of futures, having very fre-

* See Heifter's Surgery, Part III. fect. 1. chap. ii. p. 355.
† Traité des maladies des yeux, tom. i. p. 243.

quently

quently obferved that the ufe of the latter
is followed by a violent tenfion and inflammation, which caufe a laceration of the parts.
Of the juftnefs of his opinion, as well as
the fimplicity and the fpeedinefs of the operation I am fatisfied from my own experience.

On removing the firft dreffings, the third day
after the operation, the furgeon will find that
the patient opens his eye without difficulty, and
that the inflected tarfus and cilia have recovered
their natural pofition and direction. In the
partial or incomplete trichiafis, or that which
occupies only one half or a third of the length
of the tarfus in perfons whofe fkins are very
diftenfile, I have frequently had the fatisfaction
to find, on removing the firft dreffings, the
wound perfectly united.

When, however, the wound has only united
in part, and the remainder has fuppurated and
formed granulations, it fhould be covered with
a fmall ftrip of lint fpread with the ung. ceruffæ.
If there be fungus it fhould be occafionally
touched with the argentum nitratum until the
cicatrix is perfectly formed. In general the
cure does not exceed the fourteenth day from
the operation.

Hitherto I have fpoken of the radical cure of
the fecond and moft frequent fpecies of trichiafis.
As to the firft form of the difeafe, which fortunately is very rare, in which the hairs are
pointed

pointed againſt the ball of the eye, without the
tarſus having altered its natural poſition, the
treatment, if there be any, is exceedingly difficult, ſince it is demonſtrated that neither the
plucking out, nor burning the roots of the hairs
is adequate to the complete cure of the diſeaſe;
and that the everſion of the tarſus, contrary to
its natural direction, would equally ſubject the
patient to the riſk of a perpetual weeping of the
eye, and chronic tumefaction of the internal
membrane of the eye-lid. Upon this point the
art of ſurgery is yet imperfect, and the ſubject
merits a more diligent attention, than practitioners have hitherto beſtowed on it. In the
caſe hinted at in the beginning of the chapter
which came under my own obſervation, there
only appeared two or three hairs directed
againſt the eye-ball. Having however bent
outwards a ſmall part of the tarſus, oppoſite
the ſeat of the diſeaſe, I ſaw indeed that I
ſhould not ſucceed in replacing the two or
three morbidly inclined hairs in their natural direction; but that I ſhould be able
to ſeparate them ſufficiently from the cornea, and prevent their preſſing upon it without
the tarſus being ſo much turned out as to allow
the tears to fall upon the cheek. And as in
this caſe * the ſkin near the tarſus was very

* Caſe XIX.

tenſe,

tenfe, I departed from the preceding rule, by making an external incifion with the back of the lancet near the tarfus three lines in extent, and removing a piece of fkin of the fame length, and rather more than a line in breadth. When the cicatrix was complete, the operation was as fuccefsful as the nature of the difeafe admitted of, but not fuch that this method of treatment could be faid to be perfect and exempt from inconvenience in cafes of greater magnitude than the one here adduced.*

The trichiafis being cured fomething remains to be done, in order to correct the difeafe from which it has originated, as well as to repair the injury which the ball of the eye has fuftained from the friction and irritation of the inflected

---

* Dr. Crampton propofes the following operation which he ftates to have performed in one inftance, with a fuccefs which anfwered his warmeft expectations. " Let the eyelid be well turned outwards by an affiftant; let the operator then with a lancet divide the broad margin of the tarfus completely through, by two perpendicular incifions, one on each fide of the inverted hair or hairs: let him then, by a tranfverfe fection of the conjunctiva of the eye-lid, unite the extremities of the perpendicular incifions. The portion of cartilage contained within the incifions, can then, if inverted, with eafe be reftored to its original fituation, and retained there by fmall ftrips of adhefive plafter, or (perhaps what is better) by a fufpenforium palpebræ, adapted to the length of the portion of the tarfus which it is intended to fuftain, fhould one or two hairs be difplaced without inverfion of the tarfus." Effay on the Entropeon, p. 55.

hairs.

hairs. The indications in general are to strengthen the veffels of the conjunctiva, to diminifh the enlargement of the ciliary glands, and to remove the opacity of the cornea. Of thefe we fhall treat diftinctly in the chapters on *ophthalmia* and the *nebula* of the cornea.

The celebrated Albinus * is the only perfon, as far as I know, who has noticed the trichiafis of the caruncula lachrymalis. For the greater advantage of the ftudent I have thought proper to fubjoin the hiftory which he has delivered. *In fubtilibus illis pilis, quos Morgagnus in caruncula lachrymali animadvertit, trichiafis fpeciem vidi. Unus eorum increverat præter naturam, craffior longiorque atque ita fe incurvans, ut globum oculi extrema parte attingeret.* Confecuta eft oculi inflammatio dira, cruciatu tetro, et quod caufa non intelligebatur, pertinax. Adhibita fuerant quæcunque fuggerere ars potuerat, et empiria : collyria, epifpaftica, purgantia, fanguinis miffiones, fonticuli, diæta. Quum nihil proficeretur, forte itum adme. In caufam fi invenire poffem, inquirens, ecce pilus. Quo evulfo, fubfedit malum.* The author leaves us, however, to wifh for an important elucidation; whether the hair which was plucked from the caruncle was afterwards reproduced or not, and if it were in what direction it grew.

* Acad. annot. lib. iii. cap. 8.

CASE

CASE XV.

Terefa Ballerini, of Trumello, a country woman, 35 years of age, was afflicted with an obftinate chronic ophthalmia during five years, in
confequence of which her fight was nearly deftroyed. She was unable to raife the upper eye-
lid of either eye, on account of their extreme relaxed and corrugated ftate, and the tarfus and
cilia of both eyes were feen folded inwards, and
irritating the eye. A fmall degree of light was
admitted at the internal angle of the eye, as the
tarfus was lefs depreffed and folded inwards at
this part than any other. The cornea of the
right eye appeared profoundly opake, that of the
left was only a little cloudy. The hairs had
been feveral times plucked out by a furgeon in
the country, one by one, but without advantage.

The patient being received into the practical
fchool, and feated in a chair, I made a fold of
the integuments of the upper eye-lid of the left
fide, with my fingers, near the margin, taking
care to raife it more towards the external than the
internal angle of the eye-lid; and finding it fufficient to draw the tarfus and cilia outwards, I
removed it with one ftroke of the crooked fciffars.
I immediately brought the lips of the wound
together, and retained them in contact by ftrips
of adhefive plafter, and more efpecially by the
application.

application of a comprefs upon the fupercilium and the *uniting* bandage in the direction of the *monoculus.* I immediately repeated the fame operation on the upper eye-lid of the right fide.

On removing the firft dreffings, three days after the operation, the woman was able to open her eyes, and I found that the tarfi and cilia of both eye-lids had recovered their natural pofition.

A fmall wound remained at the divided part on both fides, the greateft breadth of which did not exceed two lines. By the application of the unguent. ceruffæ, fpread upon a ftrip of lint, and the occafional ufe of the argentum nitratum it healed in the courfe of twelve days. The effects of the chronic inflammation and the flight opacity of the left eye were removed in the courfe of a month by the ufe of the vitriolic collyrium, and the ophthalmic ointment of Janin; as to the right the *leucoma* was fo denfe as to be incurable.

Case XVI.

Signor Count N. . . . of Pavia, had been fubject from his infancy to a difcharge from the eyes; at the age of ten he was unable to raife the upper eye-lid of the left eye, and in a very flight degree that of the right, or only for two or three lines towards the external angle, on which account he was obliged, for the purpofe

I   of

of feeing, to hold his neck fidewife and look obliquely with the right eye. The tarfus and cilia of the fuperior palpebra of the left eye were folded inwards, and preffed almoft entirely upon the ball of the eye, and particularly upon the cornea which they violently irritated: the cartilaginous border and the cilia of the right fuperior eye-lid, near the external angle, remained in their fituation, while the reft of the hairs of the fame row ftimulated the cornea. On the left fide the cornea was very dark, and marked here and there with fmall denfe fpots: that of the right fide was merely cloudy.

The cilia were extirpated from this child five different times, and their roots touched with cauftic; but, as they always grew again more pointed and briftly than before, it was propofed to remove along with them the edges of the affected eye-lids. Such were the circumftances of the cafe when he came under my care.

As the boy was very unmanageable, principally becaufe he had been frequently tormented to no purpofe, I was obliged to confine him more fecurely, by placing him upon a fmall bed where he could be eafily held. I raifed the fkin of the fuperior palpebra of the right eye near the tarfus, by means of the forceps, making the moft elevated centre or point of the wound towards the internal angle, for the reafons before affigned, and with the crooked

fciffars

fciffars divided it at one ftroke; I then repeated
the fame operation upon the upper eye-lid of
the left fide, making the moft elevated point of
the wound on this fide, precifely in the middle
of the eye-lid. The retraction of the integuments and the denudation of the eye-lids had a
frightful appearance to the byftanders. But by
depreffing the fupercilium, and applying ftrips
of adhefive plafter, with the compreffes and
uniting bandage upon each fide, the integuments
were made to cover the eye-lids, and the lips
of the two wounds were held in perfect contact.
The boy took 3 ounces of emulfion with 9 drops
of the tincture of opium, he flept a little afterwards, and was fufficiently quiet during the remainder of the treatment.

The dreffings were removed on the fifth day,
and the boy was able to open his eyes fufficiently
well: the tarfi and cilia of both eye-lids were
now turned outwards, and fo far feparated from
the ball of the eye as not to come in contact with
it, though they could not yet be faid to be in
their proper and natural pofition. This was oc-
fioned by the wounds having fuppurated more
than ufual, and having a tendency to become
fungous which prevented the perfect approximation of the divided edges of the fkin. By
repreffing the fungus with the argentum nitratum, and covering it with the unguent. ceruffæ,
the fores healed in the courfe of two weeks; and

in

in proportion as they contracted, the tarfus and cilia of each eye-lid were feparated at a greater diftance from the eye-ball, and ultimately returned to their natural pofition.

By means of Janin's ophthalmic ointment, applied between the eye-lids morning and evening for forty days, and the vitriolic collyrium inftilied into the eye fev   times in the courfe of the day, the varicofe veffels of the conjunctiva recovered their tone. The flight opacity of the cornea of the right eye was entirely diffipated; that of the left only in part, as there were many opake fpots irremoveable.

CASE XVII.

I undertook the treatment of an old woman who for feveral years had been regarded by her friends as completely blind, in confequence of an extraordinary relaxation of the upper eye-lid of both eyes, produced by repeated attacks of ophthalmia, and an inverfion of the edges of the eye-lids. The palpebræ being forcibly feparated, the tarfi and cilia of both the upper eye-lids were feen preffing upon the eye-ball, and the cornea of each eye had in a great meafure loft its natural tranfparency. In making this examination I did not perceive that on the left fide there was alfo an inverfion of a fmall part of the tarfus and hairs of the lower eye-lid.

So

So great was the relaxation of the integuments of the two upper eye lids, that inftead of the forceps I ufed the thumb and finger
of my left hand, with which I raifed a confiderable fold of the fkin near the margin of the right
fuperior eye-lid, which I divided with the fciffars,
removing a portion of the integuments of an
oval figure, the tranfverfe diameter of which correfponded precifely to the middle of the palpebra, the longitudinal to its two angles. The
operation was repeated in the fame manner upon
the left fuperior eye-lid. I then applied upon
each the ufual dreffings, confifting of a few ftrips
of adhefive plafter, compreffes upon the fupercilium and zygoma, and the *uniting* bandage.

At the end of three days I removed the dreffings for the firft time, and found the whole in
a good ftate, as the woman was able to open
her eyes without difficulty, the tarfus and cilia
of each eye-lid had returned to their fituation,
and the wound, though not yet cicatrized, had
a healthy appearance : I obferved, however, that
in the act of opening and fhutting the left eye
a few tears efcaped from it, and that the patient
complained of a little pain in it, which was not
the cafe in the right eye. I prefently difcovered
that towards the external angle of the lower
eye-lid of the left fide there was a fmall number of hairs, which, together with the tarfus, to
the extent of two lines, was folded inwards

and

and wounded the eye. Upon everting this
part of the lower eye-lid, fome white indurated
fpots were diftinctly obferved, oppofite the inverted portion of the tarfus, which indicated the
previous exiftence of fome fmall corroding ulcers,
the cicatrices of which had drawn inwards this
fmall portion of the tarfus, together with its
correfponding cilia.

I immediately divided the fkin of the lower
eye-lid with the back of a lancet, to the extent
of nearly four lines along the inverted tarfus,
and having infinuated through this opening the
point of a fine pair of forceps,* I elevated and
removed a fmall portion of the fkin of an oval
figure, and of a fize proportioned to the degree
of depreffion and inverfion of the tarfus and
hairs, and covered the wound with a ftrip of
fimple diachylon. The wound fuppurated, and
it was neceffary to touch it frequently with the
argentum nitratum. As foon as the wound was
healed the portion of the edge of the eye-lid
folded inwards recovered its natural pofition.
The great age of the patient, who was near 60,
and the tenacity of the humour collected in the
fubftance of both the corneæ, notwithftanding
the continual ufe of the ophthalmic ointment,
and the vitriolic collyrium for a month, did not
admit of that membrane being reftored, but in a

* Plate III. fig. 8.

fmall

fmall degree, to its former. tranfparency. The
patient however towards the end of the treatment was able to diftinguifh the figures and colours of bodies, and left the hofpital very well
fatisfied in having been freed from this painful
difeafe.

CASE XVIII.

The daughter of Signor Giovanni R ... of
Rovefcalla, a child nine years of age, of a fcrofulous habit, who had contracted the *fcabies*
while at the breaft, was feized in the feventh
year of her age with a chronic inflammation of
the palpebræ of both eyes, efpecially of the right,
attended with exulceration of the internal margin
of the tarfus, and of the boundary of the fclerotic
coat with the cornea in fome points of it. In
the courfe of two years the ophthalmia, efpecially
of the right eye, refifting the ufe of a variety of
remedies, both internal and external, which had
been prefcribed for it, the child gradually loft
the power of opening this eye, except a fmall
part of it towards the external angle. The tarfi
on both fides were indurated, incrufted, and
gummed, but thofe of the right eye were alfo
drawn inwards, together with the cilia both in
the upper and lower eye-lid; the inverfion in
the lower however was confined to a fmall part
towards its external angle. The irritation which

I 4   the

the cilia excited in the right eye was so trouble-
some that the child was inceffantly carrying its
hand to it.

The child was laid upon a table with her
head a little raifed, and firmly held by affiftants,
particularly by Signor Gianni, a fkilful furgeon
of this hofpital. I formed a fold of the integuments of the upper eye-lid of the right eye with
my fingers, in fuch a manner as to elevate it
more towards the external than the internal
angle of the eye, and with a pair of very fharp
fciffars removed a convenient portion of it, of an
oval figure, clofe to the inverted portion of the
tarfus, and in a direction parallel to it. A fimilar divifion was then made of the integuments
of the lower eye-lid, but of a lefs extent, as the
inverfion of the tarfus and hairs was not fo confiderable in this as in the upper eye-lid.

The wound was wiped dry and covered in the
ufual manner with ftrips of adhefive plafter, extending from one arch of the orbit to the other;
compreffes were applied upon the fupercilium
and zygoma, and the whole fecured by the *uniting* bandage applied in the direction of the *monoculus*.

Although immediately after the operation it
was impoffible to keep the child in bed, in order
that fhe might take fome reft, for which purpofe fome drops of laudanum had been given to
her, yet no bad fymptom occurred. When
the

the firſt dreſſings were removed on the third day, to the great aſtoniſhment of thoſe around, the child opened the right eye without difficulty: the tarſus and cilia had regained their natural ſituation, and the wound in the upper as well as the lower eye-lid was perfectly healed. The great length to which the hairs that had preſſed upon the eye-ball were grown, contraſted with thoſe ſituated towards the internal angle which had preſerved their natural direction, was very remarkable.

To complete the cure, it was only neceſſary to cover the two cicatrices with a ſtrip of linen ſpread with the unguent. ceruſſæ, to ſtrengthen the varicoſe veſſels of the conjunctiva, and to remove the opacity of the cornea of the right eye, which was obtained as far as poſſible, conſidering the great and long continued thickening which had taken place, in the ſpace of forty days, by employing at firſt the Thebaïc tincture of the *London Pharmacopœia,* afterwards the ophthalmic ointment, and at intervals during the day the vitriolic collyrium.

CASE XIX.

Lorenzo Crivelli, of Montalto, a ſtrong peaſant, 26 years of age, who had never been ſubiect to diſcharges of the eyes, in the beginning of May 1798, aroſe from bed with a pruritus of
the

the right eye, fo intolerable that he could not refrain a moment from rubbing it. This inconvenience, accompanied with heat and rednefs of the whole eye, increafed in a few days to fuch a degree, that fearing he fhould lofe the fight of the eye, he came to the hofpital.

About the middle of the lower eye-lid of the right fide, to the extent of two lines, there was evidently an irregularity of the hairs, which grew in different directions. Three of thefe arofe diftinctly from the internal furface of the tarfus, were directed obliquely towards the ball of the eye, and preffed partly upon the lower portion of the cornea, and partly upon the conjunctiva near to it, which had an impreffion on it at that part, and was tinged with a fpot of blood. This had taken place without the tarfus, either in that or any other part of it, having changed its natural fituation.

Being fufficiently aware of the inutility of plucking out the hairs in this difeafe, as well as the inefficacy of the means hitherto propofed for confining them outwards by adhefive plafter, fine ligatures, and other fimilar meafures; and obferving in this cafe that a moderate everfion of the fmall portion of the tarfus to which the difeafe was confined, would be fufficient to feparate the hairs from the eye-ball without producing any remarkable deformity; I determined on this occafion, as the only means left to me, to remove a fmall portion of the integuments of the lower eye-lid near the inverted hairs.

The patient being feated with his head bent backwards, and the eye-lid firmly fixed by an affiftant preffing upon the angles, I made an incifion in the integuments with the back of a lancet, four lines in extent, immediately below the edge of the eye-lid, and clofe to the tarfus; then having raifed the divided fkin with the forceps, I removed a fmall portion of an oval figure exactly of the fame length, and about two lines and a half in its greateft breadth: The wound was covered with a ftrip of linen fpread with digeftive ointment, a comprefs was placed upon the zygoma, and the *uniting* bandage applied in the direction of the *monoculus.*

On removing the dreffing two days afterwards I found the lips of the wound confiderably approximated, and the edge of the eye-lid proportionately drawn outwards, with the three hairs correfponding to it which had been inverted, by which the patient found himfelf gradually relieved from this inconvenience, One hair only, the longeft of the three, preffed yet flightly upon the cornea; I fay flightly, becaufe the patient did not complain of it, and the mark of the conjunctiva was now almoft entirely diffipated. The wound was touched on that day and the three following with the argentum nitratum, in order to deftroy a little more of the fubftance of the eye-lid,

lid, and to caufe a ftill greater everfion of its edge oppofite this fmall point of the *trichiafis.* Five days afterwards the wound was completely healed. The long hair which alone remained out of its natural direction no longer touched the cornea, but laid in the longitudinal direction of the internal edge of the lower eye-lid, without occafioning any uneafinefs or weeping of the eye. I therefore believed that I had accomplifhed all that the cafe feemed to require, and permitted the man to return home.*

* In an effay on the Entropeon lately publifhed by Dr. Crampton of Dublin, the author endeavours to fhow, from a feries of facts, that this difeafe, but particularly the inverfion of the upper eye-lid, is owing to a thickened and contracted ftate of the conjunctiva. As this is a fubject upon which obfervation alone muft decide, I have thought it proper to fubjoin his account of the nature of the difeafe, and the operation which he propofes for its removal. " When the eye is voluntarily opened (fays this gentleman) the upper eye-lid is not drawn vertically upwards, but backwards, defcribing a line parallel to the anterior and fuperior furface of the eye, over which it moves. When the eye is completely open, the eyelid is lodged in the fpace contained between the roof of the orbit and the fuperior furface of the eye. But fhould this fpace be filled up by the thickened or contracted conjunctiva, the levator palpebræ cannot execute its functions. Every acceffion of inflammation contracts the conjunctiva; the conjunctiva terminates upon the margin of the eye-lids; which deriving no fupport from without, and being conftantly acted upon from within, readily yield and become permanently inverted." In order to remove this ftricture formed by the conjunctiva, and to reftore the parts to their natural pofition, Dr.

Dr. Crampton recommends that the extremities of the tarfi fhould be divided with a fharp-pointed biftoury introduced between the eye-ball and palpebræ, and a tranfverfe incifion made in the internal membrane of the eye-lid, from one angle of the tarfus to the other, and that the eye-lid thus liberated fhould be fupported in its natural pofition by means of a fufpenforium palpebræ, till by recovering its original healthy ftate it is enabled to perform its funētions.

CHAP. V.

OF THE RELAXATION OF THE UPPER EYE-LID.

THE operation detailed in the preceding chapter, is also employed for the cure of the relaxation of the upper eye-lid, when it is simple or
unaccompanied with a morbid inversion of the
cilia towards the eye-ball. This disease does not
injure the organ of vision, except in as much as
it prevents those who are affected with it from
being able to see, without raising the upper eye-
lid with the finger.

The excessive elongation of the upper eye-
lid is sometimes, though rarely, a congenital dif-
ease: most frequently it arises from a morbid
thickening of the parts, in consequence of ob-
stinate chronic ophthalmia, in persons of a lax
and unhealthy fibre, or from the long continued
use of emollient and relaxing applications. It
is sometimes occasioned by an atony of the elevator muscle, peculiar to the upper eye-lid, either
simple or accompanied with a paralysis of the
optic nerve, as usually happens in consequence
of violent blows upon the eye-ball, when the
eye-lids are closed, with or without laceration
                                                    of

of the upper eye-lid and extensive ecchymosis of
the conjunctiva. It sometimes takes place during short intervals, in consequence of a spasm of
the orbicular muscle of the eye-lids.

The congenital elongation of the upper eye-
lid, and the relaxation which takes place from a
morbid thickening of the parts, in consequence of
the too long continued use of emollient applications, or of the eye being kept too long closed and
compressed by bandages,· is a disease easily characterized by the combination of circumstances
which have preceded it. If the atony or complete paralysis of the elevator muscle of the eye-
lid have had any share in producing the relaxation of it, it may be known by making a transverse fold of the integuments with the fingers or
forceps, near the superior arch of the orbit. For
if this muscle have not lost its power of contraction, when it is relieved as it were from the
superincumbent weight of the integuments, the
patient is able to raise the eye-lid and open his
eye sufficiently, if otherwise the eye remains
half closed. That depression of the eye-lid, with
inability of raising it, which recurs at short intervals, which comes on and disappears suddenly,
and which depends on a temporary spasm of the
orbicularis palpebrarum, is not properly a disease,
but a symptom of some other general spasmodic
affection, as of hypochondriasis, hysteria, chlorosis,
or of diseases of the stomach, occasioned by indi-
gestion

geftion or the prefence of worms: the caufes of which affections it is not difficult to afcertain.

Among the caufes of this imperfection writers on furgery have alfo reckoned tranfverfe wounds of the upper eye-lid or correfponding fuperci- lium; of which however they have not treated with fufficient perfpicuity. For if they intend to fpeak of thofe tranfverfe wounds of the upper eye-lid or fupercilium, which deftroy or vio- lently contufe the elevator mufcle, or which greatly injure the fupraorbital nerve, the relaxa- tion of the upper eye-lid may certainly be the confequence, but not the only one, as they are very frequently fucceeded by a much more fe- rious accident, the total lofs of fight. If they mean to include every other fpecies of tranfverfe wound of the upper eye-lid or fupercilium, it is evident that if this be unattended with lofs of fubftance and heal by the firft intention, it can- not produce a relaxation of the eye-lid, and if it be accompanied with a lofs of fubftance of the integuments or fubjacent parts, and proceed to fuppuration, inftead of occafioning a relaxation, when healed, it would rather produce a contrary difeafe, the fhortening of the eye-lid.

When the difeafe is purely local and recent, in perfons not advanced in age, or affected with hemiphlegia, or paralyfis of the mufcles of the face, and when it is derived from a morbid thickening of the parts which before were foft

and

and flaccid: fome advantage may be expeƈted from the ufe of local corroborant remedies, of which cold water, with a fmall quantity of fpirit of wine added to it, friƈtions upon the relaxed eye-lid with the anodyne liquor, or tinƈture of cantharides, and the application of the foap liniment with camphor, merit a preference.

The relaxation which is fymptomatic of hypochondriafis, hyfteria, and of morbid ftimuli in the ftomach, is cured by the adminiftration of internal antifpafmodic and antihyfteric remedies, by emetics and anthelminthics.

The congenital relaxation of the upper eyelid, the inveterate humoral, and that which is accompanied with atony of the levator mufcle, provided in this laft cafe the immediate organ of vifion remain found, can only be cured by means of an operation. It is true, that in the cafe of atony or debility of the elevator mufcle, the eye can never be fo completely opened as the found one, even after the operation; the patient, however, will be able to look at objeƈts without being under the neceffity of raifing the eye-lid with his finger.

This difeafe is cured, as I have faid, in the fame manner as the trichiafis: by raifing the fuperabundant portion of the integuments of the eye-lid between the finger and thumb, and removing it by means of the fciffars; obferving however not to take away a greater or lefs quantity

K of

of fkin than is neceffary, that the eye-lid may
yield to the action of the elevator mufcle, and
by obeying it, may conveniently uncover the eye-
ball. In the moft common cafe of trichiafis, or
that which is derived from a relaxation of the
eye-lid, together with a morbid inverfion of the
tarfus and hairs, it is of the greateft importance,
as I have ftated, for the complete fuccefs of the
operation, to make the fold of the integuments
as near as poffible to the inflected tarfus, that
the edge of the palpebra may be gradually drawn
outwards; but in the cafe of fimple relaxation of the upper eye-lid, of which I am now
treating, without any morbid inclination of the
edge of the palpebra or hairs, as there is no indication to be fulfilled but that of fhortening the
integuments of the eye-lid, it is more advantageous to make the fold and excifion in the
proximity and direction of the fuperior arch of
the orbit, than near the tarfus.

The excefs of the integuments of the relaxed
eye-lid, compared with the found one, is eafily
afcertained, by directing the patient to look fted-
faftly at an object in a line horizontal to the
height of his eye; for the found and open eye
being held firmly in that pofition, will fhow
clearly how much lefs the relaxed eye-lid is raifed
than the found one. The furgeon, therefore,
having made a tranfverfe fold of the integuments at the upper part of the relaxed eye-lid,

in

in the vicinity and direction of the fuperior arch
of the orbit, proportionate to the difparity of
its length; and the fold of fkin being firmly
held by means of the forceps, he fhould direct
the patient to open his eyes. If this be performed as well on the affected as the found fide,
it will be a certain indication, as I have faid, of
the integrity and aptitude of the elevator mufcle,
to contract and exert its power upon the relaxed
eye-lid; and if at the fame time both eye-lids
are raifed to the fame height, it will be alfo a
fufficient proof of the exact quantity of integuments comprehended in the tranfverfe fold to
be removed; in the contrary cafe the fold muft
be increafed or diminifhed accordingly. Having done this, the furgeon fhould remove this
fold of the integuments with one ftroke of the
fciffars, which being more elevated in the middle of the upper part of the eye-lid, than at its
extremities will leave a wound of the figure of a
myrtle leaf. The lips of the wound fhould then
be placed in contact, and retained by means of
ftrips of adhefive plafter, but efpecially by applying a comprefs upon the fupercilium, and
another upon the inferior margin of the orbit,
and over thefe the *uniting* bandage in the direction of the *monoculus.* The cure is generally
completed in a few days, provided, as in the cafe
of trichiafis, the compreffes and *uniting* bandage

are

are exactly applied, and the latter has a proper degree of tightnefs given to it.

The cafes which I have related in the preceding chapter on trichiafis, render it the lefs neceffary for me to adduce any inftances in fupport of this operation, although I could have introduced feveral. To the young furgeon, however, it will be ufeful to read upon this fubject the cafe publifhed by Morand, in the fecond volume of his *Opufcules de Chirurgie.*

CHAP.

CHAP. VI.

●F THE EVERSION OF THE EYE-LIDS.

As the exceffive relaxation of the integuments of the palpebræ, and the morbid abbreviation of their internal membrane near the edge of the eye-lid, in confequence of fmall corroding ulcers, and the cicatrices confequent on them, occafion a morbid inclination of the tarfus and cilia towards the eye-ball; fo, occafionally, the too great relaxation and tumefaction of their internal membrane, or the too great contraction and fhortening of the fkin of the eye-lids, or of the integuments of the furrounding parts, produce a difeafe contrary to that of trichiafis; the turning outwards or everfion of the eye-lids, termed *ectropion.*

With regard to the caufes, therefore, there are two diftinct fpecies of this difeafe; the one arifing from a preternatural tumefaction of the palpebra, which not only feparates its edge from the eye-ball, but alfo preffes upon it in fuch a degree as ultimately to evert it; the other produced by a fhortening of the fkin which covers

the

the eye-lid, or that of the neighbouring parts,
by which the ciliary edge is, in the firſt inſtance,
ſeparated from the ball of the eye, and afterwards gradually turned outwards, together with
the whole of the eye-lid.

The morbid tumefaction of the internal membrane of the palpebræ, which occaſions the firſt
ſpecies of everſion, not conſidering at preſent that
of a ſimilar kind, which takes place in old age, is
generally derived from a congenital laxity of the
conjunctiva, increaſed by attacks of obſtinate
chronic ophthalmia, eſpecially of the ſcrofulous
kind, in perſons of a weak and unhealthy fibre;
or is the conſequence of a variolous metaſtaſis to
the eyes, accompanied with a relaxation of the
veſſels of the conjunctiva; of the cruſta lactea,
impetigo, or other eruptive diſeaſes of the ſkin
imprudently repelled.

While the diſeaſe occupies the lower eye-lid
only, which is moſt frequently the caſe, its internal membrane is elevated in the form of a
ſemilunar fold, of a pale red colour, reſembling
the fungous fleſh of wounds, interpoſed between
the ball of the eye and the eye-lid, which it
everts to a certain extent. But when the morbid tumefaction has extended to both the eye-
lids, the diſeaſe preſents a circular appearance,
in the centre of which the eye-ball lies as if imbedded, while the circumference preſſes upon,
and turns out the edges of both the eye-lids,
occaſioning

occaſioning conſiderable uneaſineſs and deformity. In either caſe, if the integuments of the
eye-lids are preſſed upon with the point of the
finger, it is evident that they readily admit of
being elongated, and that the eye-lids would
yield ſo as to cover the eye-ball completely, if
they were not prevented by this intermediate
tumefaction of their internal membrane.

Beſides the great deformity which this diſeaſe
occaſions, it produces a continual diſcharge of
tears upon the cheek, aridity of the ball of the
eye, frequent attacks of chronic ophthalmia, intolerance of light, and in the end nebulæ and
ulceration of the cornea.

The ſecond ſpecies of everſion, or that occaſioned by a ſhortening of the ſkin which covers
the eye-lid or ſurrounding parts, is not unfrequently
a conſequence of contractions produced by the
confluent ſmall-pox in the integuments of the face
near the eye-lids, or in thoſe of the eye-lids themſelves; of deep burns accidentally inflicted on the
ſame parts; of the extirpation of cancerous warts
or encyſted tumours of the eye-lids or circumja-
cent parts, where a ſufficient quantity of ſkin has
not been ſaved; of the malignant carbuncle; and
laſtly of lacerations of theſe parts, attended with
conſiderable loſs of ſubſtance. Each of theſe
cauſes is ſufficient to produce ſuch a contraction
and ſhortening of the integuments of the eye-

lids,

lids, as to draw them towards either of the arches
of the orbit; and confequently to feparate them
from the eye-ball, and caufe an everfion of their
edges. This effect no fooner takes place than
it is fucceeded by another no lefs inconvenient,
the tumefaction of the internal membrane of
the eye-lid, which alfo greatly contributes to
complete the everfion. For the internal membrane of the eye-lid, though flightly everted,
being inceffantly expofed to the contact of the
air, and continually irritated by extraneous fubftances, in a fhort time fwells and is elevated in
the form of a fungus; one part of which by degrees covers a portion of the eye-ball, the other
preffes the eye-lid outwards, and produces fo
confiderable an everfion of it, that its edge is not
unfrequently brought in contact with the margin
of the orbit. This fecond fpecies of the difeafe
is attended with the fame unpleafant effects as
the firft, to which it may be added, that when
either form of the difeafe has been of long ftanding, the fungous tumefaction of the internal
membrane of the eye-lids becomes indurated,
coriaceous, and almoft callous.

Although the internal membrane of the eye-
lid, in both thefe fpecies of everfion, appears
equally tumefied, yet the furgeon may eafily determine to which of the two fpecies the difeafe
belongs. For, in the firft form of the difeafe, as
I have ftated, the fkin of the eye-lid, or furrounding

rounding parts, is not disfigured with fcars, and the everted eye-lid, on being preffed upon with the point of the finger, would rife again without difficulty, fo as to cover the eye completely, if this carnous fubftance were not interpofed; while, in the fecond fpecies of everfion, befides the evident fcars and contractions which are feen upon the fkin of the eye-lid or neighbouring parts, if an attempt be made to reftore the eye-lid to its fituation, it either does not yield fo as to cover the eye-ball entirely, or it can only be reduced to a certain extent, or, from the edge of the eye-lid having contracted an adhefion to the arch of the orbit, in confequence of a very confiderable deftruction of the integuments, it does not admit of being removed in any degree from its unnatural pofition.

From comparing therefore thefe two fpecies of everfion, it muft be evident that a perfect cure of this difeafe cannot be effected equally in both forms of it, and that the latter fpecies in fome inftances is abfolutely incurable. For as the treatment of the firft fpecies of everfion, which depends only on a morbid tumefaction of the internal membrane of the palpebræ, merely confifts in removing that which is fuperfluous, the art of furgery poffeffes many efficacious means perfectly adequate to the fulfilment of this indication. But in the fecond fpecies of the difeafe, in which the principal

cipal caufe confifts in the lofs of a portion of the fkin of the eye-lid or furrounding parts, which no artifice hitherto known can reftore, a complete cure of the difeafe cannot be obtained. The furgeon muft be therefore content to remedy as far as poffible the evils attendant on it, and that in a more or lefs fatisfactory manner, according to the greater or lefs deftruction of the integuments, and to abandon as incurable thofe cafes in which the edge of the eye-lid is found to be united to the arch of the orbit. *Si nimium palpebræ deeft,* fays Celfus,* *nulla id reftituere curatio poteft.* In the treatment then of the fecond fpecies of everfion, the degree of fuccefs muft be determined in every cafe by the furgeon's obferving to what extent the eye-lid, can be reduced by gently preffing it towards the eye-ball with the point of the finger, both before and after the employment of fuch means as are calculated to produce an elongation of its integuments, fince it is to this point only that it can be reduced and maintained in its pofition permanently.

With refpect to the treatment of the firft fpecies of everfion, if the difeafe be recent, the fungous ftate of the internal membrane not confiderable, and confequently the everfion of the edge of the eye-lid fmall, of two lines in extent

* Book VII. chap. 7.

or

or little more, and in young perfons, (for in
thofe advanced in years the eye-lids are fo flaccid
that the difeafe is altogether incurable,) it may
be removed by deftroying the fuperficial fungus
of the internal membrane of the eye-lid with
the argentum nitratum, which ought to be executed in the following manner. The furgeon
fhould completely evert the affected eye-lid with
his left hand, and with his right wipe it dry by
means of a piece of linen cloth; he fhould then
rub the cauftic ftrongly upon the whole extent
of the fuperficial fungus, fo as to produce an
efchar. In order that it may occafion the patient as little pain as poffible, at the moment the
cauftic is withdrawn an affiftant fhould inftantly
cover the cauterized part with a little oil, which
will prevent the tears from readily diffolving the
argentum nitratum, and diffufing it over the
eye-ball. If, however, any portion of the diffolved cauftic fhould occafion uneafinefs, it
ought to be wafhed off, by frequently dropping
into the eye a little new milk. This application of the cauftic fhould be repeated for feveral
fucceffive days, until it has produced a fufficient
ulceration and deftruction of the fuperficial fungus of the conjunctiva, efpecially near the tarfus; after which lotions of fimple water, or barley water with mel rofæ, will be fufficient to
promote the fuppuration and cicatrization of the
wound. The refult of this treatment will be,
that

that in proportion as the internal ſurfate of the
eye-lid heals, the everſion will gradually diminiſh,
and the edge of the eye-lid will finally regain its
natural poſition.

This method of treatment, as I have juſt
ſtated, is only practicable with perfect ſuccefs in
caſes of recent and very ſlight everſion.* Where
the diſeaſe is conſiderable and of long ſtanding,
the moſt expeditious and certain method of re-
medying it, is that of extirpating the whole fungus, cloſe to the internal muſcular ſubſtance of
the eye-lid. The patient being therefore ſeated,
and his head bent ſomewhat backwards, the
the ſurgeon ſhould hold the everted eye-lid firmly
with the point of the fore and middle finger of
his left hand, and with the curved ſciſſars † in
his right ſhould include the excreſcence of the
internal membrane of the palpebra, as near to
its baſe as poſſible, and remove it completely ;
the ſame operation ſhould then be repeated on
the other eye-lid, when both are affected ; and
if the excreſcence be of ſuch a figure that it
cannot be exactly included between the ſciſſars,
it ſhould be raiſed as much as poſſible with the
forceps, or a double-pointed hook, and divided
at its baſe by means of a ſmall convex-edged

* In theſe inſtances, I believe, the diſeaſe may in general be
effectually and more ſpeedily removed by ſcarifying the internal membrane of the eye-lid with the point of a lancet.
† Plate III. fig. 3 and 4.

biſtoury.

biftoury.* The hæmorrhage, which at the commencement of the operation is confiderable, either ceafes fpontaneoufly or may be checked by wafhing the eye with cold water. The dreffing fhould confift of two compreffes, one placed upon the fuperior the other upon the inferior arch of the orbit, and over thefe the uniting bandage in the form of the *monoculus*, or applied in fuch a manner as to prefs upon and replace the edge of the eye-lid, fo that it may cover the eye-ball again. When the firft dreffings are removed, which ought to be 24 or 30 hours after the operation, the eye-lid will be found to have recovered entirely, or nearly fo, its natural pofition. The dreffing fhould afterwards confift in wafhing the fore twice a day, either with fimple water, with the aqua malvæ, or with barley water and mel rofæ, until it is completely healed. If towards the end of this period, the wound affume a fungous appearance, or if the furgeon perceive that the eye-lid is yet too far feparated from the eye-ball, it fhould be frequently touched with the argentum nitratum, in order to deftroy a little more of the internal membrane of the eye-lid, fo that when the cicatrization is completed, the contraction may be fuch as to draw the edge of the palpebra nearer to the ball of the eye. In the mean time proper meafures

* Plate III. fig. 12.

fhould

ſhould be employed to remove the cauſes by
which the everſion has been produced; as the
chronic ophthalmia, the morbid determination
of humours to the eye, and the weakneſs and
varicoſe ſtate of the veſſels of the conjunctiva,
of which I ſhall have occaſion to ſpeak in the
chapter on ophthalmia.

The indication of cure in the ſecond ſpecies
of everſion, or that which is produced by an
accidental ſhortening of the integuments of the
eye-lids or of the ſurrounding parts, is not different from that already mentioned. If the ſhortening of the integuments has been capable of
everting the eye-lid, the extirpation of a portion
of its internal membrane, and the cicatrix which
muſt enſue from it, may, for the ſame reaſons,
reſtore the eye-lid to its former poſition. But
ſince that portion of the integuments which is
loſt can never be reproduced, and in whatever
degree the whole eye-lid is ſhortened, ſo it muſt
always remain, even after the moſt ſucceſsful
operation; conſequently the treatment of the
ſecond ſpecies of everſion can never ſucceed ſo
perfectly as that of the firſt ſpecies, and the eye-
lid, though replaced, will always remain ſhorter
than natural, in a degree proportionate to the
greater or ſmaller quantity of integuments loſt.
In a conſiderable number of caſes, indeed, the
everſion appears greater than it is in reality, with
regard to the ſmall quantity of ſkin which is
deſtroyed

deftroyed; for, when the difeafe has once taken place, however fmall the contraction of the integuments may be, the tumefaction of the internal membrane gradually increafes, fo as to produce a complete everfion of the eye-lid. The operation in thefe cafes is attended with a degree of fuccefs which could not have been expected by thofe unacquainted with the nature of the fubject; for after the fungus of the internal membrane of the difeafed eyelid has been extirpated, and its edge brought towards the ball of the eye, the fhortening of the eye-lid which remains is fo inconfiderable, that in comparifon with the deformity and inconvenience which it occafioned in a ftate of everfion, the cure may be confidered as perfect; of this we have an example in the annexed figure.* Whenever therefore the retraction of the integuments of the everted eye-lid, and confequent fhortnefs of it is not fo confiderable as to prevent it from rifing again and covering the eye, if not perfectly, at leaft in a tolerable degree, the furgeon fhould undertake the operation in the manner already explained, employing, according to circumftances, fometimes the curved fciffars, at other times the convex-edged biftoury, or both. When the difeafe has exifted for a confiderable time, and the in-

* Plate II. fig. 1, 2.

ternal

ternal membrane has become hard and almoſt callous, the everted eye-lid ſhould be covered with a ſoft poultice of bread and milk for ſome days previous to the operation, in order to render it flexible and more eaſily ſeparable than in its former rigid ſtate.

It is one of the moſt certain and demonſtrable facts, that the diviſion of the cicatrices of the integuments, which have given riſe to the con-traction and everſion of the eye-lid, does not produce a permanent. elongation of it, and there-fore is attended with no advantage in the treat-ment of this diſeaſe. We ſee the ſame thing happen after deep and extenſive burns of the ſkin of the palm of the hand and fingers, in conſe-quence of which, whatever diligence be em-ployed during the treatment to keep the hand and fingers in an extended ſtate, as ſoon as the cicatrix is complete, the fingers are found irre-mediably bent. The ſame thing takes place after extenſive burns of the face and neck. Fabricius ab Aquapendente,* who was well aware of the inutility of the ſemilunar diviſion of the integuments of the eye-lids, in order to remedy their ſhortening and everſion, propoſes, as the beſt expedient, that of ſtretching them by means of adheſive plaſters applied upon the eye-lid and the ſupercilium, and tied firmly to-

---

* De Chirurg. Operat. cap. xv.

gether.

gether. Experience has taught me that whatever advantage may be derived from this practice, is equally obtained by the application of a
bread and milk poultice for feveral days, afterwards of oily embrocations, and laftly of the
uniting bandage, fo applied as to extend the
fhortened eye-lid in a direction contrary to that
produced by the cicatrix: which practice ought
to be diligently employed in every cafe previoufly to the operation being undertaken.

When the operation is determined upon, the
patient, if an adult, being feated in a chair, or if
a child, laid upon a table with the head a little
raifed, and held by proper affiftants, the furgeon,
by means of a convex-edged biftoury, fhould
make an incifion of a fufficient depth in the internal membrane of the eye-lid along the tarfus,
carefully avoiding the *puncta lachrymalia,* then
with the forceps he fhould elevate the edge of the
divided membrane, and continue to feparate it
with the knife from the whole of the internal furface of the eye-lid, in the manner ufually employed in the anatomical diffection of it, until the feparation be completed, as far as the point where
this membrane is about to leave the eye-lid, to
reach the anterior hemifphere of the eye-ball,
receiving the name of conjunctiva. The feparation being carried to this point, the furgeon,
raifing the membrane with the forceps ftill
higher, fhould entirely remove it by one or two

L   ftrokes

ftrokes of the fciffars clofe to the deepeft part of the eye-lid. The dreffing fhould confift as ufual in the application of a comprefs and the uniting bandage, in order to facilitate the return of the everted eye-lid towards the ball of the eye. On changing the dreffings, one or two days after the operation, the eye-lid will be found in a great degree reinftated, and the deformity which it occafioned confiderably leffened.

It is feldom that the operation is followed by any unpleafant fymptoms, as vomiting, great pain, or violent inflammation. If, however, they fhould take place, the vomiting may be relieved by means of an opiate clyfter, and the pain and inflammation with great tumefaction of the eye-lid leffened by the application of a poultice, or bags of emollient herbs, employing at the fame time internal antiphlogiftic remedies, until thefe fymptoms have entirely fubfided, and fuppuration has commenced upon the internal furface of the eye-lid. When the fuppuration has taken place, the part fhould be wafhed twice a day with barley water and mel rofæ, and the wound touched occafionally with the argentum nitratum, in order to keep the granulations within certain bounds, and to promote a folid cicatrix capable of retaining the reduced eye-lid in its fituation.

CASE

Case XX.

A young woman, 20 years of age, of a delicate conftitution, and of a lax and chlorotic fibre, after an obftinate ophthalmia, had both the lower eye-lids turned outwards to the extent of about two lines. The difeafe, befides disfiguring the patient's countenance, occafioned a difcharge upon the cheek of a mixture of tears and puriform matter. The everted edge of both eye-lids had a florid appearance, and was a little elevated and fungous.

After having tried the ufe of aftringent collyria for a week, without advantage, I formed the refolution of deftroying deeply the internal margin of both eye-lids by means of cauftic. For this purpofe having feparated the eye-lids, one after the other from the eye-ball, and carefully wiped them, I applied the argentum nitratum upon the fuperficial fungus of their internal margin, and preffed it upon it fo ftrongly as to produce an efchar, which was immediately covered with a layer of oil, and the patient's eyes wafhed fucceffively with new milk. This application of the cauftic was repeated fix times at different intervals, and always with evident advantage; fo that in 26 days I had the fatisfaction to fee the edges of both eye-lids raifed to their fituation. The collyrium vitriolicum

was

was employed for a confiderable time after the
cure, in order to prevent a return of the difeafe.

CASE XXI.

Giufeppa Mileri, a girl 9 years of age, a native of Pavia, of an unhealthy conftitution, incautioufly ran the point of a knife acrofs the
cornea of the right eye. This accident left a
deformed cicatrix, and occafioned a chronic
ophthalmia, which by degrees degenerated into
an enormous fwelling of the internal membrane
of the lower eye-lid, producing an everfion of
it, and giving the child's countenance a difguft-
ing appearance. At the time of her admiffion
into this fchool of clinical furgery, which was
fome months after the appearance of the ectropion, the child complained of no pain when the
fungus was touched with the point of the
finger.

I proceeded to remove the fungus with the
curved fciffars, and covered the part with a
piece of linen fpread with an ointment confifting of wax and oil, over which I applied a
comprefs and the uniting bandage. When the
dreffings were removed, four days afterwards, the
eye-lid had already rifen up confiderably, and
on the following day the fuppuration was completely eftablifhed. The eye-lid remained nearly
                                        ftationary

ftationary for a week. As foon, however, as
the wound began to heal, and confequently to
contract, the eye-lid rofe up in an equal degree,
and when the cicatrix was complete it recovered
its natural pofition.

During the whole of the treatment, which
took up about a month, no other external remedy was employed than a lotion of barley water
and honey of rofes, with fome applications of
the argentum nitratum, when the granulations
were too prominent. Afterwards an electuary,
confifting of cinchona and the antimonial æthiops,
was employed with advantage. When the
wound was completely healed I directed the
ophthalmic ointment of Janin to be ufed morning and evening for fome weeks, in order to
ftrengthen the varicofe veffels of the conjunctiva, which was attended with the beft fuccefs.
The extenfive fcar upon the cornea had entirely
deprived the child of the fight of the eye, but
the ectropion was completely cured.

CASE XXII.

A countryman, 38 years of age, was attacked
with an eryfipelas of the face, in confequence
of which the eye-lid and fupercilium of the left
fide were greatly fwollen, and the inflammation
terminated in fuppuration. The matter difcharged itfelf by burfting at three diftinct places

in the upper eye-lid, near the ſuperciliary arch.
The ſurgeon, in order to expedite the healing of
the ulcers, determined to divide and remove by
the knife the apertures from which the matter
was diſcharged; and whether in this operation
he had extirpated a portion of the integuments
of the eye-lid, 'or they had been too much deſtroyed by the ulceration, in proportion as the
ulcer healed, the upper eye-lid was obſerved to
be more and more drawn upwards and everted,
and ultimately ceaſed to cover the eye-ball. In
conſequence of which the internal membrane of
the eye-lid, from being long expoſed to the air,
became greatly tumefied and by degrees degenerated into a fungous ſubſtance. In order to
remedy this inconvenience in the beſt poſſible
manner, I made the patient ſit in the ſame poſition as in the operation for the cataract, and
with a ſmall convex-edged ſcalpel I began to
ſeparate the internal fungous membrane, commencing the inciſion near the external, and
continuing to divide it nearly as far as the internal angle of the eye, taking care to avoid the
part occupied by the *punctum lachrymale*. Having done this, I took hold of the membrane
with the forceps, and then, continuing the inciſion, I ſeparated it from the whole internal ſurface of the eye-lid, as far as where this membrane is about to reach the anterior hemiſphere
of the eye-ball, and form the conjunctiva.

As

As foon as the membrane was feparated, the eye-lid fell upon the ball of the eye, and almoft entirely recovered its former appearance. The lofs of blood was inconfiderable; but a little after the operation the patient was feized with a violent vomiting, which continued for two hours, and was checked by adminiftering opium freely by the mouth and by clyfter.

For a few days the eye-lid was moderately fwollen, but fubfided on the commencement of the fuppuration on its internal furface, and in 14 days from the operation the patient was completely well, as far as the nature of the cafe admitted.

The eye was not disfigured, although the eye-lid in reality was a little fhorter than the right. He could raife it and deprefs it at pleafure, and apply it upon the eye-ball. When he wifhed to clofe his left eye entirely, the lower eye-lid was carried upwards beyond its ufual limits, and fo fupplied the defect of length in the upper one.

Case XXIII.

A boy, 10 years of age, in the beginning of October 1790, having lain during the night wrapt in a fheet upon which ears of corn had been beaten, awoke in the morning with the eye-lids of his left eye fwollen and painful. Notwithftanding the ufe of emollient topics,

an

an abfcefs formed in the upper eye-lid, which burft below the fupercilium towards the temples, and left an opening which could not be healed by any methods of treatment which were employed. In procefs of time the upper eye-lid began to be turned outwards, and its internal membrane to fwell and protrude, and to increafe the everfion of it prodigioufly.

Towards the middle of June 1791, about eight months from the firft appearance of any difeafe, the fungous excrefcence formed by the internal membrane of the eye-lid, covered a confiderable part of the upper hemifphere of the eye-ball, and the everfion was fo confiderable that the margin of the eye-lid, efpecially towards the temples, was almoft clofe to the eye-brow. The eye-lid, however, readily yielded on being preffed upon with the point of the finger, and appeared as if it would have defcended and covered the eye had it not been for the intervention of this fungous fubftance formed by its internal membrane.

As the fungus was dry and indurated, I ordered that a bread and milk poultice fhould be applied upon it for 24 hours; I then removed the whole of it with the curved fciffars at one ftroke, carefully avoiding the fuperior lachrymal punctum.

After the extirpation it was difcovered that there was a piece of wheaten ftraw almoft an
inch

inch long and half a line thick, contained in the fold of the fungus. The whole of the fuperfluous part of the internal membrane being now removed, the eye-lid defcended over the eye fo as to cover it conveniently. The opera-tion was not followed by any unpleafant fymp-tom, and 10 days afterwards the child left the hofpital, fo far cured that no defect remained, except a fmall elevation of the eye-lid near the external opening where the abfcefs had burft.

As there can be no doubt that this piece of ftraw had prevented the ulcer of the eye-lid from healing, during eight months after the burfting of the abfcefs, fo it is fingular that this extraneous body fhould have been forced through the internal membrane of the eye-lid, without the child having been awaked by it.

Case XXIV.

Giufeppe Antonia Scanarotti, aged 36 years, living in the vicinity of Stradella, had a wart for a confiderable time near the inferior orbital arch of the right fide, which in January 1795 began to be painful. A furgeon in that neigh-bourhood applied a cerate upon it, the effect of which was, that two days afterwards he was feized with an eryfipelas, which extended over the whole of the right fide of the face. The furgeon then altered his plan, and as foon as
the

the eryſipelas began to diſappear he applied the
actual cautery upon the tubercle, and deſtroyed
it deeply, covering the eſchar with a poultice of
bread and milk, which was continued for ſeveral days. On the looſening of the eſchar the
part was found in the ſtate of a ſimple wound,
and healed in the courſe of two months.* In
conſequence of this cicatrix the lower eye-lid
was drawn a little downwards and outwards.
In proceſs of time the internal membrane of
the eye-lid began to be elevated, and to aſſume
a fungous appearance, and in about two years
from the time of the accident, the fungus became ſo exuberant as to evert the whole of the
eye-lid in the manner repreſented in the 1ſt
figure of the 2d plate. The great deformity of
the countenance, and the perpetual weeping of
the eye which the diſeaſe occaſioned, induced
the patient to come into the hoſpital the 29th
of December 1797.†

On preſſing the lower eye-lid upwards with
the point of the finger, I found that the ſkin
yielded ſufficiently to allow of its being nearly
reſtored to its natural poſition, and was therefore induced to hope that this poor man's

* Plate II. fig. 1.

† This caſe is recorded in the 1ſt vol. 4th part, p. 806, of
a journal tranſlated from the German, by Thomas Volpi,
entitled, Biblioteca della più recente letteratura medico-
chirurgicha. *Léveillé.*

condition

condition might be ameliorated. And, as the fungus of the everted eye-lid was hard and coriaceous, I covered it for three days with an ointment confifting of oil and wax fpread upon linen, over which was applied a poultice of bread and milk.

On the 3d of January 1798, the patient being placed in a chair, with the fmall convex-edged biftoury I made an incifion along the internal margin of the tarfus of the lower eye-lid, from one canthus to the other, avoiding the punctum lachrymale; and by continuing to feparate the internal membrane downwards, I removed along with it the whole of the fungus. After having covered the part with a piece of linen fpread with oil and wax, I applied a very high comprefs upon the zygoma and eye-lid, and over it the *uniting* bandage in the direction of the *monoculus.*

On the 6th the dreffing was removed for the firft time, and the eye-lid was found to have advanced more than two-thirds towards its natural pofition. I wafhed the parts with the aqua malvæ made tepid, and renewed the dreffing as at firft.

On the 9th the eye-lid had rifen up towards the eye-ball more than on the preceding days. The granulations being too luxuriant, were touched with the argentum nitratum, and the efchar was immediately fmeared with oil.

On

On the 10th, 11th, and 12th, nothing particularly occurred, except that the cicatrix began to be formed near the internal margin of the tarfus.

On the 13th, 14th, and 15th, it was neceffary to touch the ulcer towards the internal angle of the eye with the argentum nitratum.

On 21ft the wound was completely healed, by employing a wafh, confifting of the aqua calcis and mel rofæ, three times a day. The eye-lid had gained the higheft degree of elevation it was capable of attaining, and precifely as it is feen in the 2d figure of the 2d plate. The difference, though very inconfiderable, which is alfo obfervable in the figure, was proportionate to the lofs of integuments before fuftained in the part where the cicatrix was formed, a lofs not reparable by any ingenuity hitherto devifed. By this operation, however, the deformity and weeping of the eye were removed.

CASE XXV.

Maria Terefa Zeccone, of Marcignago, was afflicted at the age of fix years with a malignant carbuncle on the inferior and fomewhat lateral external part of the lower eye-lid of the right fide, which produced a confiderable deftruction of the integuments. The deformed and tenfe cicatrix which fucceeded it, occafioned afterwards

wards an enormous everfion of the eye-lid. I examined this girl's eye when fhe had attained the 16th year of her age. The everted portion was at leaft five lines in breadth; the tears were inceffantly difcharged over the cheek. The eye-lid could be pufhed upwards only in a very fmall degree, in confequence of the contraction of the integuments, efpecially towards the external angle of the eye. The great deficiency of integuments, and the rigidity of the cicatrix, did not permit me to hope for a perfect cure; however, I was defirous of alleviating her condition, and a bed was therefore allotted to her in the hofpital, on the 17th of December 1799. In order to render the integuments of the eye-lid and the cicatrix as flexible as poffible, I directed that the part fhould be anointed feveral times with lard, and that the uniting bandage fhould be applied in fuch a manner as might tend to elongate the fkin of the cheek and affected eye-lid from below upwards; which was employed until the 22d day of the fame month with great advantage.

The following day I performed the operation, by making an incifion with the convex-edged biftoury upon the internal fungous membrane of the everted eye-lid, clofe to the tarfus, from the external towards the internal angle, avoiding the inferior *punctum lachrymale,* and having feparated it in a great meafure, and detached it

as

as far as where it begins to receive the name of conjunctiva, I raifed it with the forceps and completely removed it by a fingle ftroke of the curved fciffars. I defired the patient to clofe her eye as much as poffible, and having covered the part with a doffil of dry lint, to reprefs the bleeding, I applied the uniting bandage upon the eye-lid. The dreffing was removed two days afterwards, and the eye-lid found ftraightened and confiderably elevated towards the eyeball. The wound was wafhed with warm water, and covered with a piece of linen fpread with the ointment, confifting of oil and wax, and the uniting bandage reapplied fo as to prefs the integuments of the eye-lid ftill more upwards.

On the 27th the fuppuration was very copious, and the wound had a tendency to become fungous. On the 29th this fungus had increafed fo as evidently to oppofe the farther elevation of the eye-lid, I therefore removed it at once with the curved fciffars.

On the 1ft of January 1800, the fuppuration was again abundant. The wound was wafhed feveral times a day with barley water and mel rofæ. On the 5th I ordered the ophthalmic ointment of Janin to be applied upon the internal furface of the eye-lid at bed-time, in order to reprefs the tendency which the wound always

6   had

had to the formation of fungus.   This application was continued until the 10th.

At this period the eye-lid had almoſt attained
the greateſt degree of elevation of which it was
capable, and embraced the lower hemiſphere of
the eye-ball, ſo that the tears were no longer
diſcharged over the cheek.

From the 10th to the 20th the wound
was occaſionally touched with the argentum
nitratum, and waſhed with barley-water and
honey; by means of which it was perfectly
healed.

On the 22d the girl left the hoſpital very
well ſatisfied with her improved appearance.
For no other defect remained than that depending on the ſhortneſs of the lower eye-lid, which,
however, was not very evident, unleſs when ſhe
looked upwards.

CHAP.

CHAP. VII.

OF THE OPHTHALMIA.

THERE are two fpecies of ophthalmia: the one acute and truly inflammatory, arifing from an excefs of ftimulus and reaction of the living folid; the other chronic, from debility which is moft frequently confined to the veffels of the eye or thofe of the eye-lids, but occafionally is connected with a weaknefs of the general conftitution at the fame time. The Arabian phyficians have not improperly denominated the one ophthalmia *calida*, the other *frigida*.

This diftinction, founded on obfervation and experience, is the moft certain guide which we have in the treatment of the ophthalmia. For the firft fpecies of this difeafe invariably requires the ufe of general antiphlogiftic remedies, and mild emollient applications; the other that of aftringent and corroborant remedies, either alone or conjoined with the internal adminiftration of tonics, in order to ftrengthen the patient's general conftitution.

Befides

Befides this diftinction, it is in my opinion of the greateft importance, in the treatment of this difeafe, to know that the truly acute inflammatory ophthalmia, even when treated in the moft effectual manner, is fcarcely ever fo completely refolved, that a certain period having elapfed, and the inflammation entirely ceafed, fome fmall degree of chronic ophthalmia does nQt remain in the conjunctiva and furrounding parts from local debility. This takes place either in confequence of the diftenfion of the veffels of the eye, during the period of inflammation, or of the increafed morbid fenfibility of the whole organ of vifion ; which increafed fenfibility continuing in the eye, after the acute inflammatory ophthalmia has ceafed, keeps up in that organ, and the parts furrounding it, a morbid determination of blood, which may readily lead the inexperienced to believe that the inflammation of the eyes is not fubdued.

Of the great importance of this obfervation, in determining with precifion, at the bed-fide of the patient, not only the fpecies, but alfo the different ftages of the difeafe, and confequently the felection of remedies beft adapted to each of them, I have been over and over again convinced, from the refult of my own practice and that of others. For I have frequently remarked, that thofe furgeons, who, whether guided by thefe principles or by an extenfive experience only, know how to avail themfelves

M   of

of the precife moment in which the *acute* ophthalmia changes into the *chronic* from local debility, fpeedily conduct the difeafe to a termination by fubftituting aftringent and corroborant,
for emollient and relaxing applications ; while
others, who either from ignorance or inattention
are deceived by the appearances, continue
the ufe of emollient and mild remedies, and
thus perpetuate the turgefcency of the veffels
and the rednefs of the conjunctiva, which they
fuppofe to be as much inflamed as at the beginning. It is precifely on this account that
every empiric can boaft of having cured obftinate cafes of ophthalmia with his *aqua mirabilis,*
while he impofes upon the public in vending it
as a fpecific for ophthalmia in general; fince this
collyrium, which quickly diffipates the difeafe.
in the fecond ftage, greatly aggravates it in the
firft. On this fubject, fays Hoffman;* *aufim
dicere, plures vifu privari ex imperitia applicandi
topica, quam ex ipfa morbi vi ac magnitudine*;
which is particularly applicable to the ophthalmia.

In order to place thefe general principles relative to the ophthalmia in the cleareft light,
and to render them intelligible to the young
furgeon, I have thought it neceffary to enter
into a minute detail of the phænomena of this
otherwife frequent and well known difeafe.

* Differtat. de erroribus vulgaribus circa ufum topicorum
in praxi, § 7.

The

The *acute* inflammatory ophthalmia is either mild or violent; both are accompanied with the fame fymptoms which characterize the inflammation of other parts, with the addition however of a feries of other unpleafant effects depending upon the difturbed function of the organ of vifion.

In cafes of the mild acute ophthalmia, the internal furface of the palpebræ and the white of the eye become unufually red, the patient feels a fenfe of heat in the eyes greater than natural, accompanied with heavinefs, pruritus, and pricking, as if fmall particles of fand had accidentally got into them. In that part of the eye-ball where the fenfation of pricking is moft complained of, a fmall fafciculus of blood veffels is conftantly met with upon the conjunctiva more elevated and turgid than the reft of the fmall veffels of the fame order. The patient voluntarily keeps his eye-lids half clofed, on account of the ftiffnefs and difficulty which he finds in opening them, and becaufe by this means he moderates the impulfe of the light, to which he cannot expofe himfelf, in any confiderable degree, without feeling the fenfe of heat, the pricking, and difcharge of tears increafed. If the patient poffefs much fenfibility, his pulfe becomes a little quick, efpecially towards the evening, or he is affected with laffitude, drynefs

of

of the ſkin, ſlight ſhiverings, and in ſome caſes with nauſea and inclination to vomit.

This diſeaſe is frequently of a catarrhal cha-racter, or what is commonly called a cold in the head, attended with a defluxion, in which the eyes as well as the frontal ſinuſes are affected, and ſometimes alſo the fauces and trachea. This affection is very often occaſioned by frequent variations of the atmoſphere; by imprudent tranſitions from heat to cold; by the predomi-nance of north winds; by journies performed in the ſummer through moiſt, unhealthy, or ſandy countries; by long expoſure of the eyes to the vivid rays of the ſun; and ſimilar other cauſes. It is not ſurpriſing therefore that this diſeaſe ſhould be frequently obſerved to be epi-demical, and to attack perſons of every age and ſex. In ſome particular caſes this affection ariſes principally from the ſtomach and primæ viæ, being ſtimulated by unwholeſome matters, as is frequently the caſe with thoſe who are debili-tated, or badly nouriſhed, or who are greatly ad-dicted to intoxication, or the uſe of coarſe and indigeſtible food. The preſence of ſuch cauſes is indicated by the patient's habit of body and manner of living, the nauſea which he com-plains of, the tendency to vomit, or repugnance to every kind of animal food, pain in the head reſembling hemicrania, the furred ſtate of the tongue, fetid breath, and continual flatulency.

To

To thefe caufes may be added, the fuppreffion of fome periodical fanguineous evacuation, as the menftrual flux in women, the hemorrhoidal in men, or that which takes place from the noftrils.

The mild acute ophthalmia may be fpeedily cured by a proper regimen, and by purging the patient gently with a grain of the antimonium tartarizatum diffolved in a pint and a half of the decoction of the root of the triticum repens (dog-grafs) taken in divided dofes, and occafionally repeated for fome days, provided it does not occafion exceffive purging. The external treatment, fuppofing it to be carefully afcertained that the difeafe does not arife from the introduction of any extraneous fubftance between the palpebræ and eye, confifts in wafhing the part frequently with the aqua malvæ made tepid, and in the repeated application of bags of emollient herbs boiled in new milk.* If, however, from the fymptoms before enumerated the difeafe fhould appear to arife, either wholly or in part, from fordes in the ftomach or primæ viæ, nothing will contribute more to remove the difeafe than the timely adminiftration of an emetic. Whenever likewife the ophthalmia fhall have been produced, either entirely or partly, by the fuppreffion of the menftrual or hemorrhoidal

---

* Thefe bags fhould be made of the fineft gauze inftead of linen.

flux,

flux, or of the periodical difcharge of blood
from the nofe, great advantage will be derived
from the application of leeches to the labia pudendi, or to the hemorrhoidal veffels, or in the
laft cafe to the pinnæ nafi, never omitting the
ufe of mild and emollient applications to the
eyes; and that the more affiduoufly in proportion to the obftinacy of the inflammatory fymptoms, particularly the pain and heat.

By means of this treatment the inflammatory
ftage of the mild acute ophthalmia generally
ceafes in the courfe of four or five days; which
is rendered evident by obferving, that, independently of what ufually takes place towards
the termination of inflammation in parts which
partake of the nature and actions of mucous
membranes, the patient no longer complains
of the troublefome fenfe of heat, heavinefs, ftiffnefs, and pricking in the eyes, which he felt at
firft; and that, on the contrary, he can open
his eyes without pain or difficulty, and bear a
moderate degree of light, without its increafing
the difcharge of tears or gumming of the eye-
lids.

Although, under thefe circumftances, the
white of the eye ftill continues red, and appears inflamed, it is not fo in reality. The
ophthalmia is now to be confidered as having
paffed from the inflammatory ftage into that
arifing from laxity or debility of the veffels of
the

the conjunctiva and internal membrane of the palpebræ, and the furgeon in fuch cafes would commit an egregious error if he were to continue the ufe of the emollient applications. On the contrary, he will fpeedily free himfelf from all embarraffment, if in place of thefe local emollient remedies thofe of an aftringent and corroborant nature be fubftituted, as the collyrium vitriolicum, or that confifting of eight grains of the ceruffa acetata, fix ounces of plantain water, and a few drops of the camphorated fpirit of wine, dropping it into the eyes every two hours, or immerging them in it by means of an eye-glafs. By thefe means the relaxed veffels of the conjunctiva, as well as thofe of the internal furface of the palpebræ, very quickly recover their former vigour and the ophthalmia entirely difappears.

In fome of thefe cafes of the benign acute ophthalmia, efpecially in thofe which are epidemic, from intemperance of feafon, the inflammatory ftage is extremely mild, and terminates fo quickly as to be fcarcely obferved. And this is therefore perhaps the only cafe of eryfipelatous inflammation, as the ophthalmia is in general, in which cold and repellent applications are advantageous on its firft appearance, as cold water with lemon-juice or vinegar, or the white of an egg beaten with rofe-water and a little alum. Thefe remedies employed in

other

other cafes of acute ophthalmia, though mild, but in which the truly inflammatory ftage continues for fome days, are exceedingly injurious.

The violent *acute* ophthalmia is attended with the fame concourfe of fymptoms as the mild, but they are far more malignant and fevere. In this form of the difeafe there is a fenfe of burning heat in the eyes, fpafmodic conftriction of the whole eye-ball and fupercilium, and an intolerance even of the weakeft light. The weeping is fometimes continual, copious, acrid, and mixed with mucus which tends to produce a cohefion of the eye-lids; at other times this is altogether wanting, and there is a complete aridity of the eye; the fever is fmart; the pain in the whole head, and efpecially the neck, is infupportable; accompanied with inceffant watchfulnefs. The pupil is alfo more contracted than natural, the conjunctiva appears in every part of it of a deep red colour, and the very delicate net-work of fmaller veffels, which, in the mild acute ophthalmia, is obfervable upon the anterior hemifphere of the eye, among the more elevated *fafciculi* of blood veffels, paffing from one fafciculus to another, cannot be diftinguifhed, but all are equally turgid, and as it were twifted together, compofing one excrefcence, which is elevated upon the eye-ball, and has a tendency to project between the palpebræ.

If,

If, unfortunately, the difeafe make further progrefs, and one or more veffels, by the blood being violently thrown into them, are lacerated on the fide next the eye-ball, a quantity of blood is effufed into the cellular membrane, which connects the conjunctiva to the anterior hemifphere of the eye ; in confequence of which the conjunctiva becomes gradually elevated upon the eye-ball, and projects towards the eye-lids, fo as to conceal within it the cornea, which appears as if it were depreffed. This higheft degree of the acute ophthalmia is that which is called by furgeons *chemofis.*

In general, the violent *acute* ophthalmia is principally confined to the external part of the eye-ball. Occafionally the internal part of the eye is affected alone, or at leaft in a greater degree than the external parts of it. When the difeafe affects the internal part of the eye, it is indicated by the violence of the pain felt at the bottom of the orbit, not correfponding at the moment to the changes which take place in the conjunctiva and eye-lids. I fay at the moment, becaufe the internal ophthalmia is in general very foon fucceeded by an inflammation of the external parts of the eye alfo. From confidering, therefore, the fmall alteration which appears externally, the great averfion which the patient has, even to the weakeft light, the red appearance of the iris, the great contraction of the

the pupil, and occafioually the red and turbid
ftate of the aqueous humour, it is not unrea-
fonable to fufpect, that in the higheft degree of
this difeafe, as in that which affects the external
parts, there is an extravafation of blood into
the chambers of the eye, more particularly between the choroid and fclerotic coats, to which
caufe the generally unhappy iffue of the internal
ophthalmia ought to be attributed, rather than
to any other, which, unlefs it produce a fuppuration of the eye, generally terminates in
amaurofis.

The violent acute ophthalmia demands the
moft rigorous profecution of the antiphlogiftic
plan of treatment in its full extent.   Experience
has fhown that a delay in the employment of
evacuations, and efpecially the neglect of taking
away a fufficient quantity of blood, are the
the principal caufes of the difeafe attaining
the ftate of chemofis, and threatening either
the formation of matter, or the effufion of coagulable lymph within the eye, or at leaft degenerating into the obftinate *chronic* ophthalmia,
from the exceffive diftenfion of the veffels of
the conjunctiva during the inflammatory ftage.*
In all cafes, therefore, of the violent acute ophthalmia, blood fhould be taken away quickly

* See upon this fubject the precepts and practical obfervations of Galen. De curat. rar. par fanguinis miffiones.
Cap. 17.

and

and abundantly from the veins of the arm or
foot, in proportion to the age and temperament
of the patient, and afterwards, according to circumſtances, from the neighbourhood of the eyes,
by means of leeches applied in the proximity of
the eye-lids, eſpecially near the internal angle
of the eye upon the angular vein at its junction
with the *vena frontalis, orbitalis profunda,* and
tranſverſalis faciei; always premiſing, however,
the previous abundant evacuations of blood from
the arm or foot.*   And if the diſeaſe ſhall have
appeared in conſequence of the ſuppreſſion of
ſome periodical ſanguineous diſcharge, as that of
the noſe, uterus, or hemorrhoidal veſſels, inſtead
of applying the leeches round the eye-lids, it
will be more advantageous to apply them in
the firſt caſe upon the *pinnæ naſi,* and in the
others to the internal part of the *labia pudendi,*
or to the hemorrhoidal veins. In the caſe of a
young woman, 19 years of age, who not long
ſince was attacked with a violent inflammation
in both her eyes, a little after the ſudden ſuppreſſion of the menſes, the application of leeches
to the internal part of the *labia pudendi,* after a
copious evacution of blood from the arm, pro-

---

* It appears not a little extraordinary, that no mention is
made of the diviſion of the anterior branch of the temporal
artery, or rather that this mode of taking away blood ſhould
not have ſuperſeded the employment of general bleeding
from the veins of the arm or foot.

duced

duced fo good an effect, that in lefs than 24 hours the inflammation abated, and the patient was greatly relieved. I have frequently had occafion to remark the fame thing in cafes of the violent acute ophthalmia, in confequence of the fuppreffion of the periodical hemorrhoidal flux, as well as that of the nofe.

The general and local abftraction of blood, although copious, is not always fufficient to produce a fpeedy diminution of that higheft degree of the difeafe, which is termed chemofis. In fuch urgent cafes recourfe muft be had to fome other expedient, in order to produce a fpeedy difcharge of the blood which is extrava-fated in the cellular membrane, connecting the conjunctiva to the anterior hemifphere of the eye, by which this membrane is enormoufly elevated and diftended. This confifts in the circular excifion of the projecting portion of the conjunctiva with the curved fciffars, at the part where the cornea and fclerotica unite; by means of which not only the whole of the blood which is extravafated under the con-junctiva is difcharged, and with immediate re-lief to the patient, but alfo that, which, not-withftanding the abundant general evacuations of blood, might ftill greatly diftend the veffels of this membrane. This operation is infinitely preferable to fcarification, which is practifed in fuch cafes by the greater part of furgeons; fince

the

the latter is not fufficient to difcharge the blood
which is extravafated under the conjunctiva,
and rather increafes than diminifhes the irritation, and the determination of blood to the
eye.

After the abundant general and local bleed-
ings, the patient's bowels fhould be purged by
mild antiphlogiftic aperients, as the pulp of the
tamarind, cryftals of tartar, tartarized kali, or
vitriolated magnefia; and in cafes of fordes of
the ftomach an emetic fhould be given without
hefitation; that is, for an adult, two fcruples of
ipecacuanha with a grain of the antimonium
tartarizatum; the patient fhould afterwards be
directed to take for feveral fucceffive days, in
divided dofes, a grain of tartarized antimony,
with two drams of cryftals of tartar, diffolved
in a pint of the decoction of the radix tritici
repent. (dog grafs) or milk whey.

Among the beft external remedies, efpecially
in plethoric fubjects, and after a fufficient quantity of blood has been taken away and the
bowels opened,* is defervedly ranked the application of a blifter to the neck. Not, however,
becaufe the blifter produces a difcharge of ferum
from the part to which it is applied, but because

* Hoffman Medicinæ ration. fyftem, T. 4. part 1. fect. 2.
Setacea et veficatoria non facile applicanda in plethoricis, nifi
foluta prius plethora; et alvo præfertim in cacochymicis, fub-
ducta.

it

it excites a confenfual irritation, which fufpends, as it were, the morbid procefs, by transferring it to the part which is artificially ftimulated; and it is known, from obfervation, that the neck and back part of the ear are the parts which more readily fympathize with the eyes than any other part of the head; in the fame manner as the lobe of the ear with the teeth, the peritonæum with the urinary bladder, and the fkin of the abdomen with the vifcera contained in it, &c.

With refpect to the local remedies to be applied upon the inflamed eyes, the ufe of mild and emollient applications fhould never be departed from, as bags of mallows boiled in new milk, or a poultice of bread and milk with faffron, the pulp of roafted apples, and others of that clafs, which ought to be renewed every two hours or oftener. In order to moderate the exceffive heat which is felt in the eyes, nothing is more advantageous than introducing with the point of a probe between the eye-lids and ball, the white of a frefh egg, or the mucilage of the pfyllium prepared in the diftilled water of mallows. The patient fhould be recommended to lie in bed with his head as much raifed as poffible, and not to do any thing which may impede or interrupt his perfpiration. If the edges of the eye-lids fhould have much tendency to cohere, efpecially during the night,

4   they

they fhould be fmeared at bed-time with a liniment confifting of oil and wax; as nothing contributes more to aggravate the painful effects of
the difeafe, than the confinement and redun-
dancy of the fcalding tears between the ball of
the eye and the palpebræ.

By the timely employment of thefe efficacious means, the inflammatory ftage of the violent acute ophthalmia is in general fubdued by
the 5th, 7th, or 11th day. This is marked by
the entire ceffation of the fever, by the patient
no longer complaining of the burning heat or
lancinating pains in the eyes; by the fubfidence
and flaccidity of the eye-lids, and by the patient
in general becoming eafy, and having a return
of his appetite. The eyes, which before were
either entirely dry or poured out a thin and
acrid ferum, now difcharge a quantity of mucous matter, which affords relief, the patient
opens and fhuts the eye-lids without much difficulty or averfion to a moderate degree of light,
and, laftly, the humours are not rendered turbid
by extraneous matters.

On the appearance of thefe fymptoms, notwithftanding the rednefs and tumefaction of
the conjunctiva ftill continue, it will be proper
to defift from debilitating the patient any further, and inftead of emollient and relaxing applications, (except in cafes where the excifion of
the conjunctiva has been requifite, of which I
fhall

fhall fpeak afterwards) it will be proper to fub-
ftitute thofe of an aftringent and corroborant
nature, as a collyrium confifting of the acetated
cerus and diftilled plantain water, or compofed of 6 grains of vitriolated zinc, 6 ounces of
diftilled water, one ounce of the mucilage of
quince-feed, and a few drops of camphorated
fpirit of wine, which fhould be infinuated between the eye-lids every two hours, and the
eyes immerfed in it by means of an eye-glafs.
It fhould be obferved that perfons are occafionally met with who cannot bear cold applications
to the eyes, efpecially in winter. In fuch cafes
the collyria fhould be ufed at firft tepid, and
the temperature gradually diminifhed, until the
patient's exceffive fenfibility is allayed, and they
can be employed entirely cold.

A very efficacious remedy in this ftate of the
difeafe, or when after blood has been taken away
copioufly, and the bowels evacuated, the violent
acute ophthalmia has paffed into the fecond
ftage, or that arifing from local debility, is the
Tinctura Thebaïca of the London Pharmaco-
poeia,* two or three drops of which may be in-

* Rec. Opii colati unciam unam.
       Cinnamom.
       Caryophyl. arom. an. drachmam femis.
       Vin. alb. merac. libram femis.
Macera per hebdomadam fine calore; deinde per chartam
cola. Adde, postquam colata funt, fpiritus vini tenuioris vi-
ceffimam circiter partem, ut tutiora fint a fermentatione. Re-
ponere oportet vitreis ampullis accurate obturatis.

                                  ftilled

ftilled between the eye-lids twice a day, or only at night for feveral fucceffive days, and till the patient is completely cured. At the moment this remedy is diffufed over the eye, it generally produces confiderable heat and uneafinefs; but this quickly fubfides, and on the following morning the eye is found in a clearer and much better ftate. It is neceffary, however, to obferve again, that this application, which is fo ufeful in the fecond ftage of the difeafe, is exceedingly injurious in the firft, or inflammatory ftage, and that confequently it ought never to be employed until after copious general and local bleeding, and evacuation of the bowels, and in fhort until the inflammation has entirely ceafed.* I can aver, from my own experience, that what Mr. Ware has afferted of the utility of this remedy, when employed with caution, and at a proper period, is not at all exaggerated.

When the furgeon has been under the neceffity of making a circular excifion of the conjunctiva, in order to prevent the progrefs of the chemofis, he fhould recollect that after the in-

---

* Chirurgical obfervations on the ophthalmy by James Ware. But the fpeedy advantage of this remedy is not to be expected in all cafes indifcriminately. In fome the amendment is more flow and gradual, requiring the tincture to be made ufe of for a much longer time; and a few inftances have occurred in which no relief at all was obtained from its firft application. In cafes of the latter kind, in which the complaint is generally recent, the eyes appear fhining and gloffy, and feel exquifite pain from the rays of light. P. 52.

flammatory

flammatory ftage of the difeafe is over, the ulceration which he has produced upon the eye-
ball, at the junction of the cornea and fclerotic
coat, muft contra-indicate the ufe of irritating
and aftringent collyria, fince they would exaf-
perate the difeafe, and give occafion to a re-
newal of the inflammation. In fuch cafes he
muft be fatisfied, after the inflammation has
been diffipated, with promoting the fuppuration
of the wound, by wafhing the eye frequently in
the courfe of the day with mallow-water or new
milk. The fuppuration will prefent itfelf by a
layer of mucus fpread over the whole of the whitifh circular zone, which remains after the divifion
of the conjunctiva; which zone, towards the decline of the fecond ftage of the difeafe, will gradually contract and heal, without leaving any
veftige of the wound made in the conjunctiva.

Laftly, as foon as the patient is in a ftate to
fupport a moderate degree of light without inconvenience, every kind of covering and incum-
brance fhould be removed from the eyes, except
a piece of green, or black taffeta, which fhould
be fufpended from his forehead, in order that
under this defence he may be at liberty to open
and fhut his eye-lids at pleafure, and move the
eye-ball freely. Thofe who are about the patient fhould be alfo directed gradually to admit
a greater degree of light every day into his
chamber, that he may habituate himfelf to it

as

as quickly as poffible, and be able to face the full light. For it is a certain fact, confirmed by experience, that nothing contributes more to keep up and increafe the morbid fenfibility of the organ of vifion, and confequently to prolong the difeafe, than obliging the patient to lie unneceffarily in a room completely dark, or with his eyes clofed and covered with a bandage, a longer time than the nature of the cafe requires.

What has been already delivered, relative to the phænomena and treatment of the violent acute ophthalmia in both its ftages, will be fufficient, in my opinion, to ferve as a certain guide to the young furgeon in the management of this difeafe, although it fhould occafionally be attended with fome other fymptom which is not ufual; I cannot, however, omit to mention a particular fpecies of the violent acute ophthalmia, which is diftinct from the common in this refpect, that although the inflammation and fwelling of the eyelids and conjunctiva come on with great intenfity, like the other cafes of ophthalmia of this fpecies; yet a fhort time afterwards it is attended with an extraordinary copious difcharge of matter from the eyes of a puriform appearance. This difeafe, as it is moft commonly met with in infants, a little after their birth, or attacks adults in confequence of a fudden fuppreffion of the virulent gonorrhœa, or of a tranflation of the venereal poi-

fon

son in some other manner to the eyes, is called in the first case the puriform ophthalmia of infants, in the second the acute gonorrhœal ophthalmia.

The first, as I have said, attacks infants a little after their birth, or those of an early age, while at the breast. On the appearance of this alarming disease, the eye-lids become at once enormously swollen, and in such a degree that they cannot be separated from each other, much less turned outwards. And if this is effected with difficulty, the internal membrane of the palpebræ is found converted into a villous, fungous substance, similar in some degree to the *intestinum rectum*, when it is forced out and everted in children from excessive straining. The eye-lids, during the crying of the infant, are occasionally everted of themselves, and remain in that state until they are returned by force. When the first shock of the inflammation is over, which is of short duration, a most extradinary quantity of puriform mucus is continually discharged from the eyes, which is partly secreted by the ciliary glands, but the greater part of it by the villous and fungous substance into which the internal membrane of the eye-lids and conjunctiva is converted. The fever, at the commencement of the disease is smart, the cries of the infant, the restlessness, and tremors of the whole body are incessant; and with these

symptoms

fymptoms is frequently affociated a vomiting or purging of very offenfive yellowifh mattèr.

If a prompt and efficacious treatment be not employed to reftrain this immoderate difcharge of puriform mucus from the eye-lids and con-junctiva of infants, the cornea in a fhort time lofes its tranfparency, becomes thickened, and a *ftaphyloma* is produced. On the firft appearance of the difeafe, therefore, the antiphlogiftic plan of treatment fhould be put in practice, by taking away blood from the infant, either by means of the lancet, or by the application of leeches to the temples. Afterwards a blifter applied to the neck will be found very ufeful, efpecially if the difeafe have been preceded by the retropulfion of any eruption upon the head. It will be proper alfo to purge the infant with fyrup of fuccory, conjoined with rhubarb and a little magnefia, directing the nurfe at the fame time not to. overload the child's ftomach with milk or other food as is ufual, nor to fwathe the child tightly, and drefs it in heavy clothes, as is the cuftom with our ladies, even in the hotteft weather. And if there be any reafon to believe that it is in part occafioned by the nurfe's milk being bad, fhe ought to be changed, or the difeafe, whether depending on the ftate of her ftomach or conftitution corrected.

In the poorer clafs of people this difeafe is moft frequently met with in the fecond ftage,

N 3 or

or after the inflammatory period is over, and
the copious puriform difcharge has taken place.
If it fhould happen to be obferved on its firft
invafion, befides the general remedies already
mentioned, the eye-lids fhould be covered with
bags of very fine gauze filled with emollient
herbs boiled in milk and fprinkled with camphire; or with bread and milk with faffron,
or the pulp of roafted apples fprinkled with
camphor, in order to moderate the violence of
the inflammation. As foon as the puriform
mucus is copioufly difcharged from the eyes,
which marks the commencement of the fecond
ftage of the difeafe, recourfe muft be had to
aftringent and corroborant applications, in order
to reftore the veffels of the eye-lids and conjunctiva to their former vigour, to reprefs the fungous and villous ftate of the internal membrane
of the eye-lids, and thereby check the morbid
and immoderate puriform fecretion, from which
it is principally derived. For this purpofe the
moft ufeful and efficacious application is the
introduction of the *aqua camphorata* between the
eye-lids and ball of the eye. This water is compofed of equal parts of the cuprum vitriolatum
and armenian bole, and of a fourth part of camphire, well pulverized and mixed together. One
ounce of this powder is put into a pint of boiling water; it is then taken from the fire, and
after being allowed to ftand a little until the

heavieft

heavieft parts fubfide, is decanted. The cam-
horated water thus prepared is ufed at firft, by
putting a dram of it into two ounces of cold diftilled plantain water, and afterwards increafing
the dofe of it according to circumftances. This
collyrium is injected by means of a fmall ivory
fyringe, the point of which is carefully introduced
between the eye-lids at the external angle of the
eye. In the worft cafes it ought to be employed
every hour, and in thofe of lefs magnitude two or
three times a day. The eye-lids are afterwards
covered with a piece of linen fpread with the
white of an egg beaten and infpiffated with
alum, and the cohefion of the tarfi is prevented
by frequently anointing the edges of the eye-lids
with pommade, or oil and wax.

By this method of treatment, in the courfe of
two weeks the copious difcharge of puriform
mucus from the eyes generally ceafes, the eye-
lids fubfide, and the furgeon is now able to determine precifely the ftate of the eye, and particularly that of the cornea. If there fhould
be any opacity of the latter, the moft proper
remedy for removing it is the Tinctura Thebaïca of the London Pharmacopœia, or if this
is not at hand the ophthalmic ointment of
Janin.

The violent acute *gonorrhœal* ophthalmia is
very fimilar to the ophthalmia of infants, with
refpect to the violence of the inflammation, the

copious difcharge of puriform mucus from the eyes which fhortly fucceeds it, and the tendency which the difeafe has to deftroy the organ of vifion; but it differs from it effentially, with regard to the caufe by which it is produced.

This difeafe is occafioned in two ways. The one takes place in confequence, or at leaft after the fudden fuppreffion of the virulent gonorrhœa; although every fuppreffion of gonorrhœa is not conftantly fucceeded by the appearance of fuch ophthalmia. The other is produced by the infertion of the matter of gonorrhœa, which is inadvertently carried from the genitals to the eyes.

On the fudden fuppreffion of the gonorrhœa, which ufually takes place in confequence of violent exertions of the whole body, the abufe of fpirituous liquors, long expofure of the whole body to an exceffive degree of cold, and of acrid and aftringent injections thrown into the urethra, or other fimilar caufes, the ophthalmia appears with great tumefaction of the conjunctiva rather than of the eye-lids; not long after, a copius and continual difcharge of greenifh yellow matter iffues from the eyes, fimilar to that of the virulent gonorrhœa; the difeafe is attended with great feverifhnefs, reftleffnefs, a burning heat, and acute pain in the eyes and head, and an intolerance of light, and in fome cafes alfo an incipient hypopion appears fhortly afterwards in the

anterior chamber of the aqueous tumour. In
the fecond cafe the fame effects are produced
when the patient incautioufly inferts the virus,
by rubbing his eyes with his fingers, or a cloth
imbued with the matter of gonorrhœa; with
this difference however, that the fymptoms before enumerated are not fo violent, and the inflammation fo exceffive in this inftance as the
former.

The greater part of furgeons are of opinion
that in the firft cafe there is a true metaftafrs of
the matter of gonorrhœa from the urethra to
the eyes. But to others this theory has appeared
unfatisfactory, and in my opinion with much
reafon. For the puriform ophthalmia does not
always fucceed the fudden fuppreffion of the
gonorrhœa; on the contrary, this accident may
be confidered as rare, in proportion to the fre-
quency of cafes in which the difeafe is fuddenly
fuppreffed or repelled. In the fecond place the
confirmed lues is never feen to fucceed fuch
metaftafis of the gonorrhœa to the eyes.* In
the third place the gonorrhœal ophthalmia from
inoculation with the virus, in which cafe no
doubt can be entertained that the venereal poifon
is the caufe of the difeafe in the eyes, has never
the fame powerful and immediate tendency to
deftroy the organ of vifion, as that which is de-

* The fame thing is remarked by Bell, on gonorrhœa
virul. v. i. chap. i.

rived

rived from the gonorrhœal metaftafis. Perhaps
they approach nearer the truth, who regard this
phænomenon rather as the effect of a direct confent between the urethra and eyes, than as a real
tranflation of matter; the internal membrane
of the urethra and of the palpebræ, as well as
thofe of the fauces and rectum, being produc-
tions of the cutis; and if this effect does not
take place in every cafe of fudden fuppreffion of
gonorrhœa, it is becaufe all individuals are not
endowed with the fame degree of confenfual
fenfibility.*

However

* The reafons which have led Profeffor Scarpa to doubt
the opinion of the particular manner in which the gonorrhœa
produces this affection of the eyes, would alfo I think lead one
to fufpect the exiftence of fuch a caufe altogether; but the
following communication, for which I am indebted to Mr.
Pearfon, forms a more fatisfactory argument than any pre-
fumptive evidence that can be offered.

" The venereal ophthalmia, or what Profeffor Scarpa calls the gonorrhœal
ophthalmia, whether afcribed to metaftafis, fympathy, or the application of
the matter of gonorrhœa to the eye, is a difeafe which has been defcribed by a
confiderable number of thofe writers who have treated profeffedly on venereal
complaints; but whether the greater part of them have given the refult of
their own obfervations, or have merely tranfcribed from the works of their
predeceffors, is a queftion deferving fome confideration.

" Although I am fully difpofed to treat the talents and accuracy of Profeffor
Scarpa with the utmoft deference, yet I cannot help entertaining fome doubts
of the propriety of affigning the gonorrhœa as a caufe of ophthalmia; fince,
during a pretty extenfive experience of twenty-five years, I have never feen
one fingle inftance of an inflammation of the eyes, which was evidently derived from a gonorrhœa. I am fufficiently aware of the nature and force of
negative evidence in matters depending on teftimony, not to over-rate it; and
certainly, to deny the exiftence of any attefted fact, merely becaufe it has not
occurred in the courfe of a man's own experience, would be hafty and un-
juftifiable.

However this matter may be, on the appearance of this violent acute ophthalmia, the primary indication is to fubdue the violence of the inflammation as quickly as poffible, in order to prevent the deftruction of the eye or the opacity of the cornea. Confequently, as I have faid before, blood fhould be taken away abundantly, not only generally but locally, by means of leeches, allowing it to flow in fufficient quantity ; and in cafe of *chemofis*, the excifion of the

juftifiable. In the inftance now before us, there are two points to be confidered ; the teftimony of a refpectable Prof. ffor, and the validity of his opinion ; for it is not only afferted, that thofe who are infected with a gonorrhœa may be attacked by a violent ophthalmia, but that the gonorrhœa is fome how or other the caufe of that ophthalmia. It is with reference to the latter propofition that I exprefs my doubts, which are founded upon the fact mentioned before, that, of the many thoufand cafes of gonorrhœa which have fallen under my notice, I never could, in any one inftance, trace fuch a connexion between the eye and the urethra, as that to which Profeffor Scarpa alludes.

" The puriform ophthalmia of infants, was, within my recollection, generally regarded as an indication of a venereal taint ; and much unneceffary diftrefs was often excited in families, and very improper treatment was frequently purfued, in confequence of this erroneous opinion. The nature of that complaint, and the proper method of treating it, are now much better underftood, and I conceive, that miftakes in thefe cafes are not very common at this time.

" In that form of the fecondary fymptoms of fyphilis, where the fkin is the part chiefly affected, a difeafe refembling the ophthalmia tarfi fometimes appears. It is not commonly attended with much rednefs of the tunica conjunctiva, nor is the fenfibility of the eye to light remarkably increafed : yet I have feen it, in a few inftances, in the form of an acute ophthalmia, refifting all the common modes of treatment, but yielding immediately to a courfe of mercury.

" The venereal ophthalmia refembles, in its appearance, thofe difeafes of the tarfi and tunica conjunctiva, which are derived from fcrofula : and, I believe, there are no fpecific characters by which difeafes of the eye, or eye-lids, produced by the action of the venereal virus, can be diftinguifhed from thofe which are excited by other caufes."

conjunctiva

conjunctiva ought to be performed; * it will be
also proper to employ mild laxatives, cooling
drinks, emulsions of gum arabic, the warm bath,
or at least the pediluvium, and blisters to the
neck. The patient ought to lie in bed with his
head raised, and his eyes should be frequently
fomented with bags of emollient herbs. A
small quantity of mallow-water should be injected between the eye-lids and ball of the eye,
two or three times a day, by means of a small
ivory syringe, in order to cleanse the parts; and
the white of a fresh egg, or the mucilage of the
seeds of the psyllium, extracted with mallow-
water, afterwards introduced with the point of
a probe, in order to moderate the heat and pain
which the patient so much complains of; the
edges of the eye-lids should be also anointed,
especially at night, with the ointment of wax
and oil. The surgeon should also direct that
a large poultice of bread and milk with saffron
be applied upon the perinæum, and renewed
every two hours, and that warm oil be injected

---

* Some pretend, that, in this particular case, scarifications
of the conjunctiva are rather injurious than beneficial. This
may be true with regard to scarifications, but with respect to
the excision of the conjunctiva, I can assert that it is as advantageous in the case of *chemosis* from this species of ophthalmia as in the others. Some assert, that they ought never to
be employed until the highest degree of the inflammation is
mitigated by means of general remedies and emollient applications.

into

into the urethra feveral times a day, introducing
after each injection a fimple bougie, with the
view of reproducing the gonorrhœal difcharge.
When the inflammatory ftage of the difeafe
is fubdued, which, as I have feveral times obferved, is indicated by the ceffation of fever, the
burning heat and acute pain in the eyes, and by
the diminifhed tumefaction of the eye-lids, although the fulnefs of the veffels of the conjunctiva, and the abundant difcharge of puriform
mucus from the eyes continue as at firft, the
furgeon, neverthelefs, laying afide the ufe of
emollient applications, ought to exchange them
for a collyrium, confifting of one grain of the
hydrargyrus muriatus diffolved in ten ounces of
the aqua plantaginis, which fhould be inftilled
between the eye-lids every two hours; and if
this application be too irritating, it ought to be
diluted by adding a little mucilage of the feeds
of the pfyllium: this treatment, however, is proper only in cafes where the excifion of the conjunctiva has not been requifite, for when this
operation has been executed, the ufe of ftimulant and aftringent applications, at leaft thofe
of the ftrongeft kind, ought to be defifted
from in the fecond ftage of this, as well as of
every other fpecies of ophthalmia. The fame
treatment is equally applicable to the gonorrhœal
ophthalmia, when it is produced by the infertion of the matter; except that in the latter, no
applications

applications are neceſſary to cauſe a return of
the diſcharge from the urethra, and that the
local ſtimulant and aſtringent remedies ſucceed
better in this caſe in the ſolid than in the liquid
form, as the common mercurial ointment ſmear-
ed upon the edges of the eye-lids, or inſtead of
it, the ophthalmic ointment of *Janin.*

Hitherto I have ſpoken of the two ſtages of
the benign and violent *acute* ophthalmia, and of
the treatment which each of theſe periods requires. But although the ſecond ſtage of the
violent acute ophthalmia, or that which conſiſts
in the atony of the veſſels of the conjunctiva,
and of the palpebræ, is moſt frequently ſpeedily
cured by the uſe of aſtringent and corroborant
applications; yet caſes are occaſionally met with
in practice, in which, from an unfavourable
combination of cauſes, the ſecond ſtage of this
diſeaſe is protracted to a length of time, until
it becomes in the ſtricteſt ſenſe *chronic,* and
ſlowly threatens the deſtruction of the organ of
viſion.

This unfavourable combination proceeds from
three principal ſources; either from an increaſed
ſenſibility and irritability remaining in the eye,
after the ceſſation of the *acute* ſtage of the ophthalmia; from ſome other diſeaſe in the eye, of
which the ophthalmia is only a conſequence;
or, laſtly, from ſome particular prediſpoſition of
the patient's general conſtitution.

That

That the morbid increaſe of ſenſibility in the eye is the cauſe of the diſeaſe being kept up, is inferred from the diſcharge not only reſiſting the uſe of aſtringent and corroborant applications, which produce ſuch ſpeedy and beneficial effects in caſes of ſimple debility of the veſſels of the conjunctiva and eye-lids, but alſo from the 'diſeaſe being aggravated by the uſe of theſe remedies, or even by cold water alone, from the patient's conſtantly complaining of a weight and great difficulty in raiſing the upper eye-lid, from the conjunctiva having always a yellow appearance, and from its becoming inſtantly bloodſhot, on the patient's expoſing himſelf to a moiſt and cold air, or to a more vivid light than uſual, or on uſing his eyes a little in reading or writing by candle light. If, in addition to all this, the patient's habit is weak and irritable, if he is ſubject to frequent attacks of hemicrania, to reſtleſſneſs, convulſions, ſpaſmodic tenſion of the hypochondria, or flatulency, under theſe circumſtances it is evident that the chronic ophthalmia is not only kept up by a morbid increaſe of ſenſibility in the organ of viſion, but alſo by a general nervous affection, in which the eyes participate.

With reſpect to the diſeaſes of the eye, from which the chronic ophthalmia is derived; beſides the preſence of an extraneous body between the palpebræ and ball of the eye, which has paſſed
unobſerved

unobferved by the furgeon, are reckoned the inverfion of one or more hairs of the eye-lids, or
caruncula lachrymalis, a fmall abfcefs or ulcer
in fome part of the cornea, the protrufion of a
portion of the iris, the ulcerous herpes of the
edges, of the eye-lids, the tinea of the eye-lids,
the vitiated fecretion of the ciliary glands, the
morbid enlargement of the cornea or of the
whole eye-ball.

As to the difeafes of the general conftitution,
the cure of the fecond ftage of the violent acute
ophthalmia is moft frequently retarded or prevented, either by a fcrofulous predifpofition, or
by an obftinate variolous metaftafis to the eyes,
and occafionally by the inveterate lues venerea.
The fymptoms of thefe are fo well known, even
by ftudents in furgery, that it would be unneceffary here to repeat them.

In cafes where the difeafe is kept up by an
excefs of partial or general fenfibility, the internal adminiftration of the bark, conjoined with
valerian root, animal food of eafy digeftion, gelatinous and farinaceous broths, immerfion in
the cold bath, the moderate ufe of wine,* gentle

* Hippocrates fays: oculorum dolores meri potio, aut
balneum, aut fomentum, aut venæfectio, aut medicamentum
purgans exhibitum folvit. Aph. 31. fect. vi., aph. 46. fect.
vii. Celfus has given the true fenfe of this aphorifm in the
following words: folet enim evenire nonnunquam, five tem-
peftatum

tle exercise, and the breathing a pure and tem-
perate air are attended with peculiar advantage.
Of the external applications, thofe which are of
a fedative and corroborant nature are very ufeful, but particularly the aromatic-fpirituous vapour. This is employed by putting two ounces
of boiling water, and two drams of the volatile
aromatic fpirit,* into a veffel capable of holding
three ounces, then wrapping the veffel in a hot
cloth, and conducting the vapour to the eye by
means of a fmall funnel, or by merely bringing
the veffel clofe to the eye. This fhould be repeated three or four times a day, for at leaft
half an hour, and the eye-lids and eye-brow
gently rubbed with the volatile aromatic fpirit.

The patient fhould be cautious, both during
the treatment and afterwards, not to fatigue his
eyes, and fhould defift from looking as foon as

peftatum vitio five corporis, ut pluribus diebus neque dolor,
neque inflammatio, et minime pituitæ curfus finiatur. Quod
ubi incidit, jamque ipfa vetuftate res matura eft, ab iis eifdem
auxilium petendum eft, id eft balneo, ac vino. Hæc enim, ut
in recentibus malis aliena funt, quia concitare ea poffunt, et
accendere: fic in veteribus, quæ nullis aliis auxiliis cefferunt,
admodum efficacia effe confueverunt. Lib. VII. cap. vi.
art. 8.

  * Rec. Effentiæ limonum.
       Ol. nucis mofchatæ effentialis. an. drachmas duas.
       Ol. caryophyllorum aromat. effentialis drachmam
         dimidiam.
       Spiritus falis ammoniaci dulcis libras duas.
Diftilla igne leniffimo.

    o   he

he feels the fmalleft uneafinefs or fenfe of heat
in them. In reading or writing he fhould place
himfelf in fuch a manner as to have uniformly
the fame degree of light; as the too ftrong or
too weak a light in thefe cafes is equally injurious. When the patient has once accuftomed
himfelf to the ufe of fpectacles, he ought never
to attempt to read or write, or to look at minute objects without them.

When the chronic ophthalmia is the confequence of fome other difeafe of the eye, it is
evident that the plan of treatment ought to be
directed to remove the primary affection.

Of thefe difeafes, fome have been already
fpoken of in the preceding chapters, and the reft
will be detailed hereafter. I fhall only add here
what my obfervation and experience have taught
me with refpect to the treatment of the chronic
ophthalmia, when connected with thofe difeafes
of the general conftitution which are moft frequent. As no fpecific has been yet difcovered
for the cure of fcrofula, the treatment of the
chronic ophthalmia, when connected with that
affection of the general fyftem is exceedingly limited, and is rather confined to a knowledge of
what aggravates this difeafe of the eyes, than of
any means adapted to the radical cure of it. The
chronic fcrofulous ophthalmia is exafperated by
whatever debilitates the patient: as the abftraction of blood, the frequent ufe of faline purgatives,

termed

termed antiphlogiftic, food of difficult digeftion, as hard, falted, fmoked, or fat meats, raw vegetables, acid fruits ; alfo intenfe ftudy, a fedentary life, moift and marfhy habitations, uncleanlinefs and frequent variations of temperature. On the contrary the difeafe is mitigated, as well as its effects upon the eyes diminifhed, by the ufe of detergents continued for fome time, efpecially rhubarb, the tartarized kali conjoined with the tartarized antimony in fmall and divided dofes, and if the eyes are not in a truly inflammatory and exceffively irritable ftate, the internal ufe of tonics, particularly the cinchona in powder, decoction, or cold infufion ; or the decoction of bark conjoined with the volatile tincture of guaiacum ;* or the electuary, confifting of bark, cinnaber of antimony, and gum guaiacum.† The antimonial æthiops, in dofes of half a grain a day, afterwards of 2, 3, 4 up to 20, taken for. fifty days or more. The fecond water of quick

* Rec. Decoct. cinchon. unc. 9.
　　　Aq. melis unc. 1.
A third part of this may be taken three times a day, to each dofe of which 4 or 5 drops of the tincture of guaiacum may be added for a child 10 years of age.
† Rec. Cinchon. unc. II.
　　　Cinab. antimon. unc. I.
　　　Gumm. guaiac. unc. II.
　　　Syr. cort. aurant. q. s. f. electuar.
Of which half a teafpoonful may be taken three times a day, by a child of 10 years old.

　　　　　lime

lime with chicken broth, in dofes of three ounces each, every morning fafting, and afterwards morning and evening for fome months; conftantly obferving a proper regimen. Befides thefe, fea-bathing in the fummer, and frictions with flannel, morning and evening, are attended with great advantage.

And with refpect to the external means, the fcrofulous chronic ophthalmia is exafperated by emollient and relaxing applications, and by the patient being confined in a room perfectly dark. On the contrary, thofe which afford relief are flightly aftringent collyria, as lotions confifting of a decoction of henbane (hyofcyamus niger) and the flowers of mallow boiled in milk, with the addition of a few drops of the aqua lithargyri acetati comp.; the Thebaïc Tincture of the *London Pharmacopæia*; ointments compofed of tutty, armenian bole, or aloes, in fuch proportion as not to caufe too much irritation. It is alfo advantageous to take away from the patient's eyes, every kind of covering, except a piece of taffeta fufpended from the forehead, and at a diftance from the eyes; to accuftom him by infenfible degrees to bear a moderately ftrong light, and to allow him to breathe a pure air, and to take exercife. In this manner the want of fpecific remedies is in fome meafure compenfated by the difeafe being moderated, or at leaft rendered fupportable.

I might

I might here adduce a confiderable number of inftances of patients confined for feveral months in a dark room, and abandoned as incurable, who have quickly recovered under the ufe of thefe remedies; but particularly I think from their having been very gradually accuftomed to bear a greater degree of light. It is not unworthy of remark that the fcrofulous diathefis very frequently difappears fpontaneoufly at the age of puberty, when the body is completely developed; and when this fortunate change takes place in thofe who are affe&ted with the chronic ophthalmia, the difeafe, as I have frequently had occafion to remark, difappears alfo at the fame time with the general affe&tion of the fyftem.

Not lefs difficult of cure is the chronic ftage of the acute ophthalmia from a variolous metaftafis to the eyes; or that which takes place in confequence of the fmall-pox, and not unfrequently fome weeks after the falling off of the crufts. This difeafe paffes through a fevere inflammatory ftage; and even after the moft judicious employment of antiphlogiftic remedies, refifts the ufe of corroborant and aftringent applications, which appear beft adapted to it.

One of the moft efficacious remedies in this difeafe is a feton in the neck,* kept open for feveral months. Afterwards, when the ftomach

---

* T. Hildanus Centur. I. obferv. 41. exempl. ii. iii. Journal de Médecin. de Paris, Février 1789.

and

and primæ viæ have been cleared by the opening powders,* I have found it very ufeful to order the patient, fuppofing a child 10 years old, to take morning and evening a pill, confifting of one grain of calomel, one of the golden fulphur of antimony, and four of the powder of cicuta. If the patient is poffeffed of exquifite local and general fenfibility, befides this remedy I have found it advantageous to employ a mixture compofed of three drams of Huxam's antimonial wine, and half a dram of the Thebaïc Tincture; five or fix drops of which taken in any convenient vehicle twice a day, is a fufficient dofe for a child of the fame age; and as an external application the aromatic fpirituous vapour, in the manner before recommended. Where, however, there is no increafed local fenfibility, it may be fufficient to immerfe the eyes frequently in diftilled plantain water, with a little ceruffa acetata, or camphorated fpirit of wine added to it; to apply the white of an egg with a little fugar; the Thebaïc Tincture of the *London Pharmacopœia*; or Janin's ophthalmic ointment, obferving in every other refpect the rules already laid down, not to keep the patient's

---

* Rec. Cryft. tar pulver. unciam dimidiam.
         Antimon. tartariz. granum unum.
Mifce, et divide in fex partes æquales.
One of thefe taken twice a day will be fufficient for a child of 10 years old.

eyes covered with bandages, nor to confine him for too long a time in a dark room. The fame treatment is proper in cafes of chronic ophthalmia, in confequence of the meafles.

The venereal chronic ophthalmia is ftrictly fpeaking only a fymptom of the confirmed lues. This difeafe is peculiar, in as much as it does not make its appearance with manifeft fymptoms of inflammation, but comes on infidioufly, flowly, and without much uneafinefs. It afterwards produces a gradual relaxation of the veffels of the conjunctiva, and internal membrane of the palpebræ, perverts the fecretion of the ciliary glands; caufes an ulceration of the edges of the eye-lids by which the hairs fall off, and finally renders the cornea opake. In its higheft degree, it excites a pruritus in the eyes, which increafes particularly towards the evening, and during the night, and diminifhes on the approach of morn, in the fame manner as almoft all the other fecondary fymptoms of lues venerea; laftly, it never arrives at the ftate of *chemofis.**

As the inflammatory ftage of this fpecies of ophthalmia is trifling, being fo mild as to pafs unobferved, it is never neceffary to employ the antiphlogiftic plan of treatment. The fame means, therefore, which are adopted in the cure

* See note, p. 187.

of

of the lues venerea, may, in general, be employed in this cafe, without the fmalleft delay; that is, general mercurial frictions, and at the fame time the decoction of *mezereon* bark and farfaparilla.* A few drops of the collyrium before mentioned, confifting of a grain of the hydrargyrus muriatus diffolved in 6 or 8 ounces of mallow, or diftilled plantain water, with the addition of a little mucilage of the feeds of pfyllium, may be introduced between the eyelids every two hours, and at night Janin's ophthalmic ointment. Cullen recommended, in this particular cafe, the *unguentum citrinum* of the *Edinburgh Pharmacopœia,* lowered with a double or triple quantity of lard; but I have obferved that the fame advantages are obtained from the ointment before mentioned. If much circumfpection in the ufe of mercury be required in any cafe of complicated lues venerea, it is certainly in that of which I am now treating. For if it be adminiftered in too large dofes the violent fhock which it gives to the head, never fails to aggravate the ophthalmia, and accelerate the total lofs of fight. If therefore fuch an

---

* Rec. Cort. rad. mezereon drachmam unam et femis.
　Rad. farfaparill. unc. I.
　Coque in aq. font. lib. III. ad reman. lib. II.
　　　　　adde
　Lactis vaccini recentis unc. VI.
To be taken in fmall dofes in the courfe of 24 hours.

effect fhould take place, the ufe of mercury ought to be fufpended for fome time, the patient fhould be gently purged, his fkin fhould be wafhed, and he fhould be removed into another apartment.

Laftly, it is proper to remark, that although the difeafe with which the chronic ophthalmia is connected be removed, and no traces of the latter remain upon any part of the conjunctiva which invefts the eye-ball, neverthelefs, the edges of the eye-lids very frequently continue marked here and there with fmall ulcers; which, in order that they may heal perfectly, require to be frequently touched with the argentum ni-tratum, covering the efchar immediately after-wards with a little oil.

In fome particular cafes, and efpecially in con-fequence of the crufta lactea, thefe fmall ulcers are fituated around the root or bulb of the hairs, as in the *tinea capitis*. In order to apply the cauftic to thefe ulcers accurately, and to draw it with precifion along the edge of the eye-lid, it is previoufly neceffary to pluck out the hairs with the greateft poffible care one by one, in the fame manner as in the treatment of the *tinea capitis*. This being done, and the part fomented for fome days, in order to obviate the effects occafioned by the irritation of plucking out the hairs, and to promote the fuppuration of fome fmall puftules which appear upon the

edge

edge of the eye-lids, in confequence of this operation, the argentum nitratum fhould be drawn once or twice along the tarfus; and the efchar covered with a pencil ftroke of oil.

After the exfoliation of the efchar, it will be fufficient to anoint the edge of the eye-lids for fome nights with the unguent. hydrarg. nitrat. or the ophthalmic ointment of Janin, in order that the whole feries of fmall ulcers which occupied the roots of the hairs may be fpeedily healed. It is proper to obferve, that the hairs which are plucked out, are reproduced, but not thofe which fall off fpontaneoufly in confequence of the difeafe itfelf.*

* See on this fubject the memoir of the furgeon oculift Buzzi, inferted in No. X. of the Mem. de Medic. of Dr. Giannini. The author confiders the evulfion of the hairs as the principal object in the treatment of the *tinea* of the eye-lids, and fays, that the ulcers may be readily healed by introducing three or four grains of the *unguentum ceruffæ*, between the eye-lids, at bed-time, for five or fix times, fo as to penetrate underneath them. If, after fome months, he adds, there be any appearance of the tinea re-attacking only fome of the new cilia, the affected hairs fhould be carefully extirpated, in order to prevent the difeafe from being propagated to the others, and occafioning a complete relapfe.

CHAP.

CHAP. VIII.

OF THE NEBULA OF THE CORNEA.

ONE of the evil confequences of the obftinate *chronic* ophthalmia is the nebula of the cornea. I have chofen to call the difeafe which I am now treating of by this name, in order to diftinguifh it accurately from the *albugo* and *leucoma,* or from that denfe fpot of the cornea which is feldom attended with ophthalmia, which is fometimes almoft callous, coriaceous, and of the colour of pearl; which affects the fubftance of the cornea, and confifts in a thickening of the intimate texture of that membrane from the ftagnation of gluten, or which is formed by a cicatrix in confequence of an ulcer or wound of the cornea,* attended with lofs of fubftance. The nebula, of which I am about to treat, differs from the denfe and dark fpot forming the *albugo* or *leucoma,* in as much as it is only a re-

* Avicenna, lib. iii. tract. 2. cap. 4. Scias quod albugo in oculo alia eft fubtilis, proveniens in fuperficie apparente, et nominatur *nebula*; et alia eft groffa, et nominatur *albugo* abfolute.

3 cent,

cent, flight, and fuperficial opacity * of the cornea, preceded and accompanied by chronic ophthalmia, through which the iris and pupil are feen, and which does not therefore entirely take away from the patient the power of feeing, but only caufes the furrounding objects to be feen as if covered with a veil or cloud.

This difeafe is a confequence, as I have faid, of the chronic ophthalmia, which has been long neglected, or improperly treated, in perfons of a lax fibre, and whofe eyes are weak and eafily fatigued. The veins of the conjunctiva, which is greatly relaxed in this ftage of the ophthalmia, yielding every day more and more to the blood which is retarded in them, become gradually more turgid and elevated than natural, affume an irregular and knotty appearance, firft of all in their trunks, then in their branches at the junction of the cornea with the fclerotic coat, and ultimately in their minute ramifications, which are diftributed upon the fine lamina of the conjunctiva, covering the external furface of the cornea. Whether a fimilar dilatation takes place alfo in the minute ramifications of the arteries correfponding to thefe veins, it is not an eafy matter to determine. All that can be affirmed as certain, is, that the return of blood through the veins of the conjunctiva, which

* Plate II. fig. 5. a.

have

have become varicofe, is greatly retarded by their flaccidity, their knotty and tortuous courfe, as well as by the folds which the relaxed conjunctiva forms in the different motions of the eye-ball. The minute ramifications of thefe veins upon the cornea are fortunately the laft to become varicofe, not only on account of their fmall diameter in their origin upon the lamina of the conjunctiva which externally covers it, but becaufe the lamina of the conjunctiva, being clofely united to the cornea, confines and prevents them from being fo eafily diftended by the obftructed blood, as where they are fituated upon the white of the eye, and where the conjunctiva is naturally very diftenfile, and loofely connected to the anterior hemifphere of the eye-ball. Hence it is, that although what are ftrictly called the trunks of the veins of the conjunctiva, are, in all cafes of long continued chronic ophthalmia, dilated, varicofe, and knotty, the minute ramifications of thefe veins upon the fine lamina of the conjunctiva which covers the cornea externally, are not equally fo; and this only happens in thofe cafes where the relaxation of the whole conjunctiva, including that portion of it which paffes over the cornea, and the flaccidity of its veins approaches to the higheft degree.

How confiderable the refiftance is, which the lamina of the conjunctiva almoft infeparably united to the furface of the cornea, offers to the

preternatural

preternatural dilatation of thefe venous ramifications may be inferred from cafes of violent
inflammation, particularly of *chemofis*, in which,
in a very confiderable number of inftances, the
cornea preferves its tranfparency, notwithftanding that the trunks of the veins of the conjunctiva, which are extremely turgid and twifted
together upon the white of the eye, are raifed
in a mafs above the level of the cornea, without
the blood forcing the boundary between the
cornea and the fclerotica.

In cafes, however, where not only the trunks
and branches of the veins diftributed upon the
white of the eye, but alfo their very minute
ramifications upon the cornea have become preternaturally dilated, fome fmall reddifh lines begin to appear upon that part of its furface,
around which, fhortly afterwards, a thin, milky,
or albuminous humour is diffufed, which deftroys its tranfparency in that part. The thin,
whitifh, fuperficial fpot which is thereby produced, is precifely that to which I have given
the name of nebula of the cornea. And as this
fometimes takes place in one part only, at other
times in feveral parts of the circumference of
the cornea, confequently the difeafe is in fome
cafes folitary, in others it is produced by a number of opake points diftinct from each other;
but which, collectively, darken the cornea either
partially or entirely.

The

The fpeck of the cornea, which is fometimes formed in the inflammatory ftage of the violent acute ophthalmia, differs effentially from that kind of opacity, which conftitutes the ne-bula. In the firft cafe there is an effufion of coagulable lymph from the extremities of the arteries into the intimate cavernous texture of the cornea, which tends to thicken and fubvert its ftructure; or elfe an inflammatory puftule is formed in the cornea, which afterwards fuppu-rates and produces an ulcer; the nebula, on the contrary, is formed flowly upon the external furface of the cornea, in the long protracted chronic ftage of the-ophthalmia; is preceded by a varicofe ftate of the trunks of the veins diftri-buted upon the conjunctiva of the white of the eye, and afterwards by a dilatation of their mi-nute ramifications fituated upon the furface of the cornea; and, laftly, by an effufion of tranfpa-rent or albuminous ferum, into the texture of the fine lamina of the conjunctiva, which in-vefts the external furface of the cornea; which effufion never caufes any external elevation in the form of a puftule.

In whatever part of the cornea, therefore, the nebula is fituated, there is always a fafci-culus of varicofe veins * correfponding to it upon the white of the eye, more elevated and knotty

* Plate II. fig. 5. b.

than

than the reft of the blood veffels of the fame order. And if the cornea is cloudy, in feveral
points of its circumference, there are fo many
diftinct fafciculi of varicofe veins, projecting
upon the white of the eye, which exactly correfpond to the different opake points formed upon
it. One would fay, at firft fight, that in each of
thefe fafciculi of veins, which are fo prominent
and diftinct from the others, the blood had
forced itfelf a paffage from the border of the
fclerotic coat upon the cornea. I have a preparation of an eye taken from the body of a
man affected with chronic varicofe ophthalmia
and nebula of the cornea, who died from an inflammation of the cheft. After having injected
the head by the arteries and veins, I found that
the wax with which the veins of the conjunctiva were completely filled, had not only paffed
freely into the moft elevated fafciculus of thefe
veins, but into its minute ramifications diftributed upon the furface of the cornea, at the
part precifely correfponding to the *nebula*; while
in all the reft of the circumference of the cornea the injection had ftopped, from its having
met with an infuperable obftruction. In this
eye it is aftonifhing to fee, by the help of a
glafs, the exceedingly fine net-work which the
numerous fmall branches of veins form at the
termination of the fclerotic coat, where they
elegantly anaftomofe in endlefs variety, without
any

any of them, except thofe correfponding to the *nebula,* furpaffing the boundary formed by the ftrong adhefion of the lamina of the conjunctiva at the part where it advances to cover the external furface of the cornea.

The *nebula* of the cornea demands from its commencement the moft effectual method of treatment; for although at firft it occupies only a fmall part of the circumference of the cornea, yet when left to itfelf it proceeds towards the centre of it, and the minute branches of the dilated veins, which ramify upon it, augmenting in number and extent, ultimately caufe the delicate lamina of the conjunctiva to degenerate into a denfe and opake membrane, which greatly obftructs the vifion, or tends to deftroy it altogether.

The indication of treatment in this difeafe confifts in caufing the varicofe veffels of the conjunctiva to contract, fo as to recover their natural dimenfions; and if this fhould not fucceed in deftroying the communication between the trunks of thefe veffels, and their minute branches which are diftributed upon that part of the furface of the cornea where the nebula is fituated, the former of thefe indications may be fulfilled by means of the aftringent and corroborant applications mentioned in the preceding chapter, particularly the ophthalmic ointment of Janin, provided the difeafe be incipient,

P and

and of fmall extent. But when it has advanced near the centre of the cornea and the relaxation of the conjunctiva and its veffels is very confiderable, the moft fpeedy and effectual method of treatment which has been hitherto propofed, is that of extirpating the fafciculus of varicofe veins * near their origin, that is, clofe to the nebula of the cornea. By means of this excifion the blood retarded in the dilated ramifications of the veins upon the furface of the cornea, is immediately difcharged; the varicofe veffels are enabled to recover their natural tone and dimenfions; and a fort of drain is opened at the part where the cornea and fclerotic coat unite, by which the ferous or albuminous fluid which is effufed into the texture of the lamina of the conjunctiva fpread upon the cornea, or into the cellular tiffue which connects thefe two membranes together is gradually difcharged. The rapidity with which the *nebula* of the cornea is diffipated by means of this operation is truly furprifing, as the dimnefs in that part of the cornea where it is fituated generally difappears in the courfe of 24 hours.

The extent of the excifion in thefe cafes muft be determined by the expanfion of the nebula upon the cornea, and by the number of fafciculi of varicofe and knotty veins, more elevated and

* Plate II. fig. 5. b.

diftinct

diſtinct than the others which proceed from the
ſhade or cloud of the cornea, ſo that if the nebula
is of moderate extent, and there is only one faſciculus of varicoſe veſſels * correſponding to it,
the extirpation of that alone will be ſufficient.
If, however, there are ſeveral opake points upon
the cornea, and conſequently ſeveral faſciculi of
varicoſe veins, forming a circle at different diftances from each other upon the circumference
of the white of the eye, the ſurgeon ought to
remove the whole circle of the conjunctiva at
the part where the cornea and ſclerotic coat
unite, ſince in this manner he will be certain of
including the whole of the varicoſe veſſels. On
this occaſion it ought to be obſerved, that the
mere diviſion of the vaſcular faſciculus does not
fulfil the indication of permanently deſtroying
the direct communication between the trunks
of the veſſels and their minute ramifications
upon the cornea. For when an inciſion is made,
for inſtance, with the back of a lancet, it is true
that both portions of the divided veſſel ſeparate
in a contrary direction, and leave an evident
ſpace between them; but it is equally certain
that a few days afterwards the mouths of theſe
veſſels approach and inoſculate, ſo as to recover
their former continuity. In order, therefore, to
derive the greateſt poſſible advantage from this

* Plate II. fig. 5. b.

P 2 operation

operation it is requifite to remove a fmall portion of the fafciculus of varicofe veins, together
with an equal portion of the conjunctiva upon
which it is fituated.

In order to perform this operation in the moft
expeditious manner, and with as little inconvenience to the patient as poffible, fetting afide
the ufual method of paffing a needle and thread
through the fafciculus of varicofe veffels, an
operation which is tedious, embarraffing, arfd
unneceffary, an able affiftant fhould hold the
patient's head againft his breaft, and at the
fame time feparate the eye-lids; the furgeon
then taking hold of the fafciculus of veffels with
a fine pair of forceps,* clofe to the margin of
the cornea, and raifing it a little, which, from
the flaccid ftate of the conjunctiva, it readily
admits of, fhould remove it by means of the
fmall curved fciffars, together with a fmall portion of the conjunctiva, making the fection of a
femilunar figure, and as much as poffible concentric and clofe to the circle of the cornea. If,
however, the cafe require that more than one
fafciculus of veffels fhould be removed, and that
thefe are placed at fome diftance from each
other, the furgeon fhould raife them expeditioufly, one after another, and extirpate them
in fucceffion; or if they are fituated near to

* Plate III. fig. 8.

each

each other, and occupy the whole circumference of the eye, the excifion fhould be carried completely round, following the edge of the cornea, and thus including, together with the conjunctiva, the whole of the varicofe veffels.

The divided veffels fhould be allowed to bleed freely, and their difcharge even promoted by applying a fpunge dipped in warm water upon the eye-lids, with which they fhould be fomented until the blood ceafe to flow of itfelf; the eye fhould then be covered with a cloth and bandage, and ought not to be opened until 24 hours after the operation, when the *nebula* will be found either to have difappeared entirely, or to be fo much diminifhed that the cornea may be faid to have recovered its former tranfparency. During the fucceeding days the patient fhould be directed to keep his eye clofed and covered with a piece of foft rag and bandage, and to wafh it three or four times a day with a little warm mallow-water. When the inflammation takes place upon the conjunctiva covering the white of the eye, which ufually happens on the fecond or third day from the operation, it is curious to obferve, particularly in cafes where the conjunctiva has been divided circularly, that while the greater circumference of the eye-ball becomes red, a fmall whitifh circle in the divided part forms a boundary, which prevents the rednefs of the conjunctiva

from

from extending to the cornea. By the ufe of internal antiphlogiftic remedies and emollient applications this inflammatory ftate of the con-junctiva fubfides in a few days, and that part of the conjunctiva which has been divided appears covered with a layer of mucus. From this pe-riod the wound contracts more and more, until it is completely healed. A lotion of mallow-water, ufed at firft warm, and afterwards cold, is the only local remedy which it is neceffary to employ in thefe cafes; fince every fpecies of collyrium or ftimulating ointment retards the cure.

When the wound is healed, it will not only be found that the cornea has recovered its tranf-parency, but alfo, efpecially when the excifion has been carried completely round the eye, that the preternatural flaccidity of the conjunctiva is confiderably diminifhed or entirely removed; for after a portion of this membrane has been removed in a direction concentric to the margin of the cornea, the cicatrix by its clofing draws the conjunctiva forwards, and as it were ftretches it upon the eye-ball. If, however, the con-junctiva covering the white of the eye fhould remain afterwards a little more flabby than na-tural, yellow, and marked here and there with veins which threaten to become varicofe, aftringent and corroborant applications may be employed with advantage, and the oph-

4   thalmic

thalmic ointment of Janin in the manner recommended in the preceding chapter on the
fubjeét of *chronic* ophthalmia.

Case XXVI.

Chlara Bellinzoni, of Belgiojofo, a robuft woman, 33 years of age, fubjeét from her infancy
to cutaneous eruptions, efpecially in the fpring,
was attacked fome years ago with a rednefs of
the right eye, which extended from the internal
angle towards the cornea, and which refifted
every kind of application. In the courfe of
three years, this rednefs, which evidently depended upon a fafciculus of varicofe veins of
the conjunétiva, extended fo far upon the furface of the cornea as ultimately to render it opake
for a certain extent, and to occupy even more
than two thirds of the pupil. Independently of
the patient's indiftinét vifion, the continual fenfe
of burning in the eye, occafioned by the difeafe;
and particularly the fear of lofing the fight of
that eye entirely, induced her to come into the
hofpital.

On the 3d of April 1797, while an affiftant
feparated the eye-lids, I took hold of the fafciculus of veins which extended in the direétion
of the internal angle of the eye towards the
cornea upon the fine lamina of the conjunétiva
which covers it; and colleéting the whole of

the

the fafciculus into one fold, I raifed it a little, and removed it with the curved fciffars in the form of the letter C at the parts where the cornea and fclerotic coat unite. I allowed the blood to flow, and even encouraged it, by applying a foft fpunge upon the eye-lids, fqueezed out of warm water; and afterwards covered the whole with a comprefs and bandage.

On the following day, the eye-lids were attacked with an eryfipelas, which extended over the right fide of the face, accompanied with feverifhnefs, and a greater degree of heat in the whole body than natural; an affection to which the patient had been frequently fubject for feveral years, but which fhe had never mentioned before.

I ordered her to obferve a rigorous diet, and to take a pint of the decoction of the triticum repens, with a grain of the antimonium tartarizatum, in divided dofes, for feveral days; and upon the eye-lids I applied bags of emollient herbs. The great tumefaction and tenfion of the eye-lids prevented me from examining the ftate of the cornea.

The 8th day from the operation the eryfipelas terminated by a defquammation of the cuticle. The patient was now able to open her right eye freely, and I found, with much fatisfaction, that the cornea was entirely clear, and that fhe could diftinguifh objects diftinctly. The divided part

                                        fuppurated

fuppurated kindly, no other application being employed, until the conjunctiva was perfectly healed, than a lotion of the aqua malvæ. When the wound was healed, I ordered the patient to ufe the vitriolic collyrium with a little fpirit of wine feveral times a day, by means of which the conjunctiva recovered its former tone, and the cornea its perfect tranfparency. The woman was difcharged from the hofpital, perfectly cured, in the beginning of May, which was little more than a month from the time of the operation,

CASE XXVII.

Giovanni Bonfafani, of S. Lanfranco, 50 years of age, 15 years before the appearance of the difeafe of which I am about to fpeak, was afflicted with a violent *acute* ophthalmia in both eyes; on the difappearance of which there remained on the lower part of the cornea of the right eye, a fmall but denfe and irremediable *albugo.* The left eye remained in a good ftate, but the conjunctiva of the right was always marked in feveral parts with fmall varicofe veffels. One clufter of thefe veffels, more turgid and elevated than the reft, was fituated towards the external angle, and in the courfe of fome years extended upon the cornea, and produced in that part a *nebula* through which the patient
                                                             could

could with difficulty diftinguifh objects; the
other fmall veffels of the conjunctiva alfo threatened to become varicofe, which occafioned a
troublefome fenfe of fmarting, and a perpetual
weeping of the eye.

The operation before defcribed was undertaken the 8th of May, and the blood was encouraged to flow by fomenting the parts with
warm water.

The day following I found the nebula almoft
entirely diffipated, the patient complained of a
load at his ftomach, and a bitter tafte in his
mouth; I therefore ordered him to take, in fmall
dofes, a pint and a half of the triticum repens,
with a dram of the kali tartarizatum, and a
grain of the antimonium tartarizatum, which
procured fome evacuations from the bowels, and
relieved him.

The wound was healed in the courfe of 15
days, by merely wafhing the parts frequently
with the aqua malvæ. I then ordered the patient to inject the vitriolic collyrium with a little
fpirit of wine feveral times a day, which he
continued to do for two weeks with great advantage; as the cornea entirely recovered its
former tranfparency, except at the part occupied by the *albugo*; the patient, however, faw
fufficiently well with this eye, and left the hofpital 36 days after the operation, during which
time

time it is proper to remark, he had only been confined to his bed for the firſt four days.

CASE XXVIII.

Nunciata Raffa, of Genzone, 17 years of age, of a weakly conſtitution, irregular in her menſtruation, and who had been formerly very ſubject to diſcharges from the eyes, was admitted into the hoſpital the 2d of January 1799, on account of a *nebula* upon the cornea of the left eye, which for two months had occaſioned ſome degree of ſmarting, weeping of the eye, and dimneſs of ſight.

The *nebula* occupied about two thirds of the whole cornea, and was evidently connected with a large and very elevated cluſter of varicoſe veſſels, extending from the external angle of the eye to the part upon which it was ſituated. One part of this ſuperficial ſpeck was more denſe, white, and opake than all the reſt. The faſciculus of varicoſe veſſels was elevated with the forceps, and removed by means of the curved ſciſſars, at the part where the cornea unites with the ſclerotic coat, and the part was fomented with warm water to encourage the bleeding.

Twenty-four hours had ſcarcely elapſed, when on removing the firſt dreſſings the nebula was found almoſt entirely diſſipated. The eye was afterwards covered and waſhed frequently in the

the courfe of the day, with tepid mallow-water.

On the 3d day the wound began to fuppurate, without any bad fymptom taking place, and in the fpace of 14 days was healed. The vitriolic collyrium was employed for fome weeks afterwards, which contributed to perfect the cure by completely reftoring the tranfparency of the cornea, except in that part of the *nebula* which had been always more denfe and opake than the reft.

CASE XXIX.

Giacopo Deamici, of Pavia, 52 years of age, by trade a weaver, a thin and deformed man, was affected for feveral years with a chronic inflammation of the right eye, which terminated by almoft entirely taking away the power of feeing on that fide. When he came into the hofpital, which was on the 2d of December 1794, his eye appeared to be in too hopelefs a ftate to permit him to expect any particular benefit. The cornea of the right eye was completely cloudy, and marked in feveral places with deeply opake white points, the veffels of the conjunctiva were relaxed and varicofe in the whole circumference of the eye, from whence they extended upon the cornea in the form of reddifh lines.

The

The operation, however, was undertaken, and a portion of the flaccid conjunctiva was removed from the whole circumference of the eye, at the part where the cornea and sclerotica join. The blood flowed abundantly from the wound. The next day the cornea was found much less cloudy than before.

From the 4th of December to the 29th the patient used no other external application than a lotion of mallow-water; the eye was defended from the contact of the air and light, by means of a piece of linen cloth, and he remained out of bed, as is usual with those who are in a state of convalescence.

At this period the wound was completely healed, and the cornea had almost entirely recovered its transparency, except that there remained upon it two dense white spots, neither of which was larger than the point of a needle. The patient used the collyrium vitriolicum for some time with advantage, and was then dismissed from the hospital.

Case XXX.

Domenico Robola, aged 40, a shoemaker of Pavia, excessively addicted to wine, was admitted into the hospital on the 22d of May 1795, on account of a chronic ophthalmia in both his

eyes,

eyes, which had rendered him completely incapable of following his bufinefs.

The difeafe began fix years before, by an itch-
ing and rednefs in the eyes, with tumefication
and puftules upon the edges of the eye-lids; and
from that indolence which is very common
among this clafs of perfons, efpecially thofe ad-
dicted to drinking, he neglected his difeafe until
his fight was almoft entirely deftroyed. The
conjunctiva on both fides was very much relaxed, and the blood-veffels in every part of the
circumference of the eye were varicofe and
turgid, and paffed every where beyond the border of the cornea, evidently extending for fome
way upon the fine lamina of the conjunctiva
which covers it. The cornea alfo was completely cloudy; the eye-lids tumefied, and the
ciliary glands more enlarged than ufual.

The circular excifion of the conjunctiva was
performed upon both eyes, an operation, which
in thefe cafes, is eafily executed, in as much as
the relaxed ftate of the conjunctiva readily admits of its being laid hold of with the forceps,
and elevated in the form of a fold around the
whole of the border of the cornea. The blood
was encouraged to flow, at firft by fomentations
of warm-water, afterwards by the application of
bags of emollient herbs.

The following day I found the cornea of both
eyes very much brighter. Two days after, the

patient

patient complained of naufea, and a bitter tafte in his mouth, I therefore ordered him a pint of the decoction of the root of the triticum repens with two drams of the cryftals of tartar, and one grain of tartarized antimony, in fmall dofes, which was repeated the two following days with advantage.

The mucous fuppuration upon the white circle left by the excifion of the conjunctiva, did not appear until the 8th day after the operation. By employing only a lotion of mallow-water, and keeping the eyes covered by a piece of linen fufpended from the forehead, the wound healed in the courfe of 22 days more. I then began the ufe of the ophthalmic ointment of Janin morning and evening, and the camphorated vitriolic colly-rium during the day. In two weeks more the cornea of both eyes, but efpecially that of the left, was fo much amended that the man could fee diftinctly even the fmalleft objects, and was now able to return to his former occupation.

Case XXXI.

A mendicant, 50 years of age, was admitted into the hofpital on the 12th of April 1796, with the cornea of the right eye completely darkened by a *nebula*, in confequence of an obftinate chronic inflammation of the eye, which for two months had been exafperated by a cutaneous eruption

eruption upon the whole of the right fide of the face. The whole of the cornea not only appeared fuperficially cloudy, but prefented, a little above the centre of it, a point whiter and more opake than the reft. The blood-veffels of the conjunctiva appeared highly turgid, varicofe, and relaxed, and were feen rifing upon the cornea from every part of the circumference of the white of the eye. The edges of the eye-lids were alfo tumefied, and the eye watery and gummed.

A fmall portion of the conjunctiva, and its veffels, were removed around the white of the eye, near the margin of the cornea. A confiderable quantity of blood flowed, which greatly relieved the patient of the troublefome fenfe of burning which he had before complained of. Bags of emollient herbs were applied upon the eye.

The next day the cornea prefented a degree of brightnefs which exceeded all expectation.

Three days after, an abundant difcharge of mucus took place from the ciliary glands, and that part of the conjunctiva which had been divided, which rendered it neceffary to wafh the eye frequently with mallow-water. The cornea acquired a greater degree of clearnefs; and, in order to divert more effectually the difcharge from the eye-lids, I formed a feton in the neck.

In

In three weeks more, the circular wound of the conjunctiva was perfectly healed, and I was then able to employ the vitriolic collyrium, and the ophthalmic ointment of Janin; which perfected the cure by removing the morbid ſtate of the ciliary glands, and ſtrengthening the conjunctiva. The white opake ſpot, which was ſituated a little above the centre of the cornea, remained unaltered, but did not greatly obſtruct the ſight.

CHAP.

CHAP. IX.

OF THE ALBUGO AND LEUCOMA.

THE *albugo* and *leucoma*, as I have hinted in the preceding chapter, are effentially different from the *nebula* of the cornea, in as much as the former are not produced by a flow chronic inflammation, attended with a varicofe ftate of the veins, and an effufion of thin, lacteous ferum into the texture of the fine lamina of the conjunctiva, covering the cornea; but are the effect of the violent acute inflammatory ophthalmia, in confequence of which a denfe coagulable lymph is poured out from the extremities of the arteries, fometimes fuperficially, at other times more deeply into the fubftance of the cornea: or elfe the difeafe confifts in a firm, callous cicatrix of the cornea, produced by an ulcer or wound, accompanied with lofs of fubftance. The term albugo more properly belongs to the firft of thefe, that of leucoma to the latter, efpecially if the cicatrix or denfe coriaceous fpot

occupy

occupy the whole or the greater part of the cornea.

The recent albugo, produced by the violent acute inflammation of the eye, and left upon the cornea after that affection has been diffipated by the ufe of general remedies and emollient applications, is of a clear milky colour; but when inveterate it acquires the colour of white cretaceous earth, or of pearl. Of thofe which are inveterate, fome appear to have no further dependence on the vafcular fyftem of the cornea; fince they remain infulated in the middle of the tranfparent part of that membrane, without occafioning any fmarting or fenfe of uneafinefs, without having any connection with the veffels of the conjunctiva, without the reft of the eyeball appearing in any degree difeafed, and without nature attempting any diffolution of it by abforption.

The recent albugo, provided the coagulable lymph, extravafated by the action of the extremities of the inflamed arteries, has not difforganized the intimate ftructure of the cornea, is moft frequently diffipated by the fame means which are employed in the treatment of the firft and fecond ftage of the violent acute ophthalmia; that is, in the firft ftage, by general and local bleeding, by internal antiphlogiftic remedies, and emollient applications; and in the fecond ftage, by aftringent applications of a

Q 2   gently

gently irritating and corroborant nature. For if, after the inflammatory ftage has terminated, the action of the vafcular abforbent fyftem of the cornea is excited and reftored, by means of thefe local remedies, the coagulable lymph ftagnating in that membrane, and forming the albugo, is abforbed, and the cornea recovers its former tranfparency. The cornea has a confiderable affinity to parts of a ligamentous ftructure. Like ligament it is endowed with little vitality, is not furnifhed with red veffels, and only appears to be exquifitely fenfible when it is inflamed. The inflammation of the cornea, as that of ligamentous parts poffeffing little vitality, is flowly refolved, and therefore readily leaves behind it a portion of coagulable lymph, which, during the inflammatory ftage, is effufed into its fubftance, and produces opacity; this is not neceffarily removed in any other manner, after the inflammation difappears, than by abforption, which can only be promoted by means of ftimulant applications.

But although this is frequently obtained in the recent albugo, it is not fo eafily effected, when, from the long continuance of the difeafe, the action of the abforbent fyftem of the cornea, in the affected part, has become torpid; or when the intimate texture of the cornea has been diforganized by an extravafation of denfe and tenacious lymph from the extremities of

3   the

the arteries. For whether the humour forming the albugo be abforbed or not, the injury which has been done to the internal ftructure of the cornea in this part always renders it opake. The circumftances, therefore, which are moft favourable to the cure of the albugo, are, the difeafe being recent, without diforganization of the texture of the cornea, or of the lamina of the conjunctiva covering it, and its taking place in fubjects of an early age, in whom the lymphatic fyftem is moft active, and in whom its action is more capable of being excited by external ftimuli. I have feen innumerable inftances in young children, where, in confequence of the violent *acute* ophthalmia, the fpecks or albugines, which have remained infulated in the middle of the tranfparent part of the cornea, after the difappearance of the ophthalmia, have vanifhed infenfibly in the courfe of fome months, and fometimes fpontaneoufly, contrary to all expectation. Heifter,* Langguth,† and Richter,‡ have made the fame obfervation. This phænomenon certainly, can only be attributed to the vigorous action of the abforbent fyftem in children, and to the intimate texture of the cornea, in fuch cafes, not being diforganized in

* Inftitut. chirurg. tom. i. cap. 58.
† Differt. de oculorum integritate improvidæ puerorum ftati follicite cuftodienda. § xxi.
‡ Elem. di chirurg. tom. iii. cap. 4.

the

the part where the effufion of coagulable lymph
has taken place.

Of the local remedies which are calculated to
promote abforption, whether in the recent albugo, where the inflammation has ceafed, or in
that which is inveterate, thofe from which I
have found the greateft advantage, are, the
fapphirine collyrium,* the ointment confifting
of tutty, aloes, calomel, and frefh butter,†
that of Janin, the gall of the ox, fheep, pike,
and barbel, applied upon the cornea, by means
of a fmall hair pencil, two or three times a day,
provided it does not caufe too much irritation.
The ox and fheep's gall is more ftimulating than
that of fifh.‡ In fome cafes where the eyes
were fo irritable as not to bear the action of
thefe remedies, I have employed with advantage the oil of walnuts a little rancid, directing

* This is a folution of 2 fcruples of fal ammoniacus, and
4 grains of ærugo in 8 ounces of aqua calcis, allowed to ftand
for 24 hours, and then filtered.

† Rec. Tuticæ s. p. drachmam I.
    Aloes s. p.
    Calomelan. an. gr. duo.
    Butyr. recent. unc. femis.   M. f. unguent.

‡ Stimulant applications have been advantageoufly employed in the treatment of the albugo for more than 2500
years, but it was not until the prefent time that the rational
principles of this mode of treatment were underftood. Thefe
have been deduced from the correct notions which we have
at prefent concerning the action of the fanguineous and abforbent fyftems in a ftate of health and difeafe.

                                                    two

two or three drops of it to be inftilled into the eye every two hours, and continued for fome months. In others I have found the juice of the leffer centaury with honey ufeful.

In general, however unfavourable the cafe may appear, it is proper to perfift in the ufe of fuch local and general remedies as are judged moft appropriate to the nature of the cafe, and particular fenfibility of the patient's eye, with the utmoft diligence, for at leaft three or four months before it is given over as hopelefs, and the patient declared incurable.

All the expedients which have been hitherto propofed for the cure of the inveterate coriaceous albugo, or rather leucoma, and of that which is the confequence of a cicatrix, and which confift in the fcraping of the laminæ of the cornea, the perforation of it, or the formation of an artificial ulcer upon a portion of the leucoma, are methods entirely ufelefs, invented by thofe who are ignorant of the ftructure of the parts interefted in the difeafe, and extolled by empiricifm. For whether the thicknefs of the cornea be diminifhed by means of fcraping, or by cutting it with an inftrument, fuch methods cannot in any manner reftore to that membrane the tranfparency which it has loft; and although, even immediately after the operation, a fmall degree of light fhould be admitted into the eye, this advantage would be only momentary; fince

the

the ulcer produced by the operation on healing and becoming callous again, would reproduce on the cornea its former ftate of opacity. The artificial ulceration alfo excited on the leucoma would be ufelefs, if the difeafe merely depended on a ftagnation of denfe lymph; but the fact fhows the contrary, and proves that the leucoma, which is not produced by a cicatrix, is not only formed by a denfe humour, but by a diforganization of the intimate texture of the cornea, in which confifts, as I before ftated, the difference between the *albugo* and the *leucoma.*

CHAP.

CHAP. X.

OF THE ULCER OF THE CORNEA.

THE ulcer of the cornea is a very frequent confequence of the burfting of a fmall abfcefs,
which not unfrequently forms under the fine
lamina of the conjunctiva, which covers the
cornea, or in the fubftance of the cornea itfelf,
in cafes of violent acute ophthalmia. At other
times the ulcer of the cornea is produced by
the contact of corroding, cutting, or pricking
fubftances, infinuated into the eyes, as quick
lime, particles of glafs or iron, thorns, or other
fimilar matters, capable of producing a folution
of continuity.

The fmall abfcefs of the cornea is accompanied with the fame fymptoms as the violent
inflammatory ophthalmia, particularly a troublefome fenfe of tenfion in the eye, eye-brow,
and neck; a burning heat, copious difcharge
of tears, averfion to the light, and an intenfe
rednefs of the conjunctiva, efpecially oppofite
and near the feat of the abfcefs.

This

This ſmall inflammatory puſtule, in compa-
riſon with thoſe which form upon other parts
of the body, is in general very ſlow in burſting
after it has ſuppurated. Experience, however,
has proved, that it is improper to open it with
the point of a lancet or other inſtrument, in
order to procure a diſcharge of the matter contained in it, as is practiſed by the generality of
ſurgeons; for although this abſceſs ſeem to have
arrived at its higheſt degree of maturity, the
matter which it contains is ſo tenacious and
rooted, as it were, in the ſubſtance of the cornea,
that no part of it is diſcharged by the artificial
aperture, and the orifice, on the contrary, which
is made, rather aggravates the diſeaſe, increaſes
the opacity of the cornea, and frequently occaſions the formation of another ſmall abſceſs in
the vicinity of the firſt. In ſuch caſes the moſt
certain method is to wait until the abſceſs opens
externally of itſelf, promoting its rupture by
frequently fomenting and waſhing the eye with
tepid mallow-water, and by the application of
bags of emollient herbs.

The ſpontaneous rupture of the ſmall abſceſs
of the cornea, is moſt frequently announced by
a ſudden increaſe of all the ſymptoms of ophthalmia, particularly by an intolerable ſenſe of
burning in that part of the cornea where the
abſceſs previouſly exiſted, which is augmented
by the patient's moving the affected eye-ball,

                                                      or

or even the eye-lids. This circumftance, however, is rendered evident by an excavation
which may be obferved in the part of the cornea
where the whitifh puftule was fituated, and
which may be ftill more diftinctly feen by
looking at the eye in profile.

The introduction of extraneous bodies into
the eye, which have fimply divided a part of the
cornea, or are fixed in it, provided they are immediately withdrawn, do not in general leave an
ulcer, the injured part being confolidated by
the firft intention. Thofe which abrade or burn
the furface of this membrane, or which being
fixed in it, are not immediately removed, occafion
the acute ophthalmia, afterwards a fuppuration
round the injured part, and laftly ulceration.

The ulcer of the cornea has this in common
with ulcerous folutions of continuity of the fkin,
where this integument is fine, tenfe, and poffeffed of exquifite fenfibility; that on its firft
appearance it affumes a livid and cineritious colour; its circumference is red, its margin is tumid and irregular, it is exquifitely painful, difcharges an acrid ferum inftead of pus, and has a
tendency to fpread and become deeper rapidly.
Such is precifely the character of the ulcer of
the cornea, and of thofe of the nipples, glans
penis, lips, of the tip of the tongue, which are
called aphthæ, of the tarfi, of the entrance of the
auditory canal and of the noftrils, and other
parts,

parts, where the thin tenſe and very ſenſible ſkin is inflected inwards.

The ulcers of this claſs, when left to themſelves, or improperly treated, ſpread rapidly, become deep, and deſtroy the parts which they occupy; if that of the cornea extend ſuperficially it preſently deſtroys the tranſparency of this membrane, and if it ſpread deeply in the form of a ſmall tube, and penetrate into the anterior chamber of the aqueous humour, it occaſions a diſcharge of this fluid, and afterwards a fiſtula of the cornea; if the aperture become larger, beſides the diſcharge of the aqueous humour, it gives riſe to another diſeaſe much more ſerious than the ulceration itſelf, the protruſion of a portion of the iris, the diſcharge of the cryſtalline and vitreous humours, and in ſhort the total deſtruction of the organ of viſion. This moſt ſerious accident is not unfrequently the conſequence of the violent acute gonorrhœal ophthalmia, complicated with atony or defect of vitality in the cornea; in conſequence of which this membrane is no longer ſenſible to the action of the internal and external remedies, which are directed to arreſt the progreſs of the ulceration, which, notwithſtanding the moſt efficacious meaſures extends with the greateſt celerity over the cornea, until it has completely deſtroyed it.

It is therefore of the greateſt importance, as ſoon as an ulcer appears upon the cornea to

arreſt

arreft its progrefs inftantly, as far as the nature of the difeafe permits; or fo to change the morbid procefs, that inftead of tending to the deftruction of the cornea, it may be difpofed to heal; and this fhould be aimed at the more folicitoufly, as the difficulty of converting this morbid procefs into a healthy one, increafes in proportion to the extent and depth of the ulcer; and although the healing of a large ulcer fhould be fpeedily obtained, the injury which the vifion receives, in confequence of the extenfive cicatrix which refults from it, is irreparable.

With regard to the treatment of the ulcer of the cornea, the writers who have taught that no external application can be employed with advantage, for the purpofe of healing the ulcer, before the acute ophthalmia has been either entirely, or in a great meafure fubdued, appear to me to have fallen into a confiderable error. Experience fhows precifely the contrary, and teaches that the application of fuch local remedies as are capable of quickly removing or mitigating the increafed morbid fenfibility of the ulcer, and at the fame time arrefting its deftructive progrefs, fhould be employed in the firft inftance, and afterwards thofe which are proper in the ophthalmia, provided it fhould not difappear of itfelf in proportion as the ulcer heals. It is a fact, eftablifhed by certain and repeated obfervations, that the ulcer is the caufe

of

of the ophthalmia, and not the ophthalmia of the ulcer.* It is true, that on the burfting of the abfcefs of the cornea, the fymptoms of the violent acute ophthalmia are exafperated; that the rednefs of the conjunctiva is increafed, as well as the turgefcency of its veffels; but it is equally certain that this arifes only from an augmented determination of blood to it, occafioned by the increafed fenfibility of the ulcerated part of the cornea. On the contrary, as this irritable ftate of the ulcer is allayed or diminifhed, the ophthalmia in like manner fubfides in an equal degree, and on the ulcer becoming clean, and proceeding towards cicatrization, the inflammation is gradually refolved and difappears, or at moft requires only for fome days the ufe of an aftringent and corroborant collyrium.

Similar examples come under our daily obfervation in ulcers of other parts befides the cornea, particularly in the fmall fordid fores before mentioned, which take place upon the internal furface of the lips, the tip of the tongue, the nipples, and glans penis, which, on their firft appearance, as I before faid, are covered with an afh-

---

* Except the cafe in'which the ulcer appears in the higheft degree of the violent *acute* ophthalmia ; where the primary indication muft be always that of abating the violence of the inflammation as quickly as poffible, previoufly to the treatment of the ulcer.

coloured

coloured furface, excite inflammation in the furrounding parts, and occafion a fenfe of pricking,
and a very troublefome burning heat; in order
to remove the inflammation, we do nothing
more than fpeedily allay the exceffive irritability
of thefe fores, and change the ulcerative procefs
into that which conduces to their cicatrization;
after which the furrounding inflammation is
immediately diffipated, without the neceffity of
recurring to other remedies, which are pecu-
liarly directed in the treatment of that difeafe.

The remedy, which in all thefe cafes produces fo fpeedy and good an effect is the cauftic.
This immediately deftroys the naked extremities of the nerves in the ulcerated part, and
quickly removes the morbid excefs of fenfibility; converts the cineritious furface of the ulcer
and the acrid humour with which it is imbued
into a cruft or efchar, which in the fame manner as the epidermis moderates the contact of
the furrounding parts upon the ulcer, and finally
changes its deftructive procefs into that of granulation and cicatrization.

For the purpofe of cauterizing the ulcer of
the cornea, the cauftic which is preferable to
every other is the argentum nitratum. This
fhould be cut in the form of a crayon pencil,
with the point of which, the eye-lids being well
feparated, and the upper one fixed by means of
Pellier's

Pellier's elevator,* the ulcer of the cornea fhould be touched, and the cauftic held in contact with it a fufficient length of time to form an efchar. If any part of the cauftic fhould be diffolved by the tears, it ought to be wafhed off by dropping a little milk into the eye.

During the application of the cauftic, the patient complains of very acute pain, but this exceffive uneafinefs is amply compenfated by the eafe which is felt a few minutes afterwards. For the burning heat in the eye ceafes, as if by a charm, the eye-ball and eye-lids can be moved without difficulty, the difcharge of tears and turgefcency of the veffels of the conjunctiva diminifh; and the patient is able to fupport a moderate degree of light and to take reft.

Thefe advantages continue as long as the efchar adheres to the furface of the ulcer, but as foon as the exfoliation takes place, which is on the 2d, 3d, or 4th day, the former fymptoms of the difeafe return, particularly the fenfe of pricking and burning in the ulcerated part of the cornea, the copious difcharge of tears, the difficulty of moving the eye-ball and eye-lids, and the intolerance of light; but thefe fymptoms are always lefs violent than before. On the reappearance of thefe the furgeon fhould apply the cauftic again without delay,

* Plate III. fig. 1.

taking

taking care to produce an efchar equally ftrong and adherent upon the whole furface of the ulcer, which will be fucceeded by the fame relief as before. ·And this fhould be repeated a third time, if neceffary; that is, if on the exfoliation of the fecond efchar, the exceffive fenfibility of the ulcer is not fufficiently deftroyed, and its corroding and deftructive progrefs arrefted. ·If things go on favourably it will be conftantly found, that after every exfoliation of the flough, the morbid fenfibility of the eye is diminifhed and the ulcer lefs extenfive and deep than before, and that, inftead of its former livid and afh-coloured appearance, it affumes a light flefh-colour, a certain indication that its deftructive procefs is checked, and that it is difpofed to heal. In proportion alfo as the ulcer diminifhes, the turgefcency of the veffels of the conjunctiva and the ophthalmia gradually fubfide.

At this period, when the procefs of granulation has commenced, the further application of the cauftic, which has been hitherto fo beneficial, would be improper, fince inftead of accelerating the healing of the ulcer, it would, on the contrary, reprefs the granulations, reproduce the pain, inflammation, and weeping of the eye, and the ulcer would again affume a floughy and cineritious afpect, and its edges become irregular and tumefied. This fact has alfo been

R   noticed

noticed by Platner.* *Necesse est*, says he, *ut hoc temperata manu, nec crebrius fiat, ne nova inflammatio, novaque lachryma his acrioribus concitetur.* As soon as the eye becomes easy and the process of granulation has commenced, whether after the first, second, or third cauterization, the surgeon ought entirely to desist from the further use of any powerful caustic, and confine himself to the application of the vitriolic collyrium; or that which consists of four grains of the vitriolated zinc, 4 ounces of plantain water, and half an ounce of the mucilage of quincefeed, or of psilium, which should be employed every two hours, and the patient's eye defended from the contact of the air and light by means of a soft compress and bandage. In cases, however, where, besides the ulceration of the cornea, the conjunctiva and its vessels are in some degree relaxed, it is useful towards the end of the treatment to introduce Janin's ointment between the eye-ball and eye-lids, proportioning the quantity and strength of the remedy to the particular sensibility of the subject.

With respect to the treatment of those very superficial excoriations of the cornea, in which there appears to be no excavation of the substance of that membrane, and which in reality consist only in an abrasion of the cuticle, from

* Institutiones chirurg. § 314.

the

the lamina of the conjunctiva, which covers the cornea, the ufe of the cauftic is unneceffary. It is fufficient in thefe cafes to employ the vitriolic collyrium with mucilage, or that confifting of vitriolated zinc and the white of an egg beaten together, with the addition of rofe or plantain water. The fymptoms which accompany thefe flight excoriations, or rather deprivations of the epidermis, are inconfiderable ; and provided the patient take care to inject either of thefe collyria every two or three hours, and to defend his eyes from too vivid a light, and from viciffitudes of the atmofphere, they are generally removed in a fhort time.

Hitherto I have fpoken of the ulcer of the cornea, and of the beft method of treating it, in cafes which are moft frequently met with in practice. Occafionally, however, whether in confequence of the violence of the difeafe, or of improper treatment, the ulcer, already of confiderable extent, affumes the form of a fungus elevated upon the furface of the cornea, which appears to derive its nourifhment from a fmall fafciculus of blood veffels belonging to the conjunctiva, and on this account not unfrequently gives rife to a very ferious error, the difeafe being miftaken for a *pterygium.* This difeafe, when left to itfelf, or treated with flight aftringents, generally terminates in the deftruction of the whole eye-ball ; it demands, on the contrary,

the

the fpeedy ufe of fome efficacious method
capable of deſtroying, in a ſhort time, the
whole of the fungus of the cornea, as well as the
veſſels which paſs to it from the conjunctiva, and
which has alfo the power of arreſting its de-
ſtructive progreſs. This method confiſts, in the
firſt place, in removing with the curved ſciſſars
the whole of the fungus cloſe to the ſurface of
the cornea, continuing the inciſion at the fame
time upon the conjunctiva, fo as to include
along with it the faſciculus of blood-veſſels,
from which it appeared to derive its ſupport.
Afterwards, when the blood has been allowed
to flow, the argentum nitratum ſhould be freely
applied upon all that part of the cornea which
had been previouſly occupied by the fungus, fo
as to leave a deep eſchar; on the exfoliation of
which, if the whole of the morbid part ſhould
not have been deſtroyed, it will be neceſſary to
repeat the application of the cauſtic, until the
ulcer of the cornea aſſume a healthy and granulating appearance.

In order to execute properly fo deep a cauterization, it is not ſufficient, in general, that
the upper eye-lid ſhould be firmly held by an
aſſiſtant, and the lower one depreſſed; but it
is alfo requiſite that the operator ſhould keep the
upper eye-lid raiſed by means of a ſmall ſpatula
introduced between it and the eye-ball, and
held in his left hand, while with his right he
applies

applies the cauftic upon the fungous furface of the ulcer, and retains it there a fufficient length of time to form a firm and deep efchar.

It muft be admitted that in very fevere cafes of this kind, the action of the cauftic cannot be always calculated with precifion; and it confequently happens, that together with the fungus a portion of the whole thicknefs of the cornea is deftroyed. When this accident occurs it is always followed by a protrufion of the iris through the perforation made in the cornea. This accident, however ferious it may appear to fome, is not, however, fuch as to admit of no relief, as will be fhown in the chapter on the procidentia of the iris, and provided the furgeon is able to obtain a folid cicatrix, in the part occupied by the excrefcence, which muft necef-farily prevent a return of the fungus, and the total deftruction of the eye-ball, he will have completely fulfilled the propofed indication.

Case XXXII.

Antonio Carovo, of Pavia, a boy, 14 years old, was admitted into the practical fchool of furgery, who fuffered great pain in his right eye, and was in danger of lofing it, from two fmall ulcers upon the cornea, which had fupervened in confequence of a violent acute ophthalmia.

R 3 One

One of thefe fmall ulcers occupied the inferior fegment of the cornea, the other that towards the external angle of the eye; both were
floughy and of a cineritious colour. The blood-
veffels of the conjunctiva, efpecially thofe which
correfponded to the ulcerated part of the cornea,
were extremely turgid. The boy complained
of acute pain in the eye and head, and could not
bear even the moft moderate degree of light.

Having placed him in a fupine pofture, with
his head a little elevated, I directed an affiftant
to raife the upper eye-lid, by means of *Pellier's
elevator*, while with my left hand I depreffed the
lower. This is the only method, efpecially in
children, of fixing the eye-ball fufficiently for
the purpofe of applying the cauftic with precifion to the ulcerated points of the cornea. Then
with the argentum nitratum, cut in the form of
a crayon, I cauterized both the ulcers fo as to
produce upon them a fufficiently deep and adherent efchar, wafhing the eye frequently afterwards with new milk. The patient complained
at the moment of very acute pain, but half an
hour after he was perfectly eafy in every refpect.

On the following day, he was able to fupport
a moderate degree of light, and the blood-
veffels of the conjunctiva appeared very much
lefs turgid than before the application of the
cauftic.

Three

Three days after, on the exfoliation of the efchar, the former pains in the eye returned, but were lefs violent than at firft. The ulcers were again touched with the cauftic, which occafioned lefs uneafinefs than before. It was repeated four days afterwards.

On the detachment of the laft efchar, the ulcers were much diminifhed, and their furface, which was of a pale red colour, was raifed on a level with the furface of the cornea. The vitriolic collyrium, with mucilage of quince-feed, was now fubftituted for the cauftic, and inftilled into the eye every two hours.

In the courfe of ten days more the ulcers were perfectly healed, and the ophthalmia entirely diffipated. And to render the cure more perfect, I ordered the patient to continue the collyrium for a month longer, and to introduce between the eye-lids, at bed-time, a fmall quantity of the ophthalmic ointment of Janin.

Case XXXIII.

A beggar boy, 11 years old, of a weak conftitution, and occafionally fubject to periodical fever, fome years after the fmall-pox, which had left a morbid fenfibility in the left eye, was feized with a violent acute inflammation of it; in confequence of which a fmall abfcefs formed between the laminæ of the cornea,

which

which burſt ſpontaneouſly, and left a ſmall
ſloughy aſh-coloured ulcer, of an oval figure,
which extended from the margin of the cornea,
correſponding to the internal angle of the eye,
almoſt as far as the part oppoſite the centre of
the pupil. The boy complained very much,
eſpecially on being expoſed to the light, and
there was a copious weeping of the eye. The
veſſels of the conjunctiva alſo were exceedingly
turgid, eſpecially towards the internal angle of
the eye. The argentum nitratum was applied
to the ulcer, and its action limited, by repeatedly waſhing the parts with milk, and applying
upon them bags of emollient herbs. The very
acute pain produced by the cauſtic continued
about half an hour; it then ceaſed, and the patient paſſed the reſt of the day comfortably, and
ſlept ſoundly the whole of the following night.
The next day he opened his eye freely, and ſup-
ported a moderate degree of light without uneaſineſs. The ophthalmia and weeping of the
eye were greatly diminiſhed.

On the ſeparation of the eſchar, the acute
pain in the eye, the averſion to light, and the
diſcharge of tears returned. The cauſtic was
therefore repeated, and was attended with the
ſame advantage as before.

Three days afterwards, on the ſeparation of
the ſecond eſchar, I found the ulcer very much
contracted, attended with little pain, and the
bottom

bottom of it prefenting a pale red, and granulating appearance. I ordered the collyrium vitriolicum, with mucilage, to be dropped into
the eye every two hours, and the part to be
conftantly defended from the contact of the air
and light, by means of a comprefs and bandage,
and in a few days the fore healed. The blood-
veffels of the conjunctiva, which were a little
varicofe, ftill kept up fome degree of rednefs
upon the white of the eye, and the boy was attacked with a tertian fever, attended with
violent fhiverings. I gave him the cinchona,
with a few drops of the tincture of opium; the
ufe of which was continued in fmall dofes for a
confiderable time after the fever was fubdued.
Befides the vitriolic collyrium, the ointment
of Janin was employed, which contributed
materially to invigorate the veffels of the conjunctiva, and to remove entirely the chronic
rednefs of the white of the eye. The cicatrix,
though certainly very near the pupil, did not
cover it, and confequently did not prevent the
child from feeing with the left eye.

Case XXXIV.

Giufeppe Reale, of S. Leonardo, a ftrong
plethoric countryman, 22 years of age, was attacked with a violent acute ophthalmia in both
his eyes, attended with fever and violent pain.

On

On the 7th day he came to the school of surgery, after having been once bled. His right
eye was greatly inflamed, and there was an ulcer
upon the inferior margin of the cornea, but not
very deep ; the left, which was equally inflamed,
had an ulcer upon the external margin of the
cornea, not larger in extent than a millet-feed,
but excavated and deep. The patient's pulfe
was hard and vibrating, the fever continual, and
he had an inclination to vomit. I immediately
ordered 18 ounces of blood to be drawn from the
arm, and at night 10 ounces more from the foot,
and directed that bags of emollient herbs fhould
be applied upon the eyes. He had a lefs uneafy
night than the preceding, his pulfe became foft
and undulating, and his fkin moift. As he
complained of naufea I ordered him an emetic,
which procured a copious and falutary evacuation of bilious matter ; fo that on the 4th day
from the patient's entrance into the hofpital,
the inflammatory ftage of the ophthalmia might
be confidered as having terminated. Both the
ulcers were now touched with the argentum
nitratum. In order to keep the patient's bowels
open, and to encourage a ftate of perfpiration,
I ordered him, the following day, a pint of the
decoction of the triticum repens, with two
drams of the cryftals of tartar, and a grain of
tartarized antimony, to be taken in divided dofes,
and continued for feveral days. The application

tion of the cautery allayed the violence of the pain in the eyes. When the eschars came away the ulcers were again touched with the argentum nitratum, and this was repeated three times in the course of eight days; by means of which the ophthalmia diminished, the granulating surface of the ulcer of the left eye arose on a level with the surface of the cornea, and that of the right eye was almost entirely healed. The collyrium vitriolicum, with the mucilage of psillium dropped into the eyes every two hours, was afterwards sufficient to complete the cure; and as the cicatrices of the corneæ did not extend opposite the pupil, 'they did not obstruct the vision.

Case XXXV.

Celestina Pacchiarotti, a child, two years and a half old, was brought by her mother to the school of surgery, in order that I might examine the right eye, which after a recent and severe attack of the small-pox had remained swollen, red, painful, and watery. I found upon the cornea, on the side next the nose, a small ulcer of a cineritious colour of the size of a millet-seed, and on the opposite side of the cornea, that is, towards the temples, a small incipient abscess.

I ordered that the ulcer should be immediately touched with the argentum nitratum.

The

The mother was charged to drop into the eye a little milk, and to bring the child every morning at the hour of dreffing.

After the application of the cauftic, the child remained eafy for three days, but when the efchar feparated fhe again fhowed figns of great pain and heat in the eye. The ulcer was again touched with the argentum nitratum, and on the detachment of the fecond efchar, which was four days after, I found it fo fmall and fuperficial that it might be confidered as on the point of clofing. In four days more indeed, by merely dropping into the eye the vitriolic collyrium, with mucilage, it was completely healed.

The fmall abfcefs which occupied the margin of the cornea on the fide of the temples, and which had hitherto remained ftationary, increafed and caufed a return of the pain and tenfion in the eye; it afterwards burft and degenerated into an ulcer fimilar to the firft. I inftantly applied the cauftic to this fore alfo, as I had done to the preceding. A blifter was alfo put upon the neck, and the child was repeatedly purged with the fyrup of fuccory and rhubarb. It was neceffary to touch the ulcer a fecond time with argentum nitratum before it appeared difpofed to produce healthy granulations, and to contract; which effects were obtained in fix weeks from the exfoliation of the fecond efchar. The cure was completed by the

regular

regular ufe of the vitriolic collyrium and mucilage for two weeks; which not only contributed in a great degree to heal the fecond ulcer,
but alfo to ftrengthen the veffels of the conjunctiva, and to clear the whole of the white of
the eye,

Case XXXVI.

Giufeppe Barbieri, of Pavia, aged 23, a faddler
by trade, of a flender conftitution, and occafionally fubject to intermittent fever, was attacked, towards the end of September 1796,
with an eryfipelas on the right fide of the face,
which caufed a confiderable tumefaction of the
eye-lids and conjunctiva of the right eye. This
affection difappeared in ten days, by obferving a
proper diet, and by applying upon the face, as
is the practice among the common people, the
inner bark of the elder.

A month after, on being expofed to a fharp
and cold wind, the right eye became very much
inflamed. He repeated the fame remedies as
before, but finding however that the pain, heat,
watchfulnefs, difcharge of tears, fever, and intolerance of light increafed, he came to the
hofpital. I found upon the lateral external
part of the right eye, an ulcer, a line in length,
and a quarter of a line in breadth, but very
deep.

As

As I had not at that moment an opportunity
of allowing him a bed in the hofpital, I touched
the ulcer with the cauftic and gave him proper
inftructions for profecuting the treatment at
home. He did not return for advice till ten
days after, confequently long after the exfoliation
of the efchar, and I found him in a worfe ftate
than before. A bed was allotted to him, and I
began by ordering him a bread and milk poultice to be applied upon the eye-lids, for the
purpofe of diminifhing the exceffive tenfion of
the eye and furrounding parts, and to be repeatedly purged with the *opening* powders, compofed of cryftals of tartar and tartarized antimony.

In lefs than three days the tumefaction
of the eye-lids fubfided, and I immediately
touched the ulcer with the argentum nitratum,
and produced a deep efchar. It was neceffary
to apply the cauftic three times more in the
courfe of eleven days, before the ulcer loft its
cineritious appearance, and was difpofed to
granulate and heal. By this treatment the pain
in the eye, and the chronic ophthalmia, from
relaxation of the veffels of the conjunctiva, gradually diminifhed, in proportion as the ulcer
contracted.

When the bottom of the wound was nearly
on a level with the furface of the cornea, I
                                        ordered

ordered the patient to inftil the vitriolic collyrium with mucilage of quince-feed every two
hours, by means of which the ulcer was perfectly healed, and the patient regained the entire ufe of his eye.

CHAP.

CHAP. XI.

OF THE PTERYGIUM.

THE term *pterygium* is applied by furgeons to that fmall preternatural membrane of a reddifh afh-colour, and of a triangular figure,* which arifes in general from the internal angle of the eye, near the caruncula lachrymalis, and extends by little and little upon the cornea, attended with confiderable injury to the fight.

Although this fmall membrane moft frequently originates from the internal angle of the eye, it is fometimes feen to proceed alfo from the external angle,† and in fome cafes from the fuperior or inferior hemifphere of the eye-ball. From whatever part it may arife, however, it is a conftant fact that this membrane is always formed of a triangular fhape, the bafe of which is fituated upon the white of the eye, and the apex upon the cornea, fometimes at a greater fometimes at a fmaller diftance from the centre of the cornea and of the pupil. In fome cafes,

* Plate II. fig. 3. a.
† Plate II. fig. 3. b.

though

though rarely, two or three pterygia of different fizes are met with upon the fame eye,
placed at different diftances from each other
around the circumference of the ball, with their
apices directed to the centre of the cornea,
where, if unfortunately they unite together, they
cover the whole of its furface with a denfe veil,
and produce a complete lofs of fight. This
complicated cafe appears to me to be precifely
what the ancient phyficians have called the
pannus of the eye.

The *chronic varicofe* ophthalmia, with relaxation and thickening of the conjunctiva, the
nebula of the cornea, and the pterygium, differ
from each other only in as much as they are
but greater or lefs degrees of the fame difeafe.
For all the three confift in a varicofe, relaxed,
and atonic ftate of a certain portion of the conjunctiva. In the *chronic varicofe* ophthalmia,
the preternatural fulnefs and nodofity of the
veins, as well as the flaccidity and thickening
of the conjunctiva, are confined to the white of
the eye; in the *nebula* of the cornea, a certain order of varicofe veins is dilated and
knotty for a limited extent, upon the fine
lamina of the conjunctiva, which covers the
external furface of the cornea; and in the *pterygium*, in addition to the varicofe ftate of the
veffels, which are extended over a certain part
of the cornea, there is a preternatural thicken-

s   ing

ing of the thin lamina of the conjunctiva which
covers it, upon which thefe fmall varicofe veins
are fituated. Hence it arifes that the *pterygium*
appears at firft to be a new membrane formed
upon the cornea, while it is nothing more than the
fine lamina of the conjunctiva, forming its natural
external covering, which in confequence of the
chronic ophthalmia has degenerated from a tranfparent into a thick and opake tunic interwoven
with varicofe veffels. In cafes of pterygium
therefore no new production is formed upon the
eye, the difeafe only confifting in a perverfion of
fome one of the fine and tranfparent membranes
which cover it. And a convincing proof of it,
which I fhall afterwards detail, is this, that the
incipient pterygium may be cured in the fame manner as the nebula of the cornea; that is, not by
detaching it from the furface of the cornea, but
merely by extirpating it at the part where the
cornea and fclerotica unite, in the manner employed for deftroying the communication between the minute ramifications of the varicofe
veins of the conjunctiva and their trunks, from
the former of which the *nebula* is produced and
nourifhed.

The pterygium, as I have faid on the fubject of the nebula of the cornea, would be a
difeafe no lefs frequent than the *varicofe chronic*
ophthalmia, which fo often occupies the white
of the eye, if the fine and tranfparent lamina of
the

the conjunctiva, which invests the cornea externally, were not of a texture far more dense
and compact than the reft of that membrane
which correfponds to the white of the eye, and
if the fmall veffels, which are diftributed upon
it, were not very fine, tenfe, and not fo eafily
diftended as their trunks, which are fituated
upon the reft of the conjunctiva, covering the
anterior hemifphere of the eye-ball. Hence it
is, that confidering the frequent occurrence
of the chronic varicofe ophthalmia, the pterygium is rather an unufual difeafe. If, however,
the very delicate veffels of the lamina of
the conjunctiva covering the cornea, once
yield to the impulfe of the fluid propelled into
them, and become varicofe, it neceffarily follows
that the cellular membrane, which envelopes
thefe veffels becoming gradually tumefied, the
fine and tranfparent lamina, fituated upon the
cornea, is converted into a pulpy and reddifh
coloured tunic, which is precifely that of the
pterygium.

That the *pterygium* is, in reality, nothing more
than the natural expanfion of the thin tranfparent lamina of the conjunctiva converted, for a
certain extent upon the cornea, into a pulpy,
flaccid, varicofe membrane, is rendered probable
from the folds which the pterygium and the
conjunctiva correfponding to it form, whenever
the eye-ball is rolled on the fide on which the

difeafe

difeafe is fituated; and, on the contrary, from the tenfion which takes place in the *pterygium* and conjunctiva, when the ball of the eye is turned in the contrary direction. And this is still further confirmed, from obferving, that in the former pofition of the eye-ball the *pterygium* may be as eafily laid hold of by the forceps, and raifed in the form of a fold, as the part of the conjunctiva correfponding to it, which is equally relaxed, varicofe, and red.

In the dead bodies of thofe who have had this difeafe, when the flaccid and thickened part of the conjunctiva of the white of the eye, correfponding to the part of the cornea, which is rendered opake by the *pterygium*, has been carefully feparated and removed, I have conftantly found that the pterygium * was as eafily detached from the cornea, as from the white of the eye, leaving the former in the part which it occupied denuded, and evidently deprived of the covering which it naturally receives from the fine tranfparent lamina of the conjunctiva. Nor have I been able in any inftance to diveft the cornea of its natural covering, beyond the feat of the difeafe. When befides there are feveral pterygia upon the fame eye, at different diftances from each other, there are fo many flaccid, varicofe, pulpy portions of the

* Plate II. fig. 4. a. b.

conjunctiva

conjunctiva met with forming the bafe of each of them; while the reft of that membrane, covering the white of the eye, remains clofely united to the eye-ball, without there being any appearance of varicofe veffels upon the anterior hemifphere of the eye, except in thofe parts where the relaxation of the conjunctiva, and the nodofity of the veffels have, as it were, thrown to a diftance the roots and rudiments of the pterygium.

It is worthy of obfervation, that whether the pterygium be great or fmall, and in whatever part of the circumference of the eye-ball it is formed, it conftantly retains its triangular figure ; having its bafe fituated upon the white of the eye, and its apex upon the cornea. The conftancy of this fact ought to be referred, in my opinion, to the adhefion of the lamina of the conjunctiva becoming ftronger, in proportion as it advances from the circumference towards the centre of the cornea. For in confequence of fuch ftructure and different degree of cohefion which actually exifts in the found eye, it fhould neceffarily follow, that in the firft place the progrefs of the pterygium ought to be in every cafe of fuch difeafe much flower upon the cornea than upon the white of the eye; fecondly, that from the greater refiftance which the pterygium always meets with, in proportion as it extends towards the centre of the cornea, it

ought,

ought, from mechanical neceffity, to affume a triangular form, the bafe of which correfponds to the white of the eye, the apex to the centre of the cornea. Foreftus * has particularly remarked the conftancy of this phænomenon, and fpeaking of the *pterygium,* he adds, *non cooperit oculum nifi in forma fagittæ.*

From this appearance and figure, which the difeafe invariably affumes, arifes one of its principal diagnoftic characters, by which the true *pterygium* is diftinguifhed from the fpurious, or from any other foft, fungous, reddifh coloured excrefcence, which externally darkens the cornea. For excrefcences are fometimes formed upon the cornea, which, from their colour and foft membranous confiftence, very much refemble the pterygium, although they are very different from it, being formed in reality by the fubftance of the cornea itfelf, which has degenerated into a foft and fungous fubftance. But thefe fpecies of falfe pellicles independently of their being almoft always more elevated upon the cornea than the *pterygium,* have conftantly an irregular and tuberculated figure, and never reprefent a triangle with the apex directed from the margin towards the centre of the cornea.

Another diftinguifhing character of the pterygium is, the facility with which the whole of

---

* Oper. Med. lib. ii. Obferv. 6.

it

it may be collected and raifed in a fold upon the cornea by means of the forceps; while every other fpecies of excrefcence attached to this membrane remains firmly adherent to it, and does not admit of being folded in any manner, or elevated from the furface of the cornea. This peculiarity is of the greateft importance in the treatment of this difeafe, fince the true and genuine pterygium may be cured in the fimpleft manner; while, as I have ftated at the end of the preceding chapter, the fungous excrefcence of the cornea cannot be radically extirpated and perfectly healed without the greateft difficulty.

Plenk * remarks with much propriety : *pterygia, quæ filamentis folummodo adhærent, facile, abfcinduntur, difficillimè quæ ubique accreta funt corneæ, ac in plicam elevari non poffunt.* But if this excrefcence, although of a triangular figure, and conftituting the true pterygium, adheres firmly to the cornea, and is of a deep red colour, refembling lac, bleeds readily on being touched, and occafions lancinating pains, which fhoot through the eye and temples, the difeafe threatens to become of a malignant cancerous nature, or is fo already; and therefore ought

* Ce morb. ocul. page 97.
Avicenna, lib. iii. fen. 3. cap. 23, fays; duræ, fpeaking of the cornea, denudatio quando non eft facilis, perducit ad nocumentum.

s 4 only

only to be treated by palliative means, or by the extirpation of the whole eye.

The cure of the true benign pterygium, or that which is of a triangular figure, of a cineritious or pale red colour, unattended with pain, and which may be raifed in the form of a fold, is obtained by removing this fmall triangular opake membrane in an exact manner from the furface of the cornea. But fince, from what has been ftated, the pterygium confifts in an alteration of the tranfparent lamina of the conjunctiva into a denfe and opake tunic, in confequence of the varicofe chronic ophthalmia, it neceffarily follows that this difeafe cannot be removed by any means of art, without that part of the cornea which it occupies being deprived of its natural exterior integument. And as this deprivation of the natural covering of the cornea renders a cicatrix in that part inevitable, it follows alfo, that it is impoffible to cure this difeafe by an operation, without the cornea remaining more or lefs dark in the part which was occupied by the pterygium. The young furgeon, therefore, for whom thefe obfervations are intended, fhould not fuffer himfelf to be impofed upon by the fpecious relations of thofe who affert that they have removed pterygia by the knife, and completely reftored the cornea to its original natural tranfparency. The cornea certainly appears lefs opake in that part than before;

before ; but it always remains dark, and clouded by an indelible, though fuperficial cicatrix. The advantage derived from the operation is, however, always confiderable, in as much as it prevents the progrefs of the difeafe, or the further increafe of the varicofe and thickened ftate of the thin pellucid lamina of the conjunctiva covering the cornea, and at the fame time removes the local caufe of irritation and afflux to the eye, and thereby prevents the complete opacity of the cornea. If, therefore, it has happened that after the excifion of an extenfive pterygium the patient has recovered his fight, it ought to be underftood fome degree of fight, or in that proportion which there is between a denfe membrane, which entirely obftructs the paffage of the light, and a thin fuperficial cicatrix, which does not intercept it altogether.

All that I am able to affert, from repeated obfervation, as certain and invariable, is, that after the excifion of the pterygium, the fuperficial and indelible fpeck which remains upon the cornea is always lefs extenfive than the fpace which was previoufly occupied by the pterygium. Whether this arife in confequence of the fine tranfparent lamina of the conjunctiva at the circumference of the pterygium, not being entirely diforganized, but only filled with a thick humour, and merely affected with *nebula*, which, by means of the excifion, unloads itfelf

of

of the tenacious humour which it contained, and confequently recovers its former tranfparency; or becaufe the cicatrix in the part from which the *pterygium* has been extirpated, as generally takes place in all wounds, becomes actually lefs extenfive than the parts which have been removed; certain it is, that this phænomenon is invariable, and that in a great number of cafes in which I have performed the operation, of which fome extended two lines, others two lines and a half upon the cornea towards its centre, in all, after the cure was complete, the cicatrix and offufcation of the cornea were lefs, and did not exceed one line and a half, or little more, in cafes where the pterygium was two lines in extent.

The excifion of the pterygium is an operation eafily executed. It is not neceffary for fuch purpofe to have recourfe to the curved needle, threaded with filk, with which the greater part of furgeons direct the fmall membrane to be pierced, for the purpofe of forming a noofe, by which this pellicle may be raifed, and then divided at its bafe. This method is inconvenient, not only becaufe it greatly prolongs the operation, but becaufe the blood which flows from the perforations prevents the extent of the parts which are intended to be removed from being feen with the precifion which is requifite.

The

The forceps * and very fharp fciffars † are quite fufficient for the purpofe.

The pterygium is in general removed by beginning the excifion upon the cornea, and continuing it upon the white of the eye, as far as the whole extent of its bafe in the conjunctiva, fo that when the difeafe proceeds from the internal angle of the eye, the incifion is prolonged by the generality of furgeons as far as the caruncle. The difadvantage attending this practice is, in the firft place, that the white of the eye is denuded to too great an extent; fecondly, that in confequence of the great quantity of fubftance of the conjunctiva, which is removed in the bafe of the pterygium, and the direction in which it is executed, the cicatrix which takes place upon the white of the eye, forms an elevated ridge, which, like a fmall cord, confines the ball of the eye to the caruncula lachrymalis, and prevents the freedom of its motions, particularly in the direction from the internal towards the external angle. In order to avoid this inconvenience in the treatment of pterygia, which have a very extenfive bafe upon the white of the eye, I have found it convenient to divide them, from the apex only, as far as the part where the cornea and fclerotica unite; and then to feparate them at their bafe

* Plate III. fig. 8.
† Plate III. fig. 3.

by

by a femicircular incifion,* including about a line in breadth of the fubftance of the conjunctiva, in a direction concentric to the margin of the cornea. By operating in this manner I have found that the after-treatment is much fhorter than when it is executed after the common method, that the cicatrix does not form a ridge or frænum, and that the conjunctiva being ftretched circularly and equably upon the white of the eye by the cicatrix, lofes that relaxation and varicofe ftate of its veffels which formed the bafe of the *pterygium.* This nicety is not, however, neceffary where the *pterygium* is fmall, and does not extend much upon the white of the eye.

The patient being feated for this purpofe, an affiftant behind him fhould raife the upper eyelid, with the middle and forefinger of one hand, and deprefs the lower one with thofe of the other. The operator, fuppofing the affected eye is the right, fhould place himfelf before the patient, either fitting or ftanding, as fhall be moft agreeable to him; then defiring the patient to turn his eye a little from the fide correfponding to the bafe of the pterygium, with the forceps held in his left hand a little open, he fhould take hold of the pterygium at about a line from its apex, and prefs it in the form of a fold, which

* Plate III. fig. 3. a.

he

he fhould then raife and draw gently upwards towards him, until he fhall perceive a fmall crackling, indicating the detachment of the pterygium from the fine cellular membrane which connects it to the fubjacent cornea. Then, with the fciffars in his right hand, he fhould divide the fold as clofe to the cornea as poffible, in the direction from the apex to the bafe; and having carried the incifion as far as the part where the cornea and fclerotica unite, fhould raife the fold again ftill higher, and with one ftroke of the fciffars, as concentric and clofe to the margin of the cornea as poffible, remove the pterygium, together with a portion of the relaxed conjunctiva, which formed the bafe of it. This fecond incifion fhould have the figure of a crefcent,* the points of which ought to extend a few lines beyond the relaxed portion of the conjunctiva, following the curve of the eyeball.

After the operation the blood fhould be encouraged to flow, by wafhing the parts with warm water, and the eye covered by a comprefs, either dry, or moiftened with the aqua litharg. acetat. comp. and fupported by a bandage, which fhould not comprefs the parts too much.

If no remarkable fymptoms fhould arife, as pain, tenfion of the eye, and confiderable tume-

* Plate II. fig. 3.

faction

faction of the eye-lids, it will be fufficient that the eye-ball and internal furface of the eye-lids be wafhed three or four times a day, with tepid mallow-water, and the parts carefully defended from the contact of the air, without being com-preffed. If, however, fuch fymptoms fhould occur, it will be neceffary to have recourfe to the antiphlogiftic regimen, the application of bags of emollient herbs to the eye, and the in-troduction between the eye-lids of the white of egg, or mucilage of the feeds of the *pfyllium* ex-tracted with mallow-water.

On the 5th or 6th day, in general, from the operation, the furface of the wound appears of a yellow colour, and covered with mucus; a form of fuppuration peculiar to membranes in general, and the eye-ball in particular, while its edges, and the reft of the conjunctiva furround-ing them, are red. Afterwards the wound gradually contracts itfelf every day more and more, until it entirely difappears, and the cica-trix is complete.

During the whole of the treatment, from the time of the operation, it is not neceffary to ufe any other application than a lotion of mallow-water three or four times a day. I have been convinced, from repeated obfervation, that aftrin-gent collyria, and the powders which are fo highly extolled as that compofed of the Floren-tine

tine orris and alum, occafion great irritation in the eye, and a tumefied and fungous ftate of the conjunctiva ; all of which directly oppofe the healing of the wound. And what is more difagreeable they give rife to little tufts of fungus in the centre of the fore, which are with difficulty repreffed and healed. I have feen all thefe inconveniences produced by a fingle unneceffary application of the argentum nitratum. On the contrary, by fimply wafhing the parts with the aqua malvæ, the cure proceeds regularly, the yellowifh furface of the wound contracts daily, and the cicatrization is completed in the mildeft manner in the fpace of three, or at moft four weeks. Afterwards it may be ufeful to drop into the eye three or four times a day the vitriolic collyrium, with a few drops of camphorated fpirit of wine added to it, in order to ftrengthen the conjunctiva and its veffels.

I have remarked at the commencement, that the *incipient pterygium* is in reality nothing more than the nebula of the cornea, in which the veins of the conjunctiva, invefting that part of the cornea where the difeafe is fituated, are a little more dilated than in cafes of the latter ; and that the fine lamina of the conjunctiva acquires a greater degree of denfity and opacity in that part, than when it is fimply affected

with

3

with the *nebula*.* To exprefs myfelf more
clearly, the pterygium in this cafe is not a denfe
and opake membrane, but a pellicule of the
finenefs of a fpider's web, interwoven here and
there with varicofe blood-veffels, behind which
the iris is yet fufficiently perceptible. In this
ftate of the difeafe, it is not neceffary to deprive
that part of the cornea of its natural covering.
It is fufficient, as in the treatment of the nebula
of the cornea, to deftroy by excifion the communication between the dilated ramifications of
the veins of the pterygium, and the varicofe
venous trunks fituated upon the white of the
eye. This is obtained by removing a fmall
portion of the conjunctiva of a femilunar figure,
by means of the forceps and fciffars, at the part
where the cornea and fclerotica unite, precifely
at the bafe of the incipient pterygium, in the
fame manner as in the treatment of the nebula.
After this operation the *incipient pterygium* is obferved to be gradually diffipated, or there only remains a flight opacity of the cornea, for a certain
extent of the part which it occupied, which, however, is moft frequently far lefs confiderable than
that which is left by a cicatrix of the cornea.

* This middle ftate between the nebula of the cornea, and
the confirmed *pterygium*, is denominated, by the Arabian writers, Sabel. Sabel, fays Avicenna, eft panniculus accidens in
oculo ex inflatione venarum ejus apparentium in fuperficie
conjunctivæ et corneæ; et texitur quiddam in eo, quod eft
inter eas, ficut fumus. Lib. iii. fen. 3. tract 2. cap. 19.

Acrell

Acrell, in his *chirurgical observations,* relates his having cured an *incipient pterygium* in this manner; which I have alfo frequently attempted with perfect fuccefs, but which I have thought it more proper to detail among the cafes of *nebula* of the cornea than thofe of the *pterygium,* for the reafons already affigned, and principally becaufe the morbid ftate of the lamina of the conjunctiva in thefe cafes very little exceeds that in which this covering of the cornea is found, when it is only affected with the *nebula.*

Case XXXVII.

Antonio Cantoni, of Caforati, a young countryman, 19 years of age, prefented himfelf at the practical fchool of furgery on the 12th of November 1792, with a *pterygium,* which extended from the external canthus of the right eye, upon the cornea, very near to the pupil.

On the 14th of the fame month, the patient being feated, and the triangular membrane taken hold of with the forceps, at the diftance of a line and a half from its apex, and properly raifed, I carefully feparated it from the whole of the cornea; then taking hold of the varicofe and relaxed conjunctiva, which formed the bafe of the pterygium upon the white of the eye, and elevating it a little, I removed it in the

T form

form of a crefcent clofe to the margin of the cornea, and in the fame direction.

As there was no remarkable fwelling of the eye, or eye-lids on the fucceeding days, the parts were merely wafhed with the aqua malvæ, and covered with a comprefs and bandage.

The furface of the wound, as well upon the cornea as upon the white of the eye, diminifhed daily, and on the 10th of December was completely healed. It was obfervable, that the cicatrix of the cornea did not approach fo near the pupil as the apex of the pterygium.

Case XXXVIII.

Mauro Pifani, a robuft countryman, 45 years of age, was affected with a pterygium in the internal canthus of his right eye, which he had neglected fo long, that it ultimately covered two thirds of the pupil, occafioning a great diminution of fight.

The operation was performed on the 22d of January 1793. The little membrane was very exactly feparated, by means of the forceps and fciffars, from the cornea, and a portion of the tumid varicofe conjunctiva, which formed the bafe of the pterygium upon the white of the eye, was removed, in the form of a crefcent. A greater quantity of blood flowed from the

incifion

incifion than might have been expected from
the fize of it.

On the 5th day after the operation, the
yellowifh layer of mucus, which is a certain indication of fuppuration, appeared upon the furface
of the wound. During the whole of the treatment the patient ufed no other external remedy
than a lotion of aqua malvæ three times a day,
and was fcarcely at all confined to his bed.

In 26 days the wound was perfectly healed.
All that part of the cornea which had been obfcured by the pterygium remained cloudy as
before, but with this difference, that when completely healed it occupied rather lefs of the pupil,
and the patient therefore faw more diftinctly
than before the operation.

Case XXXIX.

A ftrong man, 34 years old, a carpenter by
trade, had, for feveral years, a *pterygium* upon
the right eye, which extended from the inferior
hemifphere of the eye-ball, where it is covered
by the lower eye-lid, towards the centre of the
cornea, fo as to cover about a fourth part of the
pupil in a moderate light.

On the 12th of March 1794, the patient
being feated in the practical fchool, and the
eye-lids feparated, particularly the lower, I took
hold of the pterygium at a line and a half from

its

its apex, and having raifed it completely in the
form of a fold, I divided it a little beyond the
margin of the cornea; then taking hold of the
conjunctiva with the forceps, where it covers
the white of the eye, I removed the bafe of
the pterygium, together with a fegment of that
membrane, in a direction concentric to the margin of the cornea.

The blood was allowed to flow, and the eye
was covered with a fold of lint, moiftened in
the aqua litharg. acetat. comp. which was fupported by a bandage.

The day after, the eye-lids appeared fwollen,
red, and painful. I ordered blood to be taken
from the patient abundantly, and the eye to be
covered with bags of emollient herbs. The following day he was purged. The inflammation
was diffipated on the 7th day. The conjunctiva remained, however, exceedingly tumefied
and red, and the furface of the wound did not
yet appear covered with mucus.

On the 12th day from the operation, the mucous fuppuration began to take place, and from
that time the wound gradually diminifhed.

During the whole of the treatment, except
the application of bags of emollient herbs at the
commencement, no other external remedy was
employed than the aqua malvæ. At the end
of five weeks the wound was healed. The patient, however, ufed the vitriolic collyrium,

with

with the mucilage of quince-feed,' four times a day, for fifteen days afterwards, and anointed the edges of the eye-lids at night with the ophthalmic ointment of Janin. In this cafe alfo the cicatrix obftructed the pupil confiderably lefs than the pterygium had done.

Case XL.

Francefco Vecchi, of Calignano, a countryman, 57 years of age, of a weak conftitution, in the beginning of March 1795, made application on account of two large pterygia, one upon each eye, which had occafioned a deformity for feveral years, and finally threatened to produce blindnefs; for that of the right eye, in a moderate light, covered two thirds of the pupil, the other one half of the left. Both arofe near the caruncula lachrymalis. This man was likewife affected with an habitual chronic ophthalmia in both his eyes.

Thefe pterygia were removed in the manner related in the preceding cafes. On the following day the eye-lids and conjunctiva of both fides were enormoufly fwollen, accompanied with rednefs, pain, and fever. I directed blood to be taken from his arm, and alfo from the neighbourhood of the eye-lids, by means of leeches; he was reftricted to a low diet, and ordered to take a pint of the triticum repens, with

a grain

a grain of tartarized antimony in fmall dofes, and to apply upon the eye-lids bags of emollient herbs.

On the 8th day of this treatment he became eafy, the inflammatory ftage of the ophthalmia having ceafed, and the eye-lids greatly fubfided. The conjunctiva, however, was exceedingly red, tumefied, and almoft in a fungous ftate, and the yellowifh furface of the wound was not yet covered with mucus. Being fatisfied that the delay of the fuppuration was partly owing to the atonic ftate of the veffels of the conjunctiva, I fhould have been tempted to employ fome aftringent application, had I not been warned by fimilar cafes, in which the ufe of aftringent collyria, inftead of removing the chronic oph-thalmia arifing from relaxation of the conjunc-tiva, had, on the contrary, reproduced the in-flammation. In this cafe, therefore, and as it is now my ufual practice, I was fatisfied with ufing merely a lotion of mallow-water, and exciting an irritation in the neck, by the appli-cation of a large blifter, which was kept open for fome time, and alfo repeating it behind the ears.

On the 19th day from the operation, the tumefaction of the conjunctiva being very much diminifhed, the furface of the wound of both eyes began to fuppurate, and to be covered with mucus. From this time the wound gradually contracted,

contracted, until the 53d day, when it was completely healed.

The collyrium vitriolicum was now directed to be inftilled into the eye feveral times a day, at firft alone, but afterwards with a little camphorated fpirit of wine added to it; and the ophthalmic ointment of Janin to be ufed at night: by continuing thefe remedies for two weeks the conjunctiva recovered its vigour, and the chronic rednefs of the eyes, proceeding from the relaxation of this membrane and its veffels, difappeared.

The cicatrix of the cornea of the right eye covered only a third, or little more, of the circumference of the pupil in a moderate light; and that of the cornea of the left eye only a fourth part of the pupil.

T 4   CHAP.

CHAP. XII.

OF THE ENCANTHIS.

THE *encanthis*, in its commencement, is a small soft, reddish, or sometimes slightly livid excrescence, which arises from the caruncula lachrymalis, and neighbouring *semilunar* fold of the conjunctiva. The inveterate *encanthis* is commonly of a very confiderable size,* and extends its roots beyond the caruncula lachrymalis, and *semilunar* fold, as far as the internal mem-

* *Purmannus*, in his *Chirurgia curiofa*, page 133, has left us the defcription and figure of a tumour as large as the fift, proceeding from the internal angle of the left eye by a very flender peduncle, and hanging upon the cheek; the obfcurity, however. which pervades the whole of the defcription of this difeafe, and the little accuracy difplayed in the drawing, leave room to doubt whether this large tumour originated from the caruncula lachrymalis and neighbouring *semilunar* fold, or rather from the integuments immediately on the outfide of the internal commiffure of the eye lids. *Purmannus* fays, that he extirpated this tumour with fuccefs, by firft employing a ligature near its root, and afterwards applying upon the root itfelf the fmall button of a cautery, included in a canula.

brane

brane of either eye-lid, or of both. In confequence of its originating and being placed between the eye-lids at their internal commiffure,
which it neceffarily keeps feparated on the fide
next the nofe, it occafions no inconfiderable inconvenience to the patient, by keeping up the
chronic ophthalmia, and impeding the action of
the eye-lids, particularly that of completely clofing the eye; and partly by compreffing, and partly
removing the apertures of the puncta lachrymalia from their natural direction, it prefents
an obftacle to the free courfe of the tears from
the eye into the nofe.

This excrefcence, in its early ftate, has generally a granulated appearance, refembling a mul-
berry; or it is formed of fmall fringe-like pieces.
But when it has arrived at a confiderable magnitude, a certain part of it prefents a granulated
appearance, while the reft offers only a fmooth
fubftance of a whitifh or cineritious colour,
ftreaked with varicofe veffels, which occafionally
advances fo far upon the conjunctiva covering the eye-ball on the fide next the nofe, as
to reach the part where the cornea and fclerotica unite. When the excrefcence has arrived
at an advanced ftate, it not only conftantly involves the caruncula lachrymalis and *femilunar*
fold, but the internal membrane of one or other
of the eye-lids, or of both; befides the attachment, therefore, which the *encanthis* has, in fuch

cafes,

cafes, to the caruncula lachrymalis, *femilunar*
fold, and conjunctiva of the eye-ball, it is obferved to give off a firm and projecting appendix or procefs, along the internal furface of the
upper or lower eye-lid, in the direction of their
edges; or the middle or body of the *encanthis*
is, as it were, divided near the cornea, into two
appendices or proceffes, refembling a fwallow's
tail, one of which extends along the upper eye-
lid covered by its margin; the other runs along
the internal furface of the lower eye-lid, concealed alfo by its margin, in the direction from
the internal towards the external canthus of the
eye.

The body of the encanthis, or that middle
portion of the excrefcence, which extends from
the caruncula lachrymalis and femilunar fold
inclufively, upon the conjunctiva of the eye-ball,
almoft as far as the junction of the cornea and
fclerotic coat, is fometimes as prominent as a
hazel, or ches-nut, at other times it is of
this magnitude, but depreffed, and as if it were
flattened. The body of the excrefcence, however,
preferves the granulated appearance which it
had at firft, while one or other, or both its appendices, which are continued upon the internal
furface of either or both eye-lids, prefent, as I
have faid, rather the afpect of a lipomatofe than
a granulated fubftance. If the eye-lids are everted, thefe appendices or proceffes of the encan-
                                        this

this make an elevated projection, and when this takes place in both the eye-lids, on their being everted, thefe lipomatofe appendices form almoft a ring, which is clofely applied upon the eye-ball. This difeafe was known, and fuccefsfully treated by Fabricius Hildanus, who has called it *ficus fchirrofus ad majorem oculi canthum.**

It

* Centur. I. obferv. 2. anno 1598, 20 Febr. ad ædes D. Petri Dumantii verbi divini miniftri ad quadragenarium, habentem tumorem fchirrhofum ad magnum oculi canthum caftaneæ magnitudine colore livido, et multis venis capillaribus intertextum vocatus fui. Ille autem tumor ab una parte adhærebat conjunctivæ membranæ ufque ad iridem ; ab altera vero hærebat palpebræ fuperiori, et lachrymali glandulæ; ita ut ad oculi motum totam cooperiret pupillam fcirrhus ille. Nos (ægro purgato, prout in præcedente obfervatione fufius declaravimus) incifa item cephalica in finiftro brachio, inftitritaque optima victus rationes præfente M. Nicolao Fevotto, et Daniele le Clerc. Laufannenfibus, forcipe noftra oculari hic delineata tumorem apprehendimus. Tum attracta paulatim forcipe, et inverfa fuperiori palpebra, tumorem cultello feperatorio ad id aptato commode feperavimus. Poftea albumen ovi aqua rofacea mixtum impofuimus. Inde collyriis anodynis, et abfterfivis et tandem exfcicantibus oculum intra feptimanas tres, vifu plane illæfo, perfanavimus. Interim tamen purgationes aliquoties interavimus, et cucurbitulas cum largiori flamma fcapulis et nuchæ admovimus. Defenfivum item fronti et temporibus applicuimus.

Collyrium anodynum. Rec. Mucilag. fem. cydon, plantag. cum aqua rofacea extractæ, lactis muliebris ana uncias II. camphoræ, croci ana fcrupulum dimidium, mifce et applica tepide.

Collyrium

It appears, however, that in the cafe related by Hildanus, the encanthis had only one appendix fituated upon the internal furface of the upper eye-lid, below its margin.

The encanthis, as well as the pterygium, fometimes affumes a cancerous malignity, which is characterized by the dark red or leaden colour of the excrefeence; its extraordinary hardnefs; the lancinating pains which accompany it, and which extend to the forehead, the whole of the eye and the temples, efpecially after it has been even flightly touched; by its difpofition to bleed; and by its ulcerating in feveral points which throw out a fungous fubftance, and difcharge a thin and very acrid humour. This worft fpecies, or rather degeneration of the encanthis, admits only of a palliative treatment, unlefs the total extirpation of it fhould be attempted, together with all the parts contained in the cavity of the orbit; the fuccefs of which muft be alfo very doubtful.

* Collyrium exficcans. Rec. Aquarum plantag. rofar. ana uncias quatuor, tutiæ preparatæ, cornu cervi ufti et preparati, ceruffæ lotæ ana drachmam unam. Mifce fiat collyrium. Hic monitos velim chirurgos; collyria in quæ ingreditur lac, æftate fingulis, hyæme vero alternis diebus iteranda effe. Acefcit enim lac, et acre efficitur: hinc dolores, et inflammationes excitat.

The

The benign encanthis, whether fmall or large, may be cured by means of excifion. The fmall incipient encanthis, whether of a granulated or fringe-like appearance, which arifes from the caruncula lachrymalis and *femilunar* fold, or from a fmall part of the edges of the eye-lids alfo, where they form the internal angle or commiffure, may be elevated by the forceps, and by means of the curved fciffars, feparated clofe to its bafe from the whole extent of its origin. For the purpofe of executing this operation, it is not neceffary, as is practifed by fome, to pafs a needle and thread through the fmall excrefcence, in order to raife it and detach it with precifion from all the parts to which it adheres; as this intention may be obtained by means of the forceps, without incommoding the patient by the punctures and introduction of a thread for the purpofe of forming a noofe. In the removal of that part of the fmall encanthis, however, which originates from the caruncula lachrymalis, it is neceffary not to include more of the fubftance of the caruncle than is requifite for completely eradicating the difeafe, left by removing too much of it, an irremediable weeping of the eye fhould be produced.

After the fmall excrefcence is extirpated, the eye fhould be repeatedly wafhed with cold water, in order to clear away the blood, and fhould be covered with a linen cloth and bandage.

On the 5th, 6th, or 7th day, when the inflammation occafioned by the operation has entirely ceafed, and the mucous fuppuration is eftablifhed, the divided parts fhould be touched with a fmall button of alum, cut in the form of a crayon pencil, and the vitriolic collyrium, with mucilage of quince-feed, inftilled into the eye feveral times a day. If thefe means do not produce the defired effect of healing the wounds, but on the contrary, thofe of the caruncle and internal commiffure of the eye-lids become fungous and ftationary, they fhould be frequently touched with the argentum nitratum, taking care to avoid the conjunctiva as much as poffible, efpecially if any part of it have been included in the incifion. When the fungus has been deftroyed, the treatment may be completed by the vitriolic collyrium, or by introducing an ointment confifting of frefh butter, the powder of tutty, and armenian bole, between the eye-ball and internal angle of the eye-lids three times a day. Bidloo greatly extols the application of the powder of chalk, either fimple, or combined, with burnt alum. *Exercit. Anat. Chir. decad* II.

The large inveterate encanthis, whether flattened in its body, or projecting in the form of a hazel or ches-nut, with one or two lipomatofe appendices along the internal membrane of either or both eye-lids, is equally cured by means of excifion

cifion. The ligature cannot be employed in this cafe advantageoufly, fince the neck or peduncle of the excrefcence is never fufficiently narrow to admit of its application ; the encanthis on the contrary, when very voluminous, having conftantly extenfive attachments to the caruncula lachrymalis, femilunar fold, to the conjunctiva almoft as far as the vicinity of the cornea, and alfo one or two lipomatofe appendices along the internal membrane of either or both of the eye-lids. If, therefore, the body of the encanthis fhould be removed by the ligature, either one or both the lipomatofe proceffes would always remain to be extirpated, which fecond operation could only be executed by means of excifion. The fear of hæmorrhage, in this operation, upon which the advocates for the ligature appear to lay fo much ftrefs, is unfounded, fince the cafes of large and inveterate encanthis, which have been removed, are now fo numerous, without any unfavourable accident having happened on account of the lofs of blood (to which I could add fome of my own) that upon this point * there cannot be any room for doubt or difcuffion.

* Pellier, Recueil d'obferv. fur les malad. de l'oeil, part II. obferv. 118, relates a cafe of excifion of the encanthis, which although executed, as he fays, by an able oculift, was, however, followed by a dangerous hæmorrhage. He does not enter, however, into any detail of the nature of the difeafe, nor

difcuffion. Fabricius Hildanus, in the cafe of
the large and inveterate encanthis before cited, in
which there was only one lipomatofe procefs
along the internal membrane of the upper eye-
lid, after having taken hold of the body of the
tumour with the tenaculum, and drawn it towards him, and having everted the upper eye-
lid, fo that this appendage might projeƈt forwards through its whole extent, with a fmall
biftoury feparated this procefs from the internal
furface of the eye-lid, and by continuing the
incifion divided the body of the encanthis from
the conjunƈtiva covering the eye-ball, the femilunar fold, and caruncula lachrymalis. This
operation was attended with the happieft fuccefs, and therefore ought to ferve as a model and
guide to furgeons in the treatment of this difeafe.

When, however, the inveterate, and very
large *encanthis* has two lipomatofe appendices,
one along the internal furface of the upper, the
other of the lower eye-lid, it is then neceffary
to proceed in the following manner: the patient
fhould be placed in a chair, and the upper eye-
lid everted by an affiftant, fo that one of the

nor of the method of operating, from which one might have
been enabled to deduce the caufes of fo unuful an occurrence.
Indeed, he adds: J'ai fouvent fait cette operation a des ex-
croiffances de cette nature, et jamais je n'ai èprouvé un pareil
accident.

proceffes of the encanthis may project outwards. This being deeply divided in the direction of the edge of the eye-lid, by means of a fmall bif- toury, and then taken hold of and drawn out by the forceps,* fhould be entirely feparated from the internal furface of the upper eye-lid, longitudinally, proceeding from the external to- wards the internal angle of the eye, as far as the body or middle portion of the encanthis. The lipomatofe procefs, fituated upon the internal furface of the lower eye-lid, fhould be feparated in the fame manner. The body of the encan- this fhould be afterwards elevated by means of the forceps, or, if this is not practicable, by a double hook, and then partly by means of the fmall biftoury, and partly by the curved fciffars, completely detached from the fubjacent con- junctiva which covers the eye-ball, from the femilunar fold and caruncula lachrymalis, pene- trating more or lefs deeply into the fubftance of the latter, as the firmnefs and depth of the roots of the difeafe may render it neceffary, fince it ought to be openly acknowledged that in the treatment of the inveterate and very large en- canthis, which is deeply rooted in the caruncle, it is not always in the furgeon's power to avoid the fubftance of that part fo carefully that when the wound is healed, fome little weeping of the

* Plate III. 12. 8.

U   eye

eye may not remain in confequence of the operation.

The eye fhould be frequently wafhed with
cold water, and the after treatment in this cafe
conducted nearly in the manner recommended
in the extirpation of the fmall incipient encanthis. Frequent lotions of the aqua malvæ and
anodyne and detergent collyria are the moft
proper applications, until the mucous fuppuration in the divided parts be fully eftablifhed;
afterwards flight aftringents, and the ointment
before recommended, may be ufed with advantage. In general, the mildeft applications are
the moft ufeful, not only in the ftage preceding
the fuppuration, but afterwards; efpecially when,
together with the encanthis, a confiderable portion of the conjunctiva, covering the white of
the eye on the fide towards the nofe, has been
removed, to which the body of the excrefcence
was clofely united.

The whole of this chapter will be greatly
illuftrated by the following cafe of Marchetti.*
*Curavi quemdam canonicum polonum laborantem
meliceride magnitudinis jujubæ, quæ a caruncula
anguli majoris oculi ad totam pupillam porrigebatur.
A multis tentata curatio medicamentis, decoctis
fcilicet, collyriis et aliis hujusmodi; omnia tamen
octo menfium fpatio incaffum adhibita. Cum vero*

* Obferv. med. Chirurg. Sylloge, obf. 21.

me

me confuluiffet, ipfum tumorem evellendum cenfui;
quod cum reformidaret fpe tamen falutis operation-
em admifit, quam ftatim molitus fum, corpore prius
expurgato accuratiffime ab aliis medicis. Paravi
itaque hamulum, quo ipfam meliceridem perforavi,
et manu apprehendi, altera vero forcipe eamdem
cum folliculo feĉtione feparavi tum a caruncula,
tum a tunica adnata, et ipfa pupilla; atque ita
totum tumorem eduxi fine ulla offenfa ipfius oculi;
a quibus ftatim applicui gofsypium imbutim aqua
rofácea cum ovi albumine agitata, et portiuncula
croci, patiente tres dies hoc modo fafcia vinĉto;
adhibito poftmodum collyrio cum aqua rofarum, et
pulvere tutiæ præparatæ; quibus fpatio oĉto die-
rum omnino convaluit æger; increpante licet meam
præceptore meo ab Aquapendente *audaciam, curæ*
tamen brevi fpatio temporis id præftiterim, quod
alii medici non potuerunt perficere: idque præfen-
tibus præclariffimo Joanne Dominico Sala *cum*
multis ftudiofis.

CHAP.

CHAP. XIII.

OF THE HYPOPION

BY the term hypopion, I mean with the generality of furgeons, that collection of yellowifh glutinous humour, fimilar to matter which takes place in the anterior chamber of the aqueous humour, and not unfrequently alfo in the pofterior chamber, in confequence of the violent *acute* ophthalmia, particularly where it is internal. For, as I have faid, in fpeaking of the inflammation of the eyes, although the violent *acute* ophthalmia is, in the greater number of cafes, principally confined to the external parts of the eye, it neverthelefs occafionally attacks with an equal degree of violence both the external and internal membranes of this organ, particularly the choroidea and uvea. If, in the latter cafe, the inflammation, which affects the interior part of the eye, is not fpeedily arrefted by the moft effectual means, a coagulable lymph tranfudes from the choroid membrane and uvea, which, in proportion as it is poured into the cavity of the eye, is carried into the

chambers

chambers of the aqueous humour, paffes before the pupil, and falls to the bottom of the ante-rior chamber, fometimes filling a third part of it, at other times half, and occafionally reaching fo high as entirely to obfcure and conceal the iris and pupil.

This tenacious humour of the *hypopion* is generally called, not only by the common peo-ple, but alfo by furgeons, *matter*; but, in my opinion, very improperly, in the fenfe at leaft in which the term matter is generally received. For in this cafe it is not the product of an abfcefs or ulceration of the internal or external mem-branes of the eye-ball, but fimply the refult of a tranfudation of coagulable lymph from the internal furface of the inflamed choroidea and uvea; precifely as takes place in all other membranes of the body affected with violent inflammation, as the dura and pia mater, for inftance, the pericardium, the pleura, the peri-toneum, and the membrane proper to the vif-cera; all of which, under fuch circumftances, are covered with a glutinous furface, or thin layer of coagulable lymph, exactly fimilar to the vifcid matter which is collected in the chambers of the aqueous humour conftituting the *hypo-pion*. In the moft frequent cafes of *hypopion* at leaft, no one among the moft accurate and ex-perienced furgeons has hitherto demonftrated

that

that this difeafe has been preceded by an abfcefs of the internal membranes of the eye; or has ever obferved the *hypopion* in confequence of an ulcer of the choroidea or uvea. If, however, notwithftanding this, it fhould be infifted that there is no effential difference between coagulable lymph effufed from a membrane violently inflamed, and *matter*, it muft then be conceded that there are cafes in which matter is formed without abfcefs or ulceration, and that the *hypopion* is a difeafe precifely of this defcription.

The fymptoms which would induce one to fear a tranfudation of coagulable lymph within the eye, or the formation of an hypopion, are thofe of the violent *acute* ophthalmia in the moft exceffive degree; as great fwelling of the eye-lids, rednefs and tumefaction of the conjunctiva, as in the *chemofis*; burning heat in the eye with acute pain in it, as well as in the fupercilium and neck; fever, watchfulnefs, averfion to the weakeft light, and contraction of the pupil.

As foon as the hypopion begins to be formed, a fmall yellow line, in the form of a crefcent, is feen at the bottom of the anterior chamber of the aqueous humour, which, in proportion as the glutinous humour tranfudes from the inflamed internal membranes of the eye, paffes forwards through the pupil, and is precipitated in the aquceous humour, increafing in all its dimenfions

menfions and gradually concealing firft the lower hemifphere of the iris, then afcending as high as the pupil, and finally covering the whole circumference of that membrane. As long as the inflammatory ftage of the violent *acute* ophthalmia fubfifts, the *hypopion* continues to increafe; but as foon as this ftage ceafes, and the ophthalmia enters upon the fecond period, or that from local debility, the quantity of coagulable lymph forming the hypopion is no longer augmented, but is rather difpofed to diminifh.

This fact fufficiently fhows the importance of arrefting the progrefs of the hypopion, by employing, in the moft rigorous manner, thofe means which are moft efficacious in fufpending and repreffing the impetus of the violent acute ophthalmia in its firft ftage. In fuch cafes, therefore, copious, general, and local bleeding fhould immediately be had recourfe to, and in the cafe of *chemofis*, the divifion of the conjunctiva ; mild purgatives fhould be employed, blifters to the neck, bags of emollient herbs, and other auxiliaries of this kind, which have been already enumerated in treating of the firft ftage of th'? violent acute ophthalmia. This intention is known to be accomplifhed, by obferving, that fome days after this treatment, although the rednefs of the conjunctiva and eye-lids ftill continues, the lancinating pains in the eye have ceafed; the heat and fever have confiderably diminifhed;

minifhed; the patient's fleep and general eafe
are reftored; that the eye can be eafily moved;
and laftly, that the collection of tenacious humour forming the hypopion has become ftationary. It is not uncommon, efpecially among the
lower claffes of people, to fee patients in the fecond ftage of the violent acute ophthalmia, who
carry this collection of coagulable lymph depofited in the chambers of the aqueous humour
with the utmoft indifference, and without complaining of any of thofe fymptoms which characterize the acute ftage of the difeafe. It is
only at this period, I have faid, or when the
acute ftage of the violent ophthalmia is over,
that the hypopion ceafes to augment, and the
glutinous matter of which it is formed begins
to be diffolved, and in a ftate to be abforbed,
provided this falutary operation of nature is not
prevented or retarded by the improper conduct
of the patient.

To thofe who are little acquainted with the
treatment of difeafes of the eyes, it would certainly appear that the moft expeditious and effectual method of treating the hypopion, which
has become ftationary in the fecond ftage of the
violent acute ophthalmia, would be that of
making an incifion in the lower part of the cornea, in order to give a fpeedy iffue to the matter contained in the chambers of the aqueous
humour; particularly as this is the doctrine
which

which is commonly taught in the fchools of
furgery. Yet experience proves the contrary,
and demonftrates that the divifion of the cornea
in thefe cafes is feldom attended with fuccefs,
and that, on the contrary, it moft frequently
gives rife to evils of greater magnitude than the
hypopion itfelf, notwithftanding the modifica-
tion fuggefted by Richter;* that is, of not evacuating the matter of the hypopion all at once,
nor of promoting the difcharge of it through
the incifion in the cornea, by means of repeated
preffure or injections, but of allowing the tenacious lymph to be flowly difcharged of itfelf.
From a very confiderable number of obfervations made upon this point, I have found, that
however fmall the wound made in the lower
part of the cornea may be for the purpofe of
giving iffue to the matter of the hypopion, it
moft frequently reproduces the inflammation
and occafions a greater effufion of coagulable
lymph into the chambers of the eye than
before. And if, even after the divifion of the
cornea, the matter of the hypopion be permitted to flow out gradually and by drops, in
confequence of its tenacity fome days elapfe before it is entirely evacuated ; and the glutinous
lymph by keeping open, in the mean time, the
lips of the wound of the cornea, caufes it to fup-

* Obferv. Chirurgicarum fafciculus primus, cap. 12.

purate

purate and degenerate into an ulcer, through
which, after the tenacious fluid is evacuated, a
difcharge of the aqueous humour takes place, and
afterwards a protrufion of a portion of the iris; by
the divifion of the cornea therefore nothing more
is generally effected than changing the hypopion
into an ulcer of the cornea, with procedentia of
the iris, and fometimes even of the cryftalline. *
Nor can any particular inftance of fuccefs, in
which the matter of the hypopion has been
fpontaneoufly difcharged from a narrow fiffure
in the cornea, be adduced as an argument in
favour of an artificial divifion of this membrane
by the knife, in cafes of ftationary hypopion in
the fecond ftage of the violent acute ophthalmia.
For it is known, by experience, that there is a
material difference between the effects of the
opening of a natural or preternatural cavity of
the animal body, fpontaneoufly, or procured by
cauftic, and that made by the knife; fince in
the two former, the confecutive fymptoms are
conftantly milder than in the latter, or that of
incifion; independently of the fpontaneous burfting of the hypopion through the cornea, being
alfo not unfrequently followed by a difcharge of

* Richter fays in the fame place. Aliquando vero cum
operationem, hypopii poft ophthalmiam vehementem orti in-
ftituerem, accidit ut incifa cornea, et elapfo humore aqueo,
lens cryftallina in cameram oculi anteriorem prolaberetur, et
dilatatio ccrneæ vulunfculo eximi ex oculo deberet.

the

the aqueous humour, and afterwards by a pre-
cedentia of the iris; and therefore the fpontaneous rupture of the hypopion cannot in any
refpect ferve as a rule in the treatment of this
difeafe.

I know only one cafe in which the incifion
of the cornea, for giving iffue to the matter of
the hypopion may be confidered, not only as
ufeful, but even neceffary, that is, where the
accumulation of coagulable lymph poured into
the cavity of the eye is fo confiderable, that from
the exceffive diftention which it produces upon
all the membranes of the eye-ball, it occafions
fymptoms of fuch magnitude as to threaten,
not only the complete deftruction of the organ of
vifion, but alfo the patient's life, as I fhall have
occafion to fhow towards the end of the chapter. This particular cafe, however, cannot ferve
as a model for the treatment of the common
hypopion, or that which is moft frequently met
with in practice.

If it is certain befides, as it indubitably is,
that blood extravafated in the eye, in confequence of any violence, and that even collections of membranous flocculi of the *capfular*
cataract, pufhed by the point of the needle from
the pofterior into the anterior chamber of the
aqueous humour, infenfibly diffolve, and are
ultimately entirely abforbed, as I fhall prove in
the chapter on cataract; and that the fame
                                        thing

thing happens to the *milky* or *caseous* cataract
when broken down, and even to the cryftalline
lens itfelf deprived of its capfule and lodged
in the vitreous humour by means of the operation ; there is no caufe to doubt that the fame
abforption can take place alfo in cafes of collections of coagulable lymph, extravafated in the
chambers of the aqueous humour, when the
fource from which the glutinous humour is derived has been fuppreffed, and the power of the
abforbing fyftem of the eye at the fame time
reftored.

It appears clearly from thefe facts, in my opinion, that the refolution of the hypopion, by
means of abforption, forms the primary indication, which ought to direct the furgeon in the
treatment of this difeafe. I have remarked,
that in order to arreft the progrefs of this difeafe, the only efficacious method is that of
refifting the violence of the inflammation, and
fhortening the acute ftage of the ophthalmia,
by the rigorous employment of the antiphlogiftic treatment, and by mild and emollient applications. If this method of treatment fucceed, as it does in the greater number of cafes,
the incipient collection of coagulable lymph
poured into the bottom of the anterior chamber
of the aqueous humour, not only ceafes to augment, but in proportion as the ophthalmia difappears the abforbent fyftem takes up the hete-
                                        rogeneous

rogeneous humour, and the white or yellowifh
fpot, of a crefcent-like form, fituated at the
bottom of the anterior chamber of the eye, gradually diminifhes, and ultimately difappears altogether. *Janin* * confidered an infufion of the
flowers of the mallow applied upon the affected
eye, as a fpecific folvent for the hypopion, but
it is now known that any external emollient
application, provided it be combined with the
moft exact and efficacious internal antiphlogiftic
treatment, in order to reprefs the acute ftage of
the violent ophthalmia, is productive of the
fame beneficial effect as the decoction of the
flowers of mallows. Warm water alone is attended with the fame advantage.

" A young woman," fays the celebrated
practitioner *Nannoni*, " was ftruck upon the
eye with an ear of corn; in confequence of which
it inflamed and produced a white matter, which
prefented itfelf behind the cornea, in the form
of a crefcent, without its being poffible to determine whether it was contained in the laminæ
of the cornea, or in the anterior chamber;
whence I was afked, whether it could be evacuated by an incifion; efpecially as the patient
complained of great pain in the eye and forehead. I faid, in the prefence of Dr. Lulli and
a number of furgical ftudents, this patient being

* Mémoires et obferv. fur l'œil, fect. 9. page 405.

in

in the hofpital, that the great pain which fhe
complained of was not occafioned by the matter, but by the caufe from which the matter
originated. Which caufe confifted in an inflammation that would be probably increafed
by giving a more free accefs to the external air
than it has with the internal parts, where there
is no external wound. By fomenting the eye
and forehead with warm water, the inflammation ceafed, and the matter difappeared; a circumftance which we have now fo frequently
obferved to follow, that even in this inftance,
we may boaft of the fimplicity of the healing
art."

Such indeed is the happy termination of the
hypopion, when the difeafe has been attended to
from its commencement, and when the internal antiphlogiftic treatment, and the emollient
applications to the eye, fpeedily arreft and reprefs the *acute* ftage of the violent ophthalmia.
But it occafionally happens, either in confequence
of the inflammatory period of the ophthalmia
having refifted more than ufual the means which
are employed, or becaufe they have been adopted too late, that the quantity of coagulable
lymph poured into the eye, and collected in the
chambers of the aqueous humour, is fo confiderable that it continues for a long time, even
after the acute ftage of the ophthalmia has entirely ceafed to obfcure the eye, and intercept
the

the vifion. I have repeatedly feen patients, particularly in the lower clafs of people, as I have before obferved, in whom the inflammatory ftage of the violent ophthalmia having fubfided very flowly, either from negligence or improper treatment, the anterior chamber of the aqueous humour has remained, for a long time, almoft entirely filled with the vifcid matter of the hypopion, which, the inflammation having ceafed, they have carried about almoft with indifference, without complaining of any confiderable pain, or of any inconvenience in the eye, except the difficulty of feeing with it. It is evident, that in this fecond ftage of the ophthalmia, the diffolution of the hypopion can neither be obtained by the fame means, nor with the fame celerity, as in the firft. For in the fecond ftage of the ophthalmia, both on account of the quantity and denfity of the vifcid matter effufed, as well as of the atony of the vafcular fyftem of the eye, it is not only neceffary to allow nature time to effect a diffolution of it in the aqueous humour, and thereby difpofe it to be infenfibly abforbed along with this fluid, which is inceffantly renewed; but alfo to invigorate the diminifhed power of the vafcular fyftem of the globe of the eye, particularly that of the abforbents, by artificial means; which muft require more or lefs time, according

7

cording to the age and conftitution of the patient.

In the fecond ftage of the violent acute ophthalmia, accompanied with hypopion, the furgeon's attention therefore, fhould be confined to
remove from the eye whatever may irritate it,
or reproduce the inflammation in it; and he
fhould only employ thofe means which may
contribute to diffipate the fecond ftage of the
ophthalmia, arifing from a laxity of the conjunctiva and its veffels, and to excite, at the
fame time, the action of the abforbents. Under
thefe circumftances, therefore, he fhould, in the
firft place, carefully afcertain the degree of fenfibility of the affected eye, by introducing between the eye-lids and ball, fome drops of the
vitriolic collyrium, with mucilage of quince-
feed; and if he fhould find that this application caufes too great an irritation in the eye,
he fhould immediately defift from it, and confine himfelf for fome time to bags of tepid mallows, with the addition of a few grains of camphire, and at intervals the fpirituous aromatic
vapour mentioned in the chapter on ophthalmia, and the blifter to the neck fhould be repeated. When the exceffive morbid fenfibility
of the eye has ceafed, he fhould return again
to the ufe of the vitriolic collyrium, at firft fimple, but afterwards conjoined with a little camphorated fpirit of wine. During this treatment,
the

the furgeon will perceive, that in proportion as the chronic ophthalmia is diffipated, and the action of the abforbent fyftem of the eye excited, the tenacious matter of the hypopion is firft divided into feveral parts, or fmall maffes; that it afterwards becomes more dilute, diminifhes in quantity, and fubfides towards the lower fegment of the cornea, and ultimately difappears altogether.

The furgeon cannot always promife himfelf to obtain the fame fuccefs in the treatment of the hypopion, whether this difeafe be in the firft or fecond ftage of the violent acute ophthalmia, when the tenacious lymph, which is rapidly poured into the eye, is in fo confiderable a quantity as not only to fill completely both the chambers of the aqueous humour, but alfo to diftend them violently, and to produce confiderable preffure, particularly upon the cornea. This unfortunate circumftance, notwithftanding the moft effectual efforts of art, adapted to the peculiar ftate of the difeafe, is frequently followed by another accident of ftill greater magnitude than the hypopion itfelf, I mean the ulceration, offufcation, and rupture of the cornea, either in its circumference or centre oppofite the pupil; or in that part of it which offers the leaft refiftance.

The proximate caufe of this accident, is not fo much to be attributed to the acrid quality of

x the

the matter of the hypopion, as some pretend, as to the exceſſive degree of preſſure which it makes upon the cornea from within outwards. Mr. John Hunter,* who has left us some important reflections upon this part of ſurgical pathology, has remarked, that extraneous ſubſtances lodged in any part of the animal body, although from their nature and figure not injurious, are continually determined and propelled by the powers of nature towards the ſurface of the body ; and that the ſame, or even a leſs degree of preſſure, which, applied to the animal body externally, does not produce ulceration of the ſkin, when directed from within outwards, excites in the part which is compreſſed, the ulcerative proceſs, and that conſtantly from within, towards the ſurface of the body. The matter of the ciliary glands for inſtance, collected in large quantity, and diſtending the lachrymal ſac, which might eaſily force a paſſage through the naſal canal, rather occaſions by its preſſure, from within outwards, the ulceration of the ſac, while the ſame degree of preſſure applied upon the external part of it, would certainly not be ſufficient to produce the ſame effect. Matter confined in the frontal ſinuſes rather occaſions a corroſion of the bones and integuments of the forehead, by its preſſure

* A Treatiſe on the blood, inflammation, and gun-ſhot wounds.

from

from within outwards, than forces its natural
way into the nofe. A mufket-ball lodged
among the mufcles, in procefs of time is pufhed,
without any inconvenience, towards the furface
of the body; but no fooner does it prefs upon
the fkin from within outwards, than it occafions it to ulcerate and open a paffage for it.
Precifely in the fame manner, and in conformity with the fame law, the coagulable lymph
poured into the eye, forming the hypopion, is
continually directed towards the cornea; and if
this matter is in fuch quantity, as to prefs upon
the cornea from within outwards, beyond a certain degree not eafily determinable, the texture
of this membrane is immediately acted on by
the abforbents, ulcerated and corroded.

When this happens, the ulceration of the
cornea in general proceeds with fuch rapidity
that the furgeon has feldom fufficient time to
prevent it. And when the corrofion and rupture of the cornea has taken place in any part
of it, the redundant quantity of coagulable lymph
confined in the eye * begins to be difcharged
through this opening, with great relief to the
patient. This advantage, however, is not of
long duration; for when the glutinous humour,
which diftended the whole of the eye enor-

---

* It is on this account that this higheft degree of the
hypopion, is called, by the greater part of furgeons, the
empyema of the eye.

moufly,

mouſly, and particularly the cornea, is entirely,
or in a great meaſure, evacuated, it is very frequently followed by a fold of the iris, which
paſſes acroſs the ulcer or fiſſure of the cornea ;
from which it projects externally, conſtituting
the diſeaſe denominated the procidentia of the
iris, of which I ſhall ſpeak fully in the next
chapter.

If, under ſuch urgent circumſtances, the cornea already ulcerated, darkened, and in a great
meaſure diſorganized, is ſlow in burſting, the
violence of the ſymptoms, which ariſe from the
exceſſive diſtenſion of the eye-ball, obliges the
ſurgeon to open this membrane artificially, in order to free the patient from the violent pain, as
well as the danger of loſing his life,* which may
be

* Memoires de l'Acad. vol. xiii. 8. page 279. I paſſed
ſome days in a garriſon-town, where two ſiſters, ladies of
quality, had, at the ſame time, the ſmall-pox, one of them
20 the other 24 years of age : the variolous matter had been
transferred to the eyes ; the puſtules upon the whole of the
body had dried, and no doubt would have been entertained of
the happy termination of the diſeaſe, if the eyes had not been
affected. Their tumefaction occaſioned fever, violent pains,
accompanied with heat and throbbing. Being called into
conſultation with ſeveral ſurgeons of the town, and two or
three ſurgeon-majors of the garriſon, I propoſed to open the
eyes in order to ſave the patient's lives. My advice was not
reliſhed ; in vain I repreſented that theſe organs were irre-
coverably loſt ; the ſtrongeſt objection which was urged to
me, was, that they had never heard of ſuch an operation. A
phyſician, in particular, thought it exceedingly ſtrange that I
ſhould

be executed with the lefs exactnefs, as, in thefe cafes, he can fcarcely reckon on the prefervation of the organ of vifion., The acutenefs of the pain in the eye and the whole head in thefe cafes is fo great that it very frequently produces delirium, and excites an apprehenfion that the brain may be alfo affected by it.

If, after the evacuation of the tenacious humour, by means of the incifion of the cornea, there were any hope of reftoring to the patient, even in part, the tranfparency of this membrane, together with the action and ufe of the other parts, which conftitute the principal organ of vifion, it would be certainly prudent, that the furgeon fhould make the incifion at the lower part of the cornea, as is practifed in the extraction of the cataract. But in the cafe of *empyema* of the eye, of which I am now treating, where the cornea is every where injured by the ulcerative procefs, opake, and ready to fall into a fpecies of putridity, and where no hope can be entertained of being able to reftore any

fhould propofe to burft the eyes; but the very fpeedy death of one of thefe ladies gave the parents fome regret that they had yielded to the more general opinion. The other fifter had the good fortune to efcape, through the beneficence of nature; a fpontaneous opening taking place, through which the matter formed between the tunics of the eye was evacuated. Her eyes preferved their globular form and natural fize, but fhe remained blind, after having run the greateft rifk of her life.

part

part of it to its former tranfparency, the beft method of fpeedily relieving the patient from the intolerable pain which he fuffers, is to divide the centre of the cornea to the extent of a line and a half with a fmall biftoury, then to raife the divided edge with the forceps, and remove it circularly with a ftroke of the fciffars, leaving in the centre of the cornea an aperture of the circumference of a lentil-feed.

Through this opening, the lips of which do not come in contact, like thofe of a fimple incifion, the moft fluid part of the matter, which diftended the eye-ball, immediately efcapes; the denfe coagulable lymph, by little and little, takes the fame rout; then the cryftalline, and in a few days afterwards the vitreous humour alfo. It is very neceffary, therefore, that the furgeon fhould abftain from compreffing the eye-ball ftrongly, in order to accelerate the evacuation of the vitreous humour, as experience proves that it is advantageous in thefe cafes that this humour fhould be gradually and fpontaneoufly difcharged.

Immediately after the operation the furgeon fhould cover the affected eye with a poultice of bread and milk, which he fhould renew every two hours, not omitting the ufe of thofe general remedies which are calculated to arreft the acute inflammation, and quiet the difturbed ftate of the nervous fyftem. In proportion as the fuppuration takes place in the internal part

of

of the eye, the eye-ball diminifhes, retires to the
bottom of the orbit, and finally heals, allowing
every advantage for the appofition of an artificial
eye. From what has been advanced, therefore, it
muft be concluded that the incifion of the cornea is as neceffary and ufeful in the cafe of *empyema* of the eye, accompanied with the very
alarming fymptoms above-mentioned, and the
irremediable opacity of the cornea, which is in
a great meafure diforganized, as it is contra-
indicated and dangerous in the cafe of *hypopion,*
which is moft frequently met with in practice.

CASE XLI.

A ftrong country-woman, 35 years old, was
brought into this hofpital towards the end of
April 1796, on account of a violent acute ophthalmia in both her eyes, with which fhe had
been afflicted three days, with great tumefaction
of the eye-lids, rednefs of the conjunctiva, acute
pain, fever, and watchfulnefs. She was unable
to affign any caufe from which the difeafe had
arifen.

I took away blood abundantly from the arm
and foot, and alfo locally by means of leeches
applied near both the angles of the eyes, and I
alfo purged her. Thefe remedies were attended
with fome advantage, in as much as they con-

tributed

tributed to abate the inflammatory ftage of the
violent ophthalmia. Neverthelefs an extravafation of yellowifh glutinous lymph appeared in
the anterior chamber of the aqueous humour,
which filled about one third of that cavity.

By frequently wafhing the parts with the
aqua malvæ made tepid, and the uninterrupted
application of fmall bags of gauze filled with
emollient herbs boiled in milk, by diet, and repeated mild purges with a grain of the antimonium tartarizatum diffolved in a pint of the
decoction of the root of the triticum repens, the
fymptoms of the ophthalmia were entirely relieved, and on the 11th day the patient was able
to bear a moderate degree of light.

By perfifting in the ufe of thefe emollient applications the matter of the hypopion began to
diminifh, and by degrees, in the courfe of 12
days more, almoft entirely difappeared. I now
thought it proper to increafe the ftrength of the
local remedies, by introducing a few grains of
camphire into the bags of mallows, which produced the beft effect. For in lefs than a week·
the rednefs of the conjunctiva was entirely diffipated, as well as the fmall whitifh line of a
crefcent-like figure, which had remained at the
bottom of the cornea, depending upon the remaining part of the humour of the hypopion.

CASE

CASE XLII.

Maddalena Bignani, the wife of a gardener,
in the vicinity of Pavia, 40 years of age, of a
delicate conftitution, was feized with a violent
acute ophthalmia in her left eye, which, notwithftanding fome evacuations of blood, occafioned an *hypopion* in the anterior chamber of
the aqueous humour, fo that the cornea of that
fide appeared almoft entirely opake. The patient was admitted into this practical fchool on
the 7th day from the attack of the ophthalmia.
She complained of acute and lancinating pain
in the eye and correfponding temple.

I ordered leeches to be applied to the angles
of the eye-lids, and I purged her gently with
two drams of cryftals of tartar, and a grain of
the tartarized antimony, in a pint of the decoction of the root of the triticum repens, taken
in divided dofes. A poultice of bread and milk
with a little faffron was applied upon the eye.
In four days the acute ftage of the ophthalmia
ceafed, together with the lancinating pain in the
eye and temple; but the hypopion continued
ftationary. Nothing more was now prefcribed
to the patient than food of eafy digeftion, and
the application of bags of mallows upon the
eye, to be renewed as often as they became cold.
By this fimple treatment the matter of the hypopion,

pion, which filled the greater part of the anterior chamber of the aqueous humour, began to
be diffolved and abforbed; and in the courfe of
18 days, reckoning from the time of the ceffation of the inflammatory ftage of the ophthalmia, the pupil was clear.

Some of the tenacious matter yet remained
at the bottom of the anterior chamber, and fome
rednefs of the conjunctiva, produced by the
ophthalmia, from relaxation. I ordered a few
grains of camphire to be added to the bags of
mallows, which evidently contributed to accelerate the abforption, and in the fpace of 13 days,
to clear the white of the eye. When the hypopion was entirely diffipated, the patient ufed
with advantage a collyrium, compofed of the
acetated cerufe diffolved in plantain water, with
the addition of the mucilage of quince-feed, in
order to conftringe and ftrengthen ftill more the
conjunctiva and its veffels.

CASE XLIII.

A robuft country-woman, 20 years of age,
was ftruck upon the right eye with a piece of
wood; a violent inflammation enfued, and afterwards an hypopion, which occupied about
one half of the anterior chamber of the aqueous
humour. There was alfo on the external and
lower fide of the cornea, and apparently in the
part

part where she had been struck, a small ash-coloured and deep ulcer, of the circumference of a millet-seed, and the conjunctiva appeared excessively red and tumefied. The patient was admitted into this hospital the 5th day after the accident.

I ordered blood to be taken abundantly from the arm and foot, her bowels to be purged with small dôses of the cryftals of tartar, and the tartarized antimony, and a poultice of bread and milk, with saffron applied upon the eyelids.

On the 4th day from the patient's admission into the hospital, the inflammatory stage of the ophthalmia might be considered as having ceased, except that there was a slight pricking in the eye.

On the 6th day I found the patient more than usually tranquil. When the bag of gauze containing the poultice was raised, and the eye opened, I found the hypopion greatly diminished, and observed a small drop of the same tenacious matter ready to issue from the small ulcer upon the cornea, which, as I have remarked, had not been formed from within outwards, but from without inwards. I avoided every kind of preffure upon the eye-ball, which might contribute to the too speedy evacuation of that humour, lest the iris should follow it. I continued to foment the eye with bags of emollient herbs until the whole of the matter of the hypopion

was

was infenfibly evacuated by this opening; which
was completed in feven days. I now touched
the ulcer with the argentum nitratum, fo as to
produce a deep and firm efchar. The acute
pain which the patient felt, and the fudden increafe of the rednefs of the conjunctiva, led me
to fear a return of the inflammation ; but by
repeated ablutions with warm milk, and emollient applications, together with an opiate emulfion at night, fhe became perfectly eafy. The
efchar continued to adhere for four days. On
its exfoliation, I touched the ulcer again with
the argentum nitratum, and the fymptoms were
much lefs fevere than the firft time. On the
feparation of the fecond efchar the bottom of
the fmall ulcer was filled with granulations, and
had a tendency to heal. The vitriolic collyrium,
with mucilage, employed for two weeks longer,
was fufficient to complete the cure.*

CASE

---

* I might have extracted from my journal, a very extenfive feries of cafes, fimilar to the three preceding, had I believed that a great number of hiftories, nearly fimilar to each
other, could have afforded a clearer elucidation of the method
of treatment which I have recommended. I fhall only obferve that the hypopion in the firft ftage of the violent *acute*
ophthalmia is rarely met with in the hofpitals, as it is cuf-
tomary, particularly among the country people, to be copioufly
and repeatedly bled in inflammations of the eyes, and to employ diligently emollient cataplafms, with the hope of getting
rid of the difeafe by thefe means, as it frequently happens. But
in the cafe of hypopion, after the violence of the inflamma-

Case XLIV.

Mauro Spagnoli, a peafant, 60 years of age, was received into this practical fchool of furgery, the 20th of March 1793, who had one half of the anterior chamber of the aqueous humour of the left eye occupied by a collection of glutinous matter, which, according to his account, took place three weeks after a violent inflammation of that eye, which was removed by bleeding and emollient applications. He did not complain of any remarkable pain in the affected eye, and could bear a moderate degree of light without repugnance. The conjunctiva was red from the relaxation of its veffels.

The great age of the patient, the fmall degree of fenfibility of the eye, and the flow and almoft imperceptible diminution of the hypopion, fufficiently indicated the neceffity in this cafe of exciting the action of the abforbent fyftem, and ftrengthening the veffels of the conjunctiva, in order to diffipate the collection of tenacious lymph poured into the anterior chamber of the aqueous humour. Inftead of employing, there-

tion has ceafed, they find an extraneous matter poured into the anterior chamber of the aqueous humour, which obftructs the vifion; and it is at this period, although the difeafe does not caufe confiderable pain, that they come into the hofpital, efpecially if they are advanced in age.

fore,

fore, the antiphlogiftic method of treatment, and the emollient applications, as in the preceding cafes, I ordered the patient a nourifhing diet, proportioned to the ftrength of his ftomach, and the decoction of cinchona to be taken three times a day in dofes of three ounces. I directed the vitriolic collyrium, with the mucilage of quince-feed, to be inftilled into the eye every two hours, and a blifter to be applied to the neck. In eight days the hypopion was reduced to one half, and the conjunctiva had loft the dark red colour which it had at the commencement. The action of the collyrium was increafed by adding a little camphorated fpirit of wine to it; and in ten days more the hypopion difappeared altogether, as well as the chronic ophthalmia from relaxation.

CASE XLV.

Giovanni Nuvola, a peafant, 45 years of age, a weak fickly man, labouring in the rice-field, was ftruck upon the right eye with an ear of rice, with fuch violence that his eye became inflamed the fame day, attended with the moft acute pain; and, in a few days after, a third part of the anterior chamber of the aqueous humour was filled with a tenacious yellowifh lymph. The furgeon under whofe care he was, bled him abundantly, purged him, and ordered the eye

to

to be affiduoufly fomented with an infufion of
elder flowers and leaves of mallows.

On the 7th day, the inflammatory ftage of
the ophthalmia ceafed, and the hypopion became ftationary. The patient no longer felt
any confiderable uneafinefs in the eye, and therefore kept it only defended frôm the air and light
by means of a piece of linen fufpended from his
forehead. He now left the houfe, and attempted to purfue his labour in the fields; but
finding that, two weeks after the inflammation
had fubfided, the fight remained obftructed by
this yellowifh matter, he came to the hofpital.
The conjunctiva was affected with ophthalmia
from relaxation, and the cornea, befides the
opacity depending on the matter of the hypopion, was, in two points, flightly excoriated, as
if the epidermis had been removed.

On account of the patient's general and local
debility, I ordered him to take the cinchona,
and to obferve a nourifhing and ftrengthening
diet, and to ufe the vitriolic collyrium externally every two hours, which he could
not bear unlefs warmed. In a few days the
veffels of the conjunctiva recovered their former
vigour and the chronic ophthalmia difappeared.
The hypopion alfo gradually diminifhed, and in
fifteen days, the cornea having recovered its natural ftate of tranfparency, the patient ufed the
ophthalmic ointment of Janin for a few times
only

only at night, and then left the hofpital perfectly cured.

Case XLVI.

Filippo Saletta, 'a miller, of Calignano, 56
years of age, was received into the practical
fchool of furgery, on the 26th of December
1794, on account of an hypopion which occupied two thirds of the anterior chamber of the
aqueous humour of the right eye. The blood-
veffels of the conjunctiva were very much dilated and varicofe, the eye-lids gummed, and
there were fuperficial excoriations in fome points
of the cornea. He did not, however, complain
of much pain in the eye, and expofed himfelf
freely to the light. He related that at the
commencement of the difeafe, which had continued for a month, he had found relief from
being bled; but that afterwards, notwithftanding the application of warm, fomentations of
mallow-water, the difeafe had remained nearly
in the fame ftate as a few days after the bleeding.

I directed the patient in this cafe, as in a great
variety of others fimilar to it, to take two drams
of the cinchona three times a day, and to obferve a ftrengthening animal diet. Externally,
I ordered the vitriolic collyrium, compofed of five
grains of the vitriolated zinc, four ounces of
plaintain

plantain water and half an ounce of the mucilage of quince-feed, to be dropped into the eye
every two hours. And as the eye appeared very
little fenfible to the ftimulant and aftringent action of this remedy a fmall quantity of camphorated fpirit of wine was added to it. In 18 days,
the hypopion, as well as the chronic ophthalmia, from relaxation, difappeared. In order to
ftrengthen the part, and correct the morbid
fecretion of gum, the ophthalmic ointment of
Janin * was afterwards introduced morning and
evening, between the eye-lids of the affected
eye, and continued for 12 days.

* With regard to this remedy, I ought again to caution
the young furgeon not to ufe it at firft except with a larger
quantity of lard than is directed in the formula ; otherwife it
generally occafions too much irritation, and inftead of being
ufeful is injurious.

CHAP.

CHAP. XIV.

OF THE PROCIDENTIA IRIDIS.

THE *iris* preferves its natural pofition, and is kept at a proper diftance from the cornea, as long as the humours which fill the cavity of the eye, in which that body is immerfed and fufpended, remain in perfect equilibrium with each other, during which the *iris*, although of the moft delicate and diftenfile texture, contracts or relaxes itfelf without forming any unnatural fold. But if, after the effufion of the aqueous humour, in confequence of any accidental or artificial opening in the cornea, the preffure made by the humours of the eye behind the *iris*, is not balanced by the fluid contained in the anterior chamber, the *iris* is neceffarily pufhed forwards by little and little towards the cornea, and is in part gradually forced out of the eye, through the fame opening by which the aqueous humour was evacuated. Hence, under fuch circumftances, a fmall tumour is formed upon the cornea, of the peculiar colour of the *iris*, which, by the greater part of furgeons,

geons, is termed *ftaphyloma* of the iris, but
which I have thought proper to call with Galen * *Procidentia Iridis,* in order to diftinguifh it
from another difeafe to which the word *ftaphyloma* 'more particularly applies.

The *procidentia iridis* is occafioned by wounds
and ulcers of the cornea, penetrating for fome
extent into the anterior chamber of the aqueous
humour, and alfo by violent contufions of the
eye-ball with rupture of the cornea. If, immediately after an accidental or artificial wound
of the cornea, as that which is made in the extraction of the cataract, or for the purpofe of
evacuating the matter of the hypopion, as is
practifed by fome, the lips of the wound do not
immediately return into mutual contact, and
are not maintained in fufficient union to prevent the aqueous humour in proportion as it is
renewed from flowing out of the anterior chamber; the iris being drawn along by the current
of the aqueous humour, which is inceffantly di-

* De differentiis morborum, clafs III. cap. 13. Contin-
git vero nonnunquam, ut tunica cornea appellata profundum
habeat ulcus, qua deinceps exifa tota, aliquid ex ea tunica
procidat, quæ fecunda poft corneam ordine lita eft, uvea appellata, et ipfa pupillæ una divulfionem patiatur. Atque ex hif-
tribus quælibet paffio oculi exiftimatur: quodvis ulcus et
erofio ad folam corneam pertinet, *procidentia* ad uveam, et di-
vulfio ad pupillam.
Et tunica uvea, ut plurimum, relaxatur, cum corneam nimium erodi contigerit. De cauff. morbor. clafs III. cap. 10.

rected

rected towards the wound of the cornea, infinuates itfelf between the lips of the wound,
elongates, and by degrees a portion of it is protruded, and projects upon the cornea in the form
of a fmall tumour. The fame thing takes place
when there is a recent wound of the cornea,
and the eye-ball is unfortunately ftruck, or too
much compreffed by the bandage ; or the patient is feized with a fpafm of the mufcles of
the eye, with exceffive and repeated vomiting,
or with violent and frequent fits of coughing.
This difeafe is ftill more frequently the confequence of ulcers penetrating into the anterior
chamber of the aqueous humour, than of wounds
of the cornea, inafmuch as the folution of continuity of the cornea, in confequence of ulceration, is accompanied with lofs of fubftance, and
the lips of the ulcer do not admit of being
placed in mutual contact, in a membrane fo
tenfe and compact as the cornea. The fmall
tumour is neceffarily of the colour of the iris,
that is, brown or grey, and is furrounded at its
bafe by a fmall opake circle * of the cornea,
which is ulcerated, or has been for fome time
divided.

As the cornea is in general only perforated in
one part of its circumference, whether in confequence of wound or ulcer, fo moft frequently

* Plate II. fig. 6.

there

there is only one *procidentia* of the iris met
with in the fame eye. But if it happen that
the cornea has been wounded or eroded
in feveral diftinct places, more protrufions of
the iris take place in confequence of them in
the fame eye, and there are as many fmall tumours projecting upon the furface of the cornea
as there are apertures. I have feen a cafe in
which there were three diftinct *procidentiæ* of
the iris upon the fame cornea, in confequence
of three feparate ulcers penetrating into the anterior chamber of the aqueous humour, one of
thefe being fituated in the upper, and two in the
lower fegment of the cornea.

If we confider for a moment the delicate
ftructure of this membrane, the great number
of blood veffels with which it is fupplied, the
numerous filaments of nerves which are directed
towards it, as to a common centre, and diftributed upon it, it is eafy to conclude how violent the fymptoms which ufually accompany
this difeafe muft be, although the portion of
the iris projecting out of the cornea be fmall,
and not larger than the head of a fly. The
harfh and repeated friction to which this delicate membrane is expofed, from the motion of
the eye-lids, from the accefs of the air, of tears,
and of matter, are fufficient caufes of continual
and inevitable irritation. Added to this, that
the fmall portion of the iris, which is protruded,

Y 3 in

in confequence of the increafed afflux of blood towards the part moft irritated, acquires fhortly after its appearance a larger fize than at the time when it was forced out of the cornea; on which account it is more compreffed and irritated a little after its appearance out of the cornea, than before. In the commencement of this difeafe the patient complains of a pain, as if a thorn were fixed in the eye; this is afterwards accompanied with an uneafy fenfe of tightnefs or conftriction of the eye-ball, which is fucceeded by an inflammation of the conjunctiva and eye-lids, a difcharge of fcalding tears, and a complete averfion to the light. And as the protruded fold of the *iris* draws the reft of the fame membrane towards that part, the pupil, from mechanical neceffity, affumes an oval figure,* and is removed from the centre of the iris towards the feat of the protrufion. The intenfity of the pain, inflammation, and other fymptoms which accompany the *procidentia iridis*, do not, however, always continue to increafe; for cafes are very frequently met with in practice of long ftanding, in which the difeafe having been left to itfelf, the pain and inflammation have fpontaneoufly ceafed, and the fmall tumour formed by the iris has become almoft entirely infenfible. I lately

* Plate II. fig. 6.

faw

faw a man, 50 years of age, who had a procidentia of the iris, during 10 weeks, in the
right eye, of twice the fize of a millet-feed,
which he bore with the greateft indifference,
and without any other inconvenience, than a
little chronic rednefs of the conjunctiva, and
difficulty of moving the eye-ball freely, in confequence of the friction which the lower eye-lid
made againft the projecting portion of the iris.
When the little tumour was touched with the
point of the finger it felt hard and almoft callous. This circumftance arifes partly from the
conftriction, which, after fome time, the lips of
the wound, or ulcer, make around the bafe of
the protruded portion of the iris, in confequence of which it is deprived of its natural
exquifite fenfibility; and partly in confequence
of this tender membrane lofing its vitality, from
the induration and callofity induced upon it,
by its long expofure to the air, and tears.

With refpect to the treatment of this difeafe
in its commencement, fome recommend that
the iris fhould be pufhed back into its fituation
by means of a whalebone probe, and if there
fhould be any difficulty in this, that even the
wound or ulcer of the cornea fhould be dilated,
by making an incifion of a fufficient length, in
the fame manner as in the reduction of the
ftrangulated inteftinal hernia. Others advife,
that the portion of the iris projecting from the

eye

eye fhould be merely irritated, in order that it may contract and retire; or that the affected eye fhould be fuddenly expofed to a very vivid light, from a hope, that by the forcible contraction of the pupil, the fold of the iris confined between the lips of the wound, or ulcer of the cornea, may return to its pofition. Experience, however, has clearly proved, that all thefe methods are abfolutely ufelefs, if not dangerous. For, fuppofing it were poffible, by any of thefe methods, to replace the iris in its fituation, without tearing or injuring it in any manner, as a paffage would always remain open for the aqueous humour through the wound, or ulcer of the cornea, as at firft, the iris, when replaced, would defcend immediately afterwards, and protrude through the cornea, as it did previoufly to the operation.

It cannot be denied that the *procidentia iridis* is a ferious accident. But whoever confiders that we are not at prefent in poffeffion of any means capable of inftantly fuppreffing, or even of fufpending, the difcharge of the aqueous humour through the wound, and much lefs through an ulcer of the cornea, when either of thefe exceed certain limits, will find that in circumftances fo unfavourable, the *procidentia* of the iris, inftead of being a difeafe is rather a fortunate occurrence, and perhaps the only one which can prevent the complete deftruction of the

the organ of vifion. For the fold of the iris, by
infinuating itfelf in the form of a plug, between
the lips of the wound, or ulcer of the cornea,
puts a ftop to the complete evacuation of the
aqueous humour, which by being fpeedily collected anew in the anterior chamber, and no
longer able to flow through the cornea, prevents the further protrufion of the iris, feparates
the reft of this membrane from the cornea, and
by reftoring the equilibrium between it and the
other humours of the eye, prevents the total
deftruction of that organ. This being evident,
it muft be obvious, that any of thofe methods
hitherto propofed for pufhing back the procidentia iridis, can only be, as I have faid, ufelefs or dangerous.

Confiftently with thefe principles, there are
two principal indications which the furgeon
ought to fulfil in the treatment of the *procidentia iridis*, when it is recent ; the one, is that of
allaying the highly exquifite fenfibility of the
portion of the iris, which projects out of the
cornea ; the other, of gradually deftroying it to
fuch a depth on this fide the cornea, that
without taking away the adhefion which
it has contracted with the bottom of the
wound, on the fide next the anterior chamber
of the aqueous humour, it may not keep
the external lips of the wound, or ulcer of
the

the cornea, immoderately separated, and thereby prevent their healing.

Nothing answers thefe two indications better, than touching the portion of the iris, projecting out of the cornea, with the antimonium muriatum, or, what is more commodious and expeditious, with the argentum nitratum, fo as to produce an efchar of fufficient depth. And, in order that this may be executed promptly, and with exactnefs, it is neceffary that an affiftant placed behind the patient's head, fhould keep the upper eye-lid fufpended by means of the elevator of Pellier; and the patient, if he has attained the age of reafon, fhould hold the eye-ball fteady, by fixing it attentively upon one object. While the affiftant gently raifes the upper eye-lid, the furgeon fhould deprefs the lower with the fore and middle finger of his left hand, and with his right expeditioufly touch the fmall tumour formed by the iris, with the argentum nitratum, cut in the form of a *crayon*, and prefs it upon the centre of the protruded portion, fo as to produce an efchar of a proper depth. The pain which the patient feels at the moment is very acute; but by immediately wafhing the eye with warm milk, it quickly ceafes. The cauftic fpeedily deftroys the fenfibility of the protruded portion of iris, and by producing a fufficiently deep efchar, defends it from the

7   friction

friction of the eye-lids, and the contact of the
air and tears. And it is precifely on this account, that after the cauterization, the fenfe of
pricking and conftriction of the eye, of which
patients fo much complain, is not only relieved,
but the inflammation alfo is confiderably diminifhed, and at the fame time the copious difcharge of fcalding tears.

Thefe advantages, as in the cafe of ulceration
of the cornea, continue precifely as long as the
efchar adheres to the fmall tumour formed by
the iris. On its exfoliation, which fometimes
takes place on the fecond, fometimes on the
third day from the cauterization, all the fymptoms above enumerated return; with this difference, that they are lefs intenfe and acute
than before, and the fmall tumour of the iris is
lefs elevated upon the cornea, than it was before
the application of the cauftic. On the reappearance of thefe fymptoms, the furgeon fhould
again have recourfe to the argentum nitratum,
with the cautions already delivered, and he
fhould repeat it a third or fourth time if neceffary, that is, until the protruded portion of the
iris be fufficiently depreffed below the level of
the external lips of the wound, or ulcer of the
cornea, fo as to be no longer an obftacle to their
granulation and cicatrization.

It may be advantageous to repeat here what
has been faid on the treatment of deep ulcers of
the

the cornea. There is, as it has been remarked, when treating on ulcers of the cornea, a certain point beyond which the application of the cauftic, at firft highly ufeful, becomes exceedingly injurious, and the efchar which before allayed the pain afterwards aggravates it, and caufes the inflammation to return, with nearly the fame violence as at the commencement of the difeafe. This takes place, according to my obfervation, whenever the furgeon continues to apply the cauftic, after the fmall tumour formed by the iris has been deftroyed, below the level of the external lips of the wound, or ulcer of the cornea, and the cauftic tends to deftroy the granulation which has already commenced. In the treatment of this difeafe, therefore, as foon as the furgeon perceives that the projecting portion of the iris is fufficiently depreffed, and that the application of the cauftic, inftead of relieving aggravates the difeafe, he fhould entirely defift from the ufe of it, and merely introduce between the eye-lids, every two hours, the vitriolic collyrium with mucilage of quince-feed, or that compofed of the vitriolated zinc, and the white of an egg; and afterwards he fhould alfo employ the ophthalmic ointment of Janin, morning and evening, lowered by a double or triple quantity of lard. If the ftimulus produced by thefe applications does not difturb the procefs of nature,

6

the

the ulcer will be conftantly found to contract
itfelf by little and little, and in the courfe of
two weeks to be completely cicatrized.

The adhefion which the protruded portion of
the iris contracts during the treatment, with the
internal lips of the wound, or ulcer of the cornea, continues the fame after the formation of
the external cicatrix, and confequently during
the reft of the patient's life. The pupil, therefore, even after the moft fuccefsful treatment of
the *procidentia iridis*, is found a little inclined
towards the cicatrix of the cornea, and of an
oval figure. This change of the fituation and
figure of the pupil, however, diminifhes very
little, if at all, the power of diftinguifhing, even
the moft minute objects, and injures the vifion
much lefs than might naturally be expected;
provided the cicatrix of the cornea is not too
extenfive, and fituated precifely oppofite the
centre of the cornea. And, in the firft cafe,
the vifion is ftill lefs impeded by it, as the pupil,
which, at the commencement of the difeafe, was
narrow and oblong, and very much drawn towards the wound or ulcer, gradually enlarges
after the formation of the cicatrix, and in the
courfe of time, forms an oval lefs compreffed,*
and in fome meafure tends to occupy the fituation which it formerly had towards the centre of

* Plate II. fig. 7.

the

the *iris.* This fact has been also remarked by Richter.*

The method of treating the *procidentia iridis,* here recommended, is that which I have found more certain and useful than any other which has been yet propofed, not excluding that of removing the fmall tumour formed by the *iris* beyond the furface of the cornea, by a ftroke of the fciffars.

If the perfect fuccefs of this excifion correfponded in all cafes to what fome have promifed, nothing would unqueftionably contribute more to the fpeedinefs of the cure of the procidentia of the iris, than fuch an operation. But I am convinced, from experience, that this operation can only be executed with the hope of perfect fuccefs, in that individual cafe, in which the iris has contracted a ftrong adhefion to the internal lips of the wound, or ulcer of the cornea; and more particularly in that procidentia of the iris of long ftanding, in which the protruded portion has become in time almoft infenfible, hard, and callous, and where its bafe being ftrangulated between the lips of the wound,

* Obferv. chirurg. fafcicul. I. page 80. Omni tamen plerumque hoc vitium periculo, vel damno caret, partim cum raro vifui obfit, partim quia fponte plerumque priftinam fuam figuram pupillæ iuduit, citius quidem aliquando, interdum vero tardius. Minor pupilla fenfim latior fit, oblonga fit rotunda, deorfum tracta fenfim ad priftinum locum afcendit; atque hæc omnia fponte plerumque fiunt.

or

or ulcer of the cornea, has not only contracted
an adhesion with them, but has also assumed
the form of a fine peduncle.* Under these circumstances the excision of the inveterate procidentia of the iris is useful, and exempt from all
danger, since the prominent portion of it, which
has now formed an adhesion internally to the
ulcerated edges of the cornea, being removed
by a stroke of the sciffars, on a level with the
external lips of the ulcer, there is no risk of re-
newing the effusion of the aqueous humour,
or of giving room to the protrusion of any other
portion of the iris; and one or two applications
of the caustic afterwards are sufficient to excite
the process of granulation, and heal the ulcer of
the cornea. But this is not the case in the recent procidentia iridis, which has not yet contracted an adhesion to the internal lips of the
wound, or ulcer of the cornea. In four subjects
affected with recent procidentia iridis, after having extirpated the protruded portion of the iris,
of the size of the head of a fly, with the curved
sciffars, although I touched the divided part, as
well as the lips of the ulcer of the cornea, immediately afterwards, with the argentum nitratum, I found the next day, not without regret,
that another portion of the iris, of the same size

* I have seen a case, in which the small tumour of the iris,
from being long compressed between the edges of the ulcer of
the cornea, ultimately fell off spontaneously.

as

as the firft, had made its way through the ulcer of the cornea, and that the pupil, which was exceedingly contracted in it, approached ftill nearer the ulcer of the cornea. I had, therefore, reafon to fear that if I had perfifted in removing the fmall tumour a fecond time, it would have appeared again, and always with a greater protrufion of the iris, and ulterior ftretching of the pupil ; I therefore contented myfelf after the firft experiment, with treating the difeafe by the cauftic, in the manner before recommended; which was attended, in all the four cafes now mentioned, with fuccefs, except that the pupil having been too much drawn towards the ulcer of the cornea, remained covered more than ufual by the cicatrix.

Before I finifh this chapter, I fhall take an opportunity of directing the attention of furgeons to a particular fpecies of procidentia, much lefs frequent indeed than that of the iris, but which, however, is occafionally met with in practice, to which modern oculifts have improperly, in my opinion, given the name of the *procidentia of the tunic of the aqueous humour.**

This difeafe confifts in a fmall pellucid veficle, full of water, formed by a very fine membrane, which protrudes from the wound, or

* Chute de la tunique de l'humeur aqueufe. See Janin, Pellier, Guerin, Gleize, &c. &c.

ulcer

ulcer of the cornea, nearly in the fame manner'
as the iris does under fimilar circumftances. I
have frequently feen this fmall veficle, full of
water, projecting out of the cornea a little
after the extraction of the cataract, and fometimes alfo in cafes of ulcer of the cornea,
particularly after the excifion of the prolapfed
iris.

Oculifts are, for the moft part, of opinion, that
this fmall pellucid tumour is formed by that
fubtle, elaftic, tranfparent membrane, which
invefts the cornea internally, and which has
been defcribed by Defcemet and Demours. As
foon, fay they, as the divifion or erofion of the
cornea has expofed the thin membrane which
lines its internal furface, as this pellicle is
unable to refift the impulfe of the humours
which prefs upon it from behind forwards,
it muft of neceffity infenfibly yield, elongate,
and ultimately project out of the wound, or
ulcer of the cornea, precifely in the form of a
fmall pellucid veficle. But how remote this opinion is from the truth, muft appear to any one
who will for a moment reflect upon the following
circumftances. In the 1ft place, the fine and
elaftic pellicle, defcribed by Defcemet and Demours, cannot be feparated by any artificial
means from the internal furface of the cornea,
except near the part where the fclerotica and
cornea unite, and as *veficular procidentiæ* are met

z with

with in every part of the cornea, and in the very
centre of it, where this pellicle is not feparable
and diftinct from the compact texture of the
cornea; it muft at leaft be admitted, that the
tunic of the aqueous humour is not always that
which conftitutes the difeafe here fpoken of.
2dly. It is an admitted fact, that this *veficular procidentia* more frequently happens after
the extraction of the cataract, than on any
other occafion; in which cafe, as the tunic
of the aqueous humour muft certainly have
been divided, to allow of the paffage of the
cryftalline humour, no one can be of opinion
that the pellucid veficle which projects from the
cornea, after this operation, ought to be referred
to the diftenfion or protrufion of the tunic of
the aqueous humour.   3dly. If, in cafes of ulcer
of the cornea, the fmall pellucid veficle fometimes appears after the excifion of the prolapfed
iris, it is clear, that if it were formed by
the tunic of the aqueous humour, it ought conftantly to appear before that difeafe.   4thly. If
the furgeon remove this *veficular* body, by
a ftroke of the fciffars, on a level with the cornea, a fmall quantity of limpid fluid is obferved
to fpirt out in the act of dividing it, without
the aqueous humour of the anterior chamber
being evacuated; which inconvenience would
be inevitable, if this *veficle* were formed
by the fine elaftic pellicle which is faid to
invest

inveft the cornea internally. Befides, although the fmall pellucid tumour be taken away by ex-cifion, yet it very frequently happens, that the next day another tumour, exactly fimilar to that which has been removed, is found in the fame place. Now if this fmall tumour were formed by the tunic of the aqueous humour, protruding through the wound or ulcer, it could not be reproduced, as it is, at leaft in the fame part of the cornea. Thefe confiderations have fatisfied me that what has been commonly ima-gined to be a *procidentia of the tunic of the aqueous humour,* is in reality nothing more than the pro-trufion of a portion of the vitreous humour, which, after the extraction of the cataract, either from the too violent compreffion made upon the eye-ball, during or after the operation, or from the fpafmodic action of the mufcles, infinuates itfelf between the lips of the wound of the cornea, and appears externally, in the form now defcribed.

The fame thing happens likewife in cafes of ulcer of the cornea, when the aqueous humour being evacuated, a powerful compreffion has forced a portion of the vitreous humour towards the ulcer fituated oppofite the pupil ; or when the prolapfed portion of the iris being extir-pated, an elongation of the vitreous humour has directly infinuated itfelf between the edges of the ulcer of the cornea, without paffing through

z 2 the

the pupil. Hence it is evident why the small
pellucid vesicle is formed in both cases, although
the tunic of the aqueous humour has been divided or destroyed by the ulcer, and why this
vesicle, even after it has been removed on
a level with the cornea, very frequently re-
appears in the same place; it is because one or
more cells of the vitreous humour forming it
being removed, other cells of the same humour
filled with limpid fluid enter in succession
between the lips of the wound, or ulcer of the
cornea, in the place of the first.

The treatment of this species of *procidentia*
consists in removing by excision the small pellucid vesicle which emerges from the wound or
ulcer, and in replacing the lips of the wound of
the cornea in perfect contact immediately afterwards, in order that they may unite as exactly
as possible. In cases of ulcer of the cornea,
however, immediately after the removal of the
vesicle, the ulcer ought to be touched with the
argentum nitratum; and in such a manner that
the eschar produced by the caustic, may resist a
fresh escape of the vitreous humour, and the
ulcer of the cornea at the same time be dis-
posed to granulate and heal.

In this species of *procidentia*, that which projects out of the cornea is only a fine membrane
filled with water, and entirely destitute of 'sensibility, the separation of which from the parts
contained

contained in the eye is of very little importance;
while on the contrary, by its prefence, it produces all the difadvantages of any extraneous
body which might oppofe the union of a wound,
or the granulation and healing of an ulcer.
The divifion of this *veficular* body, therefore, is clearly indicated, and experience con-
firms the fuccefs of it. It is in general fpeedily
removed by a ftroke of the curved fciflars.
But if in any particular cafe the fmall tumour fhould not project fufficiently out of the
wound or ulcer to be included by the fcifffars,
the intention may be obtained by pricking it
with the point of a lancet or cataract needle;
for the limpid fluid which it contains being difcharged, the membrane of which it is formed
retires within the lips of the wound, or ulcer of
the cornea, and is no longer an obftacle to the
approximation of the former, or the cauterization of the latter.

If it fhould happen that the day after the excifion or puncture, the fmall pellucid tumour
fhould reappear in the fame part as before, it
will be neceffary to repeat the operation, and to
take further meafures to keep the wound of the
cornea in contact; or if there be an ulcer, to
make the efchar adhere more firmly to the
bottom and fides of it, and prefent a more
powerful barrier than before to the efcape of
the vitreous humour. In fuch cafes, therefore,

z 3 the

the furgeon fhould guard againft every thing
with the greateft poffible care, which might
prefs the vitreous humour towards the wound,
or ulcer of the cornea, and particularly the too
violent compreffion of the eye-lids, fpafm of
the mufcles of the eye, cough, fneezing, cof-
tivenefs, and other fimilar caufes, at the fame
time taking care to prevent the progrefs of the
inflammation.

Upon the treatment of this fpecies of pellucid
vefcicular procidentia, the two cafes of Pellier *
deferve to be read, to which, if further proofs
were neceffary, I might add feveral others fimilar to them, which I have met with in confequence of ulcer of the cornea, penetrating
into the anterior chamber of the aqueous humour ; the fuccefs of which has been as complete as in the two cafes defcribed by the French
oculift.

Laftly, the procidentia is a difeafe from which
the choroid coat is not wholly exempted ; I
have feen and treated this accident, in the perfon of Signor Giovanni Breffanini, an apothecary of Befcapè. In confequence of a violent
acute internal and external ophthalmia, which
was treated at the beginning with repellents, a
fmall abfcefs formed between the fclerotic and
choroid coats, at the diftance of two lines from
the junction of the cornea with the fclerotica,

* Obferv. fur l'œil, p. 350. obferv. 99, 100.

on

on the inferior hemifphere of the eye-ball. The fmall abfcefs burft, and difcharged a little denfe and tenacious lymph; a fmall blackifh body afterwards protruded from this ulcer of the fclerotica, which was formed by the choroid coat. The treatment confifted in repeatedly touching this prominent portion of the choroid with the argentum nitratum, until it was deftroyed, and reduced to a level with the bottom of the ulcer of the fclerotic coat; after which the ulcer healed. This eye remained, however, very weak, and the pupil afterwards contracted, fo as to be almoft entirely clofed.

Case XLVII.

Angiola Maria Porta, a robuft country woman, 30 years of age, after having been afflicted with a wandering gout, was attacked with a violent acute ophthalmia in the right eye, which occafioned the formation of an hypopion, and afterwards an ulcer of the cornea, with a *procidentia iridis*, of the fize of a fly's head, accompanied with very acute pain in the eye, and a difcharge of fcalding tears.

The patient was admitted into the hofpital on the 25th of May 1795. The fmall ulcer was immediately cauterized with the argentum nitratum, and in a few minutes the woman found her pain greatly relieved. As the

z 4 efchar

efchar did not adhere to the fmall tumour longer than 24 hours, I continued to apply the cauftic to it every day until the 8th of June; that is, until the protruded portion of the iris was de-ftroyed beyond the external lips of the ulcer of the cornea. Afterwards, I employed the oph-thalmic ointment of Janin for the fpace of 15 days, in which time the fmall ulcer was per-fectly healed.

Case XLVIII.

Giufeppe Borghi, of Pavia, a boy 9 years old, was brought into the practical fchool on the 22d of January 1796, on account of a *procidentia* of the iris, of the fize of a fmall lentil feed, which had formed itfelf through an ulcer fituated on the lateral and external part of the cornea of the right eye, accompanied with chronic ophthal-mia, edematofe fwelling of the eye-lids of that fide, and excoriation of the tarfi; to all which evils the poor child had been long abandoned by the exceffive negligence of his parents. Although he could not bear the light with the right eye; he gave no figns of pain when the fmall tumour, formed by the iris, was touched with the point of a probe, in confequence of this protruded portion being in fome meafure callous.

The

The fmall tumour was touched every day, for a week, with the argentum nitratum; as the efchar produced upon it did not adhere longer than 24 hours. At the end of this time the *procidentia* of the iris was deftroyed as far as the bottom of the ulcer of the cornea. On account of the tumefaction and afflux to the eye-lids, I applied, in the mean time, a feton in the neck, and purged him frequently with the tincture of rhubarb. In order to accelerate the healing of the ulcer of the cornea, after the protuberant portion of the iris was deftroyed, as well as the excoriations of the tarfi, I employed, locally, the ophthalmic ointment of Janin, morning and evening, and during the day the vitriolic colly-rium with mucilage. In 26 days the boy was perfectly cured, as he could diftinguifh with this eye the moft minute objects; the pupil, however, preferved an oval figure.

Case XLIX.

A. Catterina Cartofi, an inhabitant of Va-leggio, aged 21 years, a weak and thin woman, in attempting on the 20th of March 1797 to break a piece of wood, by bending it againft her knee, a fplinter ftruck the left eye, which di-vided the lateral and external part of the cornea perpendicularly. The iris fituated behind paffed through this fiffure, and appeared externally in

the

the form of a blackifh line, projecting upon the cornea in the direction from above downwards. The eye inflamed greatly, and it was not till the 8th day from the accident that fhe was brought to the hofpital, after having been bled. The acute pain in the eye continuing, I directed a bread and milk poultice to be applied, which gave her relief. I afterwards proceeded to touch this prominent line, formed by the iris, with the argentum nitratum. The efchar feparated a few hours afterwards, and the pain in the eye therefore returned as acutely as before, on which account I was under the neceflity of giving the patient at night an opiate draught. I repeated the application of the cauftic for three fucceffive days; which was fufficient to deftroy the blackifh line, formed by the iris, projecting upon the cornea. The ophthalmic ointment of Janin was afterwards ufed morning and evening, reduced by a double quantity of lard; by the action of which remedy the ulcer of the cornea contracted and healed, in the direction from the upper to the lower part of the fiffure. The lower extremity of the wound, however, remained ftationary, on account of the fmall portion of the iris correfponding to that part, not being deftroyed to a fufficient depth below the external lips of the ulcer of the cornea. I therefore touched this part with the cauftic twice in the fpace of three days; and afterwards

applied

applied the ophthalmic ointment, by which it was completely healed. As the perpendicular spot remaining upon the cornea, in confequence of the cicatrix, was fituated on one fide of the pupil, and as the latter being drawn towards the cicatrix, allowed a fufficient opening for the paffage of the light, it did not prevent the woman from recovering the fight of the eye.

Case L.

Signor Mauro R.. of Pavía, 40 years of age, a thin man, in the month of Auguft 1795, accidentally received a ftroke with the lafh of a whip in the external angle of the left eye, precifely at the junction of the cornea with the fclerotica. The violent contufion occafioned a fmall tumour in this part, with inflammation of the whole eye, which tumour fhortly afterwards burft, and allowed a quantity of the aqueous humour to pafs out, and after it a fmall portion of the iris, of the fize of two millet feeds put together. The relaxation of the conjunctiva near to it, and the turgefcency of its veffels formed an elevation in the external angle of the eye, which, in the form of a valve, covered a part of the *procidentia iridis.* It was particularly worthy of remark, that, although the pupil was of an oblong figure, as in all other
fimilar

fimilar cafes, it appeared more dilated than that of the found eye.

Two weeks had paffed from the time of the formation of the *procidentia iridis*, before the patient confulted me. He did not at this time complain of much pain in the eye, and not-withftanding the difeafe, frequently went out of the houfe to attend to his affairs.

I ordered that the projecting portion of the iris fhould be touched with the argentum nitra-tum; which was repeatedly executed, until the whole of it difappeared, and the ulcer was difpofed to heal; which was accomplifh-ed in 18 days. The vitriolic collyrium, em-ployed for two weeks more, completed the cure, by perfectly healing the ulcer of the cor-nea, and reftoring to the veffels of the conjunc-tiva their former vigour. The pupil remained, as ufual, of an oval figure, but from a fingu-larity, which I have not met with in any other inftance, continued, as at the commencement of the difeafe, more dilated than that of the found eye; on this account, after the patient was cured of the *procidentia iridis*, he faw better in the dark with the left than with the right eye.

CASE LI.

A poftillion, 20 years of age, afflicted from his infancy with fcrofulous tumours in the neck, and with ophthalmia, was attacked with a violent inflammation of the right eye, which occafioned an abfcefs and ulcer of the cornea, and afterwards a *procidentia iridis* of the fize of a fmall lentil feed. At the time I faw him, which was five days from the appearance of the *procidentia,* he complained exceedingly on the flighteft motion of the eye-lids. The cure was undertaken on the 11th of January 1792, by touching the fmall tumour, formed by the iris, with the argentum nitratum, and endeavouring to produce a deep efchar upon, and within it.

When the efchar was detached, the cauftic was again applied and repeated, five times in the courfe of nine days, carefully wafhing the eye each time with warm milk. At this period the portion of the iris, which protruded through the ulcer of the cornea, was deftroyed, and reduced below the level of the external lips of the ulcer. I now confined myfelf to the application of the vitriolic collyrium, which was dropped into the affected eye every two hours, by which on the 30th of the fame month the ulcer was perfectly healed. The pupil appeared

peared of an oval figure, but this was not attended with any defect of vifion.

Case LII.

Giufeppe Gaggi, of Pavia, a robuft man, much
addicted to wine, being rendered nearly blind
by an obftinate chronic ophthalmia, which
had continued 40 days with *procidentia* of the
iris, was brought into the practical fchool of
furgery on the 6th of November 1795.

There were two diftinct procidentiæ of the
iris, each the fize of a millet-feed, fituated
upon the inferior hemifphere of the cornea
of the left eye, and to complete his misfortune, the cornea of this eye was rendered
completely opake by a denfe nebula. Upon the
upper hemifphere of the cornea of the right
eye, there was alfo a *procidentia* of the iris, the
fize of the head of a fly, in other refpects it preferved its natural tranfparency. The patient
complained of intenfe heat in the eyes, but not
of acute pain.

On the 6th, 7th, and 9th of November, the
prolapfus of the iris of the left, as well as of the
right eye, was touched with the argentum nitratum, and a deep efchar was produced, which,
however, did not excite much pain.

6

On

On the 10th the efchar of the right fide feparated, and the *procidentia* of the iris was found
very much diminifhed.

On the 18th, after three more applications
of the cauftic, the two procidentiæ of the iris
of the left eye alfo were reduced to a level
with the ulcers of the cornea. Being defirous,
in this ftate of things, to ftimulate the edges of
the ulcers a little by another application of the
argentum nitratum, the patient made fome unufual contortions, and gave figns of acute pain;
to relieve which, it was neceflary to wafh the eyes
frequently with warm milk, and to cover them
at night with a poultice of bread and milk.
This fufficiently indicated the neceffity of defifting from the ufe of the cauftic. When the
laft efchar was detached, I therefore confined
myfelf to the ufe of the vitriolic collyrium,
which was introduced every two hours.

On the 13th of December, the patient being
perfectly cured of the *procidentiæ* of the iris, and
ulcers of the cornea, went into the convalefcent
ward. The ophthalmic ointment of Janin was
introduced morning and evening, with a view,
if poffible, of diffipating the denfe nebula of the
left eye; but this was not attended with the defired fuccefs. The left eye, though freed from
the procidentiæ of the iris, remained ufelefs to
him, but the right was preferved.

CHAP.

CHAP. XV.

OF THE CATARACT.

THERE are two methods of treating the cataract, the one by removing the opake cryftalline,
from the vifual axis of the eye, by means of a
needle; the other, by extracting it from the eye,
by making a femicircular incifion in the bafe of
the cornea.

It has long been difputed which of thefe two
methods ought to have the preference; and in
the warmth of difcuffion, the advantages of
the one, and the difadvantages of the other,
have been exaggerated by both parties. Obfervation and experience, however, the great
teachers in all things, feem to have pronounced
in favour of the ancient method of treating the
cataract, or that of *depreffion*; not only becaufe
depreffion is more eafily executed than *extraction*,
and can be equally employed in every fpecies of
cataract, whether cryftalline or membraneous,
folid or fluid; but becaufe *depreffion* is attended
with fymptoms far lefs violent and dangerous
than

than thofe which very frequently happen after
extraction; and if from any accidental caufe
this operation fhould occafionally prove un-
fuccefsful, it may be repeated two or three
times upon the fame eye without any rifk; a
circumftance which *extraction* does not admit
of, when that operation has not had the defired
fuccefs.

Influenced by thefe facts, I have for a confiderable time laid afide the method of treating
the cataract by extraction, and have applied myfelf entirely to the practice of depreffion, and I
fee continually great reafon to be fatisfied with
the choice which I have made. The very frequent occafions which I have had of performing
this operation, have afforded me an opportunity
of making fome ufeful alterations relative to the
means which are employed previoufly to its
execution; of which I fhall now proceed to give
a detail.

It is eafy to determine whether the operation
can be performed with a profpect of fuccefs or
not. A favourable iffue may be expected, whenever the cataract is fimple, or without any other
difeafe of the eye-ball, in a fubject not quite unhealthy or decrepid, and in whom the opacity
of the cryftalline humour has been gradually
formed, without having originated from any external violence, or habitual ophthalmia, efpecially
the *internal:* where there has not been frequent

pain

pain in the head, eye-ball, and fupercilium :
where the pupil, notwithftanding the cataract,
has preferved its free and quick motion, as well
as its circular figure, in different degrees of
light: and laftly, where, notwithftanding the
opacity of the cryftalline lens, the patient retains the power, not only of diftinguifhing light
from darknefs, but alfo of perceiving vivid colours, and the principal outlines of bodies which
are prefented to him, and where the pupil has
that degree of dilatation which it is ufually found
to have in a moderate light.

It is not equally eafy to pronounce concerning that which regards the other part of the
diagnofis; that is, whether the cataract be hard
or foft, cafeous or fluid; and whether, together
with the opacity of the cryftalline lens, the capfular membrane which envelopes it be alfo
opake. All that has been hitherto written
and taught upon this fubject, has not that
degree of certainty which can ferve as a guide
in practice, and the moft experienced oculift of
the prefent day is not able to determine with
precifion what the nature and confiftence of the
cataract is, upon which he propofes to operate,*
nor whether the capfule be yet tranfparent or
not, although the lens be evidently opake. For

* Mr. Hey ftates, that he has generally found a dark coloured cataract in old perfons of a firm confiftence.
                          Practical Obferv. in Surg. page 49.

it

it is an indifputable fact, that the capfule fometimes preferves its tranfparency, when the lens
does not. The want of accurate notions,
however, upon this fubject does not materially
influence the fuccefs of the operation; as the
furgeon ought in every cafe to be prepared to
employ fuch means as the particular fpecies
of cataract which prefents itfelf to him may
require, during the performance of the operation, whether it be hard or foft, accompanied
by opacity of the capfule, which invefts it, or
not. The firm cryftalline cataract undoubtedly
admits of being more eafily removed by the
needle from the axis of vifion than any other;
and does not rife again to its former place, if the
furgeon in removing it from the pupil ufe the
precaution of burying it in the vitreous humour. The *foft*, the *milky*, or the *membranous
cataract*, however, when met with in the operation, may be alfo removed from the pupil,
effufed or lacerated with the fame needle, without the neceffity of introducing any other inftrument into the eye.

With refpect to the hard confiftent cataract,
it fhould be obferved that the word *depreffion*,
ufed in the fchools of furgery to exprefs the
manner in which this operation is executed,
readily produces in the mind of the ftudent an
erroneous idea, that this merely confifts in preffing
the opake cryftalline with the needle, from
above downwards, until it defcends below the

pupil

pupil. If this were the cafe, as there is not
a fufficient fpace for firmly lodging the
cryftalline lens, between the corpus ciliare and
the iris, it would conftantly follow, that immediately after the operation, the cataract would
rife up again, either entirely or partially, oppofite the pupil. But the word *depreffion*, in this
cafe, has a much more extenfive fignification
than that which is commonly given to it. It
includes two motions which the furgeon makes
with the needle; one of. preffing down the
opake cryftalline, the other of burying it in the
vitreous humour, by carrying it from before,
backwards, out of the axis of vifion. By this
precaution only, is the opake lens prevented
from rifing again, and in this fenfe only ought
the term *depreffion* of the *cataract* to be explained and underftood. There is upon this point
a circumftance noticed by Parè,* which has
not been mentioned by any writer, either before
or fince his time; that, after the depreffion of
the cataract, and before the needle is withdrawn,
the patient fhould be directed to turn the eye-
ball upwards. For by this means, fays he, the
depreffed cryftalline, upon which the needle yet
refts, muft be carried from before, backwards,
and buried in the vitreous humour, a circum-

* Livre II. chap. xxii. Et étant ainfi abaiffée, la lui fait
laiffer, la tenant fujette de l'aiguille par l'efpace de dire une
paternoftre, ou environ, de peur qu'elle ne remonte, et pen-
dant faire mouvoir vers le ciel l'oeil au malade.

ftance

ftance of the greateft importance to prevent the cataract from rifing again, and which deferves to be carefully attended to by the young furgeon.

Befides this precaution of lodging the firm cataract, which is to be depreffed, in the vitreous humour, there is another of no lefs importance to the fuccefs of this operation. This confifts in lacerating the anterior convexity of the capfule of the cryftalline lens, at the time the latter is depreffed, fo that whether the capfule be opake or not, the fight cannot afterwards be obftructed by it. For it not unfrequently happens, that thofe who have not had fufficient inftruction or experience in this part of furgery, after the needle has been made to penetrate between the anterior convexity of the capfule, which is yet tranfparent and the cataract, remove the opake cryftalline from the axis of vifion, and leave the anterior portion of the pellucid capfule in its fituation, which becoming opake a few days after the operation, prefents the appearance of a denfe whitifh veil behind the pupil, which either entirely, or in part, deprives the patient of the power of feeing, and which has very properly received the name of *fecondary membranous cataract.*

To be more explicit, the moft common caufe of failure in the operation for the cataract, whatever be the method of performing it, is not owing to the cryftalline lens, however denfe it may

be,

be, but to the capfule of the lens, and more
particularly its anterior convexity. It is to be
wifhed that the art of furgery were in poffeffion
of fome eafy and efficacious means, by which
the furgeon, in every method of operating,
might be able to feparate with exactnefs, together with the opake cryftalline, the entire
capfule of the lens from the *zona ciliaris* to
which it is attached, an event which occafionally happens from a happy, but unforefeen combination of circumftances. But this fortunate
occurrence * is very rare; as the *zona ciliaris*

* Richter Obf. Chirurg. Fafc. II. page 96. * Quater in-
fcius, faltem inopinatus, extraxi lentem capfula fua obvolutam.
See Janin, Pellier, Gleize, The Edinburgh Effays, vol. 5.
It once happened to Monro, in diffecting an eye affected with
cataract, to obferve, after having removed the cornea and iris,
that by merely inclining the eye-ball in different directions,
the cryftalline with its capfule feparated by its own weight
from the *zona ciliaris*, fo flight was the union of thefe parts
with each other in this particular and very rare cafe.
Monro's Works, Num. XXV.

* It fhould be obferved, however, that this obfervation of Richter's applies
only to the extraction of the cataract, for he ftates immediately afterwards, as
will be feen by the following paffage, that the capfule is moft frequently removed along with the opake lens in the operation of couching. His experiments, however, muft be lefs decifive, in as much as they were made upon
brutes.
Qui deprimunt cataractam, lentem folummodo deprimere fibi videntur, cap-
fulamque in loco fuo remanere putant. Ego vero puto, plurimifque experi-
mentis perfuafus fum, hac operatione plerumque capfulam cum lente deprimi.
Sique itaque deprimitur facile capfula cur n n extrahatur ? Deprimi autem,
fequentia probare videntur. Saepiffime coram auditoribus operationem de-
preffionis legitumo modo peregi in oculis fullis, diffectifque dein illis lentem
capfula fua integra indutam femper reperi. Ibid. page 97.—T.

moft

moft frequently connects the capfule of the
cryftalline lens fo clofely to the vitreous humour around the *annulus* of Petit, that even in
diffecting the eye it is impoffible to feparate the
capfule of the cryftalline lens from the vitreous
humour without confiderable laceration. On
account of the extreme difficulty, therefore, of
obtaining a complete feparation of the membranous capfule of the cryftalline from its attachments, the furgeon in the greater number
of cafes has no better means left him to purfue,
than to lacerate the anterior convexity of the
capfule, through the whole circuit, which correfponds to the pupil in its greateft degree of dilatation at the moment when he removes the
opake lens from the axis of vifion; for with
refpect to the reft of the anterior convexity of
the lacerated capfule, which continues to adhere
to the *zona ciliaris* beyond the greateft difk of
the pupil when it is dilated, although it be opake,
or fhould become fo after the operation, it can
never afterwards prove any obftacle to vifion,
even in the weakeft light; as it will always remain beyond the margin of the iris.

Nor let it be objected that, although this be
obtained, the pofterior capfule of the cryftalline
remains in its fituation, which, by becoming
opake, may occafion the fame obftruction to vifion
as the anterior convexity of the capfule, when that

A A 4 has

has not been fufficiently lacerated oppofite the pupil. For not to infift on the impoffibility of depreffing and forcing the opake lens backwards,
and deeply into the vitreous humour, without
the pofterior convexity of the capfule being alfo
lacerated, in order to give paffage to the cryftalline lens, experience teaches us that, although this portion of the capfule of the cryftalline lofe its tranfparency, it is very feldom in
fo confiderable a degree as to injure the fight
materially. This fact is proved by the daily
practice of extracting the cataract, in which
operation the furgeon, after making the incifion
in the cornea, has only to divide the anterior
part of the capfule, in order to make the
cryftalline pafs out; without regarding the pofterior convexity of this fmall membranous bag,
which he leaves in its fituation, without its giving rife, or but very feldom, to any confiderable
diminution of fight. Anatomy alfo teaches us
that there are remarkable differences, in feveral
refpects, between the anterior and pofterior
portions of the capfule of the cryftalline lens.
One of the principal differences is, that the anterior convexity of this membranous bag is in
its natural ftate, at leaft three or four times
thicker and firmer than the pofterior. The
fecond difference, equally remarkable, is that
the delicate pofterior hemifphere of the capfule

fule is furnifhed with a fet of veffels peculiar to it, and altogether diftinct from that which is tranfmitted to the anterior convexity of this fac, as the firft is formed by the extremity of the *arteria centralis*, which, as if from a centre, dif- tributes branches to the circumference, while the anterior hemifphere of the capfule of the cryftalline, which, as I have already faid, is more compact than the pofterior, receives its blood-veffels from thofe of the vitreous humour, which, having paffed over the *zona ciliaris*, are irregularly incurvated, and ramify upon the an- terior furface of the capfule. I do not, however, pretend from all this to infer that the pofterior portion of the capfule of the cryftalline never lofes its natural tranfparency, but only to prove, from obfervation and experience, that even when it does become fo, it is feldom the caufe of per- fect blindnefs. It is proper to repeat, that the principal obftacle to the favourable fuccefs of the operation for the cataract, in both methods, arifes moft frequently from the anterior con- vexity of the capfule of the cryftalline becoming opake, and fometimes more denfe than in its natural ftate, or from its being converted into a foft and pulpy fubftance.

A fact of no lefs importance to be known than the preceding, but which more particularly re- lates to the operation of the cataract by depref- fion, is that the opake cryftalline removed from

the

the axis of vifion and lodged in the vitreous humour, provided it is deprived of its invefting
membrane, gradually diminifhes in fize from its
circumference towards its centre, and ultimately
difappears altogether. This phænomenon is un-
queftionable, and is proved by a very extenfive
feries of obfervations made by men of the greateft accuracy and impartiality, to which I can
add three other inftances of my own upon this
fubject. The firft was in a nobleman of Pavia,
aged 60, who died precifely a year after he had
undergone the operation of couching for a cataract in the right eye ; the other was in a woman, 43 years of age, who died three years after
the depreffion of the cataract ; and the third in
a man, 57 years of age, who died about three
years and a half after the fame operation had
been performed. In the firft of thefe three fubjects I found the cryftalline deeply imbedded in
the vitreous humour, and reduced to about one
third its natural fize; and in the other two, in
which the cryftalline was deeply fituated in the
vitreous humour below the axis of vifion, there
was only the nucleus remaining of a fize little
larger than the head of a common pin.

The depreffed cryftalline difappears even in a
fhorter time, that is, in a few weeks, when it
has degenerated into a pultaceous, cheefy, or
milky fubftance. And when it is divided, reduced to fragments, and diffolved in the aqueous
                                                    humour,

humour, it is finally abforbed, together with
the aqueous fluid, which is continually renewed. This circumftance relative to the diffolution and abforption of the depreffed cryftalline, as it is beyond all doubt,* furnifhes a
powerful argument for afferting, in oppofition
to thofe who think unfavourably of this method
of operating, that there is no fpecies of *cataract*
which may not be cured by *depreffion*.

This diffolution and abforption takes place,
not only with refpect to the cryftalline lens, but
alfo with regard to the membranous particles of
the capfule of the cryftalline; when they are detached from the furrounding parts, broken down
by the needle, and float freely in the aqueous
humour fufpended in the form of fmall flakes, or
fall to the bottom of the two chambers of that
humour. It is conftantly obferved, in this cafe,
that thefe membranous fragments of the capfule,
depofited beh nd the cornea, firft affume the
whitenefs of milk, they then become of a yellowifh colour, and afterwards liquify and dif-

---

* Many celebrated modern furgeons might be cited, who
have obferved, and recorded this very important fact; but I
fhall content myfelf with merely quoting the words of Bar-
bette on this fubject, one of the oldeft writers. Licet, fays
he, cataracta non fatis intra pupillæ regionem fit depreffa,
dummodo in particulas fit div'fa, perfecta vifio intra fex aut
octo feptimanas fæpiffime, licet tóta operatio abfque ullo
fructu peractà videatur; quod aliquoties experientia edoctus
loquor. Chirurgia Barbettiana, cap. xvi. part I.

folve

folve in the aqueous humour; finally, that they diminifh in quantity, and difappear entirely, leaving the cornea and the whole of the eye in the moft perfect ftate of tranfparency. Any one may eafily trace this falutary procefs of nature, ftep by ftep, whenever he meets with a cafe, where, either accidentally or by defign, fome membranous fhreds of the capfule of the cryftalline have been pufhed through the pupil, and depofited in the anterior chamber of the aqueous humour, that is, between the iris and the concavity of the cornea. I have had frequent opportunities of repeating this obfervation. For in feveral cafes of membranous cataract, as I fhall afterwards fhow, I have pufhed thefe membranous flocculi into the anterior chamber of the aqueous humour, in fuch quantity as to fill it on a level with the lower margin of the pupil, fo as to form the appearance of an hypopion in it. I have obferved, in thefe cafes, that this collection of flocculi and particles of the capfule confined between the iris and concavity of the cornea, has never occafioned the patient any inconvenience, that is, either inflammation or pain; and that it is alfo conftantly diffolved and removed by abforption, in a month or little more, and fometimes fooner. It is to be obferved, alfo, that the abforption of the membranous flakes takes place more rapidly in the anterior than the pofterior chamber

of

of the aqueous humour, which may depend on
the greater quantity of aqueous humour in the
anterior chamber, by which the membranous
particles are more eafily diffolved than in the
pofterior; or may be owing to the greater quantity of abforbent veffels in the anterior chamber
of the aqueous than the pofterior. If it be true,
therefore, as it indifputably is, that when the
membranous cataract, or that formed merely by
the opake capfule of the cryftalline, remaining
oppofite the pupil, after the removal of the lens,
is broken into fmall particles by the needle, and
pufhed through the pupil into the anterior
chamber of the aqueous humour, it may, by
the powers of nature, be diffolved and removed
in the fame manner as the depreffed lens is diffolved, and finally abforbed; it is evidently
proved, I think, that the *membranous cataract*
can be alfo cured by the needle, notwithftanding
the affertion of thofe who affirm that this fpecies
of cataract can only be removed by means of
extraction.

The apparatus of inftruments neceffary for
performing the operation of the cataract, by depreffion, confifts of a needle for that purpofe,
and an elevator of the upper eye-lid, which is
employed particularly in thofe cafes in which
the eye to be operated on is fmall, deeply funk,
and where the patient is very unmanageable.

The

The elevator *of Pellier* * is preferable to all others, as it collects the eye-lid, and raises it against the superior arch of the orbit, making little or no compression upon the eye-ball.

With respect to the needle, most proper for the depression of the cataract, experience has taught me, that of the great number which have been proposed for this purpose, we ought generally to prefer that which unites to the greatest fineness, such a degree of firmness as will enable it to penetrate the membranes of the eye without bending: since I have used a very fine needle, I have never had to contend with any consecutive symptoms of importance after the operation of depression, not even with suppuration of the membranes of the eye at the place of the puncture. If, indeed, the symptoms consequent on this operation are in proportion as might be expected to the injury and solution of continuity, which takes place in the parts of the eye-ball, and particularly of those which are endowed with exquisite sensibility ; it is certain that when the needle is of the finest kind, if, after it has penetrated the eye, it is merely conducted upon the capsule of the crystalline, the lens, and the vitreous humour, parts which are insensible, the operation must be always attended with very little pain, and the consequences

* Plate III. fig. 1.

of

of the puncture conftantly, or in the greater
number of cafes, of little or no moment.

With refpect to the form of the needle, I have
had an opportunity of obferving, that the one
with a ftraight point, which is commonly ufed
in this operation, is not the beft calculated for
conveniently lacerating the anterior convexity of
the capfule of the cryftalline, and of removing
the cataract, at the fame time, eafily and expeditioufly out of the axis of vifion, and lodging t
deeply in the vitreous humour. For whatever
part of the eye-ball is pierced beyond the *corpus
ciliare*, whether at a line from the union of the
cornea with the fclerotica, at two, or two lines
and a half, as fome advife, the point of the
ftraight needle, which is made to advance upon
the anterior convexity of the capfule paffes directly againft the iris, and when it has reached
it, preffes only upon one point of the circumference of the capfule and lens in the manner of
a tangent. In the motion which the furgeon
gives to the point of the needle from before
backwards, in order to prefs it firmly upon the
centre of the capfule and lens, the preffure
which he applies upon thefe parts is in reality
only made by the body of the needle, the point
of the inftrument not penetrating the anterior
convexity of the capfule and the cryftalline lens,
until thefe parts have been fo far removed from
the pupil towards the bottom of the eye by the
body

body of the needle, that its point, with refpect to the part of the eye-ball which it has penetrated, has taken a direction from before, backwards. But fince, as I have faid, in removing the capfule and lens from the pupil, the prefure is not made by the point, but the fhank of the needle; hence it very frequently happens, that in this movement, the anterior convexity of the capfule, however fmall its refiftance is not lacerated, and the cataract being compreffed, **revolves round the inftrument, and makes various gyrations above and below the pupil, and cannot after all be firmly fixed by the point of the needle,** until after having been by different motions, and repeated preffure, removed from the pupil towards the bottom of the eye, it can be directly pierced by the point of the inftrument, which is fufficiently inclined for that purpofe from before backwards. But if the cataract be of a milky, foft, or cheefy confiftence, and confequently its capfule flaccid and yielding, the fhank of the ftraight needle is only imbedded in the capfule, without opening or lacerating it, and the furgeon is then obliged to make feveral motions with the needle, in order to remove it from the pupil, to retract the inftrument, and turn the point of it backwards, that he may pierce the fore part of the capfule and lacerate it. Maître-Jan, fpeaking of the milky cataract, has made the fame obfervation.

4   " Many

" Many fruitlefs attempts are frequently made, becaufe the needle glides only upon the membrane which covers the cryftalline, which, in fuch attempts always remains entire, unlefs the inftrument be a little withdrawn, in order to carry the point of it towards the middle of the cataract, for the purpofe of preffing it upwards to break this membrane."*

Thefe difficulties are entirely, or for the moft part avoided, by ufing a very fine needle, moderately curved at the point, fuch as that which I employ.† The curved extremity of this needle

---

* Traité des maladies de l'oeil, chap. xiii.

† Plate III. fig. 10. Befides the reafons before affigned, an accident happened to me in performing the operation for the cataract with a ftraight needle, badly tempered, which proved to me the advantage of the *curved* needle over the *ftraight* one. In introducing the needle, through a very firm fclerotic coat, it happened that its point bent in the form of a *fmall hook*; which I perceived as foon as the inftrument appeared between the pupil and the capfule of the cryftalline lens. I proceeded, however, with the operation, and having pufhed the point of the fmall hook through the capfule into the firm fubftance of the cryftalline lens, I removed both from the axis of vifion with the greateft facility, and afterwards withdrew the needle very cautioufly from the eye, without producing any laceration. This circumftance happened to me in the practical fchool, in the prefence of a great number of ftudents, and the event was as favourable as poffible.

Dr. Morigi, fenior furgeon of the hofpital of Piacenza, one of the moft expert and able operators at prefent in Italy, has now adopted the ufe of this curved needle for feveral years in

the

needle is flat upon its convex furface, fharp at the edges, and has a concavity confifting of two oblique planes, forming a flightly elevated line in the middle, which is prolonged as far as the extreme point of the inftrument, fimilar to the curved needle for ftitching wounds. The handle is marked in the direction correfponding to the convexity of the curved point.*

The needle now defcribed penetrates the eyeball with the fame facility as a ftraight one of an equal degree of finenefs. When it is cautioufly pufhed forwards, and is placed between the iris and the anterior convexity of the capfule of the cryftalline, it is fituated with its convexity towards the iris, and its point in the oppofite direction towards the capfule and opake

the depreffion of the cataract, and with fo much eafe and fuccefs, that he takes every opportunity of recommending and promoting the ufe of it.

* Freytag, in his differtation inferted in the 2d volume of the Chirurgical Differtations, publifhed by Haller, mentions, that his father employed a needle with a curved point for depreffing a membranous cataract; and he adds, that he extracted the membranous cataract from the eye with the fame inftrument. The latter is certainly an exaggeration.

Bell, in the 3d volume of his fyftem of furgery, Plate XXXII. fig. 4, has given the figure of a curved needle for the depreffion of the cataract. He fays, he has frequently thought that the cataract might be more eafily depreffed by means of this needle than the ftraight one; but that he has not yet had fufficient opportunities of ufing it to be able to fpeak decifively of its advantages.

lens,

lens, which it eafily and deeply pierces by the
fmalleft motion from before backwards, without
the lens having been previoufly removed from
the pupil. By means of this inftrument the furgeon readily fucceeds in lacerating the anterior convexity of the capfule extenfively, in deeply
and firmly piercing the opake lens, conducting it
out of the axis of-vifion and lodging it fecurely
in the vitreous humour. In cafes of the cafeous, milky, or membranous cataract, the foft
pulp of the cryftalline may be broken into fmall
parts, by means of the curved point of the
needle, with the utmoft facility, and the anterior convexity of the capfule torn into fmall
flakes; which membranous flocculi may, with
equal eafe, by turning the point of the inftrument forward, be pufhed through the pupil into
the anterior chamber of the aqueous humour,
where being precipitated they are, as will be
afterwards feen, diffolved, and abforbed by the
powers of nature.

Having premifed thefe general obfervations
on the depreffion of the cataract, I now pafs to
a detail of the operation itfelf, according to the
method which I have adopted.

In general the beft furgeons do not now pre-
pare patients indifcriminately, as was formerly
the cafe, for any of the great operations, without manifeft indications for doing it; and much
lefs that which is employed in the cafe of ca-

taract,

taract, unlefs the term preparation be applied to
the diet which is for fome days· prefcribed to
the patient, or the adminiftration of a clyfter
the night previous to the operation. There are,
however, in the cafe of cataract, particular circumftances, whatever be the mode of operating, which oblige the furgeon to depart from
the general rule, and to fubject the patient
to fome method of treatment preparatory to
the operation. Thefe circumftances occur in
perfons who are dyfpeptic, or hypochondria-
cal, in women fubject to hyfterics, and in
thofe whofe eyes, independently of the cataract, are at the fame time affected with tumefaction of the edges of the eye-lids, chronic rednefs of the conjunctiva, and a copious gumming.

In cafes of dyfpepfia, hypochondriafis, and
hyfteria, it is proper, two or three weeks before
the operation, to order the patient ftrong, farinaceous, aromatic broths, and at the fame time
ftomachic bitters and corroborants, of which, the
infufion of quaffia, in fuch cafes, is particularly
ufeful, either with the addition of a few drops
of the vitriolic æther, or without, according to
the particular conftitution and fenfibility of the
patient. As a fedative and corroborant remedy,
one of the moft ufeful is a powder, confifting of
a dram of the cinchona, and a fcruple of the
radix valerianæ fylveftris taken two or three
times

times a day, the patient observing, in every other respect, a proper regulation of diet. It is a most certain and constant fact, that the less timid and nervous the patient is, the milder are the symptoms consequent on the operation.

Where the edges of the eye-lids are tumefied, incrusted, and gummed, with relaxation of the conjunctiva, chronic redness, and weeping of the eye, it is highly advantageous, two or three weeks before the operation, to apply a large blistering plaster to the neck, and to introduce between the eye-lids, morning and evening, the ophthalmic ointment of Janin, with a double or triple quantity of lard; and during the day, the vitriolic collyrium with mucilage of quince-feed, every two hours, in order to restrain the morbid secretion of the ciliary glands, and internal membrane of the palpebræ; to strengthen the conjunctiva and its vessels, and to restore the edges of the eye-lids to their natural state and flexibility, before proceeding to the depression of the cataract.

Every thing being arranged for performing the operation, the surgeon should place his patient on a low seat, on the side of a window, which has a northern aspect, so that the light coming from it may only fall upon the eye which is to be operated on laterally. The patient's other eye being covered, although affected

with

with cataract, the furgeon ought to place himfelf directly oppofite the patient, upon a feat of
fuch a height, that when he is prepared to operate, his mouth fhall be on a level with the patient's eye. And, in order to give his hand a
greater degree of fteadinefs in the feveral motions which the depreffion of the cataract requires, the elbow correfponding to this hand
fhould be fupported upon the knee of the fame
fide, which for this purpofe he fhould raife fufficiently by refting his foot upon a ftool, and
according to circumftances alfo, by placing a
fmall hard pillow upon his knee. An able affiftant fituated behind the patient, with one hand
fixed under the chin, fhould fupport the patient's head againft his breaft, and with the
other placed on the forehead, gently raife the
upper eye-lid by means of Pellier's elevator, carefully obferving to gather the eye-lid againft the
arch of the orbit, without preffing upon the
globe of the eye.

Suppofing then the eye to be operated on is
the left, the furgeon taking the curved needle
in his right hand, as he would a writing pen,
with the convexity of the hook forwards, the
point backs, and the handle in a direction parallel to the patient's left temple; fhould reft
his fingers upon the temple, and boldly perforate the eye-ball in its external angle, at rather
more than a line from the union of the cornea

7   and

and fclerotica,* á little below the tranfverfe diameter of the pupil, gradually moving the extremity of the handle of the needle from behind
forwards from the patient's left temple, and confequently giving the whole inftrument a curved
motion, until its bent point has entirely penetrated the eye-ball; which is effected with the
greateft readinefs and eafe. The operator fhould
then conduct the convexity of the needle upon
the fummit of the opake cryftalline, and by
preffing upon it from above downwards,
caufe it to defcend a little, carefully paffing
the curved point at the fame time between
the corpus ciliare and the capfule of the
cryftalline lens, until it be vifible before the
pupil, between the anterior convexity of the
capfule of the lens and the iris. Having done
this he fhould cautioufly pufh the hook with its
point turned backwards towards the internal
angle of the eye, paffing it horizontally between
the pofterior furface of the iris, and the anterior
convexity of the capfule, until the point of the
needle has arrived as near the margin of the
cryftalline and capfule as poffible, which is

---

* Albucafis. Tantum recedendum a cornea, quantum
fpecilli cufpis fpatii contineat.

F. d'Acquapendente. Si aliqua datur in fuffufione operatio tuta, eam forte futuram, ut vel acus prope corneam im-
mittatur, vel fi aliquanto longius ab illa, non tantum tamen
quantum vulgo faciunt. De Chirurg. Operat. cap. xvii.

next

next the internal angle of the eye, and confequently beyond the centre of the opake
lens. The operator then inclining the handle
of the inftrument more towards himfelf, fhould
prefs the curved point of it deeply into the
anterior convexity of the capfule, and fubftance of the opake cryftalline, and by moving
it in the arc of a circle, fhould lacerate the
anterior convexity of the capfule extenfively,
remove the cataract from the axis of vifion, and
lodge it deeply in the vitreous humour, leaving
the pupil perfectly round, black, and free from
every obftacle to the vifion. The needle being
retained in this pofition for a fhort time, if no
portion of opake membrane appear behind the
pupil, which would require the point of the
inftrument to be turned towards it, in order
to remove fuch obftacle, (for with refpect to the
cryftalline depreffed, in the manner now defcribed, it never rifes again,) the furgeon fhould
give the inftrument a fmall degree of rotatory
motion, in order to difentangle it eafily from
the depreffed cataract, and fhould withdraw
it from the eye in a direction oppofite to
that in which it had been introduced, that
is, gently inclining and turning the handle towards the patient's left temple.

In every fpecies of cataract, with confiderable
opacity and denfity of the anterior hemifphere
of the capfule of the cryftalline, the furgeon may
very

very eafily know, during the operation, whether
the curved point of the needle, infinuated between the corpus ciliare and the capfule, is expofed between the pupil and the anterior hemifphere of that membrane; or, whether having penetrated into the membranous fac of
the cryftalline, it has only advanced between
the anterior hemifphere of the capfule and
the opake lens. But when the capfule, notwithftanding the opacity of the cryftalline lens,
preferves in a great meafure, or entirely, its
tranfparency, it is an eafy matter for a young
furgeon, not fufficiently converfant with this
operation, to commit an error, and one of great
importance, that is, to remove the catarach from
the axis of vifion, and lodge it in the vitreous
humour, leaving the anterior convexity of the
capfule untouched, which afterwards gives rife
to the *fecondary membranous cataract.*

To avoid this ferious inconvenience, every
operator fhould be particularly careful to fatisfy
himfelf before making any movement with the·
point of the needle for depreffing the catarach,
that the curved extremity of the inftrument is
really, and not apparently, fituated between the
pupil and the anterior portion of the capfule,
of which he will be convinced by the degree of
light which the convexity of the hook prefents
to him, and the facility which he finds in pufhing it forwards through the pupil towards the
anterior

anterior chamber of the aqueous humour, and
in moving it horizontally between the iris and
anterior hemifphere of the capfule. In the
oppofite cafe he may be certain that the
curved point is within the membranous fac
of the cryftalline, by obferving that the extremity of the needle is obfcured and covered by
a more or lefs tranfparent veil; that he meets
with fome refiftance in pufhing it through the
pupil into the anterior chamber of the aqueous
humour; and that in doing it, this membranous
veil which covers the hook is elevated towards
the pupil; and laftly, that the point of the
needle is with difficulty conducted horizontally
between the iris and the cataract, from the external towards the internal angle of the eye.

The furgeon will remedy this inconvenience,
by giving a flight rotatory motion to the needle,
by which the point being turned forwards will
pafs through the anterior convexity of the capfule oppofite the pupil; the point of the inftrument being then turned backwards again,
fhould be paffed horizontaliy between the iris
and the anterior hemifphere of the capfule towards the internal angle of the eye; and having
reached this part fhould be boldly plunged into
the capfule, and the fubftance of the opake lens,
in order to lacerate the former extenfively, and
to carry the latter deeply into the vitreous hu-

mour

mour out of the axis of vifion, and thus complete the operation.

When, without obferving this precept, the
opake lens is removed, or, more ftrictly fpeaking, enucleated from its capfule and lodged
in the vitreous humour; and the anterior convexity of this membrane being left entire, is
flightly opake, the pupil will appear black, and
fo free from obftruction to the light as eafily to
deceive the young furgeon, and induce him to
believe that the operation has been properly
executed. But perfons experienced in this part
of furgery, will inftantly perceive, that the
pupil, under fuch circumftances, has not that
juft and perfect degree of blacknefs which
it ought to have, and that this flight dimnefs is caufed by an imperfectly tranfparent
membranous veil, placed between the pupil
and the bottom of the eye, which, when
fuffered to remain, never fails, in procefs of
time, to give rife to the *fecondary membranous
cataract.* In this cafe, the expert operator having depreffed the opake lens, fhould immediately turn the curved point of the needle forward, and pafs it through the pupil into the anterior chamber of the aqueous humour, in order
to perforate this femitranfparent membranous
veil with the greater certainty; then turning
the point of the needle backwards and making
it pafs as far as poffible between the pofterior

furface

furface of the iris and this membrane, fhould
prefs the point of the inftrument into it
and lacerate it from before backwards, making
a movement as if he had to deprefs the lens
again. In doing this he will have the fatisfaction to fee the pupil affume the deep black colour of velvet, and a degree of clearnefs which
it had not before, although the opake lens had
been completely removed from the axis of vifion.

Hitherto I have fuppofed the cataract to be
of a firm confiftence, and to refift the preffure
of the needle. But if the operator fhould meet
with a fluid cataract, the milky for inftance,
which is not an unfrequent occurrence,* when
he has paffed the needle between the corpus ciliare and the capfule, until it appears uncovered
between the pupil and the anterior hemifphere of
the membranous fac of the cryftalline lens, and
the curved point has been cautioufly advanced
between the iris and the margin of the capfule,
neareft the internal angle of the eye; at the
moment that the point of the needle is deeply
preffed into the capfule and cataract, a whitifh
milky fluid will be feen to iffue from the capfule, which, extending itfelf in the form of a

* In the greater number of cafes which have fallen under
Mr. Hey's care, the cataract has been found fo foft as to permit the needle to pafs through it in all directions.

Pract. Obferv. in Surg. p. 60.

cloud

cloud or fmoke, will be diffufed through both the chambers of the aqueous humour, and obfcure the pupil and the whole of the eye. The furgeon fhould not on this account lofe his confidence, but, guided by his anatomical knowledge, fhould make the fmall hook defcribe the arc of a circle from the internal towards the external angle of the eye, and from before backwards, as if he were depreffing a folid cataract, with a view of lacerating, as much as poffible, the anterior hemifphere of the capfule, upon which the favourable fuccefs of the operation principaily depends, not only in this, but in every other fpecies of cataract. For as to the effufion of the milky fluid into the chambers of the aqueous humour, it difappears fpontaneoufly a few days after the operation, and permits the pupil and the whole of the eye to refume their former natural brightnefs.

The method of operating which the furgeon fhould employ will be little different from this, if, during its performance, he fhould meet with a foft or cheefy cataract. The anterior convexity of the capfule fhould be lacerated as much as poffible oppofite the pupil, fo that the opening may equal the diameter of the pupil in its ordinary dilatation. And with refpect to the pulpy fubftance of the cataract, which, in fuch cafes, remains behind, partly diffufed in the aqueous humour, and partly fwimming beyond

4   the

the pupil, all that is neceſſary, is to divide the
moſt tenacious parts of that ſubſtance, that they
may be more eaſily diſſolved in the aqueous humour, and to puſh thoſe molleculæ of the ca-
ſeous ſubſtance of the cryſtalline, which cannot be ſufficiently divided, through the pupil into
the anterior chamber of the aqueous humour,
in order that they may not be carried oppoſite
the pupil, but being ſituated at the bottom of
the anterior chamber, may be gradually diſſolved and abſorbed without obſtructing the
ſight.

The *ſecondary membranous cataract*, from what
has been already ſtated, is not ſo much a diſtinct ſpecies of cataract as a conſequence of the
operation imperfectly executed, or which from
ſome particular accident has not been attended
with complete ſucceſs. For this diſeaſe is moſt
frequently formed by the anterior convexity of
the capſule of the cryſtalline remaining entire
in its ſituation, after the opake lens has been
removed, or which has not been ſufficiently lacerated to allow a free paſſage to the light
through the pupil.

The *ſecondary membranous cataract* ſometimes
appears behind the pupil in the form of membranous flocculi ſuſpended in the aqueous humour of the poſterior chamber, filling up the
pupil; at other times it repreſents triangular
membranous borders; the baſes of which are attached

tached to the *ciliary zone*, the apices extending
oppofite the pupil. When it confifts merely of
a fingle fmall membranous flake, fufpended in
the pofterior chamber of the aqueous humour,
or fine triangular membranous procefs, 'it is not
neceffary on this account to fubject the patient
to a fecond operation, fince it does not materially obftruct the fight, and in procefs of time
difappears fpontaneoufly. But when the *fecondary membranous cataract* is formed by a mafs of
membranous particles, collected in the pofterior
chamber of the aqueous humour oppofite the
pupil, in fuch a degree as entirely or in a great
meafure to clofe it up (an occurrence which
alfo happens when the anterior chamber of the
aqueous humour is fo unufually fmall and confined as not to be capable of containing the
whole of the membranous flocculi of the capfule, a confiderable part of which muft neceffarily remain behind in the pofterior chamber
clofing up the pupil;) or when the difeafe confifts in the anterior hemifphere of the opake
capfule, not being fufficiently lacerated, and adhering to the whole of the ciliary zone; then it
becomes neceffary to have recourfe to another
operation. For although, in the firft cafe, there
is fufficient ground to believe that the mafs of
membranous flocculi may in time diffolve and
difappear; yet it is not proper to leave the patient in a ftate of perplexity, deprived of fight

for

for weeks or months, when it can be fpeedily
obtained by a fafe and eafy operation; and in
the fecond cafe the operation is abfolutely neceffary, as the lacerated capfule adhering every
where to the *ciliary zone*, feldom or ever difappears; and in time rather increafes in bulk and
becomes more opake than at firft.

In both thefe cafes of *fecondary membranous
cataract*, the operation is performed in the following manner. In the firft cafe where the mafs
of the particles of the capfule loofened from the
ciliary zone clofe up the pupil, the furgeon having introduced the curved needle into the eye
with the ufual cautions, and pufhed it into the
pofterior chamber, in contact with the mafs of
membranous flakes which obftructs it, fhould
turn the inftrument towards it, and prefs the
whole of the membranous flocculi through the
pupil one after another into the anterior chamber
of the aqueous humour, precipitating them into
the bottom of this chamber, between the concavity of the cornea and the iris. I am convinced from experience that any attempts made
to remove thefe portions of membrane from the
pupil, although perfectly loofe, and to immerfe
them in the vitreous humour, in the fame manner as the lens, are quite ufelefs; for no fooner is
the needle withdrawn from the eye, than the whole
of the membranous particles, as if conducted
by a current, appear filling up the pupil again.

On

On the contrary, when they are puſhed through the pupil into the anterior chamber of the aqueous humour, they can no longer, obſtruct the pupil, but are macerated at the bottom of this cavity without occaſioning the patient any inconvenience, and in a few weeks diſſolve and diſappear altogether.

In the ſecond caſe, when the *ſecondary membranous cataract* is formed by the whole of the anterior portion of the capſule, or by ſeveral portions of it adhering to the *ciliary zone*, the ſurgeon having turned the point of the curved needle towards the pupil, ſhould perforate the membranous cataract from behind forwards : or if its borders leave any interval between them, ſufficient to admit the convexity of the inſtrument he ſhould paſs the hook through this opening; then turning the point of it backwards, ſhould conduct it horizontally between the iris and the membranous cataract, as near as poſſible to its attachment with the *zona ciliaris*, and preſſing the point of the hook into it, and into each border of it in ſucceſſion, ſometimes rotating the inſtrument between the fingers, as if to twiſt the portion of capſule round the point of it, he ſhould lacerate it as much as poſſible, in every part of its circumference, ſo as to clear the whole ambit of the pupil; and having collected all the pellicles or flocculi together, ſhould puſh them with the point of the needle

c c through

through the pupil into the anterior chamber of the aqueous humour, as has been juft ftated. In doing this the greateft care fhould be taken by the operator not to touch the iris, for on this precaution principally depends the prevention of any confecutive fymptoms of importance, notwithftanding the length of the operation, and the various movements which it may be neceffary for him to make with the needle in the eye, in order to lacerate thefe membranes, and pufh them into the anterior chamber of the aqueous humour. And if a portion of the membranous cataract fhould be found adhering to the pofterior furface of the iris, which will be known by this circumftance, that in ftretching the fmall opake membrane with the needle the pupil changes its figure, and from being round becomes oval or irregular; he fhould proceed with even greater caution than in the preceding cafe, making repeated, but fmall and gentle movements with the needle in every direction, in order to obtain the feparation of it, without endangering the laceration of the iris at its union with the ciliary ligament.

Nor will it be neceffary to vary, in any manner, the method of operating, when the fecondary membranous cataract is formed by the pofterior convexity of the capfule having become opake at any period after the operation.

For

For after the cryftalline is removed this delicate membrane is forced forwards, fo as to be in con- tact with the pofterior furface of the iris, and is pufhed, as it were, almoft within the pupil. In order to precipitate it into the anterior chamber of the aqueous humour, and thereby remove the obftruction, it is only neceffary to prefs it from behind forward with the point of the needle ; which is the more eafy as the pofterior hemi- fphere of the capfule of the cryftalline loofened · from the *ciliary zone*, has no confiderable adhe- fion to the concavity of the vitreous humour, except from the very fmall trunk of the *central* artery.

Nor will the method of operating be differ- ent from this, in thofe uncommon cafes in which the cataract is entirely, or in a great meafure, *primitively membranous*. I defign to fpeak of that particular fpecies of cataract in which the cryftalline waftes, or is diffolved and difappears, leaving only its opake capfule, or at moft a fmall nucleus not larger than a pin's head within it. This fingular fpecies of cata- ract is moft frequently met with in children, or perfons who have not exceeded their 20th year, and may be diftinguifhed from the others by a certain tranfparency and refemblance to a fpi- der's web, or by a fort of reticulated ftructure, in- terrupted with a whitifh opake fpot in its centre or circumference. Any attempt in this cafe to

lodge

lodge this membrane in the vitreous humour would prove fruitlefs, as it would rife again and reappear behind the pupil immediately after the operation. The beft and fureft practice yet propófed, therefore, is to lacerate it with the point of the curved needle, and to pufh the different particles compofing it fucceffively through the pupil into the anterior chamber of the aqueous humour, where, as it has been before obferved, it is diffolved, and in the courfe of three weeks is removed by abforption.

With refpect to the after treatment of the operation of couching, it is only neceffary, in general, that the patient fhould lie in bed, with his head a little raifed, and in a dark room, and that the eye operated on fhould be covered with a piece of dry linen pinned to his night-cap. If he fhould complain of vivid heat in the eye and eye-lids immediately after the operation, it will be proper to cover them with a comprefs of foft lint, dipped in the white of an egg and rofe water, beaten to a froth, with a fmall piece of alum. And if, notwithftanding this, the pain and tumefaction of the eye-lids increafe, it will be neceffary to cover the eye with bags of emollient herbs, and by thefe, as well as by general remedies, prevent the progrefs of the inflammation.

In perfons of exqui'te general fenfibility, in thofe affected with hypochondriafis or hyfteria,

notwith-

notwithſtanding the precautions above mentioned are taken previouſly to the operation,
nervous affections are occaſionally excited
ſhortly after the operation, as vomiting, violent headach, ſhivering, and coldneſs of the
whole body. In theſe caſes I have found nothing allay this perturbed ſtate of the nervous
ſyſtem more ſpeedily than a clyſter, conſiſting
of 8 ounces of the infuſion of chamomile, and
2 grains of opium diſſolved in it, as the opium,
when given by the mouth, is conſtantly rejected.

In very weak and timorous perſons it very
frequently happens that on the 3d or 4th day
from the operation, they are ſeized with ſymptoms of indigeſtion, accompanied with an increaſe of general heat, eſpecially during the
night, as a bitter taſte, nauſea, diſpoſition to
vomit, pain in the head, tenſion of the hypo-
chondrium, flatulency, univerſal uneaſineſs, and
watchfulneſs. A gentle purgative, and the repeated uſe of clyſters are in general ſufficient to
remove all theſe inconveniences, and conſequently prevent the ſecondary ophthalmia.

With reſpect to the diet, this ought, in the
greater number of patients, to be of the loweſt
kind, and for the firſt 24 hours ſhould conſiſt of
broths only. Perſons, however, who are much
debilitated, or ſubject to convulſions, and elderly
people, are exceptions to this rule, as a very ri-

gorous

gorous diet in fuch cafes might occafion a return, or aggravation of the nervous fymptoms. In thefe inftances, therefore, it is neceffary to allow fome foup in addition, and liquid food, which fhould be given at fhort intervals.

It is not neceffary, without particular reafons for doing it, to open the eye which has been operated on, and confequently expofe it to the light before the 3d day after the operation. It is ufeful, however, to feparate the eye-lids gently, morning and evening, and to wafh the margins and cilia with a fponge dipped in pure water, in order to prevent their cohefion.

In cafes of cataract in both eyes, I have learnt from experience, that it is not advantageous to operate upon them immediately one after the other; but that it is better to wait till the firft is well, before the operation is attempted upon the other; the delay makes little difference in the time required for the cure of both. Upon this point I have had frequent occafion to remark that, the fymptoms of the fecond operation, whether upon the fame eye, or upon that which has not been operated on, are conftantly lefs confiderable than thofe of the firft operation. Whether this arifes from the tranquillity of the patient's mind, from having experienced the little inconvenience confequent on the operation of couching, or that each eye becomes lefs fenfible to the puncture of the needle, and the motions

motions of the inftrument, after one of them has once fuffered the irritation produced by it; I am unable to decide. This I know, that I have frequently feen in women fubject to hyfteria, and in hypochondriacs, after the eafieft and moft fuccefsful depreffion of the cataract in one eye, convulfive fymptoms excited either general or confined to the head, and the eye which had been operated on; and thefe, in fome cafes, fo violent, as in a fhort time to leave the pupil dilated and immoveable, with almoft total infenfibility of the optic nerve of that fide; while in the fame patients, when the other eye has been operated on two weeks afterwards, it has not been followed by any remarkable accident.

If there be no fymptoms of any confequence to combat, which is moft commonly the cafe when the operation is executed in the manner here recommended, in general, on the 10th or 12th day from the operation, the patient is in a ftate to make ufe of his eye; which, however, he fhould do with caution, particularly at firft, that is, without fatiguing it too much, or expofing it fuddenly to a vivid light.

I confider it ufelefs here to relate any hiftory of cafes of cataract, which have been perfectly cured by means of couching, and by the method here recommended; as well as to deliver a detail of facts relative to the cure of cafeous or milky cataracts, which, after the operation, have been

c c 4   diffolved

diffolved in the aqueous humour, and then abforbed by the powers of nature ; fince a great
number of thefe facts are to be found in furgical works, in which thefe fubjects are particularly treated. I fhall only add a few cafes of
fecondary membranous cataract, the refult of which
may not be ufelefs in proving the efficacy of
the means which I have propofed in the treatment of this fpecies of the difeafe ; which I do
the more willingly, as it is to this point that the
arguments of thofe principally refer, who in-
ftruct, that in the treatment of the cataract, the
operation of *extraction* ought to be preferred to
that of *depreffion*.

Case LIII.

A peafant, 50 years old, whom I had couched
three years before, with complete fuccefs, for a
cataract of the left eye, requefted to have the
operation performed upon the right. This cataract appeared to be of a favourable kind, that
is, firm and refifting to the needle, as that of
the left eye had been; the pupil moved freely,
and the patient, notwithftanding the difeafe,
could diftinguifh the figures of bodies with this
eye. The anterior chamber of the aqueous humour of each eye was almoft the largeft I ever
faw. As the palpebræ of this eye were a little
tumefied and gummed, I directed a bliftering
                                    plafter

plafter to be applied upon the neck, and prefcribed the frequent ufe of the vitriolic collyrium for a fortnight; by means of which remedies the eye-lids recovered their natural
ftate.

I then proceeded to the operation, and although contrary to my expectation, I found the
cryftalline fomewhat foft, yet by employing
fome care I was enabled to remove it from the
axis of vifion, and to bury it deeply in the vitreous humour, freeing the pupil, as far at
leaft as I could difcover, from every obftacle to
vifion.

The operation was unattended with any particular accident; but on the 11th day, when
the patient was permitted to leave his bed, and
to begin to make ufe of his right eye, he told
me that he could not fee fo diftinctly with it
as he had done the firft days after the operation. I examined it in a clear light, and found
more than half the pupil occupied by a whitifh
irregular body, of a nature evidently membranous. The iris of this eye prefented this peculiarity, that at each motion of the eye-ball it
ofcillated and waved backwards and forwards in
a peculiar manner.

Without further delay I introduced the needle again into the right eye, and having raifed
this membranous mafs with its point, I found
that it was larger than it had appeared to be
through

through the pupil. As it was loosened from
every attachment, when I had collected the
whole with the point of the needle opposite
the pupil, I pressed it forwards, and with the
greatest ease made it pass into the anterior chamber of the aqueous humour, which, in this subject, as I have stated, was very large, to the
bottom of which it was immediately precipitated, leaving the pupil perfectly clear. The
whole of this membranous substance was as
large as a barley-corn. In the course of 25
days, however, it was dissolved and absorbed,
without having occasioned, during its lodgment
in the anterior chamber of the aqueous humour,
any inconvenience or any impediment to the
sight.

From the size and figure of this membranous
body, I am inclined to believe, that it was the
whole, or the greatest part of the capsule of
the crystalline, which, by an unusual combination of circumstances, had been completely
detached from the *ciliary zone,* but which,
in making the cataract describe a portion of a
circle, in order to lodge it in the vitreous humour, had been separated from the needle, and
remaining behind had afterwards reappeared beyond the pupil.

CASE

Case LIV.

A poor woman, very much emaciated, and subject to hysteria, was received into this practical school on account of a cataract in each eye, which she had had for several years. The colour of the cataract was blue, but interrupted here and there with whitish streaks, and there was not that convexity behind the pupil which the opake cryftalline ufually prefents. The pupil of each eye was moveable, and the patient could difcern the figures of furrounding objects. The circumftances moft unfavourable to the operation in this cafe, were the extraordinary fmallnefs of the eyes, and their being deeply funk, and more particularly the extreme narrownefs of the anterior chamber of the aqueous humour; for with refpect to the general morbid fenfibility, I flattered myfelf it might be allayed by the ufe of the cinchona with valerian root for fome time, and a more nourifhing and ftrengthening diet than this poor woman had been accuftomed to.

After a month's preparation I performed the operation upon the left eye, and having paffed the needle between the pofterior furface of the iris and the cataract, I perceived, on firft fixing and preffing the point of it upon the anterior convexity of the capfule, that this membrane

membrane became corrugated, and folded under
the inftrument; in fhort, that inftead of the
cryftalline there was only its membranous bag,
containing a fmall quantity of glutinous fluid,
which, when difcharged, was not in fufficient
quantity to render the aqueous humour fo turbid as to prevent my proceeding with the operation. This difeafe would have been denominated by fome, *atrophy* of the cryftalline. As
there was no cryftalline lens then, I merely reduced the capfule into fmall pieces oppofite the
pupil, making as many of the fragments as I
could pafs through the pupil into the anterior
chamber of the aqueous humour, but I could not
fucceed in depofiting the whole of them in it,
on account of its unufual ftraitnefs.

Immediately after the operation, the patient,
as frequently happens in cafes of hyfteria, was
feized with a violent fpafmodic affection of the
head; but no fooner was a clyfter of the decoction of chamomile flowers, with two grains of
opium adminiftered, than all her pains ceafed,
nor did any confiderable inflammation take
place in the eye afterwards.

On the 4th day the patient could fee fufficiently well; but her fight afterwards diminifhed daily, till the 18th day after the operation, when fhe was completely blind, in confequence of the pupil being entirely occupied
by a whitifh membranous body, formed by the
                                        particles

particles and flakes of the capfule, which I had
not been able to pafs into the anterior chamber
of the aqueous humour, on account of its extreme fmallnefs. I then waited a week longer,
until the membranous particles and flocculi,
which had before been precipitated into the anterior chamber, were nearly diffolved, and left
room for the others. I then introduced the
needle again into the eye, and very foon freed
the pupil from this impediment, by pufhing all
the membranous flakes into the anterior chamber, fo as to fill it on a level with the inferior
margin of the pupil. It is a conftant fact,
worthy of obfervation here, that thofe membranous fragments, which, during the firft operation, can hardly be caught by the point of the
needle, on account of their fmallnefs, after they
have been macerated fome time in the aqueous
humour, fwell, and allow of being eafily removed or pufhed forwards with the inftrument.

After the operation the pain in the head re-
curred as before, and was relieved in the fame
manner, by means of an opiate clyfter.

About 28 days after the fecond operation,
during which time the woman could diftinguifh
furrounding objects very well, the fragments and
membranous flocculi, with which the anterior
chamber of the aqueous humour had been filled
for the fecond time, were entirely diffolved and
diffipated,

diffipated, leaving the whole extent of the pupil in its ordinary dilatation, black, clear, and free from every obftacle to the light.

CASE LV.

Bartolomeo Zucchi, of Calvairate, a robuft man, 45 years of age, affected with cataract in both eyes, underwent the operation in this fchool of furgery on the 28th of April 1793. His eyes were rather fmall, and funk in the orbits.

I operated upon the left eye, in which I met with a foft cheefy cataract. Having broken the foft pultaceous fubftance of the cryftalline to pieces, I lacerated the capfule very freely all around the pupil; I then paffed the whole of the fragments and membranous flakes through the pupil into the anterior chamber of the aqueous humour, which they filled on a level with the inferior margin of the pupil. The operation was not fucceeded by any remarkable fymptom, and on the 10th day thefe fragments and flakes were diminifhed more than one half, and the patient faw diftinctly with the left eye.

I now operated upon the right eye, in which having found a cataract fufficiently firm, I was able to lacerate with precifion the anterior convexity of the capfule extenfively, and to lodge the

lens

lens deeply in the vitreous humour. Two weeks
after the operation on the right eye, the membranous particles depofited in the anterior chamber of the left eye difappeared entirely, and the
right eye was alfo capable of bearing the light.
The patient was therefore foon afterwards difcharged from the hofpital perfectly cured in
both his eyes.

Case LVI.

Maria Spigoletti, 40 years of age, had had a
cataract in the left eye for two years, and the
cryftalline of the right was becoming rapidly
opake, the eye-lids were fwollen and gummed.

She was purged with the magnefia vitriolata,
a large blifter was directed to be applied upon
the neck, and the edges of the eye-lids to be
anointed morning and evening with the ophthalmic ointment of Janin.

After three weeks preparation I attempted to
deprefs the cataract of the left eye, which I
found not diffimilar to mucus. Having therefore broken the anterior portion of the capfule,
as well as the whole of the membranous fac of
the cryftalline into fmall pieces through the
whole extent of the pupil, I made all the membranous fragments pafs through it into the anterior chamber of the aqueous humour, and
fucceeded fo as to render it free from every
impediment

impediment to vifion. A flight inflammation
enfued, which was in a great meafure confined
to the eye-lids, but fubfided in a week, by
merely employing at firft bags of emollient
herbs, and afterwards the aqua lithargyri acetati
compofita.

In the courfe of a month all the membranous
fragments depofited in the anterior chamber of
the aqueous humour, which had given the appearance of an hypopion, were diffolved and entirely removed, and the woman having recovered
the fight of this eye was difcharged from the
hofpital.

CASE LVII.

Giovanni Alberti, a country-man 66 years of
age, affected with cataract in both his eyes, was
admitted into this practical fchool of furgery for
the purpofe of undergoing the operation.

I attempted it on the left eye, and found the
cryftalline fufficiently firm to admit of being
eafily removed from the axis of vifion, and immerfed in the vitreous humour. Having accomplifhed this, I perceived, before the needle
was withdrawn from the eye, that there was a
portion of opake membrane, or a confiderable
part of the anterior convexity of the capfule,
which had not been fufficiently lacerated, floating behind the pupil. I turned the point of
the

the needle backwards again, and having carefully broken this membrane as far as the circumference of the pupil admitted, I forced the
whole of the fragments through the pupil into
the anterior chamber of the aqueous humour.
The patient had no bad ſymptom, and ſaw very
well with this eye.

Twelve days afterwards I operated on the
right eye, and the ſame thing occurred pre-
ciſely; I was able to diſlodge the opake lens
readily, but a border of the anterior portion of
the capſule remained behind, oppoſite the
pupil, that is to ſay, the capſule was lacerated with the needle, but not ſo completely
as to remove this portion of membranous veil.
I therefore turned the point of the needle, as
in the firſt inſtance, towards the m mbran-
ous border, which I lacerated in pieces, and
as I detached the portions of it, I puſhed
them through the pupil, and precipitated them
into the anterior chamber of the aqueous humour; and this I repeated until the whole circumference of the pupil appeared black. About
a month after the operation on the ſecond eye,
there was no veſtige of membranous particles
in the anterior chamber of either eye, and the
patient completely recovered his ſight.

     CASE

Case LVIII.

Paola Guagnini, of Sale, aged 45, weak, and
fubject to violent attacks of hyfteria, had been
affected for feveral years with a cataract of the
left eye, and faw indiftinctly with the right,
from an incipient opacity of the cryftalline on
that fide. The conjunctiva of both eyes was alfo
in fome degree relaxed, and the eye-lids tumefied and gummed. I therefore directed a bliftering plafter to be applied upon the neck, and the
vitriolic collyrium to be frequently inftilled into
the eyes for a fortnight; by thefe means the eye-
lids fubfided, and the immoderate vifcid difcharge ceafed. On account of the patient's
great irritability and weaknefs, I ordered her
to take ʒj of the cinchona, and ℈j of valerian root, twice a day, during the whole of this
time.

On the 21ft of November 1795, fhe fubmitted to the operation. At the moment the
point of the needle was preffed upon the cataract, in order to remove it from the axis of vifion, it burft like a fmall bladder, and a milky
fluid gufhed out, which rendered both the
chambers of the aqueous humour turbid. Notwithftanding this I could diftinguifh the nucleus
of the opake cryftalline through this cloudy
                                             fluid

fluid, which I conveyed deeply into the vitreous humour; then conducting the point of the needle again towards the pupil I detached and lacerated the anterior hemifphere of the capfule into feveral pieces, and paffed thefe membranous portions in fucceffion through the pupil into the anterior chamber of the aqueous humour.

The patient did not complain of any acute pain during the operation, and paffed the three following days without uneafinefs. On the 4th day fhe was feized with a violent hyfterical paroxyfm, with a fenfe of fuffocation, agitation of the whole body, delirium, and incoherent talking, which made me fear fome unfavourable effect on the eye operated upon. There was, however, no alteration, and contrary to my expectation, I found the day after this accident that the pupil was clear, and that the woman could diftinguifh the moft minute objects.

On the 10th day from the operation the patient was in a ftate to leave her bed, and to begin to ufe her eye in a moderate light.

The mafs of membranous flakes precipitated into the anterior chamber of the aqueous humour, which refembled an hypopion, began to be diffipated, and in the fpace of 32 days the whole fediment of the particles was entirely abforbed, and the patient was difcharged from the fchool of furgery perfectly cured. The un-

D D 2   interrupted

interrupted ufe of the cinchona with valerian root, and a few fpoonsful a day of the infufion of chamomile, with the aqua ammon. fuccinat. and the aqua canellæ, had rendered the hyfterical attacks lefs violent and frequent than before.

CHAP.

CHAP. XVI.

OF THE ARTIFICIAL PUPIL.

An accident, not frequent indeed, but which, however, occafionally happens, in confequence of the operation for the cataract, by *depreffion* or *extraction*, is that of the contraction of the pupil, which becomes entirely, or in a great meafure, clofed, attended at firft with a great diminution, and afterwards an entire lofs of fight.

This difagreeable occurrence is moft frequently produced by a violent inflammation of the internal membranes of the eye, and particularly of the iris, excited by the operation of depreffing or extracting the cataract. In fome particular inftances, however, it takes place after the operation, but without the inflammation of the internal parts of the eye, or of the iris in particular, having had any evident fhare in its production; in which cafes, at an indeterminate length of time from the depreffion or extraction of the cataract, the pupil is obferved without any evident caufe to be-

come

come daily more and more contracted, until it
is almoft entirely obliterated, and that without
the patient complaining of any uneafinefs;
in a few inftances, however, a degree of fenfibility rather greater than natural is felt in the
immediate organ of vifion, even in a moderate
degree of light.

In both cafes the pupil in general contracts
to fuch a degree as fcarcely to admit the head
of a fmall pin, and remains immoveable; the iris
around the pupil affumes a rugofe and ftellated
appearance, having an irregular aperture in the
middle, behind which, the cataract having been
depreffed or extracted, the bottom of the eye
either appears black, or a fmall fpot, or whitifh
fhade is obfervable, if, after either of thefe operations, a portion of the anterior convexity of the
capfule of the opake cryftalline lens has accidentally remained behind, and contracted an
adhefion to the iris.

Some furgical writers have been led from
theory to fuppofe, that when this morbid contraction of the pupil is derived from an exceffive diftenfion of the veffels of the iris, in confequence of violent inflammation of this membrane, it might be remedied by the ufe of local
refolvent and corroborant applications, and at
the fame time revulfives, as local and general
bleeding, purgatives, blifters, and a feton in the
neck. On the other hand, they have thought
that

that emollients, and external as well as internal antifpafmodic remedies, would be ufeful, in cafes of conftriction of the pupil produced by a fpafm of the iris, and an increafed morbid confenfual fenfibility of the immediate organ of vifion with that membrane. But however plaufible thefe indications, in the treatment of the contracted pupil, may feem, experience has fhown their inefficacy, and has fully convinced us that this difeafe can only be remedied by making an artificial aperture in the iris, which may perform the office of the natural pupil.

Chefelden, as far as I know, was the firft who ventured to propófe and make a divifion of the iris, with the intention of forming an *artificial pupil.* He introduced a couching needle, with a cutting edge on one fide only, through the fclerotic coat into the eye, at the diftance of a line and a half from the cornea; then perforating the iris on the fide next the external angle, and carrying the point of the needle through the anterior chamber of the aqueous humour, until it reached the fide next the nofe, he turned the cutting edge backwards, and retracting it, divided the iris tranfverfely.

It has been faid that this operation has had the happieft fuccefs; but Janin * has affured

* Mémoires fur l'œil, page 182, 183.

us, that having performed it in two instances
with the greatest care, no advantage was derived
from it; for after the symptoms produced by
the operation had subsided, he found that in
both patients the transverse opening made in
the iris with the cutting edge of the needle had
reunited and healed. The same thing nearly
happened to Sharp,* long before Janin, " for,"
says he, " I once performed this operation with
tolerable succefs, but a few months afterwards
the very orifice I had made contracted and
brought on blindness again."

Janin, in using Daviel's sciffars for the extraction of a cataract, accidentally included
the iris at the same time with the cornea, and
divided it from below upwards, on the side
of the pupil, which instructed him, as he
exprefses it, that the perpendicular divifion of
this membrane, on the side of the pupil, was
the only effectual method of preventing the
lips of the wound made in the iris from healing, and consequently of establishing an *artificial pupil*. It was this circumstance which led
this oculist to invent a method of operating,
and to propofe as the best means of forming
an artificial pupil, that of opening the cornea,
as is practifed in the extraction of the cataract;
and afterwards of dividing the iris with the

* Operations of Surgery, chap. 29.

sciffars

fciffars from below upwards, near the pupil on
the fide next the nofe; for in doing it on the
external fide, he afferts, that he had obferved
it to give rife to a ftrabifmus, in confequence of
the too great divergency of the optical axis.

In the fmall number of cafes of contraction
of the pupil, which has fallen within my obfervation and practice, fupervening to the operation for the cataract, by extraction or depreffion, I could never perfuade myfelf to open the
cornea, in order to make the perpendicular divifion of the iris, with the fciffars propofed by
Janin, or any other, by means of the knife, being
aware of the frequent ferious accidents which
accompany the opening of the cornea, in cafes
where the eyes have been affected after the firft
operation with violent internal ophthalmia,
fpafm, or a morbidly increafed fenfibility of the
immediate organ of vifion. Nor could I ever
induce myfelf to divide the cornea again, upon
which, after the extraction of the cataract, there
had remained an irregular cicatrix; and I have
been ftill lefs inclined to do it, knowing that it
is not fo eafy a matter as fome may perhaps
imagine, to divide the iris with the fciffars,
when it has become flaccid from the difcharge
of the aqueous humour.

I have more than once had occafion to fee a
portion of the margin of the iris two lines in
extent, feparated from the ciliary ligament,
without

without laceration of the body of this membrane, in confequence of blows upon the eyeball; and that at the part where the iris was detached from the ligamentum ciliare there remained, during the reft of the patient's life, an oval fiffure, which might, in all thefe cafes, have performed the office of an *artificial pupil*, if the immediate organ of vifion and the cryftalline humour had not been too much injured by the violence of the ftroke. I remember in a cafe of procidentia iridis, from a fmall ulcer of the cornea, where the iris was greatly ftretched, in confequence of a confiderable portion of it projecting out of the eye and having contracted an adhefion with the margins of the ulcer of the cornea, that this membrane, inftead of being lacerated in its middle, was detached for a certain extent of its circumference from the ciliary ligament, producing an artificial pupil in that part, which was very ufeful to the patient after the *procidentia iridis* was cured. In depreffing a cataract likewife, I have had the misfortune of feeing a fimilar detachment of the margin of the iris from the ciliary ligament occur, from my having pufhed the opake cryftalline a little inadvertently againft the internal margin of this membrane, at the time that it was rolling obftinately round the point of the ftraight needle, without my being able to catch it, in order to lodge it deeply in the vitreous humour and deprefs

prefs it. In different diffections of the eye likewife, I have very frequently had an opportunity
of obferving, that on taking hold of the iris with
the forceps, not only at a fmall diftance from
its greater circumference, but alfo at the very
edge of the pupil, this membrane, although
certainly of the moft delicate texture, inftead
of lacerating in the middle, has rather feparated at its union with the ligamentum ciliare.*
Laftly, it is beyond doubt, that the iris is a
membrane entirely diftinct from the choroid
coat, and has a peculiar kind of connection,
though very flight, with the ciliary ligament,
independently of the union of the choroid coat
with this ligament.

All thefe confiderations collectively, but particularly that of the weak attachment of the
iris to the ciliary ligament, and confequently of

---

* Guerin appears to me to have been better acquainted
with this important circumftance, of the eafy detachment of the
iris from the ciliary ligament, than any other modern oculift.
" *The feparation of the iris from the ciliary ligament is eafily
effected; an obfervation which ought never to be loft fight of in
the extraction of the cataract, for by forcibly extracting a large
cryftalline the iris might be entirely, or in part, detached and caufe
ferious injury, loc. cit. page* 218." All the advocates for extraction caution us, in cafes where the membranous cataract
adheres to the iris, to draw this fmall opake membrane gently,
otherwife there is a rifk of feparating the iris from the ciliary ligament; this accident being confidered as more probable than the laceration of the fubftance of the iris.

6   the

the greater facility of feparating the margin of
the iris from the ligament to which it is united,
than of lacerating the membrane itfelf, induced
me to attempt a new method of making the
artificial pupil in thofe cafes, in which, after the
extraction or depreffion of the cataract, the natural pupil might be too much contracted
or obliterated; which method of operating
confifts in feparating the outer edge of the
iris from the ciliary ligament, for a certain extent, without previoufly dividing the cornea.
The event anfwered my expectation, as will appear from the annexed cafes. The following is
a detail of the mode of performing this operation.

The patient being feated, and there held, as
in the operation for the cataract, with a ftraight
couching needle, not the thick one, which is
ufed by the greater part of furgeons, but a very
fine one,* to which I give the preference, the
fclerotic coat is perforated at the external angle
of the eye, about two lines from the union of
the tunica fclerotica with the cornea, and the
point of the needle is made to advance as far as
the upper and internal part of the margin of the
iris, that is, on the fide next the nofe. The inftrument is then made to pierce the upper part
of the internal margin of the iris, clofe to the

* Plate III. fig. 11.

ciliary

ciliary ligament, until its point is juſt perceptible in the anterior chamber of the aqueous humour; I ſay juſt perceptible, becauſe that part of
the anterior chamber being very narrow, if the
point of the needle be made to advance ever ſo
little before the iris it muſt paſs into the ſubſtance of the cornea. As ſoon as the point of the
needle can be ſeen in the anterior chamber of the
aqueous humour, it ſhould be preſſed upon the
iris from above downwards, and from the internal towards the external angle, as if with a
view of carrying the inſtrument in a line parallel
to the anterior ſurface of the iris, in order that a
portion of its margin may be ſeparated from the
ligamentum ciliare. This ſeparation being obtained, the point of the needle muſt be depreſſed,
in order to place it upon the inferior angle of
the commenced fiſſure, which may be prolonged
at pleaſure, by drawing the iris towards the
temple, and by carrying the inſtrument from
before backwards, in a line parallel to the anterior
ſurface of the iris, and the greater axis of the
eye.

Having done this, if the bottom of the eye,
beyond the artificial pupil, does not appear ob-
ſtructed by any opake body, the needle may
be withdrawn from the eye entirely. If, however, any portion of the opake capſule preſent
itſelf behind the new pupil, which has remained
after the depreſſion or extraction of the cataract,
this

this ſmall opake membrane, being broken in pieces with the point of the needle, muſt be made to paſs before the artificial pupil, and depoſited in the anterior chamber of the aqueous humour, where, as I have ſhown in the preceding chapter, theſe' membranous fragments and flakes of the capſule are gradually diſſolved and abſorbed with the aqueous humour, which is inceſſantly renewed.

In conſequence of the detachment of the iris from the ciliary ligament, it conſtantly happens, that the aqueous humour is rendered more or leſs turbid by the effuſion of a ſmall quantity of blood into it; but this diſcoloured fluid is afterwards abſorbed, and the eye recovers its former tranſparency.

During the operation the patient complains of much more uneaſineſs than in the depreſſion or extraction of the cataract; nor can it be otherwiſe, ſince by ſeparating a portion of the margin of the iris from the ciliary ligament, ſome of the filaments of the ciliary nerves which paſs through it to be diſtributed to the iris muſt be ſtretched and lacerated. The ſymptoms which enſued from this operation in the two caſes, which I have related, were neither of long continuance nor alarming. From ſome experiments made upon the dead ſubject, I am of opinion, that the curved needle which I employ for the depreſſion of the cataract, may

be

be alfo preferable to the ftraight one in the formation of the artificial pupil; which I intend
to afcertain on the firft favourable opportunity.

Case LIX.

Some years ago, I performed the operation for
the cataract before a number of furgical ftudents, upon the left eye of a countryman of
Borgo S. Siro, 50 years of age; it was at the
time when I ufed the ftraight pointed needle.
In the act of depreffing the cryftalline, I found
fome difficulty in making a firm preffure upon
it with the inftrument, round the point of which
the opake cryftalline, while rolling, was carried
fidewife againft the margin of the iris next the
nofe, feparated this membrane for a certain
extent from the ciliary ligament, and was
ready to pafs into the anterior chamber of the
aqueous humour. I retracted it in the beft manner I could, and notwithftanding a little turbid-
nefs produced by the effufed blood, after fome
attempts, I caught the firm cryftalline with the
point of the needle, and buried it deeply in the
vitreous humour out of the axis of vifion. The
eye was merely covered with a dry comprefs,
and the patient was put to bed.

Towards the evening of the fame day, the
patient felt confiderable pain and heat in the
eye.

eye. I ordered him to lose blood from the arm plentifully, and the eye to be covered with bags of gauze filled with emollient herbs boiled in milk. The following day he was purged with cryſtals of tartar, and confined to a rigorous diet. The eye-lids and conjunctiva, however, were confiderably ſwollen until the 5th day, and it was therefore neceſſary to repeat the bleeding; the tumefaction afterwards gradually fubſided, and on the 14th day had entirely diſappeared.

Upon examining the eye attentively, I found that the aqueous humour had not yet regained its former tranſparency, that the natural pupil, which was exceedingly contracted and almoſt obliterated, was removed from the internal towards the external angle of the eye, by the depreſſion of the portion of the iris, which had been ſeparated from the ciliary ligament; that, laſtly, at the part where the ſeparation had taken place there was an oval fiſſure two lines and a half in extent, through which the patient could diſtinguiſh objects fufficiently well. In two weeks more the eye recovered its natural tranſparency. There being a cataract in the right eye alſo, I performed the operation upon it a few days afterwards, and with the beſt poſſible fuccefs.

CASE

Case LX.

Maria Guerini, an inhabitant of the Genoefe mountains, a ftrong woman, 45 years old, but occafionally fubject to rheumatifm, which affected her fometimes in the back, at other times in the neck and head, had for a long time loft the ufe of her left eye, in confequence of cataract, and finding that fhe was likely to experience a fimilar misfortune alfo in the right, fhe was admitted into this fchool of furgery to undergo the operation.

I depreffed the cataract of the left eye with fuccefs, and all went on very well till the 4th day, when the patient was fuddenly feized with a ptyalifm, rheumatifm in the neck and the whole of the left fide of the head, with acute pain, violent inflammation, and fwelling of the eye-lids and ball of the eye; the conjunctiva was tumid and prominent as in the *chemofis*. I ordered blood to be drawn copioufly from the patient's foot, as well as locally by means of leeches, and I directed a blifter to be applied upon the neck. She was repeatedly purged with a grain of tartarized antimony diffolved in a pint of the decoction of the radix tritici repent. and during the day fhe made ufe of a tepid infufion of elder flowers. The eye was fo-

E E   mented

mented with fmall bags of emollient herbs.
The inflammation both of the external and internal parts of the eye was fuch that an hypopion feemed inevitable. This ftate of perplexity
continued a week, when the rheumatifm and
ophthalmia gradually difappeared. The patient,
however, had no more fight with the left eye
than before the operation. The pupil was fo
much contracted as to appear obliterated. I did
not think it proper to meddle with the eye again
at that time, but advifed the patient to return to
the hofpital in a few months, which fhe did.

The patient having been purged with fmall
dofes of the antim. tart. and confined for fome
days to a proper diet, was fubjected to the operation for the artificial pupil. Having pierced
the fclerotic coat with a very fine ftraight needle, I paffed the point againft the fummit of
the margin of the iris next the nofe, and as foon
as I could juft difcern the point of the inftrument I preffed it downwards, and drawing the
iris towards the temple, I feparated a portion of
its margin from the ciliary ligament, and I continued to do this, defcending to the extent of
two lines and a half; I then withdrew the
needle from the eye. The woman gave figns
of acute pain, and the aqueous humour was
rendered a little turbid.

As foon as fhe was put to bed I ordered blood
to be drawn from the foot, and the eye to be
6   covered

covered with bags of gauze, filled with emollient
herbs boiled in milk, and I directed an emulfion
with twelve drops of the tincture of opium, to
be taken at bedtime. She paffed a comfortable
night.

There was afterwards a flight inflammation
of the conjunctiva and eye-lids, which was fubdued in a few days by emollient applications
only, and on the entire ceffation of the inflammatory ftage, the aqua lithar. acet. comp. was
employed with advantage.

On the 11th day from the operation I could
examine the eye commodioufly. The aqueous
humour had not yet entirely regained its perfect
clearnefs. The perpendicular fiffure formed
between the internal margin of the iris and the
ciliary ligament, performed the office of a pupil;
by which the woman diftinguifhed the furrounding objects. After a months conva-
lefcence, the obfcurity produced by the blood
effufed into the aqueous humour was diffipated,
and the woman left the hofpital cured.

CASE LXI.

A mendicant who had loft his left eye from
the extraction of a cataract, in one of the hofpitals of Piedmont, and the pupil of whofe
right eye was fo contracted, after a violent inflammation, as fcarcely to admit the head of a

fmall

small pin, and was therefore of little use to him, was brought into this practical school of surgery, in consequence of a fall upon the ice, by which he had dislocated his left hand. After he had recovered from this accident, I proposed to him to make some attempt to better his sight, to which he assented.

Having introduced a straight needle into the right eye, as in the operation of couching, I passed the point of it to the internal and superior margin of the iris, which I pierced as near its edge as possible; then partly by pressing the iris from above downwards, and partly by drawing it towards the temple, I separated it from the ciliary ligament to the extent of more than two lines; after which I withdrew the needle, leaving the aqueous humour somewhat turbid.

In the act of detaching the iris from the ciliary ligament, the patient gave signs of exquisite pain, but as soon as the eye was covered with a small bag of gauze filled with emollient herbs boiled in milk, he became easy.

On the 3d day the eye-lids and conjunctiva were considerably inflamed. He was bled largely, and purged with the crystals of tartar; and the emollient applications were continued. On the 10th day the acute ophthalmia was dissipated, and was succeeded by that from local debility, which was removed by means of the vitriolic collyrium, with mucilage of quince seed.

On

On the 20th day from the operation I found that the artificial pupil perfectly anfwered the intention for which it had been made; as the patient could diftinguifh objects fufficiently well. In lefs than a month afterwards the flight tinge which the aqueous humour had received from the blood entirely difappeared.

CASE LXII.*

In the year 1788, a woman came to me who had had a cataract extracted from the left eye. The pupil had clofed, in confequence of a violent inflammation, which, according to her account, continued 50 days. She had been deprived of the right eye in her infancy, by a fuppuration of the cornea after the fmall-pox. Under thefe circumftances, there was no other means of reftoring fight to this unfortunate woman, than by the formation of an *artificial pupil* in the left eye, which was executed in the following manner.

* This cafe has been communicated to me by Signor *Francefco Buzzi*, a very able furgeon and oculift of Milan, already known as an anatomift by his difcovery of the *yellow fpot* at the bottom of the eye, fince defcribed by *Soemmerring*. Perfuaded of the imperfection of the common methods of making the artificial pupil, he had for a long time adopted and practifed the new mode of operating which is here defcribed.

The

The patient being placed in a chair, an affiftant, fituated behind, held the head, fupported
againft his breaft, by placing his right hand under the chin. With the fore and middle fingers of his left hand, he elevated the upper eye-
lid of the left eye, while I in the fame manner
depreffed the lower. With a fpear-pointed
needle in the right hand I pierced the fclerotic
coat at about the diftance of two lines from the
circumference of the iris, and afterwards pufhing the inftrument forwards, I penetrated the
iris towards its upper part, about a line from
the contracted pupil; and after having paffed
the needle in a direction parallel to the anterior
furface of the iris, I inclined its point downwards, and at the fame time preffed it backwards towards the centre of the vitreous humour, feparating the iris forcibly at the upper
part, for at leaft a third part of its circumference.
This I executed with as much quicknefs as in the
depreffion of the cataract, otherwife the blood
which is difcharged from the ruptured veffels of
the iris, fills the anterior chamber, and prevents
the iris from being feen; and therefore, if this
precaution is neglected, the operation may be
rendered imperfect, or perhaps even ufelefs.

A few hours afterwards the patient felt a painful tenfion in the eye-ball, which extended to
the orbit, the cheek, and one half of the head.
I now employed the general remedies, in order

to

to prevent a violent inflammation. After 35 days confinement to bed, the blood, extravafated in the anterior chamber, was entirely removed ; and I could perceive that this detached portion of the iris was fo far removed towards the temple, that at the part where it had been feparated there was a large oblong *artificial pupil.* The patient was afterwards able to walk freely by herfelf, and to read and write with the affiftance of cataract fpectacles.

I have hitherto fpoken of the artificial pupil, in cafes where the natural pupil is unufually contracted or obliterated, in confequence of the operation for the cataract.

I have not much difficulty in perfuading my-felf that that fpecies of contraction of the pupil, which is accompanied with an adhefion of the anterior convexity of the capfule of the opake cryftalline, may be alfo remedied by means of the needle. For, befides a very confiderable number of cafes recorded by authentic writers on thefe fubjects, I might relate fome of my own, relative to the cataract, complicated with confiderable contraction and immobility of the pupil, which have been fuccefsfully difplaced by the needle, fo that after the operation, the pupil, which had been contracted and immoveable, has recovered its natural fize

and

and mobility. But if even, in fome particular cafes, the adhefion of the anterior convexity of the capfule of the opake cryftalline to the pofterior furface of the iris were fuch as to elude every poffible attempt to feparate it by means of the needle, I am of opinion that it could not be productive of any other confequence than that of feparating the iris for a certain part of its circumference from the ciliary ligament, and confequently of producing an artificial pupil.* The elucidation of this point muft, however, depend upon further obfervation and experience, as I have propofed to affert nothing upon thefe fubjects which has not been dictated by practice, and confirmed by a fufficient number of facts.

---

* It is lately afferted that, in this particular cafe, the celebrated oculift Demours has fortunately fucceeded in making an artificial pupil, by piercing the cornea and iris with a biftoury, near the fclerotic coat, and removing a portion of the iris, with the fciffars, of the fize and figure of a forrel-feed, and that without at all difplacing the found and tranfparent cryftalline.

CHAP.

CHAP. XVII.

OF THE STAPHYLOMA.

THAT difeafe of the eye-ball is termed ftaphyloma, in which the cornea lofes its natural
tranfparency, is elevated upon the eye, and gradually projects beyond the eye-lids in the form
of an oblong tumour of a whitifh or pearl colour, which is fometimes fmooth, at other times
tuberculated, attended with a total lofs of fight.

This difeafe not unfrequently attacks infants
a little after their birth, and is moft commonly
a fequela of the puriform ophthalmia ; or it appears in confequence of the fmall-pox, and
what is extraordinary, never during the eruptive
or fuppurative ftage of that difeafe, but on the
deficcation of the puftules, and even after the
crufts have defquamated.

In a great number of cafes, when the ftaphyloma has arrived at a certain elevation upon
the cornea, it becomes ftationary, or only increafes in exact proportion with the eye-ball; in
others

others the fmall tumour gradually increafes in all its dimenfions, and in fuch a difproportion, with refpect to the reft of the eyeball, that it ultimately projects confiderably beyond the eye-lids, occafioning great uneafinefs and deformity.*

This difeafe is juftly ranked among the moft dangerous to which the eye-ball is fubject; fince to the total and irremediable lofs of fight which accompanies it, are added the evils which neceffarily arife from the augmentation and protuberance of the ftaphyloma, when the tumour

* I had lately occafion to fee a fingular difeafe of the cornea, in a woman 35 years of age, which if it be not referable to the ftaphyloma, I do not know in what clafs of difeafes to place it. The eyes were naturally prominent; the cornea of each fide, without any evident caufe, became elevated in the centre and gradually projected outwards, fo that it no longer formed a regular fegment of a fphere applied upon the fclerotica, but a pointed cone. When the cornea was viewed fidewife it refembled a fmall tranfparent funnel with its bafe applied upon the fclerotica. In particular motions of the eye-ball, the point of this cone appeared rather lefs tranfparent than its bafe, in others not fo; but even where it appeared leaft tranfparent, it was not in fuch a degree as to prefent any confiderable obftacle to the fight. When the eyes were placed directly oppofite a window, the apex of the cone reflected the light fo powerfully, that it had the appearance of a luminous point: and as this took place precifely oppofite the pupil, which was now contracted, the woman could only fee objects diftinctly in a moderate light, in which the pupil was fufficiently dilated; in a ftrong light her vifion was weak and confufed.

of

of the cornea has acquired fuch a magnitude as
not to admit, of being enclofed and covered by
the eye-lids. For in fuch cafes, the continual
expofure of the eye-ball to the contact of the
air, and the particles floating in it, the friction
which the cilia make upon it, and the inceffant
difcharge of tears upon the adjacent cheek, are
caufes fufficient to occafion the eye to become
gradually painful and inflamed, and fympathetically to affect the found one; and finally
to produce an ulceration of it, together with the
lower eye-lid and the cheek upon which it
refts.

It has long been the opinion of furgeons,
that in the formation of the ftaphyloma, the
cornea yields to the diftenfion produced by
the turgefcence of the proper humours of the
eye, in the fame manner, nearly, as the perito-
neum yields to the preffure of the vifcera contained in the abdomen when an inteftinal hernia is formed. Richter * has oppofed this theory,
by remarking that the ftaphyloma is moft frequently formed without its having been preceded by any of thofe morbid predifpofitions
which are generally regarded as capable of
weakening the texture and elafticity of the cornea; that the cornea, degenerated into ftaphyloma, acquires a much greater thicknefs than

* Obferv. Chirurg. Fafcicul. II.

that

that which it poffeffes in a natural ftate, and that confequently the ftaphyloma, inftead of being internally concave, is quite compact and folid, while it ought to be precifely the contrary if this tumour were the effect of an exceffive diftenfion of the cornea from within outwards, with an attenuation of its natural texture.

In conceding to Richter the encomiums to which he is entitled for his diftinguifhed merits in all the branches of the healing art, I cannot but remark on this occafion, that the illuftrious author in advancing, as he has done, a matter of fact, relative to the origin and nature of ftaphyloma, has extended his doctrine too far, in admitting no difference between the ftaphyloma recently appearing in infants, and that of adult fubjects, in which laft, the ftaphyloma, has acquired fuch a magnitude as to project confiderably beyond the eye-lids. I fully agree with Richter as to the certain and demonftrable fact, that the recent ftaphyloma in infants is entirely compact and folid from the increafed thicknefs which the cornea affumes in this difeafe; but it is equally certain, as I have found from repeated obfervation, that in the ftaphyloma, which originally is perfectly folid and compact, after a feries of years, and in perfons of a mature age, where the tumour has acquired fuch a fize as to project out of the

the eye-lids, the cornea, properly fo called, is
conftantly thinner, or certainly not thicker than
natural, that is to fay, the tumour is not perfectly folid internally, unlefs with regard to its
ftate of fulnefs, as it contains the iris and the
cryftalline and not unfrequently alfo a portion
of the vitreous humour; which parts leaving
their natural fituation, are pufhed gradually fo.-
wards to occupy the concavity of .the cornea,
which is proportionally formed and enlarged.

The cornea of infants, in its natural ftate, is
in proportion, at leaft twice as thick and pulpy
as that of adults; and confequently the anterior
chamber of the aqueous humour is proportionally fo contracted, in comparifon with
that of adults, that in very young infants the
cornea may be confidered as almoft in contact with the iris. Such alfo is the natural
foftnefs, flexibility, and fucculency of the cornea
in infants at an early age, that when feparated
from the reft of the eye in the dead fubject,
and rubbed between the fingers, it lofes at leaft
one half of its bulk and thicknefs, which does
not take place in adults. And the cornea is fo
pliant and diftenfile at this early period, that, if
in the fine injections of the head, the injected
fubftance is extravafated in large quantity
within the eye-ball, the cornea, compreffed
from behind forwards, is confiderably elevated
in the body of the infant towards the eye-lids,

3   which,

which, under such circumstances, never happens in the eyes of adults.

In consequence of this natural softness, succulency, and flexibility of the cornea of infants, as well as from the natural straightness of the anterior chamber of the aqueous humour, it not unfrequently happens, that when they are attacked soon after birth with the *puriform* ophthalmia, or variolous metastasis, their cornea, more readily than that of adults, gives admission within its spongy texture to the thick and tenacious humour which is propelled into it; by the stagnation and condensation of which, the cornea at that early period not only loses its natural organization and transparency, but also swells, becomes much thicker than natural, and in a short time degenerates into an acuminated, whitish, or pearly tumour, completely solid, without any internal vacuity, and perfectly in contact, and adhering to the iris, to which the cornea of infants, as I before observed, is naturally very closely situated.

In the course of some years, however, the disease undergoes new modifications. For the whole eye increasing in volume in proportion to the age, the iris and crystalline, from causes not fully known, abandon their natural situation, and are continually forced forwards; to which perhaps the preternatural fluidity and turgescency

turgefcency of the vitreous humour contributes,
which, when the difeafe is of long ftanding, is
conftantly found in large quantity, and of a
watery confiftence. Now thefe parts, the cryftalline and iris, when the cornea is not perfectly hardened and firm, gradually prefs this
membrane from within outwards, and in time
diftend it in all its dimenfions, fo as to caufe it
to project beyond the eye-lids, rendering it at
the fame time thinner in proportion to the volume and capacity which it acquires. I have
never met with a large ftaphyloma protruding
out of the eye-lids in adult perfons, which had
not originated in infancy; and I have conftantly found that the thicknefs and denfity of
the cornea, both in the living and dead bodies
of thofe who were affected with this difeafe
were in an inverfe proportion to the age. In
the inveterate ftaphyloma, which projects confiderably beyond the eye-lids, the iris may be diftinctly feen in different parts of it contained within
it; and if this is not equally evident in all the
parts of the tumour, it is becaufe the conjunctiva
which externally covers the cornea, and the
veffels of this membrane having become varicofe,
throw over it a ftratum of fubftance of unequal denfity and opacity. And it is precifely
this denfe ftratum of the lamina of the conjunctiva covering the cornea, which in the ftaphyloma that has arrived at a confiderable fize

and

and amplitude may eafily deceive, the fubftance of the cornea appearing to acquire greater denfity and thicknefs, in proportion to the increafe of the tumour, whereas quite the contrary takes place, the increafed denfity of the lamina of the conjunctiva, which covers it externally, only fupplying in part the diminifhed thicknefs of the true texture of the cornea; a means which nature providently employs on many occafions, in order to prevent the injuries which fome important parts might receive, when deprived of their natural covering, and expofed to the action of external agents. It is not to be prefumed, that of the many able furgeons and accurate obfervers of every age, who have frequently, in the courfe of their practice, deftroyed inveterate ftaphylomata of the largeft fize, no one fhould have perceived that in this higheft degree of the difeafe, the cornea inftead of being diminifhed in thicknefs, according to the common opinion, is, on the contrary, a body entirely compact and folid internally. On the contrary I find them, when fpeaking of the deftruction of large ftaphylomata, projecting much beyond the eye-lids, by means of the ligature, delivering cautions to draw the thread only lightly for fear of the cornea, rendered thin in thefe cafes, being eafily lacerated. And Gunz*

* De Staphilom. differt. fee the Difput. Chirurg. of Haller.

relates

relates his having been an ocular witnefs of fuch
an unfortunate accident, in a cafe where a ligature had been applied upon the ftaphyloma, by
means of a needle and thread.

The doctrine of Richter, therefore, upon the
nature of this difeafe is true, when it is confined
to the recent ftaphyloma of infants. But it appears to me to admit of exceptions as it regards
the thicknefs of the cornea, in the ftaphyloma
of long ftanding, which has arrived at a confiderable fize, and projects out of the eye-lids.

Some pretend that the fclerotic coat alfo is
fubject to ftaphyloma, that is, to a partial diftenfion and elevation of its anterior hemifphere
in the white of the eye; others entertain a
doubt of the exiftence of this difeafe. It has
never occurred to me, indeed, even once, to fee
any tumour or elevation of the fclerotica on its
anterior furface, correfponding to the white of
the eye, in the form of ftaphyloma; and on the
contrary, what may feem extraordinary, I have
twice happened to meet with the ftaphyloma of
the fclerotic coat in its pofterior hemifphere,
in the dead fubject, where I do not know that
it has been feen or defcribed by any other.
The firft time was in an eye taken from the
body of a woman 40 years old, for another purpofe. This eye * was of an oval figure, and

* Plate II. fig. 9.

F F   upon

upon the whole, larger than the found one of the oppofite fide. On the pofterior hemifphere of this eye, and on the external fide of the entrance of the optic nerve, or on the part correfponding to the temple of that fide, the fclerotica was elevated in the form of an oblong * tumour of the fize of a fmall nut. And as the cornea was found and pellucid, and the humours ftill preferved their tranfparency, on looking through the pupil, there appeared within it, towards the bottom, an unufual brightnefs, produced by the light penetrating that part of the fclerotica, which had become thin and tranfparent where it was occupied by the ftaphyloma. When the eye was opened, I found the vitreous humour entirely diforganized and converted into limpid water, and the cryftalline lens rather yellowifh, but not opake. When the pofterior hemifphere of the eye was immerfed in fpirit of wine, with a few drops of nitrous acid added to it, in order to give the retina confiftence and opacity, I could perceive diftinctly, that there was a deficiency of the nervous expanfion of the retina within the cavity of the ftaphyloma; that the choroid coat was very thin and difcoloured at this part, and wanted its ufual vafcular plexus; and that the fclerotica, particularly at the apex of the ftaphyloma, was

* Plate II. fig. 9. a.

rendered

rendered fo thin as fcarcely to equal the thicknefs of writing paper. I knew that the woman
from whom the eye had been taken, had loft
the faculty of feeing on that fide fome years before, during an obftinate ophthalmia, attended
with a moft acute and almoft habitual pain in
the head.

The fame obfervation I had an opportunity of
making on an eye, accidentally taken from the
body of a woman 35 years of age, and politely
fent tò me from Milan by Dr. Monteggia, who
has diftinguifhed himfelf by his excellent medical
and furgical writings. This eye was alfo of an
oval figure, and larger than the oppofite one.*
The ftaphyloma of the fclerotic coat † occupied
its pofterior hemifphere on the external fide of
the entrance of the optic nerve, or on the fide
next the temple. The vitreous humour was converted into water; the capfule of the cryftalline
was exceedingly turgid, with a whitifh diluted
fluid; the cryftalline, yellowifh and lefs than natural; the retina, deficient within the ftaphyloma; the choroid and fclerotic coats, forming
the tumour, were rendered fo thin as to admit
the light. Dr. Monteggia could not furnifh me
with any thing pofitive refpecting this woman's
fight before her death. It is remarkable, that
in both the cafes now defcribed, the ftaphyloma

* Plate II. fig. 10.
† Plate II. fig. 10. a.

of

of the fclerotic coat was fituated on the external fide of the entrance of the optic nerve. Further obfervations may, perhaps, hereafter enable
furgeons to eftablifh the diagnoftic fymptoms of
the ftaphyloma of the fclerotic coat; but from
its deep fituation and the nature of the difeafe, I
doubt very much whether the art will ever ar-
rive at an effectual method of arrefting its progrefs, much lefs of curing it.

Returning to the ftaphyloma of the cornea,
as this part of the eye-ball, in fuch cafes, is rendered irremediably opake, the aim of the furgeon in the treatment of this difeafe, when recent, and in infants, muft be neceffarily confined to prevent the diforganized tumour of
the cornea from increafing in fize, and to deprefs and flatten it as much as poffible; and in
the large inveterate ftaphyloma projecting beyond the eye-lids, to effect fuch a reduction of
its fize, that it may re-enter and be deeply lodged
within the orbit, fo as to allow an artificial eye
to be fixed, and thereby leffen the deformity of
the countenance.

In recent cafes of ftaphyloma, Richter propofes to produce an artificial ulcer upon the bafe
of the tumour of the cornea, by means of the
reiterated application of the argentum nitratum or the antimonium muriatum, and to keep
it open by the repeated ufe of thefe cauftics;
in order to evacuate by means of this fmall cauterization,

terization the thick and tenacious humour, which is the immediate caufe of the opacity and preternatural tumefaction of the cornea. The author afferts, that he has frequently obtained a diminution of the ftaphyloma by means of this fmall drain made in the fubftance of the cornea, and in one particular cafe, that he has even reftored the tranfparency of the cornea; which has always appeared to me one of the moft extraordinary and wonderful cures of the many which are found recorded on the difeafes of the eyes; particularly as it was completed in 14 days. " *Ter repetita operatione, quarto fcilicet, feptimo et decimo die, ne veftigium quidem morbi die decimo quarto fupererat.*"*

I am forry to be obliged to declare, that although I have frequently adopted this method of treatment in the recent ftaphyloma of infants, and that with the fulleft confidence of fuccefs, not only from a perfuafion that this plan of treatment proceeded from certain and evident premifes founded on the nature of this difeafe, when recent and in fubjects of an early age, but becaufe in fo doing I was guided by one of the moft authentic writers in furgery; yet I have never had the gratification to obtain fuch fuccefs, either with regard to reftoring the tranfparency of the cornea, or diminifhing the fize of the fta-

* Obferv. Chirurg. Fafcic. II.

phyloma,

phyloma, as in any degree to equal that obtained and related by Richter. In three children, one a year and a half old, and the other
two, little more than three years of age, recently attacked with ſtaphyloma in one of the
eyes, in conſequence of the ſmall-pox, in which
I excited and kept open a ſmall ulcer at the
baſis of the cornea, by means of the argentum
nitratum, for more than 30 days, I derived no
advantage from it with reſpect to the diminution of the tumour, and ſtill leſs with regard to
the opacity of the cornea. In a boy five years
of age, who had been a ſhort time affected with
a ſtaphyloma in one eye, after a violent *chemoſis,*
having produced an ulcer upon the baſis of the
cornea, by penetrating a ſmall depth into the
ſubſtance of the diſorganized and tumid cornea
with a lancet, and afterwards keeping the ulcer
open for five weeks, by means of a ſolution of
the argent. nitrat. I obſerved that the ſtaphyloma was a little depreſſed, and had loſt the
acute point which it had in the centre,* but the
cornea remained every where opake as at firſt.
In two other ſubjects, nearly of the ſame age,
under the ſame circumſtances, and treated in
the ſame manner, although the ulcer of the cor-

---

* The conical figure which the cornea aſſumes in this diſeaſe, is a characteriſtic mark by which the ſtaphyloma may be
diſtinguiſhed from the leucoma with complete opacity of the
cornea.

nea

nea was kept open for 50 days I could obtain no depreffion or diminution of the ftaphyloma, and confequently the pointed tumour in
both remained of a pearl colour, as at firft.

If, however, by means of further trials made
by perfons of ability, this plan of treatment
fhould be found to be advantageous, not with
a view to reeftablifh the tranfparency of the
cornea, but merely to reftrain and deprefs the
recent ftaphyloma of infants, I am of opinion
that no one will perfuade himfelf that this mode
of treatment can be of any utility in obtaining
a diminution of the fize of the inveterate ftaphyloma in adult perfons ; or that which protrudes beyond the eye-lids and preffes upon the
cheek. For what advantage can be expected
from an artificial ulcer made in the fubftance of
the cornea, which is no longer foft and pulpy,
nor thickened merely by a tenacious humour
effufed into its cavernous texture, but which,
in procefs of time, has become arid, coriaceous,
prominent by the exceffive diftenfion from
within outwards, and covered by a callous ftratum formed by the lamina of the conjunctiva,
and its varicofe veffels ? It is certain, that whenever the inveterate ftaphyloma, projecting beyond the eye-lids, happens to become accidentally ulcerated from external violence, from the
acrimony of the tears, or from the long continued preffure of the parts upon which it refts, a

diminution

diminution in its fize has never been obfervable
in confequence of fuch ulceration; on the contrary, it is ftated to have happened frequently in
fuch cafes, that the exulcerated inveterate ftaphyloma has degenerated into a fungus of a malignant nature.

In the higheft degree of this difeafe, therefore, when the ftaphyloma projects out of the
eye-lids, the moft effectual means of arrefting
the progrefs of the difeafe, and removing the
deformity, which we are at prefent in poffeffion
of, is the excifion of the ftaphyloma, and when
the wound is healed, the application of an artificial eye.

Of this operation Celfus * expreffes himfelf
in the following manner. *Curatio duplex eft.
Altera ad ipfas radices per medium tranfuere acu
duo lina ducente; deinde alterius lini duo capita ex
fuperiore parte, alterius ex inferiore adftringere inter
fe, quæ paulatim fecando id excidant. Altera in
fumma parte ejus ad lenticulæ magnitudinem excindere; deinde fpodium; aut cadmiam infricare.
Introlibet autem facto, album ovi lana excipiendum,
et imponendum; pofteaque vapore aquæ calidæ foven-
dus oculus, et lenibus medicamentis unguendus eft.*

Although the firft method, or that of deliga-
tion, is at prefent laid afide, as admitted by all
to be lefs proper; the greater part of furgeons,

* De Medicin. lib. vii. cap. 7.

neverthelefs,

neverthelefs, continue to pierce the bafe of the
ftaphyloma with a needle and thread, not indeed
with a view of making a ligature upon the tumour, but to form a loop, by which a commodious hold may be taken, for the purpofe of
retaining the eye-ball firmly at the time when
the extirpation is performed. But fince this
advantage, as I fhall hereafter fhow, may be
obtained by a more fimple, expeditious, and lefs
inconvenient method to the patient ; I am perfuaded that the apparatus of the needle and
thread will, ere long, be abandoned, not only as
a method of treatment, but as an auxiliary in
the operation.

With refpect to the fecond mode of removing the *ftaphyloma*, or that by excifion, it appears to me that fufficient attention has not
been paid to what has been delivered by Celfus
on this fubject. For he does not direct that the
ftaphyloma fhould be divided circularly at its
bafe, as is practifed in the prefent day, but that
the excifion fhould be made in the centre or
extreme point of the tumour, and that a circular portion of the fummit or apex of the ftaphyloma, equal in fize to a lentil-feed, fhould
be removed. *In fumma parte ejus ad lenticulæ
magnitudinem excindere.* The great importance
of this precept of Celfus, in the treatment of
the ftaphyloma, can only be eftimated by thofe
who have had frequent opportunities of comparing

paring the advantages of his mode of operating, with the very ferious inconveniences which arife from the common practice of removing the ftaphyloma circularly at its bafe, and the ftill greater evils which are produced by the circular divifion of this tumour, including the fclerotica, according to the practice of Wolhoufe; as fuch a mode of treatment is invariably followed by violent inflammation of the eye-ball and eye-lids, the moft acute pain in the head, watch-fulnefs, convulfions, copious fuppuration, and fometimes gangrene of the eye and eye lids. It is, in my opinion, a certain fact, eftablifhed by an extenfive feries of obfervations, that the further the femicircular excifion of the ftaphyloma is made from the centre or apex of the tumour towards its bafe, and confequently the nearer the fclerotic coat, the more confiderable are the fymptoms confequent on this operation; and vice verfa.

Confiftently with thefe facts, the following is the method of effecting the deftruction of the inveterate ftaphyloma, which I have adopted. The patient being feated, I direct the head to be properly held by an affiftant, then with the fmall knife,* which is ufed for the extraction of the cataract, I pierce through the ftaphyloma at a line and a half or two lines from the centre or

* Plate III. fig. 7.

apex of the tumour, in the direction from the
external to the internal angle of the eye; and
paffing the knife precifely in the fame direction as in the extraction of the cataract, I divide
the apex of the tumour downwards in a femicircular manner. Having done this, I take hold of
this fegment of the ftaphyloma with the forceps,* and turning the cutting edge of the
fcalpel upwards, I finifh the operation by removing the apex of the ftaphyloma circularly;
fo that the detached portion is two, three, and
fometimes four lines in diameter, according to
the fize of the ftaphyloma. And as a portion
of the iris is generally included in the fection of
the apex of the ftaphyloma, from this membrane having contracted an adhefion to the cornea at the commencement of the difeafe, as
foon as the circular divifion of the fummit of
the ftaphyloma is completed, the cryftalline, or
its nucleus, is immediately difcharged from the
eye, and after it a portion of the diffolved vitreous humour. In confequence of this evacuation the eye-ball is frequently fo much diminifhed as to admit of being covered by the
eye-lids, over which I immediately apply a dry
comprefs and bandage.

The pain produced by the excifion is trifling,
and it is. common to fee patients very eafy

* Plate III. fig. 8.

during

during the three or four firft days after the operation. On the 4th day, in general, the eye
and eye-lids begin to be painful, inflamed, and
tumefied. On the appearance of thefe fymptoms the eye fhould be covered with a bread and
milk poultice, with a view of promoting and
accelerating the fuppuration of its internal membranes. Indeed, where the progrefs is regular,
the fwelling of the eye-lids fubfides towards the
7th or 9th day, and fome puriform matter is
feen upon the poultice, mixed with the diffolved
vitreous humour, which flowly iffues from the
bottom of the eye ; thefe are fucceeded by the
matter becoming thicker and whiter, the patient becoming eafy, and by a manifeft diminution of the whole eye-ball, which not only retires within the eye-lids, but deeply within the
orbit.

If the eye-lids be gently feparated at this period, the conjunctiva is found tumid and reddifh, and the edge of the divided portion of the
ftaphyloma appears as if it were formed by a
fmall circle of white fkin. On the feparation
of this gelatinous circle, which feldom exceeds
the 12th or 14th day from the operation, the
margin of the wound becomes florid ; it then
contracts daily more and more, and laftly clofes
entirely. A fmall flefhy prominence remains
only for a few days in the centre of it, refembling a fmall reddifh papilla, which, by a few
applications,

applications of the argentum nitratum, retires completely and heals.

The fymptoms occafioned by this operation, are fo far from being confiderable, that in the greater number of cafes, the furgeon is obliged to irritate the eye for feveral days after the operation, in order that it may inflame, partly by leaving it for a long time uncovered and expofed to the air, and partly by enlarging the wound made in the centre of the ftaphyloma, by removing another circular portion half a line in breadth, and thus facilitating ftill further the difcharge of the humours, and the admiffion of the air to the cavity of the eye. When the inflammation has once commenced in the internal part of the eye, and is fucceeded by fuppuration, the reft of the treatment proceeds regularly, by the ufe of emollient applications only, and is fpeedily completed. And as, by adopting the method of deftroying the ftaphyloma here recommended, the confequent contraction of the eye-ball takes place equally around the greater axis of this organ, the mutilated part which remains is alfo regular in its whole circumference, and offers an eafy and convenient fupport to the artificial eye.

CASE

Case LXIII.

Regina Fedele, a female peafant, 19 years of age, living in Caffanmagnago, had, from her infancy, a ftaphyloma of the left eye, in confequence of the fmall-pox, which gradually increafed, fo as to project without the eye-lids for more than an inch. The deformity, as well as the inconveniences arifing from the perpetual weeping, and the frequent attacks of ophthalmia, which, by confent, were alfo propagated to the found eye, induced the poor girl to apply to this hofpital for relief on the 20th of November 1785.

I ingenuoufly acknowledge, that experience had not then fufficiently inftructed me in the beft method of operating in cafes of ftaphyloma, and although I was of opinion that the removal of a portion of the fclerotic coat with the tumour ought to be profcribed from practice, yet it appeared to me a matter of little confequence that the excifion fhould be made in the very borders of the cornea with the fclerotic coat. With the knife, therefore, which is ufed for the extraction of the cataract, I pierced through the bafe of the ftaphyloma, at the part where the cornea and fclerotica unite, and divided it downwards; then with the forceps and fciffars I removed the whole tumour of the cornea circularly. The

eye-ball

eye-ball was prefently emptied of the humours, and retired within the eye-lids. On examining the detached cornea, which had formed the ftaphyloma, attentively, I found that this membrane was entirely diftinct from the callous ftratum of the conjunctiva covering it; and that it was not thicker than natural, but in fome parts even thinner. At the moment the ftaphyloma was extirpated, the patient felt acute pain. After the operation the eye-lids were covered with a dry comprefs and bandage; and as the patient was plethoric I ordered blood to be taken from the arm. Half an hour afterwards the patient was feized with vomiting and univerfal fhiverings, which returned at intervals during the day and following night, notwithftanding the ufe of Riverius's mixture and opiate enemata.

The following day the eye-lids and ball of the eye appeared unufually tumid, and of a dark red colour, threatening gangrene. The fever was very fmart, the pulfe hard, with rednefs of the countenance, and very acute pain in the head. I therefore ordered blood to be taken away from the foot, and at night directed that leeches fhould be applied upon the left temple, and the eye-lids covered with a poultice of bread, milk, and faffron. During the night of the 2d day the patient was delirious, and was feized at intervals with univerfal rigors.

On

On the 3d day, obferving that a blackifh fubftance prefented itfelf between the edges of the
tumefied eye-lids, refembling clotted blood, I
carefully feparated them, and there gufhed out
half a table-fpoonful of grumous blood mixed
with aqueous humour, which was attended with
relief to the patient and a diminution of the general fymptoms.

On the 6th day, as the exceffive tumefaction
of the eye-lids was a little diminifhed, I found
the eye-ball fullied with matter which was diluted and fetid. The edge of the wound was
floughy, and a fmall abfcefs the fize of a pea
was alfo formed in the conjunctiva, correfponding to the external angle of the eye, which I
opened with a lancet. From the bottom of
this fmall abfcefs arofe fhortly afterwards a fungus which gave me fome uneafinefs. I continued, however, the application of the emollient
poultices, and the internal ufe of a grain of the
tartarized antimony in a pint of the decoction
of the triticum repens, taken in fmall dofes,
which kept up the perfpiration, and procured
one or two motions daily.

It was not till the 13th day after the operation, that the fuppuration began to affume a
healthy appearance, and the fever, and the pain
in the head to abate. The eye-lids and ball of
the eye afterwards fubfided gradually, and the
fungus of the conjunctiva became ftationary.

The

The healthy fuppuration continued copious for a month, during which the margin of the wound of the ftaphyloma remained dark and floughy. When the fuppuration of the internal part of the eye was greatly diminifhed, this floughy margin feparated in the form of an efchar, and left a fmall wound of a healthy afpect. The fungus of the conjunctiva in the external angle of the eye difappeared, and the diminifhed eye-ball retired towards the bottom of the orbit. In three weeks more the fmall wound in the centre of the remaining part of the eye-ball was perfectly healed.

By means of the decoction of the cinchona, and a proper diet, the young woman recovered her former ftrength, and about ten weeks from the operation, after having fuffered the moft acute pain, with great hazard of her life, returned home perfectly cured, as far as the nature of the difeafe admitted.

Case LXIV.

Maria Antonia Bariola, of the valley Salinbeni, 30 years of age, of a delicate complexion, was disfigured from her infancy with a ftaphyloma of the right eye. The tumour had gradually increafed, fo as to protrude out of the eye-lids, particularly from the age of four years, after receiving a blow upon that eye. The ftaphyloma

G G

phyloma frequently inflamed, and produced a
correfponding affection of the left eye alfo,
which, on her admiffion into the hofpital, was
not only inflamed, but ulcerated upon the
cornea.

After fome time had been taken up in the
treatment of the ulcer and ophthalmia of the
left eye; I propofed to the patient to fubmit to
the excifion of the ftaphyloma, which occupied
the right eye, left the left eye, which frequently
participated in the inflammation with which
the other eye was affected, fhould be ultimately
loft alfo. The patient affented to it, and on
the 6th of February 1796 I pierced the moft
pointed part of the ftaphyloma, with the knife
ufed for the extraction of the cataract, at the
diftance of a line and a half from the centre or
apex of the tumour, forming a femicircular border at the lower part, which being raifed with
the forceps and turned upwards I removed
circularly with the fame inftrument, taking
away a portion of the apex of the tumour of
the cornea three lines in diameter. The brown
and diforganized lens paffed through this aperture, and afterwards a confiderable portion of
the diffolved vitreous humour. On carefully
examining this circular portion of the cornea,
feparated from the reft of the ftaphyloma, I
found it thinner than that membrane is in a found
ftate, except that fome parts of it were thickened

by

by the induration and callofity of the lamina of
the conjunctiva, which covered it. The eye-ball
was a little diminished, and the eye-lids being
clofed, I directed them to be covered with a dry
comprefs and bandage.

The patient did not feem to feel much pain
from the operation, nor during the five following days, neither were the eye-lids or eye-ball
at all inflamed. A fmall quantity of mucila-
ginous humour only, iffued from the eye daily.
As the inflammation and fuppuration of the
internal part of the eye, however, was neceffary to obtain the propofed intention, and feeing that after fix days from the excifion of the
ftaphyloma there was no appearance of its taking place, I ordered the patient to remove the
bandage, and expofe this eye as freely to the air
as the found one. It was thirty hours after
this expedient before the eye and eye-lids began
to inflame and tumefy, which was attended
with moderate pain and flight feverifhnefs. A
poultice of bread and milk was now applied,
and after three days the fuppuration was feen
to proceed from the internal part of the eye-
ball, at firft of a ferous, but afterwards of a
good quality. The margin of the wound was
pale and floughy.

In eight days the fuppuration abated, and
fhortly afterwards, on the feparation of this
fmall floughy circle, the wound contracted fo

that there was no longer any aperture in its centre, but a small reddish fleshy papilla, which I touched several times with the argentum nitratum. The emollient poultice was now discontinued, and the vitriolic collyrium substituted in its stead, which was dropped into the eye several times a day. The eye-ball very much diminished, and flattened at the part previously occupied by the staphyloma, preserved its motion, and .presented a very good support for the application of the artificial eye. The cure was completed in little more than a month from the period at which the eye began to be inflamed.

In comparing this case with the preceding, the advantage which results from the small circular excision of the apex or summit of the staphyloma, in the manner taught by Celsus, must be obvious, contrasted with the alarming symptoms which succeed the removal of this tumour at the-line where the cornea and sclerotica unite, and more particularly if it be executed in the sclerotic coat itself.

I shall not subjoin any other cases on this subject, to these now delivered, since those which I shall relate at the end of the next chapter, will equally contribute to a fuller confirmation of this practical point.

CHAP

CHAP. XVIII.

OF THE DROPSY OF THE EYE.

In all the cavities of the animal body, moiftened by a ferous vapour, as in thofe deftined to contain a certain and determinate quantity of aqueous and limpid fluid, there is fuch a reciprocity of action between the fecerning extremities of the arteries, and the mouths of the abforbent veffels, that the fluid poured into thefe cavities is held in circulation, and inceffantly renewed, without ever accumulating beyond a certain degree, or a determinate quantity. If this relation of action between thefe two vafcular fyftems be interrupted or deftroyed, in confequence of general or local indifpofition, the cavities, no longer lubricated by the ferous vapour, contract and are obliterated; or, on the contrary, become unufually diftended by the exceffive quantity of ferous or watery fluid inceffantly collecting and ftagnating in them, and acquire an immoderate and much greater fize than any one unacquainted with thefe fubjects might imagine.

G G 3   The

The eye, confidered merely as a cavity deftined to contain a certain and determinate
quantity of ferous, limpid, aqueous fluid, is
fometimes fubject to one and fometimes to the
other of thefe two difeafes, the firft of which is
denominated *atrophy*, the latter *dropfy* of the
eye. In the firft cafe, the eye-ball gradually
diminifhes, fo as to contract itfelf and wafte
away; and as the abforbent fyftem never ceafes
to act fo, where there is a defect of fluid to be
abforbed, it takes up, by little and little, the folid
parts of the eye-ball, which it infenfibly diminifhes, and in procefs of time even deftroys.
In the fecond cafe the eye becomes of a fize
greater than natural, and fometimes fo extraordinary in its bulk as to protrude out of the eye-
lids, at firft with great weaknefs, and afterwards
with complete lofs of fight.

The generality of furgeons teach, that the
immediate caufe of the dropfy of the eye is
fometimes the increafe of the vitreous, at other
times of the aqueous humour. In all the cafes
of dropfy of the eye which I have operated
upon, or have examined in the dead body,
in different ftages of the difeafe, I have conftantly found the vitreous humour, as the difeafe was inveterate or recent, more or lefs diforganized and in a ftate of diffolution; nor
have I been able, in any inftance, to diftinguifh, on account of the increafed quantity,
which

which of thefe two humours, vitreous or aqueous,
had had the greater fhare in the formation of
the difeafe. Among the moft efteemed modern
oculifts there are fome who believe that
the principal caufe of this difeafe ought to be
referred to the contraction of the inorganic pores
of the cornea, through which the aqueous humour
being no longer able to tranfude, ftagnates
within the eye, and there produces the
dropfy. In afferting this, they appear not fufficiently
acquainted with the activity of the abforbent
fyftem in the animal œconomy, and
feem not to have confidered, that in conformity
with their theory, the dropfy of the eye ought
conftantly to fucceed the *pannus* of this organ,
the *leucoma*, and extenfive cicatrices of the cornea,
a circumftance which is contradicted by
daily obfervation and experience.

Laftly, I have diffected an eye affected with
dropfy, in a child about three years and a half
old, who died of marafmus. In this eye, the
vitreous humour was not only wanting, and the
cavity which it occupied filled with water, but
the membrane of the vitreous humour was alfo
converted into a fubftance, partly fpongy, and
partly lipomatofe. This eye was a third part
larger than the found one. The fclerotic coat was
not thinner than that of the found eye, but was
flaccid and yielding, and when feparated from
the choroid coat could not fupport itfelf or preferve

ferve

ferve the globular form. The cornea was a
third part larger than that of the found eye,
had loft its natural pulpy quality, and was fenfibly thinner than that of the found eye. Between the cornea and the iris there was a confiderable quantity of aqueous humour of a faint
red colour. The cryftalline lens, with its opake
capfule, was pufhed a little into the·anterior
chamber of the aqueous humour, where it could
not advance further in confequence of its capfule having contracted a firm adhefion with the
iris around the edge of the pupil. When this
capfule was opened the cryftalline paffed out,
one half of which was diffolved, and the reft
very foft. It was impoffible to feparate the
pofterior capfule of the cryftalline from a hard
fubftance, which appeared to be, as it was in
reality, the membrane of the vitreous humour
altered in its texture. On dividing the choroid
coat from the ligamentum ciliare to the bottom
of the eye, a confiderable quantity of reddifh
water iffued from the pofterior part of the eye,
but not a particle of vitreous humour. Inftead
of vitreous humour there was a fmall cylindri-
cal fubftance, partly fungous, partly lipomatofe,
furrounded by a confiderable quantity of water,
which ran through the longitudinal axis from
the entrance of the optic nerve to the corpus
ciliare, or to that hard fubftance to which the
pofterior convexity of the capfule of the cryf-
                                             talline

talline ſtrongly adhered. This ſmall cylinder, for two lines and a half from the entrance of the optic nerve forwards, was covered by a ſtratum of whitiſh ſubſtance folded upon itſelf, as the omentum is, when it is drawn upwards towards the fundus of the ſtomach. I ſuppoſe that this ſtratum of whitiſh ſubſtance was the remains of the diſorganized retina ; for on pouring ſome rectified ſpirit of wine upon the whole internal ſurface of the choroid coat, and upon this little cylinder, I found no trace of retina upon the internal ſurface of the choroid, and this white ſubſtance, folded upon itſelf, acquired a conſiderable degree of firmneſs, preciſely as the retina does when immerſed in ſpirit of wine. The little cylinder, as well as the hard ſubſtance which occupied the place of the corpus ciliare, was evidently the membrane of the vitreous humour, emptied of water, and converted into a maſs, partly ſpongy, as I have ſaid, and partly lipomatoſe. It is not eaſy to determine whether this fungous and lipomatoſe degeneration of the membrane of the vitreous humour had preceded the dropſy of the eye, or had been the conſequence of it. This caſe, however, added to ſeveral others of dropſical eyes which I have examined, in which no vitreous humour was found in the poſterior part of the eye, but only ſome water or bloody lymph, contributes greatly to prove, that this diſeaſe conſiſts principally

in,

in a morbid fecretion of fluid from the fmall
cells of the vitreous humour, and fometimes,
alfo, in a fingular degeneration of the alveolar
membrane, of which the vitreous humour is
compofed.*

The increafed fecretion of aqueous fluid,
both into the fmall cells compofing the vitreous
humour, and into other parts of the eye-ball;
the rupture of thofe cells from exceffive diftenfion; and at the fame time the diminifhed
energy of the abforbent fyftem of the affected
eye, are moft probably the caufes of the morbid accumulation of the humours of the eye.
From the ftagnation and gradual increafe
of the vitreous and aqueous humours, it neceffarily follows, that the eye-ball affumes at
firft an oval figure, terminating in a point
at the cornea; then, by enlarging in all its
dimenfions, it arrives at a fize greater than
the other, and ultimately protrudes out of the
orbit, fo as no longer to admit of being covered
by the eye-lids, disfiguring the patient's countenance, as if an ox's eye had been inferted in
the place of the natural one.

* A cafe, nearly fimilar to this, is related in the Medical
Obfervations and Inquiries, vol. iii. art. 14.   It is to be obferved, however, that in the child mentioued in this work,
the eye firft began to diminifh in fize, and afterwards to become dropfical, and to acquire a very confiderable bulk,
which, if it had taken place in the cafe that came under my
obfervation, could not have been known.

This

This difeafe is fometimes preceded by blows upon the eye or correfponding temple, or by an obftinate internal ophthalmia; at other times by no other inconvenience than a trouble-fome fenfe of fwelling and diftenfion in the orbit, difficulty in moving the eye-ball, and confiderable diminution of fight: and laftly, by none of thefe caufes, nor by any other fufficiently evident; efpecially if the difeafe happens in children at a very early age, from whom no account can be obtained. As foon as the eye has affumed the oval figure, and the anterior chamber has become larger than natural, the iris appears placed more backwards than ufual, and is in a fingular manner tremulous on the flighteft motion of the eye-ball. The pupil remains dilated in every degree of light; and the cryftalline is fometimes brown from the commencement of the difeafe, at other times it only becomes fo in the higheft degree of it. When the difeafe becomes ftationary, and the cryftalline lens is not profoundly opake, the patient can diftinguifh light from darknefs, and, in a fmall degree, the figures of bodies, and the moft vivid colours; but when the eye increafes ftill more in bulk, and the cryftalline is entirely opake, the retina is, as it were, rendered paralytic, by the exceffive diftenfion, and confequently is no longer fenfible to the few rays of

light

light which pafs through the edges of the opake
cryftalline to reach the bottom of the eye.

In the laft ftage of this difeafe, or when the
dropfical eye-ball protrudes out of the orbit, and
can no longer be covered by the eye-lids, to the
ill effects already enumerated, are added thofe
which arife from the aridity of the eye-ball, the
contact of extraneous bodies, the friction of the
cilia, the difcharge of matter and tears, the ulceration of the lower eye-lid, upon which the
eye-ball preffes, and the excoriation of the eye-
ball itfelf; in confequence of which, the dropfical eye is occafionally attacked with violent
ophthalmia and fevere pain in the affected part,
and the whole of the head. Nor does the ulceration always keep within certain bounds, but
fpreads, firft rendering the cornea opake, and
afterwards deftroying the fclerotica, and, in proportion, the other component parts of the eye-
ball.

On the firft appearance of the dropfy of the
eye, furgical writers advife the internal adminiftration of mercurials, the extract of cicuta,
that of the pulfatilla nigricans (anemone pra-
tenfis); and externally, aftringent and corroborant collyria, a feton in the neck, and compreffion upon the protruding eye-ball. As far,
however, as I have confulted the refult of the
obfervations of the beft practitioners upon this
fubject, I have not met with a fingle hiftory

6   correctly

correctly detailed of a cure of the dropsy of the eye by means of these internal remedies. And, with respect to the external applications, I know from my own experience, that when the disease is manifest, astringent and corroborant collyria, as well as pressure upon the protuberant eye, are highly injurious. In these cases, I have succeeded in quieting, for some time, the uneasy sense of distension within the orbit, and upon the forehead and temple of the same side, of which patients in this state complain so much, particularly when they are affected with recurrent ophthalmia, by means of a seton in the neck, frequent ablutions with the aqua malvæ, and the application of a plaster made of the same plant. But as soon as the eye-ball begins to protrude from the orbit, and to pass beyond the eye-lids, there is no means of preventing the unhappy consequences of the disease, but by an operation which consists in evacuating the superabundant humours of the eye, by means of an incision, and thereby obliging its membranes, in consequence of a mild inflammation and suppuration of the internal part of the eye, to contract themselves, and retire to the bottom of the orbit. To defer this operation longer, would be to abandon the patient to the inconveniences of an habitual ophthalmia, the danger of ulceration of the eye-ball and

subjacent

fubjacent eye-lid, and even to the carcinoma of the whole eye, with the hazard of his life.

To fulfil this indication of emptying the eye-ball of the fuperabundance of aqueous hu- mour ftagnating in it, the *paracentefis* of the eye- ball was formerly highly commended. *Nuck,** one of the advocates for this operation, punc- tured the eye by means of a fmall trocar, p e- cifely in the centre of the cornea. Afterwards it was judged more proper to puncture the eye- ball through the fclerotic coat, at about two lines from its union with the cornea, for the purpofe of more eafily evacuating the vitreous humour alfo, together with the aqueous, in fuch quantity as might be thought fufficient to diminifh the morbid enlargement of the eye- ball.

This method of operating in the dropfy of the eye, notwithftanding the approbation it re- ceived from the moft celebrated furgeons, is at prefent fallen into difufe, as ineffectual and in- adequate to the purpofe. Nor will this appear furprifing to thofe who are acquainted with our prefent notions upon the animal œconomy, par- ticularly with refpect to the abforbent fyftem, and who are not unaware how little can be reckoned upon the favourable fuccefs of the paracentefis, as a mode of treatment in chronic

* De Duct. Ocul. Aquos, page 120.

dropfies

dropfies in general, but particularly that of the
tunica vaginalis, or *hydrocele*. For the radical
cure of the latter is never obtained, unlefs, after
the water is evacuated, the adhefive inflammation takes place in the tunica vaginalis and albuginea, or when both thefe membranes fuppurate, ulcerate, and contract a firm adhefion to
each other, by which the poffibility is taken
away of any further collections of water in the
fcrotum. And if it has occafionally happened
that the puncture has effected a radical cure of
the hydrocele, it is becaufe by an unforefeen accident it has excited an inflammation of the
tunica vaginalis and albuginea, and has thereby
produced a coalefcence of thefe two membranes.

According to thefe principles, the paracentefis of the eye, directed only to evacuate the fuperabundant quantity of fluid contained in it,
cannot be a means of curing the dropfy of this
organ, unlefs the puncture made by the trocar
excite an inflammation and fuppuration, and
afterwards a coalefcence between the membranes
compofing it. Nuck relates, that, in a young
man of Breda, on whom he performed the operation, he was obliged to puncture the eye five
times at different periods; that at the 6th time
it was neceffary to employ fuction through the
canula, in order to evacuate the greateft poffible
quantity of vitreous humour; and laftly, that

4 he

he was under the necessity of introducing a plate
of lead between the palpebræ and eye, for the
purpose of maintaining a continual preffure upon
the empty and diminished eye-ball. In a woman
of the Hague, he fays, that he punctured the
eye twice without advantage, and that she was
two or three times more fubjected to the fame
operation, without, however, adding what was
the refult of it. I have not much difficulty
in believing, that the radical cure of the dropfy
of the eye may have been fometimes obtained
by means of the puncture, after repeated intro-
ductions of the trocar, and other fimilar harsh
modes of treatment with the canula of this inftrument, introduced into the eye-ball; but
this fuccefs cannot be attributed to the fimple
evacuation of the fuperabundant quantity of
vitreous and aqueous humour; but to the irritation produced by the canula, and to the con-
féquent adhefive inflammation or fuppuration
excited in the internal membranes of the eye.
It is not furprifing that Woolhoufe, after having
learnt this from experience, wifhing to fecure
the perfect fuccefs of the *paracentefis*, for the
radical cure of the dropfy of the eye, fhould
afterwards have taught that when the canula
has been introduced into the eye, it ought to be
rotated between the fingers at leaft fix times;
and, according to the fame rule, Platner fhould
have propofed, that after the humours of the

eye

eye have been difcharged by means of the trocar, a tepid fluid fhould be injected into the eye
through the canula; and Mauchart, that the
aperture made in the eye fhould be kept open
by means of a fmall tent of lint. If all thefe
circumftances prove on the one hand the infuf-
ficiency of the paracentefis in the radical treatment of the dropfy of the eye, they evidently
fhew on the other, that the perfect cure of this
difeafe can only be obtained by emptying the
eye of its humours, and at the fame time exciting in its internal membranes, a certain degree
of inflammation and fuppuration.

In order to obtain this completely, the moft
eafy and expeditious method hitherto propofed,
is, without doubt, that which I have detailed in
the preceding chapter on the radical treatment
of the inveterate ftaphyloma, which projects beyond the eye-lids. Upon which I cannot but
repeat alfo upon the prefent occafion, that the
circular excifion of the dropfical eye-ball in the
fclerotic coat is highly difadvantageous, if not
dangerous. For this operation is conftantly followed by the moft alarming fymptoms, as repeated hæmorrhages, collections of grumous
blood in the bottom of the eye-ball, violent inflammation of the eye-ball, of the eye-lids, and
head; inceffant vomiting, convulfions, and delirium, with great hazard of the patient's life.
Thofe modern writers indeed, who have faith-

fully communicated to the public the refult of
their practice upon this fubject, in the number
of whom, after Louis,* Marchan,† and Terras,‡
deferve much praife, have ingenuoufly declared
that in fome cafes of dropfy of the eye, in which
they have performed this operation, they have
had much reafon to regret their attempt.

The circular incifion made in the upper part
or centre of the cornea of the dropfical eye, of
the circumference of a large lentil-feed, or rather more, in the manner defcribed by Celfus on
the fubject of ftaphyloma, is exempted from
thefe very unpleafant confequences. · By means
of this operation, which is in no degree painful,
an opening is made for the difcharge of the humours, and an inflammation is promoted in the
internal parts of the eye. And this is obtained
without occafioning that fudden evacuation and
fubfidence of the membranes of the eye, which
neceffarily happens when the circular incifion is
made in the fclerotic coat, which greatly affects
the nerves of this organ, and the parts which
fympathize with it, as the head and ftomach;
this intimate confent not being perhaps the leaft
of the caufes from which the unhappy confequences before mentioned are produced; independently of thofe which neceffarily arife from

* Mémoires de Chirurg. T. xiii page 286. 290.

† Journal de Med. Paris. Janvier 1770. Sur deux ex-
ophthalmies ou groffeurs contre nature du globe de l'œil.

‡ Ibidem Mars 1776. Sur l'hydrophthalmie.

the

the almoft fudden expofure of a large furface of the bottom of the eye to the contact of the air, and the frequent ufe of lotions which are employed in thefe cafes.

With refpect to the method of operating, it is precifely the fame as that detailed in the preceding chapter. The furgeon, therefore, whether the cornea be tranfparent or not (fince, as I have faid, the immediate organ of vifion, in thefe cafes, is irremediably loft) fhould pierce this membrane with the fmall knife, at the diftance of a line and a half from its fummit or centre, and paffing the inftrument from one canthus of the eye to the other, fhould divide it downwards in the form of a femicircle, then having raifed this fegment of it with the forceps, and turned the cutting edge of the knife upwards, he fhould complete the operation by removing a circular portion of the centre of the cornea, of the fize of a large lentil-feed, or three lines in diameter in the cafe of an adult. Through this circular opening in the centre of the cornea, the furgeon, by a gentle preffure, fhould force out as much of the fuperabundant humours of the eye, as may be fufficient to allow the diminifhed eye-ball to re-enter the orbit, and be covered by the eye-lids. For the remainder, which is left ftagnating in the eye, will gradually flow out through this circular aperture in the centre of the cornea,

without

without the affiftance of further preffure. Until the appearance of the inflammation on the 3d or 5th day from the operation, the eye fhould be covered by a dry comprefs and bandage. But as foon as the eye and eye-lids begin to be inflamed and fwollen, the furgeon fhould, if neceffary, employ the internal remedies fuited to moderate the inflammation, and fhould cover the eye-lids with a poultice of bread and milk, which ought to be renewed every two hours at furtheft. It very frequently happens, both in the cafe of ftaphyloma and in the dropfy of the eye, that on the firft appearance of the inflammation, the eye which has been operated on increafes in fize, and protrudes out of the eye-lids again, nearly as much as before the operation. In 'this cafe it will be ufeful to cover the projecting portion of the eye-ball with a fmall piece of fine linen fpread with a liniment compofed of oil and wax, or with the yolk of an egg and the oil of St. John's wort, over which the poultice of bread and milk fhould be applied.

When the fuppuration of the internal part of the eye has commenced, which will be evident by the dreffings being moiftened with a tenacious lymph mixed with a portion of the humours of the eye, which will inceffantly flow from the opening in the cornea, and by the margin of the incifion affuming a pale floughy appearance, the eye-lids will fubfide, the eye-ball diminifh

diminifh in fize and gradually re-enter the orbit, and will continue to contraƈt itfelf more and more. The fmall floughy margin of the wound in the cornea will afterwards feparate in the form of an efchar, and leave a fmall ulcer of a healthy colour, which in the fame manner as the eye-ball will gradually contraƈt till it is clofed and entirely healed, leaving fufficient room between the eye-lids, and the mutilated portion of the eye-ball, for the appofition of an artificial eye.

Although the circular excifion of the centre of the cornea of the fize of a large lentil-feed, be fufficient in the adult to excite a mild inflammation and fuppuration in the internal part of the eye; yet if this fhould not manifeft itfelf before the 5th day, it will be neceffary to expofe the eye to the air, or as I have faid, in fpeaking of the ftaphyloma, to remove a circular portion of the cornea, by means of the forceps and curved fciffars, a line or rather more in breadth; which occafions the patient no inconvenience or pain, and produces the defired effeƈt of ultimately exciting an inflammation and mild fuppuration of the internal part of the eye, without which a complete cure cannot be obtained.

CASE LXV.

A peafant boy, 13 years of age, of a healthy and robuft conftitution, had no other complaint,

except

except an immoderate enlargement of the right eye, which projected fo much out of the orbit that the eye-lids were not fufficient to cover it. The cornea of this eye, although not clear, allowed the deeply-feated iris to be yet feen through it, the pupil dilated, and the cryftalline of a dark colour. His mother informed me that at two years of age, a little after the deficcation of the fmall-pox, he was afflicted with a violent inflammation in both his eyes with a denfe cloud, particularly in the right eye ; that by means of repeated blifters to the neck and behind the ears, and other external and internal remedies, he finally recovered the ufe of his left eye ; but that the right remained in the fame ftate ; and that it afterwards enlarged gradually till it acquired the enormous fize which it had when I faw him ; without his having ever complained of violent pain in it. The boy being taken into the hofpital I agreed to perform the operation upon him, which was on the 8th of June 1797.

Having pierced through the middle part of the cornea with the fmall knife which is ufed for the extraction of the cataract, and elevated the lower fegment of it with the forceps, I removed a circular portion of the centre of the cornea with Daviel's fciffars, rather more than two lines in diameter ; and as the cryftalline did not advance by a flight preffure, I opened

its

its capfule with the point of the knife, from
which a milky humour immediately efcaped,
and afterwards the dark coloured nucleus of the
cryftalline, and by a moderate degree of preffure, a confiderable quantity of vitreous humour
in a ftate of diffolution, by which the eye-ball
was fo much diminifhed, that on directing the
patient to clofe his eye-lids, they were' fufficient to cover it completely.

The boy did not feem to feel much pain during the operation, and paffed the firft and fecond
day out of bed, without experiencing any inconvenience. On removing the comprefs and
bandage from time to time, they were moiftened
with a glutinous humour, which had all the
appearance of being the diffolved vitreous humour. On the 4th day I found the eye-lids
fwollen, red, painful, and a little feparated, and
the eye-ball inflamed, with a flight pain in the
head, and a little fever. I ordered a poultice of
bread and milk to be applied upon them, and to
be renewed every two hours.

On the 7th day the fuppuration commenced
in the internal part of the eye-ball, at firft of a
ferous, and afterwards of a mucous and good
quality, with a diminution of the fever and
pain. The fuppuration continued in larger or
fmaller quantity for two weeks, and in the
mean time the palpebræ and eye-ball fubfided
greatly, and the latter very much diminifhed in

fize,

fize, retired towards the bottom of the orbit. The fmall floughy circle which furrounded the incifion in the centre of the cornea, feparated entirely, and left a fmall wound of a florid colour, which in a week clofed, and by a few applications of the argentum nitratum healed entirely. The deficiency of the eye might have been eafily fupplied by an artificial one.

Case LXVI.

A young lady, 16 years of age, of a delicate conftitution, in other refpects healthy and regular, was affected with an enlargement of the left eye, which increafed in all its dimenfions, fo as in the courfe of nine years to become twice the fize of the oppofite one, projected out of the orbit, and did not admit of being covered by the eye-lids.

Her parents attributed this difeafe to a fall which fhe had had when a child upon a heap of wood and rubbifh, by which fhe ftruck and violently bruifed her left eye, which was greatly difcoloured externally. The cornea of this eye was, to fome extent, become opake; but the pupil, notwithftanding, could be feen beyond it irregularly dilated, and the cryftalline dark.

While the eye-ball remained on a level with the orbit, the patient complained of no greater inconvenience than that of blindnefs, but as foon

6

as

as it could be no longer covered by the eye lids an ophthalmia fupervened, which became habitual, and was occafonally communiçated to the found eye; and this was accompanied with a very troublefome fenfe of tenfion in the enlarged eye, and in the temple of the fame fide. Aftringent applications, compreffion, and the internal ufe of the pulfatilla nigricans had, as far as it appeared, augmented the pain in the head and eye, and had rendered the attacks of ophthalmia more frequent than before.

On being confulted, I propofed to empty the dropfical eye by the excifion of a portion of the cornea, as the only expedient capable of arrefting the progrefs of the difeafe, and preferving the found eye. The patient, as well as her friends, rejected this project as too violent and extreme. In order to allay the pain in the eye and head, and the troublefome fenfe of tenfion in the orbit, I prefcribed to the patient the application of fmall bags of mallows with a little camphire, and the emulfion of gum arabic with a few drops of the tincture of opium to be taken at night.

Two mouths after the confultation, the fame inconveniences returned with fo much violence, that the patient demanded to have the operation inftantly performed; which was executed precifely as in the preceding cafe, that is, by removing a circular portion in the centre of

the

the cornea, of the ſize of a large lentil-ſeed. Some aqueous, and a large quantity of thin vitreous humour flowed out, and alſo the dark cryſtalline in a ſtate of diſſolution. The eyeball retired a little within the orbit, ſo as to be covered by the eye-lids.

The patient found great relief from this evacuation of the eye, and continued perfectly eaſy till the 5th day. Finding, however, that the eye was ſlow in inflaming, I directed the patient to keep it expoſed to the air the whole of the 6th day. On the night of the 7th the eye-lids were tumefied, and the eye-ball began to inflame, and gradually to enlarge ſo much as to be ready to project out of the eye-lids again. The fever, however, and the pain in the eye and head were moderate. The eye-lids and eye were covered with a cloth ſpread with the yolk of an egg and oil of St. John's wort; and over it was applied a poultice of bread and milk. The general treatment was limited to ſome emollient clyſters and a low diet.

On the 11th day the ſerous ſuppuration appeared, and afterwards the mucous, which continued abundant for 20 days longer, on the appearance of which, the fever and pain in the eye entirely abated, and the tumefaction of the palpebræ and eye-ball gradually ſubſided. The ſmall ſloughy circle around the inciſion in the cornea was afterwards detached as uſual; the

little

little ulcer of a good colour contracted, forming in the centre a kind of flefhy papilla, which was repreffed by the argentum nitratum, and finally healed entirely. The young lady, though cured, could not bear the application of the artificial eye, till eight months after the evacuation of the eye-ball.

CASE LXVII.

In the beginning of June 1799, Signor Vincenzo Vifconti, a very able apothecary of this city, came to me with his infant fon, about a year and a half old, who had been juft brought to him from the country, where he had been nurfed, that I might examine the left eye, which had become confiderably more turgid and prominent than the right, with tumefaction of the eye-lids of that fide, and a fpecies of fugillation of the conjunctiva, particularly towards the internal angle. The father conjectured that it had arifen from a fall or blow upon the left eye; but the nurfe ftrongly denied it. The child did not feem to be in pain, and appeared as if he could fee with this eye. I ordered the little patient to be gently purged, and refolvent fomentations to be applied externally.

Thefe remedies were of no advantage, and the eye-ball increafed in fize with fuch rapidity, that by the middle of November of the fame year it projected out of the orbit prodigioufly,

and

and was so large as not to admit of being covered by the eye-lids; which, as well as the conjunctiva, were occasionally inflamed, without any evident cause, on which account it was sometimes necessary to take away blood locally, by means of leeches. At this period the sight of the left eye was greatly diminished, if not entirely lost.

The rapid enlargement of the eye-ball, the inutility of the remedies hitherto employed, the deformity of the countenance, and more particularly the danger of the sound eye being affected by it, or the dropsy degenerating into a much worse disease, determined me, together with Signor Volpi, surgeon of this hospital, to empty and diminish the size of the dropsical eye.

On the 21st of November, therefore, the child being placed upon a table, and held by proper assistants, with the small knife, which is used for the extraction of the cataract, I pierced through the cornea of the dropsical eye, near the centre of it, and taking hold of the divided semicircular border with the forceps, and turning the cutting edge of the knife upwards, I removed a circular portion of the centre of the cornea, of the diameter of a small lentil-seed. I chose, in this, case, to remove as little of the centre of the cornea as possible, not only as I was desirous of ascertaining again, whether the

symptoms

fymptoms confequent on the evacuation of the eye-ball, are in proportion to the extent of the circular incifion made in the cornea, but be-caufe I greatly feared, that in fo young a child, a fudden and violent inflammation of the eye and eye-lids might be attended with fatal con-fequences.

Through this fmall aperture formed in the centre of the cornea, the femifluid and diffolved cryftalline efcaped, and a large quantity of thin vitreous humour; fo that the eye ball inftantly retired within the eye-lids, which were covered with a comprefs and bandage. The child flept a little after the operation, and afterwards got up and paffed the reft of the day as ufual, in play, without fhewing any fign of pain.

From the 21ft to the 28th, fome fluid re-fembling the diffolved vitreous humour flowed from the eye, and the eye-ball and palpebræ fubfided daily; but no appearance of inflam-mation prefenting itfelf in the internal part of the eye, I ordered that the child's eye fhould be uncovered, with the precife view of caufing it to inflame; which, however, had no effect.

On the 30th of November, I obferved that a portion of the vitreous humour, not diffolved, but confiftent and globofe, protruded out of the circular aperture formed in the centre of the cornea, and the eye-ball appeared lefs diminifhed than it was on the preceding days. With a

ftroke

ftroke of the fciffars I removed this obftacle
formed by the vitreous humour, and on preffing
upon the eye-ball gently, a confiderable quantity of bloody ferum flowed out, after which
the eye-ball became as fmall as on the preceding days.

On the 2d of December fome figns of inflammation in the eye-lids and conjunctiva appeared. The child feemed defirous to lie-in
bed. I ordered a bread and milk poultice to be
applied upon the tumid eye-lids.

On the 8th of December, the inflammation
of the eye-lids and conjunctiva, inftead of extending, as I had hoped, within the eye-ball,
had, on the contrary, entirely ceafed, and a
portion of the iris prefented itfelf at the fmall
opening made in the centre of the cornea,
which completely clofed up this aperture, and
the eye-ball, in the mean time, became again
turgid. I pufhed back this procidentia of the
iris with the point of a probe, and immediately
a remarkable quantity of bloody ferofity flowed
out.

Convinced now, that the circular aperture
formed in the centre of the cornea was too fmall,
and lefs than was requifite for exciting an inflammation of the internal membranes of the eye;
by means of the forceps and curved fciffars I removed a circular portion from the border of the
cornea, fo as to render this opening of a circumference

ference equal to a large lentil feed. After this
an inflammation was fpeedily excited in the
internal parts of the eye-ball, which had a very
mild courfe, never obliging the child to lie in
bed, nor caufing it any acute pain. The internal inflammation having terminated in fuppuration, true pus began to appear upon the poultice : from this time the cure proceeded with
the greateft regularity to the end, without the
child's ordinary mode of living, or its ufual good
humour being interrupted.

In proportion as the difcharge of matter proceeding from the internal part of the eye diminifhed in quantity, the eye-lids fubfided, and
the eye diminifhed in fize, and funk towards
the bottom of the orbit, leaving at laft a regular
furface, which would ferve at pleafure for the
convenient fupport of an artificial eye.

The refult of this hiftory proves, in the moft
convincing manner, what has been afferted in
the two laft chapters; that the violence of the
fymptoms confequent on the operation of the
ftaphyloma and dropfy of the eye, are in proportion to the extent of the circular incifion made
in the eye-ball, for the evacuation of the humours. That therefore the very ufeful precept
of Celfus, of removing only a circular portion
of the centre of the cornea, of the fize of a lentil-feed, admits of fome exceptions. For if this
incifion be too fmall to allow the humours to

7   be

be readily difcharged, and the blood which afterwards colle&s within the eye-ball, or be fuch as
to be eafily clofed up by fome portion of the
vitreous humour, which is not diffolved, by a
portion of the iris, or by grumous blood, it gives
occafion to new colle&ions of bloody ferofity
within the cavity of the dropfical eye, and prevents the inflammation and fuppuration of its
internal membranes; a circumftance abfolutely
neceffary to obtain the end which the furgeon
propofes in the treatment of this difeafe.

CHAP

C H A P. XIX.

OF THE AMAUROSIS AND OF THE HEMERA-
LOPIA.

THE celebrated furgeons Schmucker and Richter, guided by obfervation and experience, have
treated this fubject with fo much precifion and
clearnefs, that it only remains for me at prefent to add fome reflections and facts, which
tend to confirm the truth and utility of the
doctrine of thefe two illuftrious writers, and thus
facilitate the ftudies of the young furgeon.

The amaurofis is *perfect* or *imperfect, inveterate
or recent, continual or periodical.* The *perfect inveterate amaurofis,* with organic injury of the fubftance conftituting the immediate organ of vifion, is a difeafe abfolutely incurable. The *imperfect recent amaurofis,* particularly that which
is *periodical,* generally admits of a cure, fince it
is moft frequently connected with a difordered
ftate of the ftomach and primæ viæ, or is dependent on caufes, which though they affect the
immediate organ of vifion, may be removed

without

without leaving any trace of diforganization, either in the optic nerve or retina.

In general, thofe cafes of amaurofis may be regarded as incurable which have exifted for feveral years, in perfons advanced in age, and whofe fight has been weak from their youth; thofe which have been flowly formed, at firft with a morbid increafe of fenfibility in the immediate organ of vifion, and afterwards with a gradual diminution of perception in this organ to complete blindnefs; thofe in which the pupil is immoveable, without being much dilated, but where it has loft its circular figure, or when it is fo much dilated as to appear as if the iris were wanting, having alfo an unequal or fringe-like margin; in which the bottom of the eye, independently of the opacity of the cryftalline lens, has an unufual palenefs, fimilar to horn, fometimes inclining to green, reflected from the retina as if from a mirrour;* which are accompanied with pain of the whole head, and with a conftant fenfe of tenfion in the eye-

---

* The retina of a found eye is tranfparent, and, therefore, in any degree of dilatation of the pupil, the bottom of the eye is of a deep black colour. This unufual pallor then which accompanies the amaurofis, indicates that a confiderable change has taken place in the fubftance of the optic nerve forming the retina, which, according to all appearance, is become thickened, and rendered permanently incapable of tranfmitting the impreffions of light. This fign, therefore, is one of the moft unfavourable.

ball;

ball; which have been preceded by great and protracted incitement of the whole nervous fyf-tem, and afterwards by general debility and languor of the whole conftitution, as after the long abufe of fpirituous liquors, manuftupration, or premature venery; thofe which have been preceded or accompanied by attacks of epilepfy, or by frequent and violent hemicrania; which have come on in confequence of violent and obftinate internal ophthalmia, at firft with an increafed, but afterwards diminifhed fenfibility of the retina, and flownefs of motion in the pupil; which, befides being inveterate, are the confequence of blows upon the head; which have been occafioned by direct blows upon the eye-ball; which have appeared after violent contufion and laceration of the *fupraorbital* nerve,* whether this has taken place immedi-ately after the blow, or fome weeks after the healing of the wound of the fupercilium; which have been occafioned by extraneous bodies pe-netrating the eye-ball, as leaden fhot,† &c.; thofe which are derived from the confirmed lues venerea, in which the prefence of one or more exoftofes upon the forehead, upon the fides of the nofe, or upon the maxillary bone,

---

* Of the numerous cafes of amaurofis of this kind, I do not know that any one has been cured, except that related by Valfalva, in his Differt. II. § XI.

† Neffi, Inftituzioni de Chirurgia, T. iii. page 282.

lead

lead to the suspicion that there may be also similar exostofes within the orbit: lastly, those which are conjoined with a manifest change of figure and dimension of the whole eye ball, as when it is of a long oval figure, or of a preternatural bulk or smallness. Maitre-Jan certainly alluded to these causes of amaurosis, when he said, *c'est rechercher la pierre philosophale que de vouloir chercher des remedes pour guérir le goute fereine; cette maladie est absolument incurable.*

On the contrary, those cafes of *recent imperfect amaurosis*, most frequently at least, if not always, admit of a cure, which, although the patient be almost, or even completely deprived of fight, have not been produced by any of those causes which are capable of contusing, or destroying, the organic texture of the optic nerve or retina; in which the immediate organ of vision preserves some, though little, sensibility to the light, whether in the direction of the axis of vision or laterally; those cafes of sudden or recent amaurosis, in which, although the pupil is preternaturally dilated, it is not excessively fo, and is regular in its circumference; behind which the bottom of the eye is of a deep black colour, as in a natural state; which have not been preceded or accompanied by violent and continual pain in the head and eye-brow, nor by a fense of constriction in the eye-ball; which have originated from violent anger, excessive

grief

grief or terror; thofe which have fucceeded an exceffive fulnefs and crudity of the ftomach, plethora either general or confined to the head, the fuppreffion of accuftomed fanguineous dif- charges from the nofe, uterus or hæmorrhoids; thofe occafioned by an evident metaftafis of va- riolous, rheumatic, herpetic, or gouty matter; which are the confequence of profufe lofs of blood; which are to be referred to a nervous debility not inveterate, in perfons who are young, and which is confequently yet fufcep- tible of being remedied; thofe produced by convulfions and violent efforts during a laborious parturition; thofe which accompany the course or decline of acute or intermittent fevers; and thofe, laftly, which are *periodical,* or which come on and difappear at intervals, every day, every three days, every month, or at a certain feafon of the year.

By an attentive examination of the nature and caufes of the imperfect amaurofis which admits of a cure, it is found, from the careful obfervations of Schmucker and Richter, that this difeafe is moft frequently derived from a morbid excitement or irritation in the digeftive organs, either alone or accompanied with general nervous debility, in which the eyes participate fympa- thetically. According to thefe principles, in the greater number of cafes of *recent imperfect amau- rofis,* the principal indication of cure which the

I I 3   furgeon

furgeon ought to fulfil in the treatment of this
difeafe, is that of unloading the ftomach and
primæ viæ of the faburræ and morbific ftimuli;
and afterwards of ftrengthening the gaftric fyftem, facilitating the digeftion, and at the fame
time exciting the whole nervous fyftem, and
particularly that of the eyes, which are affected
and rendered torpid by a fympathetic connection.

With refpect to the firft part of the treatment of the *imperfect amaurofis*, the intention is
perfectly anfwered by emetics and internal refolvents. In the clafs of emetics, experience
has taught that the *antimonium tartarizatum* is
preferable to every other, and that when given
afterwards in fmall and divided dofes, it anfwers
the purpofe of a refolvent medicine, the action
of which may be increafed by conjoining it with
gummy or faponaceous fubftances. In the
treatment of the imperfect amaurofis, therefore,
which is moft frequently fympathetic, and depending on acrid matters in the primæ viæ, it
will be proper at firft, in the greater number of
cafes, to diffolve for an adult, 3 grains of tartarized antimony in 4 ounces of water, of which
2 table-fpoonsful may be taken every half hour,
until it produces naufea, and afterwards abundant vomiting. On the following day he fhould
be ordered to take the refolvent powders, compofed of one ounce of the cryftals of tartar and

one

one grain of the tartarized antimony, divided
into fix equal parts, of which the patient fhould
take one in the morning, another four hours
afterwards, and the third in the evening, during
eight or ten fucceffive days. This medicine
will produce a flight naufea, and fome evacuations of the bowels more than ufual, and perhaps, after fome days, even vomiting. But if,
during the ufe of this opening powder, the patient make ineffectual efforts to vomit, and
complain of.a bitter tafte and want of appetite,
without any amendment of the fight, the emetic
fhould be repeated, and even a third and fourth
time, if the prefence of the morbific ftimuli in
the ftomach, bitter tafte, tenfion of the hypochondria, acid eructations, and tendency to
vomit require it. For it not unfrequently happens, that the patient, on the firft evomition,
throws up only water with a little mucus, but on
repeating the emetic, after the naufeating powder has been ufed for fome days, a confiderable
quantity of yellowifh green matter will be
thrown up, which will greatly relieve the ftomach, head, and eyes.

The ftomach being cleared, the opening pills
of Schmucker fhould be prefcribed,* or thofe of
Richter,

* R. Gum. Sagapen.
  Galban.
  Sap. venet. an. drachmam j.
  Rhei opt. drachmam unam et femis.

I I 4

Antim.

Richter.* The phænomena which are usually observed to happen in consequence of this treatment, are the following: the patient, after having vomited copiously, feels more easy and comfortable than before. Sometimes on the same day on which he has taken the emetic he begins to distinguish the surrounding objects; at other times this advantage is not obtained till the 5th, the 7th, or 10th day; and in some cases not till some weeks after the adhibition of the emetic, and the uninterrupted use of the opening powders or pills. As soon as the patient begins to recover his fight the pupil is found less dilated than before, and is also more contracted when exposed to the vivid light of a candle; and in proportion as the power of vision augments, this contraction and mobility of the pupil increases. Upon the whole, the cure

Antim. tartariz. grana xvj.
   Suc. liquirit. drachmam unam F. Pilul. gran. unius.
The patient should take 15 of these pills, morning and evening, for the space of 4 or even 6 weeks.

* R. Gumm. Ammoniac.
   Aff. fœtid.
   Sap. venet.
   Rad. Valerian, s. p.
   Summit. arnicæ an. drachmas duas.
   Antim. tartariz. gran. xviij. F. pilulæ granorum
      duorum.
The patient should take 15 of these pills 3 times a day for some weeks.

is feldom completed in lefs than a month, during which time the ufe of local remedies calculated to excite the languid action of the nerves of the eye fhould not be neglected, as will be hereafter mentioned.

When the furgeon fhall have fufficient reafon to believe, that by means of thefe remedies the offending matters which ftimulated the ftomach have been perfectly eliminated, and efpecially after the patient has, in a great mea-fure, regained his fight, the plan of treatment fhould be directed to ftrengthen the ftomach, and invigorate the nervous fyftem in general, and that of the nerves of the eye in particular. He fhould therefore prefcribe a powder compofed of one ounce of the cinchona and half an ounce of valerian root, divided into fix equal parts; of which the convalefcent fhould take one in the morning and another at night, in any convenient vehicle, and fhould continue the ufe of this medicine for at leaft five weeks. In the mean time he fhould live on tender fucculent food, and cooling broths, fhould take a moderate quantity of wine, and ufe gentle exercife in a falubrious air.

As a local application, both during the continuance and decline of the imperfect amaurofis, in order to roufe the languid action of the nerves of the eye, the vapour of the aqua ammoniæ puræ properly applied to the affected eye is of the
highest

higheft advantage. This remedy is employed
by placing a fmall veffel containing it near the
patient's eye; fo that the very penetrating vapour with which it, is furrounded may excite a
pricking fenfation in that organ ; by the action
of which, in lefs than half an hour, the eye
which is expofed to it, becomes red and waters
copioufly. It is then proper to defift from it,
and repeat it three or four hours afterwards,
and continue it in this manner until the amaurofis is perfectly cured. If both the eyes are
affected with this difeafe, it is unneceffary to
obferve that it is requifite to have two fmall
veffels filled with the aqua ammoniæ puræ, or
if one only be employed, that it will be neceffary to hold it firft to one eye and then to the
other, until both water abundantly, and become red. It is neceffary to renew the aqua
ammoniæ puræ every 3d day, in order to preferve its activity. This very ufeful application
ought to be employed from the commencement
of the treatment of the imperfect amaurofis, or
at leaft immediately after the patient's ftomach
has been unloaded of the offending matters, by
means of an emetic, and continued for a length
of time, even after the amaurofis is diffipated.
Thilen,* befides many others, affures us, that
he has alfo ufed this local remedy in fuch cafes

---

* Medicinifche und chirurgifche Bemerkungen § Amaurofis.

with

with advantage. The action of the vapour of the cauftic volatile alkali applied to the eyes affected with incomplete amaurofis, may be alfo affifted by other external ftimuli applied to parts of the body which have a clofe confent with the eyes, as blifters to the neck, friction upon the eye-brow with the anodyne liquor, and irritation of the nerves of the internal noftrils by means of fternutatory powders, as that compofed of two grains of the hydrargyrus vitriolatus, and a fcruple of the powder of the leaves of betony; and laftly, the electric fluid. Electricity has been propofed as one of the principal means of curing the amaurofis, but experience has fhown that no confidence is to be placed in it, except as a fecondary remedy; and Mr. Hey,* one of the moft zealous promoters of this practice, confeffes, that electricity is only ufeful in cafes of recent amaurofis, and, moft frequently only when combined with appropriate internal remedies, among which, refolvents are the principal.

With refpect to the *imperfect periodical amaurofis*, every practitioner would be difpofed to believe that the cinchona ought to be the fpecific; experience, however, has proved the contrary, and convinced us that this excellent remedy, which is fo efficacious in intermittent

* Medical Obfervations and Enquiries, vol. v. page 26.

fevers

fevers and other periodical difeafes, rather aggravates the *imperfect periodical amaurofis*, and
renders its attacks more frequent, and of longer
duration than before. This difeafe, on the contrary, is moft frequently cured in a fhort time,
by emetics and internal refolvents; and laftly,
by corroborants and the cinchona, which before
was ufelefs or injurious.

This plan of treatment in the *imperfect amaurofis* of recent date, is, in the greater number of
cafes, employed with perfect fuccefs, fince the
difeafe, as it has been remarked before, is only
fympathetic, and principally dependent upon
the morbid ftate of the digeftive organs. There
are, however, as I have alfo obferved, cafes of
imperfect amaurofis, to the formation of which,
befides the more common caufes enumerated,
others concur, which require the employment of
particular methods of treatment, befides thofe
which I have mentioned. Such is, for inftance,
the *imperfect amaurofis*, which takes place fuddenly, in confequence of exceffive heat, infola-
tion, violent anger in plethoric perfons, which
demands, before every other meafure, the general and partial abftraction of blood, cold fomentations to the eyes, and the whole head; afterwards an emetic, or the purges with the kali
tartarizatum, or antimonium tartarizatum, in
fmall dofes. Schmucker relates, that he had
frequently, by means of bleeding and an emetic,
                                         reftored

reſtored the. ſight to ſoldiers who had loſt it by making forced marches, when heavily loaded, in very hot weather. An emetic, after the eva-cuation of blood, is the more indicated, as in all theſe caſes the patient complains at the ſame time of a bitter taſte, of tenſion of the hypo-chondria, and continual nauſea. Richter men-tions a prieſt, who being violently enraged, be-came inſtantly blind, and to whom having given an emetic the next day, on account of his hav-ing evident ſymptoms of bilious ſaburræ, he re-covered his ſight the ſame day.

So likewiſe, in the treatment of the recent imperfect amauroſis, from a ſudden ſuppreſſion of the catamenia, the principal indication pre-viouſly to the uſe of an emetic, is evidently that of reproducing the diſcharge of blood from the uterus, by means of leeches applied to the internal ſurface of the labia pudendi, and by pediluvia; and afterwards that of a vomit, of the opening pills before mentioned, or thoſe of Bek-ker, or thoſe compoſed of a grain of aloes and two of myrrh and ſaffron. If theſe ſhould not ſucceed in reproducing the menſtrual flux, much confidence may be placed in electric ſhocks paſſed from the loins through the pelvis in all directions, and from that part to the thighs and feet repeatedly, and without abandoning the hope of ſucceſs, although the good effects of this treatment ſhould not be evident for ſome

weeks,

weeks, fince I am perfuaded from experience, that it is one of the moft powerful means which we poffefs, both of reproducing and accelerating the difcharge of blood from the uterus.

In the treatment of the imperfect amaurofis alfo, occafioned by the fuppreffion of an habitual profufe hæmorrhoidal flux, and accompanied with tenfion of the hypochondria, congeftion of blood in the head and eyes, difficult refpiration and crudities of the ftomach, previoufly to the ufe of an emetic, the moft efficacious method of treating the blindnefs is that of the application of leeches and warm fomentations, to the hæmorrhoidal veins, in order to obtain a copious difcharge of blood from them; afterwards an emetic will be neceffary, and the opening pills of Schmucker, or inftead of them, thofe compofed of aloes.

So in the treatment of the recent imperfect amaurofis produced by the variolous, rheumatic, herpetic, or gouty metaftafis, or from the impetigo of the head imprudently repelled, the furgeon's attention fhould be directed to eliminate the acrid matters ftimulating the ftomach, and at the fame time determine the peccant humour from the eyes to fome other part, by means of a confenfual irritation excited in the neck by blifters or fetons, or blifters to the arms, hands, or feet; and in the cafe of impetigo of the head, or of herpetic eruptions imprudently repelled,

pelled, after the ftomach has been unloaded
of the faburræ, it will be very ufeful to give
Huxham's antimonial wine, with the extract
of aconite, the extract of aconite with calomel,
and the golden fulphur of antimony (fulph.
antimon. præcip.) of the third precipitation, in
divided dofes, the kermes mineral, the decoction
of the woods, and the warm-bath.

The method of curing the imperfect amaurofis, in confequence of fevers improperly
treated; that derived from deep grief, fear, profufe hæmorrhage, profound meditation, or forced
and intenfe exercife of the eyes upon very minute or bright objects, does not differ at all, or
very little, from that which has been already delivered; and confifts principally in removing the
fordes of the ftomach, and afterwards in ftrengthening the nervous fyftem in general, and particularly that of the eyes.

Indeed, in this confenfual *imperfect amaurofis,*
in confequence of fevers improperly treated, the
the practitioner's attention is immediately called
to the morbid ftate of the organs of digeftion ; as
in this difeafe, befides the blindnefs or great diminution of fight, the countenance appears pale and
tumid, the digeftion is flow, the appetite wanting
or depraved, there is a bitter tafte in the mouth,
vertigo of the head, difturbed fleep, and a turgid
abdomen with flatulence. In this combination
of circumftances, nothing contributes more to

6   the

the reftitution of the patient's fight than the ufe
of an emetic, and the refolvent pills; afterwards
the cinchona, bitters, preparations of fteel, and
externally the vapour of the aqua ammoniæ
puræ.

Deep grief and terror have a direct action, as
it were, at the fame time, upon the nerves of
the eyes and the organs of digeftion, the function of which latter is fo perverted by thefe affections, that bilious acrid faburræ fpeedily accumulate in them, from the ftimulus of which
the nervous fyftem in general, and particularly
that of the eyes, is confenfually affected, and, I
might fay, almoft rendered torpid. If, therefore,
an emetic be indicated in any cafe of recent
imperfect amaurosis, as one of the principal
means of diffipating incomplete blindnefs, it is
certainly in the cafe where the difeafe is derived
from grief or terror; the good effects of which
have been repeatedly confirmed by experience.
When the ftomach and inteftines are unloaded
of the bilious acrid matters, by means of the
tartarized antimony, or refolvent pills, the treatment in this cafe alfo is completed by the cinchona, conjoined with valerian root; and by
fumigations of the aqua ammoniæ puræ; by
nourifhing and eafily-digeftible food; by divert-
ing the mind and directing it to agreeable objects; and by moderate exercife of the whole
body. It is to be obferved only, that the imperfect

perfect amaurofis, occafioned by fear, demands
the continuation of thefe remedies for a much
longer time than that produced by grief.

The *incomplete amaurofis*, which arifes from
general nervous debility, in confequence of profufe hæmorrhage, convulfions from *inanition*, or
long continued application to deep ftudies, efpecially by candle-light, is lefs in reality an *amaurofis* than a weaknefs of fight, from exhaufted
energy of the nerves, particularly of thofe which
conftitute the immediate organ of vifion. This
inconvenience is cured or diminifhed, if recent
and in young perfons, by fmall and divided dofes
of the tincture of rhubarb, in order to cleanfe
the ftomach and primæ viæ; afterwards by
corroborant and cardiac remedies, and by the
patient defifting from whatever debilitates the
nervous fyftem, and confequently the fight.
Laftly, when the ftomach is cleared of the faburræ; the decoction of cinchona with valerian
may be prefcribed with advantage, the infufion
of quaffia, with the addition of a few drops of
vitriolic æther in each dofe, nutritious animal
food of eafy digeftion, and viper broth. The
aromatic fpirituous vapour mentioned in the
chapter on ophthalmia may be ufefully employed as a local application, and if this fhould
not fucceed, much advantage may be derived
from that of the aqua ammoniæ puræ. The
patient fhould take exercife on foot, horfeback,

K K   or

or in a carriage, in a pure and dry air, and in warm weather he fhould ufe fea-bathing. He fhould avoid as much as poffible mental anxiety, and fhould not fix his eyes on very minute or lucid objects,* In proportion as he takes nourifhment and regains ftrength, and the action of the nervous fyftem in general is invigorated, his fight will gradually amend; to preferve and improve which, he fhould keep in mind, above all, to maintain the tone and vigour of the ftomach, and to moderate the impreffion of light upon the eyes, which he may eafily do by never expofing himfelf to a vivid light, unlefs when they are defended by plain green glaffes.

* It occafionally happens that patients, in thefe cafes, cannot look at a very near object, with one or both the eyes, without experiencing fatigue and pain in one or both of them, while they feel no inconvenience from looking at an object at a certain diftance. And when the difficulty which they find in looking at a near object is confined to one eye, it is accompanied with ftrabifmus and double fight. This depends upon a debilitated ftate of the mufcles of the eyes, in confequence of which the patient cannot conveniently accommodate the eye-ball to very near objects, or maintain it for a length of time in this pofition; and when the debility is confined to the mufcles of one eye, this being unable to concur in the actions of the other, ftrabifmus and double vifion are the neceffary confequences. This inconvenience is alfo remedied by the general and local corroborants before mentioned, and by avoiding to ftrain the mufcles of the eyes. And if the debility be confined to one eye only, and occafion the ftrabifmus, it will be advantageous to keep the affected eye covered for fome time.

The

The *hemeralopia* or *nocturnal blindnefs* is, ftrictly fpeaking, only an *imperfect periodical amaurofis*, moft frequently fympathetic of difor- der of the ftomach, the attacks of which fuper- vene towards the evening, and difappear in the morning. This difeafe is in fome countries en- demical, and in others epidemical at certain fea- fons of the year.

Thofe who are affected with this difeafe, fee objects at fun-fet as if covered with a greyifh veil, which by little and little is converted into a denfe cloud, interpofed between them and the furrounding objects. The pupil both during the day and the night is more dilated and lefs moveable than it is ufually in a ftate of health. In the greater number of cafes, however, the pupil is more or lefs moveable in the day, and always enlarged and immoveable during the night. If the patient be placed in a room faintly lighted by a candle, where other perfons can fee fufficiently well, the objects are either difcerned with difficulty, or cannot be feen at all, or he can only diftinguifh light from darknefs; much lefs is he able to diftinguifh any thing by moon- light. On the approach of morning he recovers his fight, which remains perfect during the whole day, until fun-fet.

The difeafe is generally cured, and frequently alfo in a fhort time, by treating it in the fame manner as the imperfect amaurofis; by emetics,

the

the opening powders or pills, and by blifters to the neck; and locally, by the vapour of the cauftic volatile alkali; and laftly, by the cinchona conjoined with the valerian root. In cafes where the difeafe has been preceded by plethora or fuppreffed perfpiration, bleeding, and fudorifics are alfo indicated.

By this method of treatment I fucceeded in curing three patients attacked with it. The firft was a boy 14 years of age, who, for feveral weeks, had ufed fumigations of boiled fheep's liver without advantage. The fecond was a waterman, and the third a hufbandman of our neighbouring rice-fields. They were between 30 and 40 years old, each meagre, with a yellowifh tumid countenance. The boy after having vomited copioufly, by means of a grain and a half of tartarized antimony, diffolved in four ounces of water, and taken in fmall quantities in the fpace of two hours, made ufe of the opening powders during the following days; which occafioned fome naufea, and two, or fometimes three copious motions every day. On the 5th day at night, he began to diftinguifh the furrounding objects by the very weak light of a lantern. The vapour of the cauftic volatile alkali was ufed conftantly from the firft day after the emetic, and on the 16th day he was perfectly cured. The waterman, after three dofes, vomited a large quantity of yellowifh vifcid matter. He afterwards ufed the opening

ing powders, which, on the third day, produced a fecond vomiting, and expofed his eyes
regularly every four hours in the day to the action of the vapour of the cauftic volatile alkali.
He did not begin till the 11th day to diftinguifh
objects at night by the weak light of a candle.
The hufbandman vomited only once in large
quantity, but was afterwards greatly naufeated
by the opening powders for nine fucceffive days,
and had every day a copious evacuation from
the bowels of greenifh matter; he ufed alfo the
vapour of the cauftic volatile alkali, as a local
application, and on the 14th day at night, began to fee by the light of a candle, and continued to acquire a greater power of feeing objects at night, until he was perfectly well. Towards the end of the treatment I ordered this
patient to take the cinchona with valerian
root.

But the moft fpeedy recovery that I have
known, was in the fpring of the prefent year,
in the cafe of Mauro Bonini, of Donelafco, a
robuft farmer, 22 years of age. In the month
of March he began to difcover, that at fun-fet
he could only diftinguifh objects very imperfectly. This indifpofition increafed to fuch a
degree, that in the beginning of May, he became, towards night, almoft entirely blind.
On the 10th of May he came to this hofpital.
On examining him in the day-time I found the
pupil of both his eyes unufually dilated, and al-

moft

moft immoveable; and towards night I made the experiment, and fatisfied myfelf that he was blind. The patient complained of a bitter tafte, heavinefs of the head, and his tongue was furred. On the 11th of May I prefcribed an emetic, which did not produce all the effect that I expected; on the following day, therefore, I gave him one more powerful, compofed of ʒjfs of ipecacuanha, and gr. ij of tartarized antimony. This caufed him to vomit a large quantity of yellowifh green matter; the patient immediately afterwards found his head relieved, and the bitter tafte removed; the pupil of both eyes was a little contracted, and appeared to be in a flight degree fenfible to the impreffion of a vivid light. He began to ufe the vapour of the cauftic volatile alkali externally. On the evening of the fame day the patient's fight appeared to be improved. On the 13th no remedy was employed, except the vapour. On the 14th the patient complained again of a bitter tafte, and his tongue appeared furred. I ordered him to take the opening powders every three hours, which produced naufea and repeated evacuations from the bowels. The ufe of the vapour was continued. Towards the evening the patient diftinguifhed very well all the objects which were prefented to him. On the 16th the fymptoms of indigeftion entirely difappeared, and the pupil of both eyes was

contracted,

difeafe, recommended bleeding, the ufe of emetics, when the patient is fafting, or the evacuation of the bowels by purgatives or clyfters, and
fternutatories. This practice was followed by
all the phyficians who fucceeded them, and
was the fame at the time of Foreftus* and
Timeus.† Hildanus,‡ who attributed much
efficacy in the treatment of this difeafe to a
feton made in the neck, ftates, however, that
he had only employed this method after the
repeated ufe of cathartics. The fame thing
is met with in the works of Smetius,§ Pla-
terus,‖ Adolphus,¶ and Trew.**

St. Yves,†† one of the moft diftinguifhed
oculifts of his time, mentions an ecclefiaftic,
who, a few days after he had loft his fight, having given him an emetic, and opened the jugu-
lar vein, recovered his fight; which was afterwards ftrengthened by means of the vapour of the
fpirit of wine, properly directed to the eyes. He
alfo ftates, that he reftored the fight of a young
canon by the repeated ufe of purges, cooling
broths, and the application of fpirituous va-

* Obf. et cur. med. lib. xi. obf. 32. fchol. obf. 38.
† Cafus medicinal. lib. i. caf. 24.
‡ Centur. 1 obferv. 24. Centur. 5. obf. 13.
§ Mifcellan. med. page 546.
‖ Praxis. med. page 104.
¶ Act. n. c. vol. ii. obf. 87.
** Commerc. Norimberg. T. 7. an. 1737. N. 1.
†† Traité des Maladies des yeux, chap. 27, 28.

pours;

Celfus,* in the chapter on the Mydriafis, adds the following words. *Quidam fine ulla manifefta caufa fubito obcæcati funt. Ex quibus nonnulli cum aliquandiu nihil vidiffent, repentina profufione alvi lumen receperunt. Quo minus alienum videtur et recenti re, et interpofito tempore, medicamentis quoque moliri dejeciones, quæ omniam noxiam materiam per inferiora depellant.* This paffage of Celfus relates, in my opinion, not only to the treatment of the dilated pupil, but alfo to that of the imperfect amaurofis, which takes place fuddenly; and it appears to me to merit the attention of practitioners.

The firft of thefe obfervations made by Celfus, that perfons affected with amaurofis for fome time, have recovered their fight on the fupervention of a diarrhœa, appears to be con-

fufficient for a radical cure. I have known obftinate foldiers who have been unwilling to do any thing for three weeks: and I have fometimes even permitted it, in order to afcertain whether the remedy was as efficacious in an inveterate as a recent affection. I have found no difference, and as I now believe, I have made every neceffary experiment to convince myfelf, I oblige them to fubmit to this treatment whenever I am aware of it. I fhall not fubjoin the names of thofe who have been cured in this manner. There are at prefent in the regiment more than 250 men who have been treated in this manner, and even more than 60 at the end of March, and the beginning of laft April, 1787.

Dupont Mémoire fur la goutte fereine nocturne épidémique, ou nyctalopie.

* De Medicin. lib. vi. cap. 37.

firmed

firmed by a cafe related by Dr. Pye,* of a man
40 years old, who had been afflicted for two
months with a periodical amaurofis, which, for
a certain length of time, attacked him regularly
every evening, afterwards irregularly and at
different intervals, with great dilatation of the
pupil, and fuch obfcurity of vifion towards night
that he could not even diftinguifh the light of
a candle. The man was feized with a diarrhœa.
Dr. Pye ordered him the faline mixture, which
he took for nine days; and afterwards an electuary, compofed of the cinchona, nux mofchata,
and fyr. e cort. aurant. Thefe two articles were
added to the cinchona on account of the diarrhœa,
which ftill continued. On the fecond day of
ufing this electuary the diarrhœa increafed, and
the patient vomited copioufly; after which he
recovered his fight almoft inftantly, fo as to diftinguifh objects as well in the night as in the
day. The diarrhœa continued, and after having
employed the electuary for two days it was neceffary to fufpend the ufe of it. The diarrhœa
was accompanied with a very violent fever, and
it was remarked, that in the acme of the fever,
although the patient became extremely deaf, he
did not lofe his fight either day or night. Dr.
Pye does not ftate what means were employed
for moderating the fever, but only that it proved

* Med. Obferv. and Enquiries, vol. i. art. 13.

fatal.

fatal. The fact, however, is certain, that this spontaneous evacuation of the bowels had entirely relieved the patient of the periodical imperfect amaurofis. I have no doubt, that if an attentive examination were made of the numerous cafes recorded in medicine, a great number of fimilar facts might be met with, proving the influence which offenfive fubftances, ftimulating the ftomach, have upon the organ of vifion, and confequently of how much advantage the fpontaneous evacuations of the bowels may be in the cure of this difeafe.

But, however rare or little noticed may be the examples of incomplete amaurofis difappearing, in confequence of fpontaneous vomiting or copious dejections, promoted merely by the powers of nature; we are now in poffeffion of fo many cafes of the fuccefsful treatment of this difeafe, by means of fuch evacuations procured artificially with emetics and internal refolvents, that no doubt can be longer entertained of the juftnefs of the fecond part of Celfus's obfervation, relative to their propriety in this difeafe, *et recenti re, et interpofito tempore, medicamentis quoque moliri dejectiones, quæ omnem noxiam materiam per inferiora depellant.*

The accurate cafes related by Schmucker and Richter, afford numerous certain and fatisfactory proofs of this; but the confidence which

we

we repofe in the method of treating the imperfect and the periodical amaurofis now delivered,
muft be increafed, if we reflect that the moft
authentic of the ancient writers, in the greater
number of thefe cafes, have alfo cured this
difeafe, by no other means than thofe of
emetics and purgatives, although in their writings they have attributed the fuccefs of the
treatment to other caufes, or to the efficacy
of other remedies which they prefcribed con-
jointly with the emetics and refolvents. Ga-
len,* Ætius,† Ægineta,‡ Actuarius,§ Rhazes,||
Avicenna,¶ in fpeaking of the treatment of this

* Lib. de oculis, part iv. cap. 11, 12.

† Sermo feptimus, cap. 48. 52. cap. 46. de nemeralopia.
Si vero per hæc non fuccefferit, rurfus purgatorium dandum
eft, quale eft hoc. Scammoniæ obol. iij, caftorei obol. ij,
falis obol. iij. In deoilioribus autem fcammoniæ obol. ij, injice.
Talis autem purgatio fæpe et veftigio liberavit, aut multo
meliorem conditionem induxit. Poft paucos dies dandum eft
purgatorium pituitam et bilem ducens.

‡ Lib. iii. cap. 48.

§ De method. med. lib. iv. cap. 11. poft fanguinis mif-
fionem fternutationes movendæ funt, et ante cibum vomitibus
utendum.

|| De œgritud. ocul. cap. 4. Cum prolongatur ftatus
morbi, provocentur fternutationes, et vomitus jejuno fto-
macho; deinde curetur cum collyriis valentibus ad hoc.

¶ Lib. iii. fen. 3. tractat. 4. Quandoque hoc fit propter
communitatem ftomachi et cerebri. . . . . . Quod fi fuerit
ab humiditate, adminiftrantibus tunc illud quod refolvit poft
evacuationes. Vomitus autem qui fit cum facilitate, eft
ex iis, quæ conferunt.

difeafe,

contracted, as in a state of health. On the 17th
the patient left the hospital perfectly cured.

The ancients have very highly commended,
in the treatment of this disease, fumigations of
sheep's liver roasted, conveyed to the eyes by
means of a funnel, as well as the eating of the
liver thus prepared. This remedy, even at the
present time is generally accredited, not only on
the assertions of the vulgar, but also of profes-
sional persons; and some writers add, that it
succeeds in a surprising manner among the
Chinese, where this disease is said to be very
frequent. I cannot relate any case of my own
in confirmation of this; in the boy before mentioned, it appeared to me to be of no advantage. If, however, the effiacy of this remedy
is a matter of fact, we may boast of having
another means of curing the *nocturnal blindness,**
besides that which I have delivered.

Celsus,

---

* It was an old soldier who imparted to his comrades the
remedy which I am about to describe, when there was so
large a number affected with nocturnal blindness at Strasbourg
in 1762. The soldiers cook a slice of ox's liver, weighing
about half a pound, in an earthen pot newly varnished, and
just large enough to hold four pints of water. When the
liver is done, so as to be fit to eat, and the vapour is of a sup-
portable heat, they place the pot upon the bed, and inclining
the head very near it, they throw over a covering so as exactly
to enclose them. They remain there until the liver ceases to
produce any vapour, or the difficulty of breathing obliges the
patient to come out. One application only, is, in general,
K K 4   sufficient

pours; and exprefsly ftates, that he had frequently fucceeded in curing the *amaurofis* whenever he had undertaken the treatment of it,
immediately on its acceffion, by taking away
blood, and ordering an emetic to be taken once
or twice in the interval of two days.

Heifter * imagines that he had cured an
amaurofis by means of falivation only. From
the narration which he gives, however, it appears, that previoufly to the patient's ufing
mercury, he ordered him an hydrogogue purgative; and that the following day, on his complaining of naufea and inclination to vomit,
an emetic compofed of two grains of tartarized
antimony and a fcruple of fugar, by means of
which he vomited copioufly, and his naufea
was relieved; that after all this he ordered him
fome pills made with calomel and the extract
of fumaria, and the fize of a bean of mercurial
ointment to be rubbed into the parotid glands;
and that on the 9th day, the falivation having
fcarcely commenced, the patient could diftinguifh light from darknefs. Now from this account, and from comparing it with what we
know at prefent, of the efficacy of emetics and
purgatives in the cure of this difeafe, it is eafy
to infer, that the cure of the imperfect amaurofis obtained by Heifter is not to be attributed to

* Syftem of Surgery, T. 1.

the

the mercurial falivation, but to the removal of the offenfive matters ftimulating the ftomach.

The fame writer* alfo, in a woman affected with amaurofis, and threatened with complete blindnefs from exceffive grief, and from having fixed her eyes too long on lucid objects, obtained a cure by means of a fingle bleeding, and fome cathartic pills compofed of calomel and jalap. He † likewife reftored the fight of a fervant, which had gradually diminifhed without any apparent difeafe in the eye, but who complained of continual naufea, by prefcribing to him a powder compofed of 25 grains of ipecacuanha, and ten grains of vitriolated kali, to be taken in the morning; and an infufion of Euphrafia, hyfop, and faffafras during the day, befides a blifter to the neck, and a ftimulant refolutive collyrium.

Ribe ‡ mentions a young man, 22 years of age, who had loft his fight three months before he was examined by him, which was re-ftored by the ufe of an emetic repeated feven times at different intervals. Helvig § and Schroëk ‖ have tranfmitted to us feveral hiftories of the imperfect amaurofis, fympathetic of the

* Med. chirurg. u. anat. Wahrnehm. 1. Band.
† Loc. cit. Band 75.
‡ Act. Svecic. vol. i. Trim. 1. N. 1.
§ Obferv. phyfic. med. obf. 33.
‖ Mifcellan. nat. eur. decad. 2. an. 5. obf. 217.

ftomach

ftomach, and primæ viæ, cured by refolvent purgatives only.

Vandermonde * relates the hiftory of a girl, eight years old, who, from faburræ and worms in the ftomach, had recently loft her vifion and fpeech. The prefence of worms in this cafe was indicated by a rapid movement of the tongue, like that of a ferpent; and continual expiration by the nofe, great anxiety, and copious perfpiration of the head. The girl took an emetic, and brought up, with other matters, a round worm half a foot long; fhe then took purgatives, conjoined with anthelmintics, and very quickly recovered her fight and fpeech.

Fabre † mentions a certain Jean Barricot, who, ten days after he had been afflicted with the colic, loft the fight of both his eyes, and who had loft blood twice without advantage, and had ufed a collyrium of rofe water and the white of eggs. Fabre prefcribed to the patient four grains of tartarized antimony, and two days afterwards, a draught made with half an ounce of fenna, half a dram of the *pulvis e tribus,* and one ounce of manna ; in two days more four grains, as before, of the tartarized antimony, and fo for nine days following; afterwards fome pills compofed of calomel and fcammony, an infufion of euphrafia, and the fudorific and laxative

* Journal de med. de Paris. T. x.
† Ibidem T. xx.

ptifan

ptifan of the Paris pharmacopæia for eight days.
The vapour of fpirit of wine and coffee was applied externally, directed to the eyes by means of
a funnel. On the 4th day of this treatment,
Barricot began to diftinguifh the light from
darknefs; on the 12th day he could diftinguifh
colours at a fmall diftance; and by the 20th,
recovered his fight entirely.

Thilen * relates two very interefting cafes of
imperfect amaurofis, cured by the ufe of the
tartarized antimony, firft as an emetic, and afterwards as an opening medicine, fometimes
given alone, at other times conjoined with faponaceous fubftances, and the extract of *arnica*.

Whytt † mentions a woman, whofe fight was
greatly diminifhed whenever fhe had acidity of
the ftomach. She was relieved from this inconvenience by means of an emetic, fome abforbent
powders, and bitter ftomachic corroborants. I
know alfo a very refpectable perfon, who happened frequently, before he was aware of the
caufe, to experience for fome hours after dinner
a great dimnefs of fight, approaching to a degree of blindnefs, in confequence of eating fifh
fried in olive oil. It is very remarkable that the
digitalis purpurea, the *ftramonium*, the infufion of tobacco, and many other fimilar articles,

* Medicinifche und chirurgifche Bemerkung. § Amaurofis.
† Delle affez. ipocond. ed ifter. cap. 1.

6   produce

produce blindnefs almoft as foon as they are taken into the ftomach.

In the *French Mercury* for the year 1756,* there is an account of a cure performed by Fournier, of feveral perfons affected with *hemeralopia.* The firft were three foldiers, to whom, after being bled, he gave an emetic. On the following day, as they yet complained of heavinefs of the head and naufea, he repeated the bleeding and emetic. By thefe means all the fymptoms were removed, and the three foldiers were cured. Fournier employed the fame method of treatment, with equal fuccefs, in eight other foldiers, belonging to the fame garrifon, attacked with this difeafe.

Pellier † cured the *hemeralopia* in the captain of the fhip Micetti, with fmall dofes of tartarized antimony, blifters to the neck and cooling aperient ptifans. The fame writer afferts,‡ that he had frequently cured the recent imperfect amaurofis, by fmall dofes of tartarized antimony only (émétique en lavage), and by local aromatic fumigations.

To this feries of facts, and many others which may be found recorded on this fubject, not only by the ancient but by modern furgeons, I fhall add fome cafes of my own, to prove, in the moft

* Fevrier, page 168.
† Recueil de mem. et. obf. fur l'œil, obf. 132.
‡ Ibidem, obferv. 136. 138.

convincing

convincing manner the utility and efficacy of
the method of treating the recent imperfect
amaurofis here recommended, which, as I have
already ftated, is only an affection derived from
fympathy with the ftomach,* depending upon
morbific ftimuli in the organ of digeftion, with
nervous debility, either general or confined to
the eye.

It is to be remarked, that in the treatment of
the recent imperfect amaurofis, both among the
ancients and the greater part of the moderns,
the general, or partial, evacuation of blood is very
frequently and indifcriminately made to pre-
cede the ufe of an emetic or cathartic. Further obfervation on the treatment of this difeafe has taught us that it is not to be regarded
as a general rule, and that the abftraction of
blood ought only to be employed in thofe cafes,
in which it is clearly indicated by particular circumftances; as in cafes of recent imperfect
amaurofis accompanied with affections of the
ftomach, and at the fame time plethora, either
general, or confined to the head, in young and
ftrong fubjects, or in perfons in whom the
amaurofis has been produced or kept up by the
fuppreffion of fome accuftomed fanguineous
evacuation. In other cafes the abftraction of

* Experientiæ fuffragium firmum eft, ut in omnibus capitis
et nervorum morbis, fic etiam in iis qui oculos detinent, ven-
triculi et virtutis ipfius digeftivæ rationem effe habendam.
Hoffman Differt. de morbis præcipuis recta medendi ratione.

6   blood

blood is not indicated; and in perfons extenuated
and affected with general nervous debility, afflicted with exceffive grief, or where there is a
difpofition to convulfions, it may rather prove
injurious.

So likewife with refpect to the felection of
remedies proper for unloading the ftomach and
inteftines of the *morbific fomes,* and at the fame
time roufing the activity of the nervous fyftem
generally, it is worthy of remark, that, except
the cafe above mentioned, of perfons very delicate and extenuated, in whom the tincture of
rhubarb is more properly indicated, the antimonium tartarizatum as a vomit, or in divided
dofes as a refolvent, either alone or combined
with gummy and faponaceous fubftances, fo as
to excite naufea, and gently open the bowels, is
preferable to the draftic medicines, and acrid
purging clyfters, which were formerly in ufe.
It is not improbable, that in the treatment of
the recent *imperfect amaurofis,* produced by faburræ, and accompanied by fuppreffion of perfpiration, with metaftafis to the eyes, the tartarized antimony given in fmall and repeated
dofes is preferable to every other internal purgative, from its particular mode of action upon
the ftomach, and fympathetically upon the
whole fyftem; not only by expelling from the
ftomach and inteftines the acrid bilious impu-
rities, but by its peculiar ftimulus, ftrengthening

the

the activity of the nervous fyftem, and reftoring the perfpiration and the action of the abforbent veffels.

Case LXVIII.

Giacomo Migliavacca, of Pavia, 32 years of age, by trade a carpenter, of a weak conftitution and emaciated, towards the middle of March 1798, after exceffive grief, began to feel an ob-tufe pain in the eye-brow, general laffitude, tenfion of the abdomen, and lofs of appetite. On the 7th of April following, three hours after rifing out of bed, he fuddenly loft the fight of both h's eyes.

The next day he was admitted into the prac-tical fchool of furgery. On examining his eyes, I found the pupils very much dilated and im-moveable to the ftrongeft light, but regular in their circumference, and the bottom of the eye behind the pupil of a deep black colour.

I ordered the patient, without delay, two grains of tartarized antimony, diffolved in four ounces of water, to be taken by fpoonful at fhort intervals, until it produced naufea and vo-miting. The patient having taken the whole of the folution, vomited at three times a very confiderable quantity of mucus and bilious greenifh matter, fo acrid, that for fome hours afterwards he complained of an intolerable heat

in

in the tongue and fauces. He had alfo, on the fame day, two colliquative motions; he afterwards paffed a good night, and the following day found himfelf relieved of the pain in the head and fupercilium. I ordered him to take the opening powder, compofed of one ounce of cryftals of tartar and a grain of tartarized antimony, divided into fix equal parts, one of which was taken three times a day, and continued for feveral fucceffive days. The powder produced each time naufea, and one or two abundant evacuations from the bowels every day, with great relief, not only to his head, but his general conftitution; fince after the ufe of thefe opening powders for a few days, he ceafed to complain of proftration of ftrength, and tenfion of the hypochondria. In the mean time I directed him to hold a fmall veffel, containing the aqua ammoniæ puræ near his eyes three times a day, until at each time they fhould begin to water and become red.

During the firft four days there was no fenfible alteration in the patient's eyes; but on the 5th day (13th of April) he faid, that he could fee the candle diftinctly, which was brought near him. The pupils being then examined, I found them a little contracted. The opening powders were continued, but only twice a day.

On the 19th of April, the patient could fufficiently difcern the furrounding objects in a

moderate

moderate light. I found the pupils, alfo more
contracted than on the 13th, and as the patient
had been hitherto kept on a low diet, and
found his appetite returning, I allowed him the
diet of convalefcents. In order to ftrengthen
his ftomach and invigorate his nervous fyftem,
inftead of the opening powders, I ordered him
thofe compofed of ℥j of the cinchona, and ℥fs
of the valerian root, divided into fix equal parts,
of which he took one morning and evening,
without ever omitting the ufe of the vapour of
the cauftic volatile alkali. From the 19th of
April the patient's fight improved daily, and on
the 22d of May he was difcharged from the
hofpital in a ftate capable of following his bufinefs, which he alfo prefently purfued.

Case LXIX.

Stefano Barbieri, a pale weakly boy, 14 years
of age, belonging to the hofpital for orphans in
this city, was attacked in March 1797 with a
peripneumony, for which he was freely bled.
While he was recovering, he complained that
he could fcarcely difcern any thing with the
right eye, and that he felt occafionally violent
and deep pains in that eye, and the correfponding fupercilium. Antifpafmodics and tonics
were prefcribed for him; but without advantage, as the fight of this eye diminifhed daily;
the

the pupil was contracted and become immove-able, and a fmall whitifh line prefented itfelf beyond the pupil, which appeared to be an in-cipient opacity of the capfule of the cryftalline lens.

He remained in this ftate two years, as his left eye ferved him fufficiently well ; when, in the beginning of September 1799, he was fud-denly deprived of almoft the entire fight of his left eye, with this peculiarity, that on his firft waking in the morning, he could, with diffi-culty, diftinguifh light from darknefs. Having examined him, I found the pupil of the left eye greatly dilated and immoveable, while, as I have faid, the pupil of the right, already greatly de-teriorated, was immoveable and contracted.

I chofe, in this cafe, to try the effect of the pulfatilla nigricans. I ordered the patient to take three grains of it morning and evening; I then increafed it half a grain twice a day, until the boy took nine grains of it night and morn-ing. At the end of 15 days I was obliged to omit this remedy, as it was attended with no advantage to the fight, and occafioned violent pains in the head, vertigo, and little lefs than general convulfions. I was contented to do no-thing till the 24th of December of the fame year, when I purfued the following plan of treatment.

I prefcribed

I prescribed two grains of tartarized antimony dissolved in four ounces of water, of which the boy took a table spoonful every half hour. After he had taken about three parts of the medicine, he vomited half a bason full of greenish, bilious, tenacious matter, and towards night had two alvine evacuations. He passed a good night, and on awaking the following morning distinguished the objects near him, and the persons who passed through the ward; which he had not been able to do for some months before. I immediately put him upon the use of the opening powders, composed of ʒj of crystals of tartar, and gr. ij of tartarized antimony, divided into eight equal parts, of which he took three a day; and these powders produced nausea and two evacuations regularly every day. The vapour of the caustic volatile alkali was used with the greatest diligence three or four times a day.

On the 1st of January, an hour after having taken the first opening powder, the boy vomited violently, and threw up a large quantity, as at first, of greenish viscid bilious matter. The medicine was suspended for that day, and was afterwards reduced to two doses only of the powder, one morning and evening, until the 8th of January.

At this time the boy could distinguish objects very well with the left eye, the pupil of which was less dilated than before, and showed some mobility on being exposed to a strong light.

The

The pupil of the right eye remained as at firft, contracted and immoveable; and the boy could diftinguifh light from darknefs. He 'had not the yellowifh livid appearance in his coun- tenance that he had before, and felt a good ap- petite.

I had now recourfe to Schmucker's opening pills, of which the boy took four morning and evening, without omitting the frequent ufe of the vapour of the cauftic volatile alkali. The pills produced naufea for a few minutes, and afterwards purged him twice a day, without occafioning debility.

On the 16th of January he was feized with a diarrhœa, without any evident caufe; it was therefore neceffary to fufpend the opening pills, which were, however, refumed on the 22d, but in half the dofe; and as thefe alfo purged him too much, they were employed every fecond day, without omitting the ufe of the vapour of the aqua ammoniæ puræ.

' On the 9th of February, the boy finding the fight of his left eye tolerably re-eftablifhed, left the houfe without leave, on a very rainy day, and returned completely wet from head to foot. This occafioned, two days afterwards, a conti- nued fever of the remittent type, which was removed with the cinchona conjoined with va- leriǎn. The left eye, however, even in the ftrongeft

3

ftrongeft paroxyfms of the fever, retained its vigour.

On the 26th of February I left the boy in a good ftate of health, both with refpect to his general habit and the fight of the left eye, with which he could diftinguifh the fmalleft objects. The right eye remained imperfect, as it was at the commencement of the treatment.

Case LXX.

Giovanni Sciguagni, a carrier, about 30 years of age, a man of a ftrong temperament and good habit of body, in 1791 was feized one morning, as he was going out of church, with a weaknefs of fight in both his eyes, which progreffively increafed to fuch a degree, that in a few minutes he found himfelf completely blind.

Being brought to the hofpital, his countenance appeared flufhed, his pulfe was hard and full, the conjunctiva was ftreaked with fome blood veffels, and the pupil dilated and immoveable; he complained of no inconvenience except the blindnefs.

Blood was taken from the arm, and afterwards 14 leeches were applied to the temples, and the anterior circumference of the neck, from which an abundant difcharge of blood was obtained; the patient was at the fame time ordered

dered a proper diet, aqueous drinks, and a purgative. By these measures a diminution of the strength of the body generally was obtained, but no advantage with respect to the blindness.

The next day two sinapisms were applied to the feet, and a large blister to the neck, which were of no benefit. On the 4th day of the disease he took, in small quantities, a pint of the decoction of arnica, and at night a pill made with the extract of arnica and the pulsatilla nigricans. But as these remedies, which were daily increased in dose, produced no advantage in the space of 15 days, although continued with diligence and exactness, recourse was had to Schmucker's pills.

At the end of six days, the patient experienced a small degree of relief from these pills, which gradually increased every day, and in the space of 27 days he recovered his sight perfectly, which remained good for two months; but afterwards relapsed in consequence of his indulging in indigestible food and spirituous liquors.

This second time, after having a small quantity of blood taken from him, he resumed the use of Schmucker's pills, and by those only, without any external application, except cold lotions to the eye, he recovered in the course of 32 days, and had no further relapse.

CASE

Case LXXI.

Giuſeppe Antonio Goſſi, of Stradella, 60 years old, of a lively and ſtrong temperament, was attacked towards the end of 1794, with an obſtinate quartan fever, with which he was ſo afflicted for 13 months, notwithſtanding the means which were employed, that on the final ceſſation of it, five months of good living were ſcarcely ſufficient to put him in a tolerable ſtate of health. At this time, his former ſtrength not being yet perfectly re-eſtabliſhed, he began to ſee black ſtreaks before the left eye, which gradually increaſing, in the ſpace of 15 days he was completely deprived of the power of ſeeing with that eye. Some medicines which were preſcribed for him rendered his ſight a little better, but it was of ſhort duration; and he continued ſometimes loſing almoſt entirely the ſight of the left eye, at other times regaining it ſo as to be able to walk without danger.

He paſſed ſeveral weeks in this ſtate, alternately better and worſe, and in the hope that nothing further would enſue: the right eye remaining ſound, he was unwilling to ſubmit to any further treatment; when ſuddenly the ſight of the right eye alſo became ſo diminiſhed, that in a few days he found himſelf reduced to the

neceſſity

neceſſity of being conducted, in order to walk with ſafety.

All the remedies which are adminiſtered on theſe occaſions being found ineffectual, and the patient reduced alſo to the greateſt diſtreſs, by being deprived of the employment by which he gained a livelihood, he came on the 8th of June 1796 to this city for relief.

On an attentive examination the pupils were found exceedingly dilated and immoveable, and the bottom of the right eye, beyond the pupil, was very dark.

On account of the diſorder, principally of the organs of digeſtion, increaſed by violent affections of the mind, with which the patient for ſome months had been exceſſively agitated, four grains of tartarized antimony diſſolved in eight ounces of water were preſcribed for him, of which a large table-ſpoonful was to be taken every two hours. The firſt doſe of this ſolution excited only nauſea. It was repeated the following day, and he had ſcarcely taken ſix ſpoonsful of it when he was ſeized with a violent vomiting, by which he threw up a large quantity of very bitter yellowiſh-green mucus, and had two alvine evacuations.

On the 11th I preſcribed 16 grains of the antimonium tartarizatum diſſolved in 12 ounces of peppermint water, with the addition of Ʒſs. of the ſyrup of orange-peel; of which a

ſpoonful

spoonful or two was to be taken three times a day. He was alfo ordered to drink, now and then, in fmall quantities, during the day, an infufion of a dram of the folia arnicæ in a pint and a half of water. On the two firft days, a few hours after having taken one or two fpoonsful of the folution of tartarized antimony, he vomited more or lefs bile; but afterwards the medicine only excited naufea.

On the 14th the black ftreaks which appeared before the left eye began to be diffipated, and in a few days were entirely loft. The pupil of both eyes became a little moveable, and on the 12th day from the commencement of the treatment, he was already able to diftinguifh very large objects.

The folution of the tartarized antimony was now omitted, and he was ordered Richter's opening pills, of which at firft he took 15 three times a day; afterwards 18, and laftly 24, never omitting, however, the ufe of the infufion.

He had not taken the pills 15 days before his fight was ftrong enough to enable him to walk without a guide; and in about fix weeks, by the uninterrupted ufe of thefe pills, and the affiftance of fpectacles, which he ufed before he was affected with the imperfect amaurofis, he was able to read and write. On examining his eyes at this period, there was no appearance of difeafe,

difeafe, except that the fight was rather lefs perfect in the left than in the right eye.

The pills produced only naufea occafionally,
and regularly every day a loofe motion. He
was allowed to return home at his own requeft,
upon condition that he would continue to take,
at intervals, another entire dofe of the pills.
He was not fubject afterwards to any alteration
in his fight.*

CASE LXXII.

Giufeppa Pizzi, a girl 16 years of age, of
Belgiojofa, of a delicate conftitution, who had
not yet menftruated, towards the end of May of
this year, 1801, was affected with a morbid appetite, fo diftreffing that fhe could fcarcely fatisfy herfelf by eating every kind of grofs food
in large quantity, efpecially bread made with
Indian corn (zea mays). The girl being alfo
fatigued by the hard labour of the country, to
which fhe had not yet been fufficiently accuftomed, perceived that her fight became dim.
Her immoderate appetite fuddenly ceafed; fhe
had a bitter tafte, and began to feel a fenfe of
weight in the region of the ftomach, accom-

---

* The progrefs and treatment of this difeafe is perfectly
known to *Volpi*, a fkilful and expert furgeon of this hofpital.

panied

panied with naufea and continual head-ach;
fhe then loft the fight of the right eye entirely,
and in a great degree that of the left. The pupil of both eyes was exceedingly dilated, and
almoft immoveable to the ftrongeft light, and
fhe alfo appeared as if fhe had an incipient ftrabifmus. In this ftate fhe was brought into the
practical fchool of furgery, on the 4th of June
1801.

On the 4th of June the girl took a table
fpoonful of a folution of four grains of tartarized
antimony in five ounces of diftilled water,
which occafioned great naufea for a long time;
but fhe only vomited a little vifcid whitifh
matter.

On the 5th, the emetic was repeated, and
given in the fame manner. It produced a more
copious vomiting than on the preceding day;
but always of mucous whitifh matter. The
pain in the head was, however, greatly diminifhed, as well as the fenfe of weight in the
region of the ftomach. The naufea, however,
and furred tongue ftill continued. The pupil
appeared a little moveable to a very vivid light,
and when the left eye was covered, the patient
could diftinguifh whether it was light or dark.
She began to ufe the vapour of the aqua ammoniæ puræ, which was repeated every two or
three hours.

                                                        On

6th. Little pain in the head; the taſte leſs
bitter than on the preceding days; the pupil
acquires ſome mobility. The opening powders are preſcribed, of which the patient takes
three in the day, and continues to apply the vapour of the cauſtic volatile alkali to the eyes
every two or three hours.

7th. Very little pain in the head. The
opening powders produce nauſea for a few
hours; afterwards two abundant evacuations
in the courſe of the day. The pupil contracts
a little, and the patient can diſtinguiſh the
figures of large objects.

8th. The pain in the head is entirely gone,
as well as the bitter taſte and furred ſtate
of the tongue. The pupil is more ſenſible to
the impreſſion of the light than on the preceding day.

9th, 10th, 11th, and 12th. The patient
continues to take the opening powders, and
to uſe the vapour of the cauſtic volatile alkali
externally.

13th. The patient complains again of head-
ach and bitter taſte, and the tongue is furred. Inſtead of the opening powders I ordered her an emetic, compoſed of half a dram
of ipecacuanha, and one grain of tartarized antimony, to be taken at once. The patient vomited much yellowiſh-green matter. The head-

ach

ach immediately ceafed, and the girl could then diftinguifh fufficiently well the objects that were prefented to her. She continues the ufe of the vapour.

14th. She is very well. The pupil of the right eye, or of that moft affected with amaurofis, is even more contracted than that of the left.

15th. The patient refumes the ufe of the opening powders, and continues to employ the vapour of the cauftic volatile alkali externally.

16th. There is a gradual amendment. The patient can diftinguifh a fmall needle with the right eye.

17th, 18th, 19th, and 20th. The opening powders produce daily two abundant evacuations, without debilitating the patient. She has a good appetite and digeftion.

21ft. The ufe of the opening powders is omitted, and the decoction of cinchona with the infufion of valerian root, taken in dofes of three ounces three times a day, fubftituted in place of them.

22d, 23d, 24th, 25th, 26th, and 27th. The girl can fee the moft minute objects as well with her left as her right eye. She acquires a healthy complexion; and the ftrabifmus has almoft entirely difappeared.

28th. She leaves the hofpital perfectly cured. She is advifed, however, to continue the ufe

of

of the vapour for a week longer, and internally, morning and evening, a powder compofed of a ʒj of the cinchona, and ʒfs of valerian; and alfo to obferve a regular diet, and to avoid the burning rays of the fun.

CHAP.

CHAP. XX.

OF A CALCULOUS CONCRETION OF THE IN-TERNAL PART OF THE EYE.

AMONG the very confiderable number of dif-eafed eyes, which the friendly condefcenfion of Dr. Monteggia, a celebrated phyfician and furgeon of Milan, has afforded me an opportu-nity of examining, I have found one almoft en-tirely transformed into a ftony fubftance.*

This eye, taken from the body of an elderly woman, was about one half the fize of the found one. The cornea was dufky, behind which the iris appeared of a fingular figure, being concave, and without foramen or pupil in the middle. The reft of the eye-ball, from the termination of the cornea backwards, felt unufually hard to the touch.

By making an incifion I found the fcleroticaf and the choroidea‡ nearly in a natural ftate, and a fmall quantity of limpid fluid iffued from the

* Plate II. fig. 8.   † Plate II. a. a.   ‡ Plate II. b.

anterior

anterior chamber of the aqueous humour. Beneath the choroid coat there appeared two hard calculous *fcutellæ*, united together by means of a compact membranous fubftance; one of which was fituated pofteriorly, the other anteriorly. The former * occupied the bottom of the eye; the latter † the fituation of the corpus ciliare and the cryftalline lens.

Having made an incifion through the compact membrane, which united the margins of the two calculous *fcutellæ*, I found within this cavity, inftead of the vitreous humour, fome drops of a glutinous bloody fluid, and along the axis of it a fmall foft cylinder, ‡ which running anteriorly from the bottom of the eye along the greater axis of the ball, went to be implanted in an elaftic cartilaginous fubftance, fituated in the centre of the anterior calculous *fcutella*, precifely at the part, which, in a natural ftate, is occupied by the cryftalline lens and its capfule; both of which parts were entirely wanting.

The pofterior furface of the iris had contracted a firm adhefion with the middle part of this cartilaginous fubftance, fituated in the centre of the anterior calculous fcutella; confequently when the iris was viewed on the fide next the cornea and anterior chamber of the aqueous hu-

* Plate II. c. c.　† Plate II. d. d.　‡ Plate II. f.

mour,

mour, it appeared, as it was in reality, concave in the middle.

The optic nerve degenerated into a thread, paffed through the fclerotic and choroid coats,* advanced through the centre or bottom of the pofterior calculous *fcutella*, and was loft in the fmall foft cylinder,† which, as I have ftated, went to be inferted in the cartilaginous fub-ftance, fituated in the centre of the anterior cal-culous fcutella, or in the part which is naturally occupied by the cryftalline lens and its capfule. The greater part of this fmall cylinder, efpe-cially near the ciliary body, was apparently no-thing more than the membrane of the vitreous humour emptied of its fluid, wafted, contracted, and converted into a compact fubftance. The fame thing was obferved in the diffection of the dropfical eye before mentioned.‡

Haller has met with a fact fimilar to this, and has given us the defcription of it, which, from its great refemblance to the one here de-tailed, is worthy of being related and confronted with it.

In furis cadavere, fays he,§ *quod an.* 1752, *diffecuimus, diritas quidem non tanta, raritas au-tem etiam major fuit. Cum enim in eo homine nervos oculi folicite pararemus, cæcum fuiffe eo la-*

* Plate II. e.　　† Plate II. f.　　‡ Page 294.
§ Obferv. Patholog. oper. min. obferv. 65.

*tere, atque in cicatricem in cornea esse, et durita-
tem in oculo ipso adparuit. Cum dissectione de-
functi essemus, adparuit mira mali causa. Cho-
roideæ membranæ suberat, retinæ loco, lamina ossea,
aut lapidea (nam fibras osseas nullus vidimus),
cui ipsa choroidea adhærebat, ut alias retinæ solet
concentrica, hemisspherio cavo similis, nisi quod du-
plici lamina fieret, et in altero latere duobus quasi
loculis excavaretur. Is quasi scyphus accurati ro-
tundo foramine perforabatur, qua nervus opticus
subit, ut eo magis induratam retinam esse adpa-
reret.*

*Intra hanc osseam caveam multum vitreum legiti-
mum corpus, sed nervum, quasi albam nempe cylin-
drum riperimus quæ per foramen ossei cyathi transf-
missa metiens ejus diametrum denique adhærebat
osseo. confuso corpori, quod potuisses pro corrupta
lente crystallina habere. Ei corpori undique et
iris, et processus ciliorum cognomines connascebantur,
et cornea denique, ad quam iris pariter conferbuerat.
Nunc sive retinam, ut ego persuadeor, sive quid-
quam aliud fuisse velis, quod in os cavum et hemis-
phæricum mutatum sit, in oculo tamen tenerrima
parte corporis humani indurationem perfectam natam
esse adparet; nihil ergo in corpore nostro dari, quod
indurari nequeat. Lapillos aliquos in lente crystallina repertos fuisse legi; ejusmodi autem morbus,
nescio an visus sit, qualem hæc opportunitas nobis
obtulit.*

Distinct

Diſtinct mention is made of calculous con-
cretions of the internal part of the eye, by F.
d'Hildanus,* Lanciſi, as quoted by Heiſter,†
Morgagni,‡ Morand,§ Zinn,‖ and Pellier.¶

* Centur. I. obſerv. 1.
† Vindiciæ de cataracta, page 97.
‡ De ſed. et cauſ morb. Epiſt. 13, 9. Epiſt. 52. 30.
§ Mem. de l'Acad. R. de ſciences an. 1730.
‖ Hamburg, Magaz. De retina oſſificata, 19. B.
¶ Recueil de mem, et obſ. ſur l'œil, obſ. 239.

INDEX.

I N D E X.

A.

Bandage,

INDEX.

I N D E X.

Fiftula

INDEX.

3

Hypopion,

Puriform

INDEX.

N N   Sciffors,

EXPLANATION

PLATES.

PLATE I.

a. b, The lachrymal fac.

c. The tendon or ligament of the *orbicularis* mufcle of he eye-lids.

d, The fuperior lachrymal punctum.

e. The inferior lachrymal punctum,

f. The caruncula lachrymalis.

g. A portion of tne orbicularis palpebrarum which co-vered the lachrymal fac, feparated in a great meafure from the ligament c. and everted.

PLATE II.

Fig. 1, The everfion of the lower eye-lid, occafioned by a fhortening of the integuments, in confequence of an ex-tenfive cicatrix formed a little below it.

Fig. 2. The ftate of the lower eye-lid (fig. 1.) after the operation, In confequence of the greater fhortening of the integuments towards the temples than the nofe, the lower eye-lid is feen to be lefs elevated towards the external than the internal angle. It embraced the lower part of the eye-

6   ball

ball however, fufficiently to prevent the defcent of the tears upon the cheek, and to correct the deformity.

Fig 3. Two pterygia of different fizes upon the fame eye, taken from a dead fubject.

a. The larger pterygium fituated upon the eye-ball on he fide next the nofe.

b. The fmaller pterygium on the fide next the temples. The two lines, one ftraight, the other femicircular, marked upon the pterygium a, denote the double direction which ought to be given to the incifion in the extirpation of the difeafe.

Fig. 4. Diffection of the conjunctiva of the eye (fig. 3.) which evidently proves that the pterygium is nothing more than a morbid thickening of the fine lamina of this membrane, which naturally covers the external furface of the cornea.

Fig. 5. a. The nebula of the cornea.

b. The fafciculus of varicofe blood veffels of the conjunctiva, by which the nebula of the cornea is, as it were, nourifhed and kept up.

Fig. 6. a. Procidentia of the iris through a fmall ulcer of the cornea. In this figure is feen the whitifh margin of the ulcer, the contracted and preternaturally difplaced ftate of the pupil, and the oblong figure which it affumes in fuch cafes.

Fig. 7. The ftate of the eye (fig. 6.) after the cure of the procidentia of the iris. The pupil in fome degree recovers its natural figure.

Fig. 8. Calculous concretion of the internal part of the eye.

a. a. The fclerotica turned back.

b. A portion of the choroidea.

c. c. Calculous concretion in the form of a fmall cup or fcutella, which occupied the bottom of the eye precifely in the fituation of the vitreous humour.

d. d. The

d. d. The other calculous concretion in the fituation of the corpus ciliare.

e. The entrance of the optic nerve into the cavity of the eye-ball through the centre of the calculous fcutella c. c.

f. The foft funnel-fhaped body, which extended from the bottom of the eye as far as the fituation of the capfule of the cryftalline lens.

Fig. 9. Staphyloma of the fclerotic and choroid coats fituated at the bottom of the eye.

Fig. 10. Another ftaphyloma of the fclerotic and choroid coats fimilar to it.

PLATE III.

Fig. 1. An elevator for the upper eye-lid.

Fig. 2. Crooked or probe-fciffars for the divifion of the integuments of the eye-lids in cafes of Trichiafis, or of exceffive relaxations of them.

Fig. 3. Small fciffors very convenient for removing any portion of the internal part of the eye-lids, or of the conjunctiva.

Fig. 4. Sciffors curved upon the back, commonly called by the French *cifeaux à cuiller*.

Fig. 5. 6. Apparatus for cauterizing the os unguis and pituitary membrane which covers this bone on the fide of the cavity of the noftril.

Fig. 7. Small knife for the divifion of the cornea.

Fig. 8. Forceps very ufeful in the various operations which are performed upon the eye-lids, conjunctiva, and eye-ball.

Fig. 9. A folid leaden tent, furnifhed with a fmall plate, for the purpofe of compreffing the external part of the lachrymal fac.

Fig.

Fig. 10. The needle with a curved point, for the depreſ-ſion of the cataract.

* The point of the inſtrument magnified.

Fig. 11. The ſame needle with a ſtraight point.

Fig. 12. A ſmall convex-edged biſtoury, very uſeful in removing the fungoſities of the internal ſurface of the eyelids, and encyſted tumours of thoſe parts.

T. Bensley, Printer,
Bolt Court, Fleet Street, London.

Plate I.

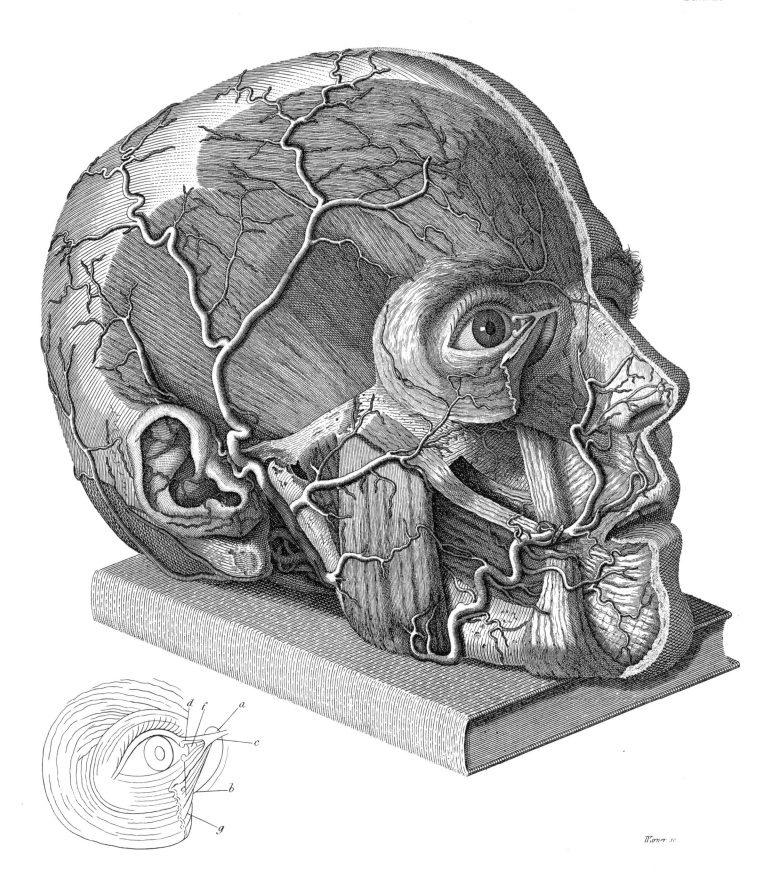

Warner sc.

Published Sept.r 15.1806. by T Cadell, and W. Davies Strand.

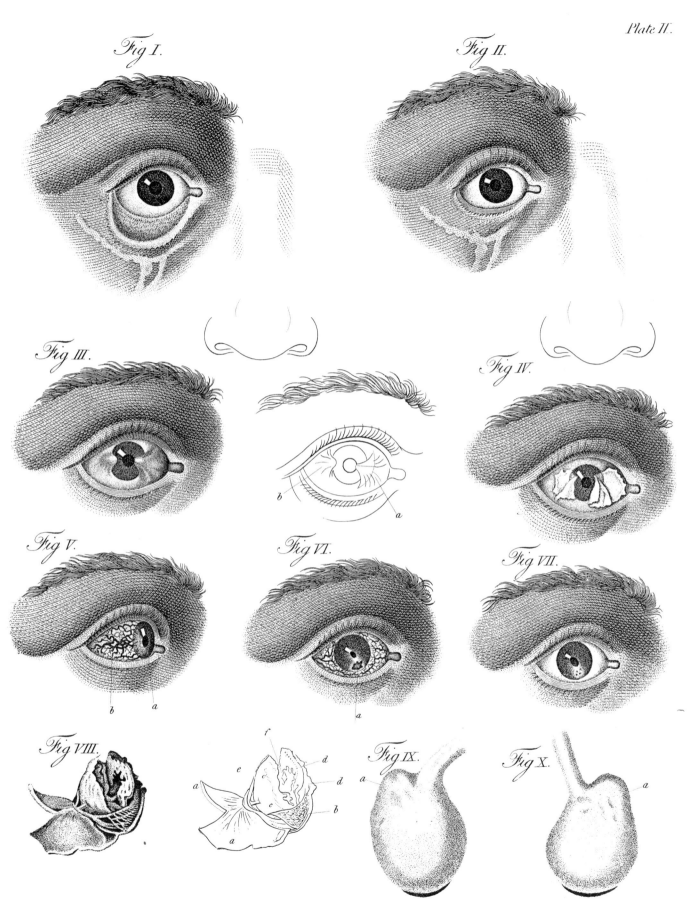

Plate II.

Fig I.

Fig II.

Fig III.

Fig IV.

Fig V.

Fig VI.

Fig VII.

Fig VIII.

Fig IX.

Fig X.

Published Sept.r 15. 1806 by T. Cadell and W. Davies. Strand.

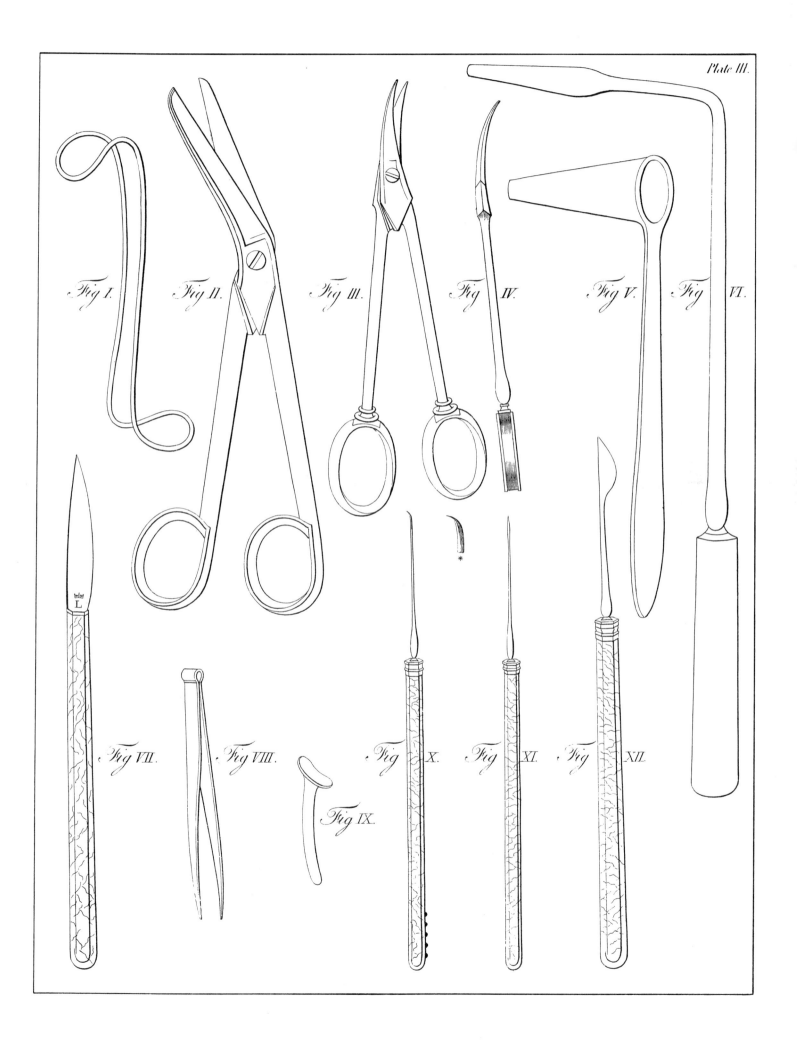

Plate III.

Fig I. Fig II. Fig III. Fig IV. Fig V. Fig VI.

Fig VII. Fig VIII. Fig X. Fig XI. Fig XII.

Fig IX.

CORRIGENDA.

P. 24. l. 9. *after* flough *dele* refembling cotton.

— 55. l. 6. f.b.——— whitifh *dele* or cottony.

— 59. l. 12. ———fubftance *dele* refembling cotton.

— 33. l. 6. *for* Ægnieta *read* Ægineta.

—263. l. 4. f.b. — Ce morb. ——— De morb.

—188. l. 4. *after the words* blifters to the neck, *add*, Schmucker imagines that a powder confifting of gr. vj of Rhubarb and ℈ j of nitre, taken every three hours, contributes greatly to reproduce the gonorrhœa, in confequence of the diuretic property of thefe medicines

P. 194. l. 20. *after the words* moft frequent, *add:* A fact which for its conftancy merits the attention of practitioners, is, that every *chronic ophthalmia,* whether fcrofulous, variolous, morbillous, herpetic, or venereal, invariably affects the internal membrane of the eye-lids and the ciliary glands, in preference to the conjunctiva, which covers the anterior hemifphere of the eye, while on the contrary the *acute ophthalmia,* from whatever caufe or predifpofition it may be derived, conftantly occupies in preference the conjunctiva of the eye-ball.

This special edition of

P R A C T I C A L O B S E R V A T I O N S O N T H E

Diseases of the Eyes

has been privately printed for the members of The
Classics of Medicine Library by the Rae Publishing
Co. Engravings were printed by the Meriden Gravure
Co. Film was prepared from the first English edition
of 1806. New type matter was composed by Eastern
Typesetting Co. in Baskerville. The text paper was
especially made for this edition by The Monadnock
Paper Mills. The volume has been bound in top grain
genuine cowhide, with end leaves in a marbled design, by the Tapley-Rutter Co., Bookbinders. Edges
are gilded, and covers are brass die stamped in 22-
karat gold. Cover stampings, design and production
of the edition by Max M. Stein.

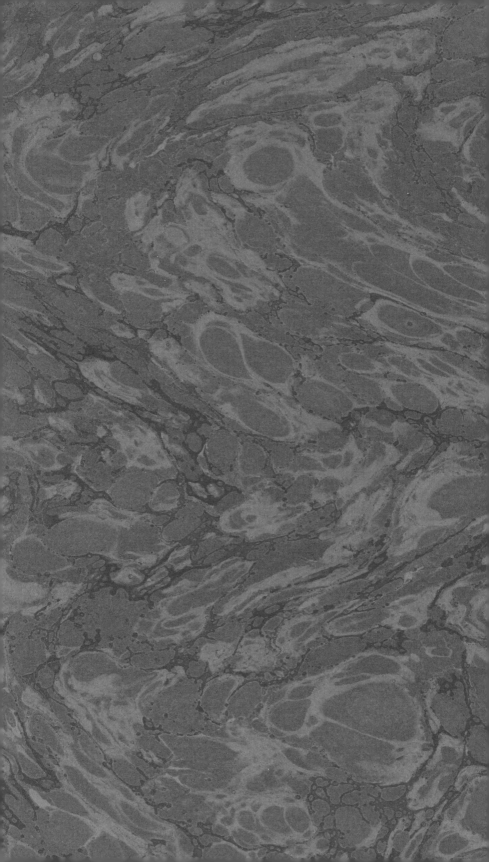